# (DIS)CONNECTED EMPIRES

# (Dis)connected Empires

*Imperial Portugal, Sri Lankan Diplomacy, and the Making of a Habsburg Conquest in Asia*

ZOLTÁN BIEDERMANN

OXFORD

UNIVERSITY PRESS

# OXFORD
UNIVERSITY PRESS

Great Clarendon Street, Oxford, OX2 6DP,
United Kingdom

Oxford University Press is a department of the University of Oxford.
It furthers the University's objective of excellence in research, scholarship,
and education by publishing worldwide. Oxford is a registered trade mark of
Oxford University Press in the UK and in certain other countries

Published in the United States of America by Oxford University Press
198 Madison Avenue, New York, NY 10016, United States of America

British Library Cataloguing in Publication Data
Data available

Library of Congress Control Number: 2018947664
ISBN 978–0–19–882339–1

To my mother, in loving memory

# Preface

When the idea for this book emerged around the turn of the millennium, global history writing was entering its golden age. The historiography of the Portuguese empire in Asia, in contrast, seemed past its prime. It had discretely pioneered global connective methods for three decades, gone through a moment of fame thanks to some widely read books written by Sanjay Subrahmanyam in dialogue with the best Portuguese scholars of his generation, and then failed to keep up with the hype. Over the past fifteen years, much has been written about Portuguese empire building in Asia of course, but very little has caught the attention of the wider profession, especially those doing their readings in English.

It was a frustrating situation at the time, and remains of concern now. Why should anyone not working specifically on Sri Lanka, the Portuguese, or the Asian fringe of the Spanish Habsburg empire read this book? Only one of the three polities in the title figures as an empire in John Darwin's widely applauded *After Tamerlane*.[1] In the great house of global history described by Jan de Vries, our story appears to live a modest life on the ground floor, far from the 'mega-processes' of globalization dwelling upstairs, in the 'penthouse'.[2] Yet that is precisely the problem. By separating apparently peripheral, minor interactions from an imagined canon of 'great empires', something crucial has been pushed out of the frame. Only once we appreciate the full range of European-Asian interactions that occurred beyond the great land-bound empires of Asia *and* before the arrival of British imperialism in the region will we be in a position to go ahead with two fundamental historiographical operations that are still largely absent from the panorama today. On the one hand, we shall be able to further our understanding of the beginnings of modern European imperialism and colonialism in Asia in conjunction with, rather than as a departure from, earlier encounters. On the other, we may start at last to explore the contrasts and connections between European expansion in Asia and the colonization of the New World.

When I came across, some years after completing the original research for this book, Philip J. Stern's retelling of the story of the English EIC, I realized just what a treasure trove I was sitting on.[3] Here are two comparable stories of empires apparently built on trade, but with an agenda of conquest written into their DNA. Both convinced themselves only gradually that it might be a good idea to take over territories in Asia. Both saw their histories told in ways that still hinder genuinely complex interpretations of their trajectories. There were some differences, too.

---

[1] John Darwin, *After Tamerlane. The Rise and Fall of Global Empires, 1400–2000* (London: Penguin, 2007).

[2] Jan de Vries, 'Reflections on doing global history', in *Writing the History of the Global. Challenges for the 21st Century*, edited by Maxine Berg (Oxford: Oxford University Press, 2013), p. 32.

[3] See Philip J. Stern, *The Company-State. Corporate Sovereignty and the Early Modern Foundations of the British Empire in India* (New York: Oxford University Press, 2011).

In the Portuguese case, part of the explanation for the territorialization of the Asian empire in the late sixteenth century had always been that, once Phillip II of Spain had taken the throne in Lisbon in 1581, policy changes occurred as a matter of Castilian influence. This meant that my study had to involve a critical incursion into the history of another body politic, which happened to be the greatest empire of its time. The other aspect distinguishing the story of the Portuguese in Sri Lanka—the largest territorial conquest in the region before the EIC campaigns of the late eighteenth century—was that, whilst the original DNA of the empire did in fact offer the possibility of conquest, the real driving force behind the blossoming of conquest discourse had been an Asian polity with its own imperial tradition: the seemingly obscure kingdom of Kōṭṭe which, for decades, fed its imperial ideas into Portuguese channels of communication. The challenges this poses to Eurocentric narratives of globalization are riveting. I wondered how such a powerful story could have evaded the attention of historians for so long.

Most of us are painfully aware of the complexity of early modern encounters across the early modern world, the unsettling combinations of commercial, diplomatic, military, and cultural exchanges they tended to involve. The study of Iberian-Asian materials, often neglected by global historians, is key for a deepened understanding of those dynamics. In many ways, the complexity of Iberian interactions in Asia prefigures and, from 1600 onwards, accompanies those of Dutch and especially British expansion. Sri Lanka is in fact an outstanding example of how similar developments occurred repeatedly in the same place, as *three* European powers in a row went—to put it bluntly for a moment—from commerce to conquest. Clearly, the way forward is not to depoliticize early expansion in Asia by dismissing it as merely commercial, or redistributive, or predatory in a petty way, but to re-politicize every bit of it.[4] This is not just to reiterate how 'merchant empires' and 'company states' were common, and the early modern world full of 'corporate bodies politic and hyphenated, hybrid, overlapping, and composite forms of sovereignty'.[5] It is also to emphasize how every individual leaving a trace in the colonial archive—be it as a governor, a *rāja*, an ambassador, a monk, a merchant, or a mercenary—needs to be seen as part of the process that, without ever having been linear or inescapable, prepared the ground for European hegemony.

There are abundant opportunities here for global historians. Since in the Atlantic the comparison of British and Iberian colonialism has made significant progress, the doors stand open for similar endeavours in Asia. There is scope to emulate John Elliott's *Empires of the Atlantic World* or Jorge Cañizares-Esguerra's *Puritan Conquistadors*.[6] Similarly, whilst much is known now about the ways British rule

---

[4] Cf. most frustratingly Darwin, *After Tamerlane*, pp. 53–4, with a dismissal of Portuguese imperialism on grounds of M. N. Pearson, *The Portuguese in India* (Cambridge: Cambridge University Press, 1987).

[5] Stern, *The Company-State*, p. 3.

[6] John H. Elliott, *Empires of the Atlantic World. Britain and Spain in America, 1492–1830* (New Haven, CT: Yale University Press, 2006); Jorge Cañizares-Esguerra, *Puritan Conquistadors. Iberianizing the Atlantic, 1550–1700* (Stanford, CA: Stanford University Press, 2006); Stern, *The Company-State*, pp. 218–19 gives a list of the most valuable comparative works for Asia, including Sanjay Subrahmanyam, ed., *Maritime India* (Oxford: Oxford University Press, 2004), which offers a reprint

relied on local elites, almost nothing has been written about how such interactions extended their roots into earlier centuries.[7] It is revealing that a book as ground-breaking as Sujit Sivasundaram's *Islanded* could produce a bold new interpretation of early British rule and its capacity to reinvent Sri Lanka as an island colony, whilst refraining almost entirely—for its own strong reasons, to be sure—from engaging with earlier processes of a comparable nature.[8]

This book has been written in the hope that new bridges may be built, and there is no objective reason why imperial and global historians at large should not embrace the story it tells. But what about Sri Lanka? Is it legitimate to revisit the early colonial past of a country just emerging from almost three decades of civil strife? The scars that societies carry away from war are not always immediately perceptible, and sometimes people feel that they may be best left untouched. Yet such scars tend to linger on in the depth of collective bodies. To examine them is one of the most rewarding and, at the same time, daunting challenges a historian can face. In Sri Lanka, a little more than four centuries ago Europeans began to engage in a process of conquest and colonization that was only reversed in 1948. On the surface of it, many aspects of colonial culture have been well integrated into the fabric of Lankan society. English is a widely spoken language, Christian schools educate the nation's elite, and western tourists are encouraged to spend time in the quaint colonial towns of Negombo and Galle.[9]

Against this backdrop, the past decade has also seen grievances re-emerge against European powers that brought their languages, religion, and material culture to replace the island's own. Connected history—to which I will turn in this book—does not always go down well with Asian audiences. Before we dismiss such anxieties as signs of academic immaturity, it is worth pointing out that there is a potentially pernicious politics to global and connected history writing, especially when it emphasizes trade or culture *over* war and exploitation. As David Washbrook has put it, there is a danger that the 'connections' and 'networks' favoured by global historians may 'stand in for relations of force and coercion'.[10] This is particularly disturbing when one considers how, on the European side of the post-colonial divide, so much remains to be done to engage with the wrongdoings of the past. Time may give poetry to a battlefield, as Graham Greene had it, but it does so in very different ways among the victors and the vanquished. Whilst many in Sri Lanka

---

of Kenneth McPherson's *The Indian Ocean: A History of the People and the Sea*, Sinnappah Arasaratnam's *Maritime India in the Seventeenth Century*, and Furber's *Rival Empires of Trade in the Orient, 1600–1800*.

[7] See C. A. Bayly, *Indian Society and the Making of the British Empire* (Cambridge: Cambridge University Press, 1988).

[8] Sujit Sivasundaram, *Islanded: Britain, Sri Lanka, and the Bounds of an Indian Ocean Colony* (Chicago, IL/London: University of Chicago Press, 2013). Earlier processes of a comparable nature are explored in Alan Strathern, *Kingship and Conversion in Sixteenth-Century Sri Lanka. Portuguese Imperialism in a Buddhist Land* (Cambridge: Cambridge University Press, 2007) and Michael Roberts, *Sinhala Consciousness in the Kandyan Period 1590s to 1815* (Colombo: Vijitha Yapa Publications, 2003).

[9] For a general overview of Sri Lankan history, John Rogers, *A Concise History of Sri Lanka* (Cambridge: Cambridge University Press, 2019).

[10] David Washbrook, 'Problems in global history', in *Writing the History of the Global. Challenges for the 21st Century*, edited by Maxine Berg (Oxford: Oxford University Press, 2013), p. 27.

still count the losses suffered four centuries ago, Portugal and Spain (like other European countries) have abundantly studied and often celebrated their expansionist past without engaging in a sustained way with its darker side. Conquest often stands as an abstract, or indeed tacitly glorified concept in a vacuum, as if it had not involved massacre, rape, plunder, and enslavement on a colossal scale. A key text such as the Portuguese inventory of the objects pillaged from the Temple of the Tooth in Kōṭṭe in 1551, for example—an event that would have its equivalent in the emptying and desecration of Notre Dame of Paris by Ottoman or English invaders—has never been studied in any depth.[11]

All this does not mean, though, that we surrender to local nationalist narratives involving the sectarian targeting of religious and linguistic minorities, accused of being 'less Lankan' than others.[12] There is a quandary but, as Steve Stern put it in 1992 regarding the challenges that New World historiography faced at the time, 'the solution to the quandary is to welcome it'.[13] I can see no other way forward than to tackle blunt simplifications of the past with full vigour, and mobilize scholarship against rose-coloured narratives of encounter as well as aggressively nationalistic, exclusionary stances. Once we are willing to set simple and straightforward, often chauvinistic readings of the sixteenth-century materials aside, a window opens up onto a richly textured, if painfully complicated past. It is a past of violence, conflict and usually brutal negotiations, but not a past that we can by any means lay to rest. There is no contradiction here between a revisionist reading of the early modern period (one that embraces the principles of connected history) and a firmly anti-colonial stance (one that observes critically early signs of hierarchization).

As Gary Tomlinson put it, postcolonial historiography should be about building a past that 'resists our intellectual attempts to occupy it even while it takes its shape from us'.[14] My hope is that once the reader reaches the end of this book, any reservations about the legitimacy of revisiting colonial history from the comfortable warmth of a European university department will have dissipated. This is not an attempt at whitewashing colonialism by devolving historical agency to people in the distant 'South'. It is an exercise in digging deep into a dirty past that will always be hard to digest to all parts involved. This book does tell a story of connections and exchanges, but ultimately the story is also part of a larger process, which saw the emergence of a European project to dominate the world. The ideas of conquest dissected here may have been a tiny seed in the beginning, ignored, even ridiculed

---

[11] Sousa Viterbo, *O thesouro do rei de Ceylão* (Lisbon: Typographia da Academia Real das Sciencias, 1904). An English translation is under preparation.

[12] The most virulently chauvinistic approach of recent times is in Susantha Goonatilake, *A 16th Century Clash of Civilizations. The Portuguese Presence in Sri Lanka* (Colombo: Vijitha Yapa, 2010). A slightly more moderate work is C. Gaston Perera, *The Portuguese Missionary in 16th and 17th Century Ceylon: The Spiritual Conquest* (Colombo: Vijitha Yapa, 2009).

[13] Steve J. Stern, 'Paradigms of Conquest: History, Historiography, and Politics', *Journal of Latin American Studies*, 24 (1992), p. 34.

[14] Gary Tomlinson, 'Unlearning the Aztec *cantares* (preliminaries to a postcolonial history)', in *Subject and Object in Renaissance Culture*, edited by Margreta de Grazia, Maureen Quilligan, and Peter Stallybrass (Cambridge: Cambridge University Press, 1996), p. 261.

by Iberian authorities during much of the sixteenth century. Yet they grew into something mighty enough to have left a lasting imprint on the globe we inhabit.

*

This book was born in the archives of Portugal, Spain, and India, allowed to take shape in my mind during a prolonged stay in Sri Lanka, and written over the years in Paris, Lisbon, Los Angeles, Providence, Madrid, and London. It has been much too long in the making, and the debts that I have incurred are very substantial indeed. First and foremost, I wish to thank Dejanirah Couto and Luís Filipe Thomaz for supporting me as supervisors at the École Pratique des Hautes Études of Paris and the Universidade Nova of Lisbon between 1999 and 2006, and ever since as friends. Jean-Claude Waquet ploughed through my Portuguese dissertation with great intellectual vigour, bringing into focus the key aspects I wished to see recognized. Anthony Disney and Roderich Ptak offered scholarly and personal guidance in challenging times with a warmth that I did not dare to expect. Anthony Pagden and Sanjay Subrahmanyam helped me find my place in academia by taking me on as a post doc on the 'Imperial Models in the Early Modern World' programme at UCLA. Onésimo de Almeida gave me shelter at Brown University from the bureaucratic chores that threatened to derail the project after I started to work in London, and Sabine McCormack offered to publish this study at Notre Dame, shortly before her untimely death. Over the years, I received generous financial and logistic support from the Portuguese Foundation for Science and Technology (FCT), the William Andrews Clark Memorial Library (UCLA), the American Institute of Sri Lankan Studies (AISLS), and the Arts and Humanities Research Council (AHRC) of England. I can only hope that others will be able to benefit from such support in the future.

Alan Strathern, Chandra Richard De Silva, Gananath Obeyesekere, John Rogers, Jorge Flores, Michael Roberts, and Sujit Sivasundaram have been the most wonderful companions in my endeavours to understand Sri Lanka—and far beyond. Without their writings and suggestions, I would have struggled to grasp what my questions might be. Without their encouragement, I may well have given up on answering them. Amal Gunasena from SOAS did what he could to make me fluent in Sinhala. Among the colleagues at Birkbeck and UCL who supported me over the past nine years, I wish to give my special thanks to Carmen Fracchia, John Kraniauskas, Luís Trindade, Philip Derbyshire, Stephen Hart, Debbie Martin, and Alexander Samson. For Lisbon, Paris, and Colombo, the list of people who made the writing of this book possible is naturally longer. My special thanks go to André Murteira, Andreia Martins, Ângela Barreto Xavier, Catarina Madeira Santos, Francisco Bethencourt, Francisco Roque de Oliveira, Ira Unamboowe[†], Ivo Veiga, Joana Estorninho, João Paulo Oliveira e Costa, Jorge Santos Alves, K. D. Paranavitana, Nuno Senos, Paulo Varela Gomes[†], Pedro Cardim, Rui Loureiro, and Teresa Castro.

None of this would have been possible without the loving support of my family. I thank my father Reinhard, my brother Gábor, my wife Eva, and my daughter

Hannah for all the love and care that has kept me going over the years. Jean, José, and Érica Nieto McAvoy in Madrid have showered me with patience and affection, for which I thank them from the bottom of my heart. I dedicate this book to the memory of my mother Ildikó, who started it all off by travelling between worlds at a time when few people did.

# Contents

# List of Illustrations and Maps

# Introduction
## Querying the Origins of European Conquest in Asia

Why conquer? Taking possession of lands in Asia was not an idea that came to Europeans instinctively. It did not occur to Marco Polo, as has been famously noted, when he travelled to Cathay.[1] Nor did it appear *ex machina* to Vasco da Gama when he reached Calicut in 1498, at a time when Columbus inaugurated Castilian possessive operations—first rhetorical, soon military—in the New World. As the Portuguese, and then their English, Dutch, Danish, and French followers ventured into Asian waters, the thought of taking over parts of the continent only came to them gradually. This is, then, the primary objective of this book: to explore how connections were established across cultural boundaries, how conversations arose between Iberian and South Asian agents of empire, and how the ground was slowly prepared for one of the largest European territorial possessions in the East before the advent of the British empire: the *Conquista de Ceilão*, or Conquest of Ceylon.

### GLOBAL HISTORIES BETWEEN CONNECTION AND DISCONNECTION

Much emphasis has been placed during the past twenty years—since the publication, in 1997, of Sanjay Subrahmanyam's widely received article on the 'connected histories' of early modern Eurasia—on the study of global connections.[2] Connected histories are now everywhere, and rightly so. Less has been said, however, about how exactly connections worked or failed to work in local contexts, and how, in some instances, they paved the way for disconnection and colonial endeavour. This is, in part, to do with the ambition of 'connected history' to dismantle old Eurocentric narratives where agency had been too tightly bound up with expanding western nations. The de-centring and levelling of the playing field has been one of the great achievements of the past two decades.[3] But since the fact remains that

---

[1] Stephen Greenblatt, *Marvelous Possessions. The Wonder of the New World* (Chicago, IL: University of Chicago Press, 1991), p. 53.

[2] Sanjay Subrahmanyam, 'Connected Histories: Notes towards a reconfiguration of Early Modern Eurasia', *Modern Asian Studies*, 31, 3 (1997), pp. 735–62.

[3] This change is amply reflected in the structure and contents of the recent sixth volume of the *Cambridge World History*: Jerry H. Bentley, Sanjay Subrahmanyam, and Merry E. Wiesner-Hanks, eds., *The Construction of a Global World, 1400–1800 CE* (Cambridge: Cambridge University Press, 2015).

parts of South and Southeast Asia were invaded by Europeans at various moments after 1500, and not vice versa, it is also crucial to ask where and when precisely connections evolved in such a way that conquest became a possibility.

As Jeremy Adelman recently put it, we need 'narratives of global life that reckon with disintegration as well as integration, the costs and not just the bounty of interdependence'.[4] To be sure, it would be unfair to say that global historians have ignored disintegration and disconnection, and that on such grounds connected history itself is obsolete. Global and critical connective methods remain powerful and legitimate tools for an understanding of how the world changed after 1500.[5] But it certainly is worth emphasizing how a nuanced picture cannot emerge if we fail to come to terms with the forces that, within the freshly interconnected universe of the 1500s, and *from its very inception*, drove disconnection and hierarchization. How was it that some societies engaging in trans-continental diplomatic and commercial exchanges, often facing each other with comparable confidence, gradually drifted apart, *while they were talking to each other*, in such a manner that one could dream up the conquest of the other? Were divergences in political cultures, and ultimately disconnection, aspects as characteristic of the early modern world as connectivity was?

To answer such questions, this book goes on a global journey (see Figure 0.1). It explores the diplomatic, cultural, and military triangle built during the sixteenth century by the Portuguese empire, the imperial polity led by Kōṭṭe in Sri Lanka, and the Catholic Monarchy of the Spanish Habsburgs. Obviously, each of these imperial formations had very distinctive sizes, shapes, and histories. Portugal had pioneered explorations in the Atlantic, settled a number of uninhabited islands, waged wars in the North of Morocco, and established trading posts along the West African littoral during the fifteenth century. The rulers of the House of Avis, a young dynasty established in the late 1300s with a connection to the House of Lancaster, developed wider commercial and political ambitions and, in 1498, established the first maritime link between Europe and Asia. By the middle of the sixteenth century, there were Portuguese coastal establishments from Brazil to Japan, and tributary agreements with numerous rulers especially in the Indian Ocean region. Historians have, over the past decades, unveiled the tentative, often erratic nature of Lusitanian inroads into Asia in particular, offering a healthy departure from earlier, nationalist tales of a highly centralized empire.[6] It has also been shown, however, that amidst all the improvization and internal rivalry, imperial ideas did play a role alongside with commercial and other considerations. To maintain that there was no Portuguese imperialism in Asia in the sixteenth century is

---

[4] Jeremy Adelman, 'What is global History now?', *Aeon* (2017), https://aeon.co/essays/is-global-history-still-possible-or-has-it-had-its-moment (last accessed 20 September 2017).

[5] See a rebuttal to Adelman, with abundant bibliography, in Richard Drayton and David Motadel, 'Discussion: the futures of global history', *Journal of Global History*, 13, 1 (2018), pp. 1–21.

[6] See above, Luís Filipe F. R. Thomaz, *De Ceuta a Timor*, 2nd ed. (Lisbon: Difel, 1994); Sanjay Subrahmanyam, *The Portuguese Empire in Asia 1500–1700. A Political and Economic History* (London: Longman, 1993); Romain Bertrand, *Le long remords the la conquête. Manille-Mexico-Madrid: l'affaire Diego de Ávila (1577–1580)* (Paris: Seuil, 2011).

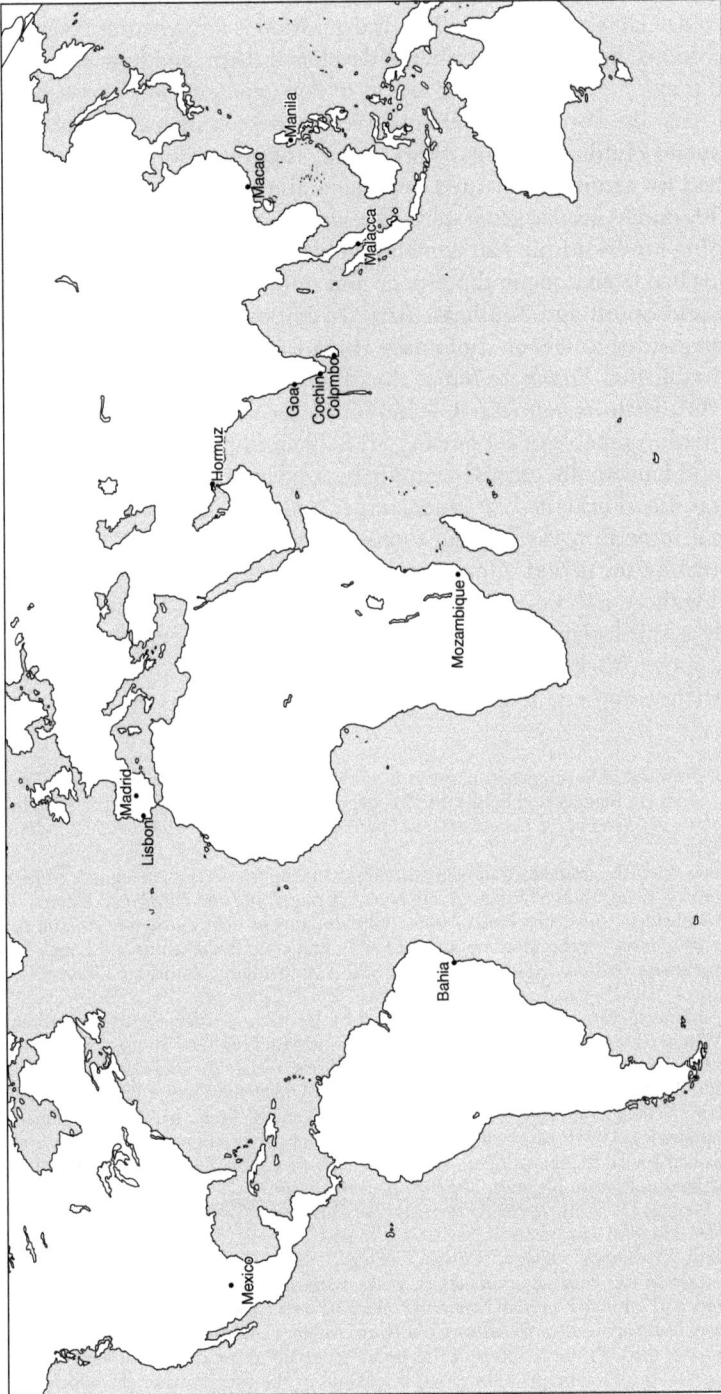

**Figure 0.1** Nodes of global communication in the Iberian-Lankan encounter.

today as untenable as older interpretations attributing the origin of all imperial evils to Vasco da Gama's arrival in 1498.[7] The question is not whether Portugal had imperial ambitions, but where and when it developed them, and how plans of conquest gained traction even when some sectors of Portuguese society opposed them.[8]

In South Asia, the Portuguese were observed with keen interest by the elites of the Buddhist and Hindu kingdoms of Sri Lanka. These kingdoms—above all, that of Kōṭṭe—had for centuries nurtured imperial ambitions in a regionally confined and, by 1500, purely insular geography. The Universalist symbolism of *cakravarti* ('wheel-turning') overlordship had come to fill little more than the space of Lanka itself, but this had been done in diplomatic and military cooperation with polities across mainland South and Southeast Asia. To impose their authority at home, Lankan rulers tended to rely on diplomacy abroad. It made much sense to engage the newly established *Estado da Índia*, the official apparatus of Portuguese possessions in Asia with its centre at Cochin and later Goa, as yet another Indian political formation capable of supporting Sri Lankan imperial projects. Gradually, Portuguese and Lankan discourses of empire became intertwined. Lankan imperial ideas were transfused into the Portuguese imperial system. Despite the fact that the match proved imperfect, the Lankan imperial ideal showed great resilience and vitality throughout the period. Almost nothing that happened before the 1590s can be explained without a thorough consideration of Lankan politics and diplomacy.[9]

Eventually a third player, the empire of the Spanish Habsburgs, entered the stage. It had grown back-to-back with the Portuguese empire, expanding mostly across the Atlantic and establishing ample colonial possessions in the Caribbean,

---

[7] An explicit dismissal of Portuguese expansion as not being imperial is in Darwin, *After Tamerlane*, p. 53. The idea of an era inaugurated by the 1498 voyage is at the heart of K. M. Panikkar, *Asia and Western Dominance. A Survey of the Vasco da Gama Epoch of Asian History, 1498–1945* (London: Alan & Unwin, 1953).

[8] There is now a relative abundance of overview works in English on the Portuguese empire. The best points of entry are Anthony Disney, *A History of Portugal and the Portuguese Empire*, 2 vols. (Cambridge: Cambridge University Press, 2009); Subrahmanyam, *The Portuguese Empire in Asia. A political and economic history* (London: Longman, 1993); Francisco Bethencourt and Diogo Ramada Curto, eds., *Portuguese Oceanic Expansion, 1400–1800* (Cambridge: Cambridge University Press, 2007); Jorge Flores, 'The Iberian Empires, 1400–1800', in *The Cambridge World History*, vol. 6; *The Construction of a Global World, 1400–1800 CE*, edited by Jerry H. Bentley, Sanjay Subrahmanyam and Merry E. Wiesner-Hanks (Cambridge: Cambridge University Press, 2015), pp. 271–96.

[9] The key reference works on Sri Lankan history are still the *University of Ceylon History of Ceylon*, vol. I, parts 1 and 2, edited by H. C. Ray (Colombo: Ceylon University Press, 1959–1960), followed by the *University of Peradeniya History of Sri Lanka*, vol. II, edited by K. M. de Silva (Peradeniya: University of Peradeniya, 1995). Much of the factual history of the Portuguese presence in Sri Lanka has been established by Tikiri Abeyasinghe, *Portuguese Rule in Ceylon 1594–1612* (Colombo: Lake House, 1966); Chandra Richard De Silva, *The Portuguese in Ceylon 1617–1638* (Colombo: H. W. Cave & Co., 1972); George D. Winius, *The Fatal History of Portuguese Ceylon. Transition to Dutch Rule* (Cambridge, MA: Harvard University Press, 1971); Jorge Flores, *Os Portugueses e o Mar de Ceilão, 1498–1543. Trato, Diplomacia e Guerra* (Lisbon: Cosmos, 1998). The most sophisticated, theoretically informed study of the Portuguese materials, written specifically to tackle questions of Lankan kingship, religion and ethnicity, is Alan Strathern, *Kingship and Conversion in Sixteenth-Century Sri Lanka. Portuguese Imperialism in a Buddhist Land* (Cambridge: Cambridge University Press, 2007). Much of it resonates through the chapters of this book, especially those concerned with the reign of Bhuvanekabāhu VII. It also contains a thorough discussion of the source materials, which are overwhelmingly in Portuguese. Also see, more recently, Stephen C. Berkwitz, *Buddhist Poetry and Colonialism: Alagiyavanna and the Portuguese in Sri Lanka* (Oxford: Oxford University Press, 2013).

Central America, the Andes, and the River Plate region from the 1490s. In 1581, a decade and a half after the nominal conquest of the Philippines launched from New Spain, it incorporated the global Lusitanian empire and became a realm where, as Phillip II enjoyed hearing, the sun never set. Under the Iberian union of crowns (1581–1640), Sri Lanka became a theatre of state-sponsored Iberian conquest and colonization. The question arises whether this shift reflects a transmission of *conquista* tactics from the New World to the Old, as has been suggested, or something more complex. In what ways had sectors of Portuguese society prepared the ground for the shift? To what extent did the Lankan imperial project continue to shine through even the thickest layers of Iberian *conquista* discourse? Can the Spanish-Portuguese conquest be compared with other European endeavours in Asia, namely those of the English EIC and the Dutch VOC?[10]

The vibrancy and complexity of the relationships at stake, their global nature, but also the challenges posed to historians interested in trans-continental connectivity, emerge vividly from the reception, in 1542, of an ambassador from Sri Lanka at the royal court in Lisbon. In many ways, the event is a perfect example of how global connections could work. When Śrī Rāmarakṣa, a Tamil minister dispatched by Bhuvanekabāhu VII of Kōṭṭe (r.1521–51) to negotiate an inter-imperial agreement with John III of Portugal (r.1521–57), traversed hall after hall of a palace built on Lisbon's riverfront to celebrate the oceanic expansion of the Avis dynasty, both parties stood in awe of each other's magnificence. The Portuguese courtly elite marvelled at the refined gifts carried across the palace, testimonies to the economic prosperity, imperial ambition, and artistic sophistication of a distant Asian court. There were finely carved ivories and even, according to one account, a gold statue representing a Sinhalese prince soon to be crowned by the Portuguese monarch.

The prince, a three-year old child called Dharmapāla, had been chosen by the ruler of Kōṭṭe, Bhuvanekabāhu VII, to succeed him on the Lankan imperial throne. He was not next in line, but the embassy was sent precisely to secure him that position. Whilst bending the rules of succession was no novelty for the Lankan elite, the geography of the mission was. For the first time in history, legitimation for the next potential *cakravarti* of Sri Lanka was to be sought not within the island, nor even on the Indian or Southeast Asian subcontinent, but in a Christian land on the other side of the globe. Two royal dynasties were talking to each other over thousands of miles of distance and across deep cultural divides with relative success.

The principal events of the diplomatic encounter as imagined by the Lankan royal court are represented on a finely chiselled ivory casket (see Figure 0.2). On the left side of the panel, the Sinhalese prince is presented to the Portuguese monarch, his hand placed into the hands of John III as a widely readable sign of allegiance. On the right, John places a Lankan crown on the head of the prince, symbolically

---

[10] In contrast with the vast amount of literature available on imperial Spain and its New World colonies, little has been written about Spanish activities in Asia, and even less about their impact on the Portuguese *Estado*. See Rafael Valladares, *Castilla y Portugal en Asia (1580–1680). Declive imperial y adaptación* (Leuven: Leuven University Press, 2001) and Romain Bertrand, *Le long remords the la conquete. Manille-Mexico-Madrid: l'affaire Diego de Ávila (1577–1580)* (Paris: Seuil, 2011). Further references to New World historiography are given below, in Chapter 5.

**Figure 0.2** Dharmapāla meets John III. Front panel of the 'coronation casket', Kōṭṭe, c.1541. Munich, Bayerische Verwaltung der staatlichen Schlösser, Gärten und Seen, Residenz München, Schatzkammer, Inv.-Nr. 1241.

committing to his defence. Connections and converging imperial ideas were at the heart of the deal. For the ruling elite of Kōṭṭe, this was a moment of mutual recognition allowing two polities with commensurable and connectable imperial ambitions to cooperate; a moment, in fact, of mutual conquest. As Alan Strathern put it in his groundbreaking study of Lankan kingship in the sixteenth century, the iconography asserts how 'one could be emperor and vassal at the same time' in Sri Lanka, ambitioning hegemony on the home front whilst skilfully playing the global diplomatic game abroad.[11] Kōṭṭe, it was thought, could maintain its claims to suzerainty within the island of Lanka while the Portuguese empire would thrive on the seas surrounding it—and, crucially, invest resources in the maintenance of the Lankan political order. Bhuvanekabāhu VII appears on the left and right hand ends of the casket in full majesty, riding a royal elephant and sitting on the lion throne of Kōṭṭe, displaying all the signs of authority of the foremost ruler of Sri Lanka (see Figure 0.3). For another five decades to come, Kōṭṭe was to maintain its symbolic prominence in Lanka against stiff competition from other polities thanks to the Portuguese connection.

All this being said, however, the story is also one of gradual divergence and, eventually, communicational breakdown. The house of Kōṭṭe intertwined its destiny with a society that began, roughly at the time when the embassy returned home, to forge new plans for its own imperial future in Asia. Whilst on the casket the Sinhalese king appeared in full imperial majesty, his and his successor's days as truly independent, Buddhist rulers of Lanka were numbered. Reports of Śrī Rāmarakṣa's diplomatic mission have reached us through works with such ominous titles as the *Temporal and Spiritual Conquest of Ceylon*, by the Jesuit Fernão de Queiroz, or the *Spiritual Conquest of the Orient*, by the Franciscan friar Paulo da Trindade. Whilst

---

[11] Strathern, *Kingship and Conversion*, p. 66. For an exploration of this and other caskets, with further bibliography, see Zoltán Biedermann, 'Diplomatic Ivories: Sri Lankan Caskets and the European-Asian Diplomatic Exchange, 1500–1600', in *Global Gifts. The Material Culture of Diplomacy in Early Modern Eurasia*, edited by Zoltán Biedermann, Anne Gerritsen, and Giorgio Riello (New York: Cambridge University Press, 2018), pp. 88–118.

**Figure 0.3** Bhuvanekabāhu VII as overlord of Lanka. Side panel of the 'coronation casket', Kōṭṭe, c.1541. Munich, Bayerische Verwaltung der staatlichen Schlösser, Gärten und Seen, Residenz München, Schatzkammer, Inv.-Nr. 1241.

1542 produced important gains for Kōṭṭe and is a delight to historians looking for global connections, the diplomatic offensive also prepared the ground for much more sinister developments, including the assassination of Bhuvanekabāhu VII in 1551; an increasing pressure on rulers to convert to Catholicism; and the gradual infiltration of the Lankan imperial project by Iberian ideas of spiritual and temporal conquest. There is a distinct possibility that Lankan indigenism itself was reinforced precisely through the confrontation with Portuguese aggressivity.

By 1557, king Dharmapāla was baptized and became Dom João. In 1580 he signed a will leaving his kingdom to the Portuguese crown in case he died without having produced a Sinhalese heir, and by the time he passed away in 1597 a military campaign aiming for the conquest of the island, ordered by Phillip II of Spain, was fully under way. The coastal lowlands of Sri Lanka became one of the largest theatres of terrestrial warfare involving any European power in Asia before the advent of British rule. And when the Portuguese were ousted in 1658, it was thanks to an alliance of a Lankan ruler in the mountainous interior with the Dutch, who soon replicated the Portuguese experience of going from maritime control to territorial conquest—only to be followed, after 1796, by the British, who conquered the island in 1815 and held it until 1948.[12]

At one level, the story of the collapse of the Luso-Lankan dialogue calls to be linked up with the developments described by Lauren Benton in *A Search for Sovereignty*. The imperial triangle unravelled tragically, towards the end of the period under consideration, under the weight of the binding together, in European minds, of royal authority with the notion of full territorial control.[13] It was the new mental construct of sovereignty, I shall argue, that exploded into Sri Lanka around 1600 to cause the greatest damage after almost a century of softer, suzerainty-based interactions. This said, the bulk of the story is chronologically anterior to Benton's, and it unfolds at a different level, in a more labyrinthine and culturally interconnected terrain. It is a story of connections that worked whilst being increasingly put under strain; and a story of a breakdown announced many decades before it materialized. A picture will emerge of the various layers of (dis)connectivity that prepared the ground, during the sixteenth century, for the disruptions of the early seventeenth century. Interactions during this period gained traction from the way that *together* South Asian and Iberian policy-makers cultivated, often against many obstacles, commensurable imperial ideas—but also considered the possibilities of not continuing the dialogue. This is a process that takes us not so much into the realm of laws and clashing legal cultures, but first and foremost into a world of ideas and utterances, at the heart of which we find what Frances Yates so aptly described, forty years ago, as the 'Imperial Theme'.[14]

## CHAPTERS OF THE LUSO-LANKAN ENCOUNTER

As we delve into the making of the global sixteenth century, we are confronted with a fundamental question: do we study empires (as they grow and confront each other), or empire (as an idea that resonates across the globe)? Yates found it notable how imperial ambitions proliferated across Europe precisely at the time when Charles V saw his dominions grow across the globe as the one and only legitimate *Imperator*. As Habsburg Spain expanded, France and England developed

[12] Intriguingly little has been written about the transitions between colonial powers. See, however, Alicia F. Schrikker, *Dutch and British Colonial Intervention in Sri Lanka, 1780–1815: Expansion and Reform* (Leiden: Brill, 2007) and Zoltán Biedermann, *The Portuguese in Sri Lanka and South India. Studies in the History of Empire, Diplomacy and Trade, 1500–1650* (Wiesbaden: Harrassowitz, 2014), pp. 103–48.

[13] Lauren Benton, *A Search for Sovereignty. Law and Geography in European Empires, 1400–1900* (Cambridge: Cambridge University Press, 2009).

[14] Frances A. Yates, *Astraea. The Imperial Theme in the Sixteenth Century* (London: Routledge and Kegan Paul, 1975), p. 33.

their own imperial discourses. One symbolic figure in particular rose to glory in this context: Astraea. The virgin goddess under whose just government humanity would find its way back into the Golden Age, the child 'destined to rule a reconciled world', was at the heart of countless ramifications of European discourses on empire. This, Yates argued, was the key to understanding European politics in the Renaissance.

To Yates, Astraea and the reign of Saturn were a quintessentially European affair. Today, as I argue in Chapter 1, we are in a position to go further, and ask new questions about transcontinental connections and commensurable cultures of political violence. The imperial theme is a much broader occurrence than Yates was able to see in the 1970s, and one that can be made to work for us as it helps explain many of the contradictions of the early modern world. What makes it most fascinating is how its European expressions resonated with thriving, deeply rooted imperial themes in the Americas, in Africa, and in Asia. Sri Lanka, the case study at the heart of this book, carried on a heritage of Aśōkan, Buddhist-inspired imperialism that proved connectable with the Iberian Renaissance emulations of the Augustan imperial ideal against many odds. The question here is not so much what formations like the Portuguese *Estado da Índia* or the kingdom of Kōṭṭe *were* (though this book ventures some thoughts in this regard), but what people believed them to be. Even a network-like entity such as the *Estado* or a territorially undefined polity such as Kōṭṭe could think and act imperially with consequences going far beyond their geographical limits. Empire was a common vision of Iberians, South Asians and other peoples across the globe, notwithstanding diverse material conditions and many cultural differences. It was an idea with devastating consequences as it helped pave the ground for conquest and colonization. But it was a shared idea nevertheless, and opened up numerous opportunities for cross-cultural communications.

Chapter 2 delves into the beginnings of the Lankan-Portuguese encounter, highlighting the early obstacles to the unfolding of an inter-imperial dialogue. It dwells on the stark contrast between the lack of curiosity shown by early Portuguese agents of empire in Ceylon, and the vivid interest taken by the Lankan elites in the Portuguese. While Ceylon disappeared from the Portuguese imperial imagination, overshadowed by countless other fields of opportunity emerging across Asia, the elite of the kingdom of Kōṭṭe began to labour with remarkable diplomatic perseverance to entice Portuguese leaders into visiting the island. Requests were made for the establishment of a military base at Colombo, which, it was hoped, might help consolidate the authority of the ruler of Kōṭṭe in a highly unstable political environment against the fierce competition of other Lankan rulers. The culmination of the diplomatic efforts of the ruler of Kōṭṭe, Bhuvanekabāhu VII, with the 1541–3 embassy mentioned above, is the subject of Chapter 3. In addition to the ivory casket already mentioned, significant archival materials survive today to give us a detailed picture of how the inter-imperial deal—following what I have called the 'Matrioshka principle' of nesting empires—was imagined in the Lankan capital. The papers also go some way to show, however, the limitations of the conversation that Bhuvanekabāhu wished to maintain: the Portuguese monarch, John III, accepted some requests whilst rejecting others, ignoring some of the most fundamental needs of his vassal. From this mosaic of mutual understandings and misunderstandings, a picture emerges that is at once wondrous in the way it contains two commensurable imperial models, and ominous in the way these two models do not quite talk to each other in the way the elite of Kōṭṭe expected.

Chapter 4 explores the ways in which rulers and princes across Sri Lanka followed Bhuvanekabāhu's initiative to capture the attention and the resources of the Portuguese crown. Conversion to Catholicism, I argue, became a key diplomatic tool during the 1540s in the competitive quest for alliances with the *Estado*. This served the interests of Lankan rulers in the short term, but also prepared the ground for larger transformations in the longer run. Increasingly, Portuguese adventurers and decision-makers were encouraged by the local political elites to intertwine the Lankan imperial project with ideas of Catholic Universalism and, ultimately, a confessionalized Portuguese imperial mandate. Sri Lanka as a territory of the mind began to emerge precisely at this moment, combining Lankan ideas of the island as a repository of empire with a new notion of spiritual conquest. The road from here to subjugation was, however, not a straightforward one. As I show in Chapter 5, much of the second half of the sixteenth century was spent—even after the brutal looting in 1551 of the most sacred site of Lankan Buddhism, the Temple of the Buddha's Tooth at Kōṭṭe—in wars where Portuguese troops essentially followed Lankan orders. If comparisons with the New World can be made, then it is not so much with reference to the 'Middle Ground' paradigm coined by Richard White, as to the 'Native Ground' identified more recently by historians such as Kathleen DuVal and Pekka Hämäläinen. Portuguese individuals became increasingly involved in terrestrial warfare and diplomatic activities across the lowlands and the mountainous central areas of Sri Lanka. They were active in many ways, but they also lacked an official Portuguese mandate. The kingdom of Kōṭṭe itself, with its allies, was in a defensive position, constantly besieged by rival Lankan forces during the third quarter of the century. This situation functioned as a pressure cooker, however, generating an increasingly complex Mestizo society at Colombo, especially after this city absorbed the militarily untenable royal court of Kōṭṭe, in 1565. The new *caput regni* remained politically dependent on the old imperial project of Kōṭṭe, but also became a potential breeding ground for plans—some inspired by distant Spanish deeds—that could not be controlled indefinitely by the Lankan elite.

Chapter 6 analyses the transformations that finally paved the way, in the 1580s and 1590s, for a policy turn towards an officially sanctioned conquest of Ceylon. The 1580 donation of Kōṭṭe to the Portuguese crown, which would itself fall into Habsburg hands soon after, emerges as a key moment along with the dramatic military and political developments in other parts of the island. The growth and collapse of the rival empire of Sītāvaka in the interior is shown to have triggered perceptions of opportunity among some Portuguese leaders, but wider connections were also essential for change to occur. Crucial new links emerged connecting Colombo with Malacca, Manila, and Madrid, the imperial capital where, ultimately, conquest orders were issued by 1595. And yet, even in this phase of transition, the local initiatives of Luso-Lankan and Sinhalese war-makers remained a driving force.

The clash of legal and political cultures that unfolded as the idea of conquest finally began to materialize is the subject of Chapter 7. The main question addressed is whether the new policy supported by the Habsburg administration can be explained in terms of 'Spanish influence' on the Portuguese imperial model. Whilst an affirmative answer may seem self-evident, a more detailed analysis shows very clearly that the Iberian Union of crowns was not in itself the cause for transformation, but an opportunity for Portuguese reformist forces to change the status quo. Although orders for the conquest of Ceylon were issued in Madrid, an intricate web of communications spanning half the globe was ultimately a more powerful source of political change than any of the central authorities of the Catholic Monarchy. Before we hurry to conclusions, again, emphasis must be placed on the commonalities of Iberian and Lankan political culture, on the possibilities of joint empire-building as well as the impossibilities.

In Chapter 8, I argue that the final years of the sixteenth century and the first decade of the seventeenth century brought about one of the great misunderstandings of the early modern period: the reading of Kōṭṭe's suzerainty-based imperial project, by the Habsburg authorities, as a project of sovereignty-oriented conquest. The resulting wars that dragged on during the following decades resulted largely from this widening gap in political culture. This, I venture in the conclusion, may allow us to make some further extrapolations on the merits and shortcomings of connected history. Do commensurability and the potential for mutual understandings logically increase as societies talk to each other and learn each other's languages, or can they also decrease? What can the lessons learned from this case tell us about the interdependence of the global and the local in the sixteenth century? Does Sri Lanka offer us a model that may enrich our understanding of the making of global power dynamics elsewhere? Far from suggesting that Sri Lanka offers a general template—it is, of course, a particular case very different from others such as the Mughal empire, Ming China or Safavid Persia—I do ask whether it may be worth engaging more systematically than before in something like '(dis)connected history': an approach that explores the global connectivity of early modern polities whilst also integrating systematically the obstacles arising to it. The most desirable option in my perspective is that we examine the profound, inextricable intertwinement of deeply contradictory processes of convergence and divergence as a core characteristic of early modernity at large.

# 1

# (Dis)connecting Empires
## Towards a Critical History of Early Modern Imperial Connections

Global history has promised redemption from the compartmentalized understandings of the past that dominated the world less than three decades ago. Yet some fundamental spatial and temporal divisions—between early modern and modern, or between Atlantic and Indic—remain in place. The question is: how do we labour against those divisions without losing sight of the faultlines that shaped the lives of people in the past? Where exactly do we draw the line between our own ambitions to overcome compartmentalized approaches to history, and the undeniable fact that past societies did not communicate unrestrictedly across the globe? Can we be critical of the local and the regional without creating an ultimately meaningless hegemony of the global?[1] It is my contention that a critical connected history genuinely concerned with the local as much as with the global is our best bet to face the challenge. Along the way, we may be able to answer questions about temporality, communication, periodization, and the nature of historical change in contexts where formerly disconnected societies began to interact.

## 'CONNECTED HISTORY' AND THE PROBLEM OF SCALE

Whilst global connections between Sri Lanka, Lisbon, Madrid, Rome, Manila and many other places are one theme highlighted in this book, much of the action explored unfolds in relatively confined geographical spaces. Many historians face this dilemma. Letters may have travelled thousands of miles, but they were still written and read in specific loci. An order might have been issued in Madrid in reaction to news coming from Colombo or Goa, and this emerging, global dimension of human agency is clearly a key characteristic of the sixteenth century. Yet actions feeding into the news or resulting from the orders (for example, someone's coronation or death) still occurred first and foremost locally, in smaller environments, the shape and size of which depended on the mobility that would fit in

---

[1] On the regional as an important category sitting between the local and the global, see R. Bin Wong, 'Regions and global history', in *Writing the History of the Global. Challenges for the 21st century*, edited by Maxine Berg (Oxford: Oxford University Press, 2013), pp. 83–105.

one day after another of human activity on the ground. Naturally, these more confined places were not isolated either, and might well have multiple, long-distance connections of their own—but they seem different from the emergent global space nevertheless. Where, then, *is* the ground upon which global historians interested in connections labour? If we had to point it out on a world map, what movements would our fingers perform?

One approach is to see the global and the local as two separable categories, fundamentally differing on grounds of their scale. At its simplest, the global is big, and the local small. In fact, in an era of material-based communications the global and the local tend to inhabit different temporalities, which may well offer the firmest anchor for any considerations about scale: whilst in a local theatre of war actions produced consequences within minutes, days or weeks, it could take years for news to travel from, say, India to Iberia and back. Under such a lens, the local appears to relate to the global as a part to the whole. The local inhabits the global, nesting in spaces left untouched by the latter, rather than vice versa. Historians can engage with these complementary dimensions by looking at the past through a zooming lens. They can zoom in, zoom out, then zoom in again somewhere else, and enjoy the complementarity of micro and macro developments unfolding under their eyes.

But where precisely does a zooming-in-and-out approach leave us in our quest to understand the articulations between the local and the global? Among the challenges global history faces today, this remains one of the most demanding. Much recent writing on early colonial interactions boils down, as Jorge Cañizares-Esguerra has pointed out, to local history in new clothes. Even what is by now identifiable as the new mainstream borderland historiography in the Americas often delivers little more than an ultimately infertile succession of studies that, whilst paying lip service to global questions, fail to address the relation between their local subjects and the formation of the global power structures we ultimately wish to understand.[2] The shortage of conceptual firepower at a supra-local level may well be at the heart of the new historiography's frequent failure to provide a compelling alternative to imperial history.[3] Crucially, the inverse is also sometimes the case. Much work has been done to reveal the movement of individuals, commodities and other artefacts across the globe in the early modern period. Global historians have been able to build compelling narratives about the making of the world we live in—writing, as Maxine Berg put it, 'the history of the global'.[4] Yet the resulting picture of a profusely interconnected world traversed by itinerant people, ideas and things of all sorts is often, as John-Paul Ghobrial has recently taken the courage to warn, impressionistic at best.[5] One does not have to listen

---

[2] Jorge Cañizares-Esguerra, 'Entangled Histories: Borderland Historiographies in New Clothes?', *American Historical Review*, 112 (June 2007), pp. 789 and 799. More on borderlands below, in Chapter 5.

[3] Pekka Hämäläinen and Samuel Truett, 'On Borderlands', *Journal of American History*, 98, 2 (2011), p. 339.

[4] Berg, ed., *Writing the History of the Global*.

[5] John-Paul Ghobrial, 'The Secret Life of Elias of Babylon and the Uses of Global Microhistory', *Past and Present*, 222, 1 (2014), p. 56.

very hard to pick up the signs that global history may be heading into a crisis. 'The neatly packaged narrative of ever-increasing globalization, interconnectedness and universalization', a growing number of historians will now agree, may well prove 'too abstract to be meaningful'.[6] Studies on immobility are starting to appear alongside the mainstream preoccupation with mobility.

Connective approaches do remain, I believe, our best hope for linking up not only one place with any other, but also the local with the global. Yet clearly, some conceptual refinement is needed. 'Connected history', elevated to paradigm status around the turn of the millennium, has been described as 'an approach to history that focuses on [...] connections that transcend politically bounded territories and connect various parts of the world to one another'.[7] A 'focus on interconnections' was almost naturally at the heart of the new global history journal project launched in Britain in 2006, partly in reaction to what was perceived as the excessively broad and abstract theorizing of American 'world' historians.[8] But exactly what 'connections' should consist of, or how they might be theorized in terms of temporality and scale, has never quite been clarified. When the motto of connected histories appeared in the late 1990s, it was sufficiently enthralling for no one to feel hampered by the vagueness of the terminology.[9] It may have been tempting to see the method as an antithesis to comparative history—after all, the 1997 article was written in reaction to Victor Liebermann's ongoing work on Eurasian 'parallels'—but in much of the work of Subrahmanyam himself, the two methods appear as mutually compatible.[10]

Where is it, then, that we are heading? Identifying more and more connections has become, like identifying the movement of people and things per se, of limited significance. Clearly, the fifteenth and sixteenth centuries saw a drastic increase in long-distance connections, but we also need to ask questions about how precisely the new links worked or failed to work, and why. In other words, we may need some sort of connection history to consolidate the notion of connected history before the latter becomes so pervasive that it loses relevance—or indeed gives rise to an unhelpful, localist backlash, which is the last thing we need.[11] The current

---

[6] Maryam Patton, 'Global Microhistory: One or two things that I know about it', Blogpost on *JHIBLOG* (September 2015), https://jhiblog.org/2015/09/09/global-microhistory-one-or-two-things-that-i-know-about-it/ (last accessed 19 October 2017).

[7] Sanjay Subrahmanyam, 'Connected Histories: Notes towards a reconfiguration of Early Modern Eurasia', *Modern Asian Studies*, 31, 3 (1997), pp. 735–62. Sven Beckert in the AHR Conversation 'On Transnational History', *American Historical Review*, 111, 5 (2006), p. 1446.

[8] William Gervase Clarence-Smith, Kenneth Pomeranz and Peer Vries, 'Editorial', *Journal of Global History*, 1, 1 (2006), p. 2.

[9] On the role that vagueness can play in scholarship, see Patrick Gardiner, *The Nature of Historical Explanation*, reprint (Oxford: Clarendon Press, 1980), p. 81.

[10] Prasannan Parthasarathi has called comparison 'the poor stepchild of global history' in 'Comparison in global history', in *Writing the History of the Global*, p. 69. Subrahmanyam has repeatedly underlined the importance of systematic comparative work. See e.g. 'A Tale of Three Empires. Mughals, Ottomans, and Habsburgs in a Comparative Context', *Common Knowledge*, 12, 1 (2006), pp. 66–92.

[11] For a fresh take on failed dialogues, see Ralf Hertel and Michael Kivak, eds., *Early Encounters Between East Asia and Europe: Telling Failures* (Abingdon/New York: Routledge, 2017).

thinking about 'Global Microhistory' is important.[12] In this renascent subfield, two strands have appeared: one exploring the global lives of individuals, and another exploring concentrations of global connections in specific places.[13] Ultimately, such approaches seem to feed on Giddensian structuration theory, and that is in itself an auspicious proposition. Here, the global is 'a function of system integration or interaction between individuals away from each other in time or space or both', and thus 'it is the global that reappears inside the local in the form of distant influences impinging on personal lives and daily activities'.[14]

We should make sure that we aim for more than just a peppering of global history with micro-stories, or the exploration of particular individuals and places traversed by a high concentration of global forces. Those narratives are at their most valuable where they engage with the more disconcerting challenges of the 'glocal' turn, and the often unstraightforward interactions between the global and the local. The term 'glocal' may be awkward and imperfect, but as early modernists we face more than just the duty of keeping an eye on the global when talking about the local, or remembering the local when exploring the global. We need to think about genuinely complex explanations of the past where the local *makes* the global, and vice versa. And where the global *challenges* the local, and vice versa, without linearity. Localization theory as proposed by O. W. Wolters—emphasizing the way societies engage proactively with the foreign and integrate it into their own power structures—shall spring up repeatedly over the following chapters because it offers such a valuable departure from more static, often unidirectional models.[15] It helps explain how overarching, transcontinental forces might be digested into local power structures, but also offers glimpses into how local processes feed into the making of global power structures—and so on, in a pendular movement that ends up transforming everything, from the most remote Sri Lankan town to the global empire, in intensely, but never straightforwardly interconnected ways. Connections as such are, in other words, both large and small in scale; they allow the local to inhabit the global and vice versa; they offer opportunities for the local to produce the global and vice versa; and they will typically do all this whilst facing considerable obstacles, both structural and conjunctural, which call to be studied in depth.

Historians of Iberian expansion in Asia are in a privileged position to make suggestions in this regard. Sanjay Subrahmanyam's formulation of the connected

---

[12] Francesca Trivellato, 'Is There a Future for Italian Microhistory in the Age of Global History?', *California Italian Studies*, 2, 1 (2011), online publication.

[13] See Brodie Waddell, 'What is microhistory now?', Blogpost at *Many-headed-monster* (June 2017). https://manyheadedmonster.wordpress.com/2017/06/20/what-is-microhistory-now/ (last accessed 5 November 2017). Waddell cites as examples for the 'global lives' approach John-Paul Ghobrial's 'The Secret Life of Elias of Babylon and the Uses of Global Microhistory', *Past and Present*, 222, 1 (2014), pp. 51–93, and for the 'global places' approach Benjamin Kaplan's *Cunegonde's Kidnapping: A Story of Religious Conflict in the Age of Enlightenment* (New Haven, CT/London: Yale University Press, 2014), along with the current unpublished work of Maxine Berg on British Columbia.

[14] Jean-Sébastien Guy, 'What is Global and What is Local? A Theoretical Discussion Around Globalization', *Parsons Journal for Information Mapping*, 1, 2 (2009), pp. 1–2.

[15] O. W. Wolters, *History, culture, and region in Southeast Asian perspectives*, 2nd revised edition (Ithaca, NY: Cornell University Press, 1999).

histories method emerged in the 1990s precisely out of his engagement with the then burgeoning historiography of the Portuguese empire in Asia. Acknowledging the importance of Iberian-based transcontinental connections, sticking to solid archival methodologies, *and* questioning the pertinence of a binary division between Europe and Asia at the same time, had been at the core of a lively historiographical school initiated in the 1970s by the French historians Jean Aubin and Denys Lombard, developed in the 1980s by their disciple Luís Filipe Thomaz and other Portuguese scholars, and finally digested for the Anglophone public in the 1990s by Subrahmanyam.[16] For the followers of the so-called 'Luso-Asianist' approach, the *Estado da Índia*, the political formation built by the Portuguese in the East along with numerous other, unofficial forms of mercantile, missionary and military presence, functioned as an intricate hub of connections messing rather thoroughly with traditional notions of scale and with the customary metageography of continents. It was both tiny (being based in seaports) and vast (establishing navigational links between India and Europe). It was both insignificant when compared to the great landbound empires of the time, and yet highly influential, when connected with its surroundings, as suggested by the deep transformations that societies in and around those contact nodes underwent. Rather than seeing the *Estado* as a European polity in Asia, historians began to understand how it functioned as an Asian polity in its own right or, more pointedly, a polity participating in the emerging realities of an early modern Maritime Asia intertwined with Maritime Europe, gradually forming something that was novel to all sides involved.[17]

## 'CONNECTED HISTORY' AND THE PROBLEM OF INTERCULTURAL COMMUNICATION

To understand this transcontinental, in-between space where the established metageography of 'Asia' versus 'Europe' can begin to dissolve without glossing over other boundaries that did in fact exist, the study of communications was and is key. There are, to begin with, materialities to be understood that conditioned the way information and ideas moved across the world or not—perhaps a daunting perspective, but not an uninteresting one if we think of a 'material turn' that grounds power in materiality, and vice versa.[18] Words might be written on goldleaf

---

[16] Sanjay Subrahmanyam, *The Portuguese Empire in Asia 1500–1700. A Political and Economic History* (London: Longman, 1993).

[17] See especially the journal *Mare Luso-Indicum* (École Pratique des Hautes Études/Libraire Droz) published under the direction of Aubin and Geneviève Bouchin, with the occasional participation of M. N. Pearson, in the 1970s, and its successor *Moyen-Orient et Océan Indien, XVIe–XIXe siècles* (Société d'histoire de l'Orient/L'Harmattan) since 1984. The journals *Mare Liberum* (CNCDP, Lisbon) and *Anais de História de Além-Mar* (CHAM, Lisbon) have carried on some of the legacy, though gradually retreating into less transnational terrain. One of the most accessible antologies of the Luso-Asianist scholarship remains the collection of articles in Sanjay Subrahmanyam, ed., *Sinners and Saints. The Successors of Vasco da Gama* (New Delhi: Oxford University Press, 1995).

[18] See Tony Bennett and Patrick Joyce, 'Material powers: Introduction', in *Material Powers: Cultural Studies, History and the Material Turn*, edited by Tony Bennett and Patrick Joyce (London/New York: Routledge, 2010), pp. 1–22.

or paper, passed through palace doors or the gates of a fort, carried along jungle paths or kept in ship cabins by soldiers, traders or priests, whispered in the middle of the night, lost in a shipwreck, or proclaimed with pomp to large audiences. For the present study, these aspects are more important than the economic backdrop against which communications occurred. I have not found a clear enough link between the political developments covered in this book and fluctuations of prices or trade patterns to pursue an integrated political-economic approach. My attempts at thinking about the shift to conquest in relation to the cost of procuring cinnamon, for example, were dispiriting. I have, in contrast, found abundant signs that communication methods and—to borrow an expression put to good use by John-Paul Ghobrial—'information flows' played a key role.[19]

Naturally, the most fascinating aspect to emerge from these materials is not just how, after 1500, people from Portugal were suddenly able to travel a long distance around the Cape. It is the way Portuguese and Lankan men and women could, for the first time in history, see each other in flesh and blood, hear each other's voices, exchange gifts and goods, fight or convene to engage in increasingly complex negotiations, with increasingly wide-ranging implications. The challenge then becomes to explore the mechanisms by which people established meaningful connections and kept them alive or not, often against significant linguistic, social, and political odds, on grounds of imperfect acts of communication—so much so that the present enquiry into the history of early imperial connections can be read as a communications-based history of political change.

How were people at the beginning of the early modern period to communicate if they barely understood each other's language? Is it not the case that, as a historian of Portuguese literature once put it, the expansion into a world full of 'unknown' languages must have generated countless 'zones of communicational silence'?[20] Portuguese and Sri Lankan political discourses became connectable, I will argue, because the historical actors involved developed an interest in treating them as connectable and maintaining a meaningful interaction even when they knew that it might not be perfect. People keep communicating even in a world full of flawed translations because, as Sidney Mintz forthrightly put it, meanings arise 'out of use, as people use substances in social relationships'.[21] As every linguist knows, communication is about more than just the unambiguous rendering of verbally presented contents. It generates mutual understandings and misunderstandings through the performance of communicational and speech acts, often

---

[19] Which is not to say that a revisiting of the enormously important work of Portugal's greatest economic historian, Vitorino Magalhães Godinho, would not be desirable. I have, for example, come across a fair amount of documents that could be used to correct established chronologies of the cinnamon price evolution, although the panorama remains patchy. Cf. *Os Descobrimentos e a Economia Mundial. 2a edição correcta e ampliada*, 4 vols. (Lisbon: Presença, 1981–3). On the notion of 'information flow', see John-Paul Ghobrial, *The Whispers of Cities. Information Flows in Istanbul, London, and Paris in the Age of William Trumbull* (Oxford: Oxford University Press, 2013), pp. vii–viii.

[20] Maria Leonor Carvalhão Buescu, *O estudo das línguas exóticas no século XVI* (Lisbon: Instituto de Cultura e Língua Portuguesa, 1983), pp. 21–5.

[21] Sidney Mintz, *Sweetness and Power: The Place of Sugar in Modern History* (New York: Viking Press, 1985), p. 17.

across considerable semiotic gaps. Fortunately, early modernists are today inclined to consider communicational processes in the larger sense of the word—that is, including the acts surrounding the utterance of words and writing of texts—as key historical factors, namely in the formation of the state.[22] Some of the most stimulating scholarship produced in recent years pertains to what has been designated in France and Germany as the 'cultural history of the political' (*histoire culturelle du politique/Kulturgeschichte des Politischen*).[23] Communication, representation, and performance constitute vital links in this thriving new historiography between individual and group agency on the one hand and the creation of new power symbols and structures on the other. The symbolic communication that powered (perhaps excessively) Geertz's 'Theatre State' has been brought to early modern Europe, and is changing the nature of the game.[24]

Ironically, of course, much of this scholarship remains primarily preoccupied with the formation of European states,[25] but it is beginning to open doors to an integrated study of European, African, and Asian power structures in the early modern period. Cultural historians of the political have decided to embrace an ample and open concept not only of communication, but also of culture.[26] European early modernists remained long fixated on the role played by political philosophy and the rise of new institutions in the making of the state. South Asianists, in their turn, long cultivated a comparable obsession with the political role of religion. In both cases, the focus on a single aspect not only obscured the rest of the picture, it also hindered historiographical connections between the continents. To adopt a transversal approach centred on the study of communication, translation, and representation appears as a refreshingly simple way forward to de-reify and decompartmentalize continental histories, whilst still maintaining the possibility of disruption. It is, as Nicholas Dirks once put it, a matter of concentrating on the 'cultural construction of power', whichever part of the world and whichever aspect of culture we are looking at, and even if more than one culture is involved.[27]

---

[22] See for example Ronald Asch and Dagmar Freist, eds., *Staatsbildung als kultureller Prozess. Strukturwandel und Legitimation von Herrschaft in der Frühen Neuzeit* (Cologne: Böhlau, 2005).

[23] Barbara Stollberg-Rilinger, ed., *Was heißt Kulturgeschichte des Politischen?* (Berlin: Duncker & Humblot, 2005).

[24] Clifford Geertz, *Negara: The Theatre State in Nineteenth-Century Bali* (Princeton, NJ: Princeton University Press, 1980). Barbara Stollberg-Rilinger, 'Rituals of Decision Making? Early Modern European Assemblies of Estates as Acts of Symbolic Communication', in *Political Order and the Forms of Communication in Medieval and Early Modern Europe*, edited by Yoshihisa Hattori (Rome: La Viella, 2014), pp. 63–95.

[25] See Birgit Emich, 'Frühneuzeitliche Staatsbildung und politische Kultur. Für die Veralltäglichung eines Konzepts', *Zeitschrift für historische Forschung*, 35 (2005), pp. 191–205.

[26] Which is not to say that this comes without further risks. As Anne Kane put it, 'while it is now widely accepted that culture [...] is as constitutive of social structure, social order, and social change as material and institutional forces, and causally significant in historical events, transformations, and processes, the problem of how to access and deploy the explanatory power of culture in historical accounts remains vexing'. 'Reconstructing Culture in Historical Explanation: Narratives as Cultural Structure and Practice', *History and Theory*, 39, 3 (Oct. 2000), p. 311.

[27] Nicholas B. Dirks, *The Hollow Crown. Ethnohistory of an Indian Kingdom* (Cambridge: Cambridge University Press, 1988), p. 5.

Early modern global interactions, especially those of the sixteenth century, are best understood as open-ended communicational processes involving multiple, dynamically evolving groups and polities, rather than clearly delimited entities pertaining to the domain of 'us' encountering 'them', or 'them' reacting to 'us'. Change occurs historically as agency itself takes successive different forms and goes through variations of scale. Communication and imperial expansion can and have been theorized as structures rather than events—integral building blocks, that is, of the unfolding project of western hegemony—but the approach I favour especially for the period before 1600 is less clear-cut.[28] It aspires to a dissection of early imperial interactions as processes shaped by cross-cultural, performance-laden dialogues unfolding in a world marked by quickly evolving capabilities for translation, shifting borders, and power relations. 'Evolving', to be sure, is not to be read as signalling linear development, let alone a linear movement towards modernity. Quite the contrary.

## FROM 'COMMERCE' TO 'CONQUEST'? TACKLING THE GHOST OF PHASEOLOGY

A focus on the *shifting* dynamics of interaction and communication is fundamental in our field. Observing the unfolding of asymmetric power relations between 'discoverers' and 'discovered' has been a preoccupation among historians for some time. Much has been written about transitions from 'contact' to 'annihilation' (Peter Mancall) or to 'removal' (James Merrell), about the successive stages of 'alliance, conquest, and conversion' (Steve J. Stern) or, in one of the most remarkable pieces of New World revisionism, on the possibility that 'domination' may have preceded—and indeed done well without—'dominance' (Gonzalo Lamana).[29] Analogous ideas have been around for Asia, where the differences between early and high colonial interactions are even more manifest than in the Americas, for many years. In contrast to the advocates of the 'Vasco da Gama epoch' approach, who in the post-independence years embraced the notion that the Portuguese explorer single-handedly disrupted the natural flow of Asian history,[30] historians including Holden Furber, Michael N. Pearson, Blair King or Anthony Reid began

---

[28] Cf. Patrick Wolfe, 'Settler Colonialism and the Elimination of the Native', *Journal of Genocide Research*, 8, 4 (2006), pp. 387–409.

[29] James H. Merrell, *The Indians' New World. Catawbas and their Neighbors from European Contact through the Era of Removal* (Chapel Hill, NC: University of North Carolina Press, 1989). Steve J. Stern, 'Paradigms of Conquest: History, Historiography, and Politics', *Journal of Latin American Studies*, 24 (1992), pp. 1–34. Gonzalo Lamana, *Domination without Dominance: Inca-Spanish Encounters in Early Colonial Peru* (Durham, NC: Duke University Press, 2008).

[30] See K. M. Panikkar, *Asia and Western Dominance. A Survey of the Vasco da Gama Epoch of Asian History, 1498–1945* (London: Alan & Unwin, 1953). The expression resurfaces repeatedly, as in A. J. R. Russell-Wood, *A World on the Move. The Portuguese in Africa, Asia, and America, 1415–1800* (Baltimore, MD: Johns Hopkins University Press, 1993), p. 6, or Coral Bell, *The End of the Vasco da Gama Era. The Next Landscape in World Politics* (Sydney: Lowy Institute for International Policy, 2007).

from the late 1960s to talk about a prolonged age of 'partnership' or 'commerce' leading up to the better-known period of 'dominion' (Pearson).[31]

Such approaches have been extremely valuable and important. They do involve, however, the risk of reinforcing linear interpretations of the past. A rigid handling of the notion of process may here end up implying inevitable progressions from 'commerce to conquest', logically entailing a degradation of relations from consensus to confrontation.[32] Such theories are problematic: first, because conquest sometimes preceded commerce, and much of the time war and trade were inextricably intertwined affairs anyway;[33] and second, because the phases into which global interactions have been sliced up are often still grounded in the temporality of European expansion.[34] The lack of integration between the history of what is presumed to be the expanding party, and that of the receiving side, reveals a doggedly entrenched overestimation of the push versus the pull factors. If one considers the very different receptions of the Portuguese in two such proximate places as Calicut and Cochin, within the same few months in 1498, the picture simply does not square with the phases so nonchalantly thrown around by historians. Different Asian elites had different interests and approaches. One struggles to see any valid alternative to observing *both* sides as equivalent, fully proactive agents of encounter, at least in order to understand how things got going. Romain Bertrand has branded this approach as an *'histoire à parts égales'* (nodding, with a critical twist, to Lucien Febvre's *histoire à part entière*), a history where all sides involved are given equal standing per principle, regardless of the outcomes that hindsight tells us about.[35] In general, such stories involve complicated combinations of continuity and change, rather than clear-cut progressions from one stage of interaction to the next. Early modern interactions involve confusing fluctuations, intertwinements, bifurcations, and inversions. As we shall see, there were misunderstandings even as communications grew, and signs of mutual understanding even as dialogues collapsed.

[31] Holden Furber, 'Asia and the West as Partners before "Empire" and After', *Journal of Asian Studies*, 28, 4 (1969), pp. 711–21; Blair L. King and M. N. Pearson, *The Age of Partnership: Europeans in Asia before Dominion* (Honolulu: University Press of Hawaii, 1979); Anthony Reid, *Southeast Asia in the Age of Commerce, 1450–1680* (New Haven, CT: Yale University Press, 1988).

[32] See Mark T. Berger's portentous review article 'From Commerce to Conquest: The Dynamics of British Mercantile Imperialism in Eighteenth-Century Bengal, and the Foundation of the British Indian Empire', *Bulletin of Concerned Asian Scholars*, 22, 1 (1990), pp. 44–62, which does, despite the title, pay attention to the inextricable intertwining of commercial and political dynamics or, as the author puts it, to the existence of 'a number of complementary impulses' (p. 60).

[33] See, most pertinently, the analysis of this intertwinement in overseas politics under Manuel I by Luís Filipe F. R. Thomaz, 'Factions, interests and messianism: The politics of Portuguese expansion in the East, 1500–1521', *The Indian Economic and Social History Review*, 28, 1 (1991), pp. 97–109. A preoccupation with this complexity may well have prompted Charles Boxer to invert the order of 'commerce and conquest' in the title one of his later books: *Portuguese Conquest and Commerce in Southern Asia, 1500–1750* (London: Variorum Reprints, 1985).

[34] Raymond F. Betts, *Europe Overseas: Phases of Imperialism* (New York: Basic Books, 1968). Perhaps a good alternative to 'phases' is indeed 'faces', as in Phillip Darby, *The Three Faces of Imperialism: British and American Approaches to Asia and Africa, 1870–1970* (New Haven, CT: Yale University Press, 1987).

[35] Romain Bertrand, *L'histoire à parts égales. Récits d'une rencontre, Orient-Occident (XVIe–XVIIe siècle)* (Paris: Seuil, 2011). Lucien Febvre, *Pour une histoire à part entière* (Paris: SEVPEN, 1962).

## THE PERVASIVENESS OF VIOLENCE:
## REVISITING THE 'AGE OF PARTNERSHIP'

Any approach to inter-cultural communication and connected histories will inevitably run into the challenge of redistributing agency without downplaying the brutal realities of encounter. The subtext in the Age of Partnership theory has often been that, prior to the arrival of the Europeans, the Asian seas were a neutral space, a quiet home to peaceful cosmopolitan trade. This amounts to a watered-down version of Polanyi's and Revere's old theory of protected and unmilitarized commercial spaces on the fringes of great land-bound empires.[36] Against such a backdrop, partnership during the early modern period often appears as a survival of older practices *despite* the European intrusion, while breakdowns then result *from* it. This is only useful inasmuch as it allows for a due recognition of the resilience of Asian societies. There is indeed no way around the fact that in the sixteenth century it was often the Portuguese who felt 'discovered' by their Asian counterparts, compelled to occupy unstable positions in diplomacy, warfare, and trade despite all the glorious fuss of the chronicles, usually written decades later.[37] One could thus argue that during the early colonial period the older logics of Asian political and commercial culture prevailed over the gradually emerging forces of the new European system, and were *then* steadily eroded.

However, it is also becoming increasingly clear that what characterizes the system in Maritime Asia before 1500 is not so much a staunch commitment to peaceful transnational commerce, but some of that—especially at the symbolic level—along with a deeply rooted, pervasive culture of violence commensurable to that of other parts of the world. It may be time to take a critical distance from such theories as that, for example, of Sheldon Pollock about the fundamental contrasts between 'Indic' and 'Latin' empire building. For Pollock, the so-called Sanskrit cosmopolis expanded peacefully through conviction, as opposed to the Roman empire, which grew through conquest—in a contrast that, for the author, remained meaningful even centuries after the demise of Rome.[38] Clearly, the essentializing impulse carrying the entire comparison calls to be revisited. Already it is clear that, as Alan Strathern has pointed out most recently, precisely on the fringes of the Sanskrit cosmopolis the beautiful and the sacred, from which this particular formation is supposed to have drawn its strength, appears thoroughly 'plunged into the dirty work of political competition and group struggle in a way that is all

---

[36] Robert Revere, '"No Man's Coast": Ports of Trade in the Eastern Mediterranean', *Trade and Market in Early Empires*, edited by Karl Polanyi (Glencoe, IL: Free Press, 1957), pp. 38–63.

[37] Jorge M. Flores, '"They have discovered us". The Portuguese and the Trading World of the Indian Ocean', in *Encompassing the Globe. Portugal and the World in the 16th and 17th centuries*, edited by Jay Levenson (Washington, DC: Freer and Sackler Gallery, 2007), vol. II, pp. 185–93.

[38] Sheldon Pollock, *The Language of the Gods in the World of Men: Sanskrit, Culture, and Power in Premodern India* (Berkeley/Los Angeles: University of California Press, 2009), pp. 163–88. For a recent romanticized vision of the pre-Portuguese Indian Ocean, see Akhil Gupta, 'Globalization and Difference: Cosmopolitanism before the Nation-State', *Transforming Cultures e-Journal*, 3, 2 (2008).

too familiar from other parts of the world'.[39] The closer one looks, the more one doubts whether a peaceful pre-European Indian Ocean is anything else than the projection of a twentieth-century dream.

Whilst the Portuguese as newcomers to the region certainly brought with them new military tactics and technologies (not gunpowder itself, but canons mounted on high board ships, for example), the militarization of the ocean and its ports was no novelty. A system of navigational permits imposed by force had been in place in the Red Sea centuries before it was adopted by the Portuguese.[40] Instances of militarization in the waters around India, Persia and Arabia were, as highlighted by Sebastian Prange, numerous.[41] Violence was commonplace on the land and on the sea, explaining the fast adaptation of Muslim commercial warlords to Portuguese tactics, soon matched by the Portuguese apprenticeship of South Asian methods.[42]

That the harsh realities thus emerging mirror the systemic violence described by historians of late medieval Iberia amounts to a significant historiographical convergence.[43] In both instances, the recognition of the pervasiveness of violence corrects earlier romantic ideas about the tolerational nature of medieval spaces— namely Iberia before the Inquisition and the Indic before the Portuguese—whilst also limiting the scope for a simplistic denunciatory stance. To recognize a certain permanence of conflict helps us, perhaps better than anything else, integrate early European activities into Asian history. It opens the door to a world of communications built around the possibility of politically and socially meaningful, mutually understandable violence. In fact, this is why the notion of 'contained conflict', thrown into the debate by Subrahmanyam almost three decades ago, is so appealing.[44] It comes as a recognition that there was a pressing propensity on all sides involved in the early modern encounter to constantly measure forces, to extort concessions and thus make the markets, as well as political and social structures, work. Force was seen as a virtue across the board. It is precisely its pervasiveness and legitimacy that allowed it to remain contained. Only gradually—and this can of course be read as the more significant part of the story—did one side come up with a *kind* of violence leaving no space for compromise, dislodging commensurable

---

[39] Alan Strathern, 'The digestion of the foreign in Lankan history, c. 500–1818, in *Sri Lanka at the Crossroads of History*', edited by Zoltán Biedermann and Alan Strathern (London: UCL Press, 2017), p. 225.

[40] Luís Filipe F. R. Thomaz, 'Precedents and Parallels of the Portuguese *Cartaz* System', in *The Portuguese, Indian Ocean, and European Bridgeheads, 1500–1800: Festschrift in Honour of Professor K. S. Mathew*, edited by Pius Malekandathil and Jamal Mohammed (Tellicherry: IRSSH, 2001), pp. 67–85.

[41] Sebastian R. Prange, 'A Trade of No Dishonor: Piracy, Commerce, and Community in the Western Indian Ocean, Twelfth to Sixteenth Century', *American Historical Review*, 116, 5 (2011), pp. 1269–93.

[42] On adaptations in terms of naval technology, see Vítor Rodrigues, 'A evolução da arte da Guerra dos Portugueses no Oriente (1498–1622)' (PhD dissertation, Insituto de Investigação Científica Tropical, Lisbon, 1998). On 'apprenticeship' see Jean Aubin, 'L'apprentissage de l'Inde. Cochin, 1503–1504', *Moyen-Orient et Océan Indien, XVIe–XIXe siècles*, 4 (1987), pp. 1–96.

[43] David Nirenberg, *Communities of Violence: Persecution of Minorities in the Middle Ages* (Princeton, NJ: Princeton University Press, 1996).

[44] Sanjay Subrahmanyam, *The Political Economy of Commerce: Southern India, 1500–1650* (Cambridge: Cambridge University Press, 1990), especially pp. 252–4.

power practices and upsetting the relative balance of forces. To recognize the pervasiveness of violence does not entail minimizing the impact of European activities, it simply introduces an important nuance.

As we shall see, in 1506 there was not even a moment of hesitation on the South Asian side to co-opt the Portuguese as military allies and mercenaries for local warfare, that is, to harness their violent potential. If the Portuguese had such a success in Sri Lanka and South India as power brokers during the sixteenth century, it was above all due to, and not in spite of, the political and social frameworks in which they came to act. Societies were prepared for considerable levels of physical violence to be exerted regularly by exogenous as well as indigenous agents. It is within a larger transcultural system pervaded by political and social uses of violence—often expressed of course, as we shall see, through a language emphasizing the ultimately harmonious goals of the measuring of forces—that the dialogue between Portuguese and Sri Lankans can be found to be most firmly anchored. But dialogue about what?

## EMPIRES AS NETWORKS: THE PROBLEM OF MAPPING IMPERIAL SPACE

Empires and the imperial have been the focus of much attention over the past decades, but there is still remarkable uncertainty surrounding those words. If communications evolved unstraightforwardly and violence was a crucial, transversal factor underlying the early imperial encounter, it is equally important to emphasize the obvious, namely that none of this was practised by state actors in the modern sense of the word. The autonomous state with its increasingly efficacious attempts at monopolizing violence and creating coherent, mutually exclusive spaces of sovereignty interconnected by formal diplomatic channels was just about starting to appear on the horizon. Whether we speak of empires, kingdoms or other political formations for this period, one thing that the historiography of the last four decades has made visible is the fragility and fragmentedness of such bodies politic.

The recognition of the fragility of polities traditionally seen as precursors of modern nation states has been at the heart of key scholarly transformations in South Asia *and* Iberia. We are now in a position to connect the histories and the historiographies of the two regions. Historians of Portugal have, since the 1980s, radically questioned the monolithic nature of the late medieval and early modern state. This revisionism, especially in António Hespanha's *The Vespers of Leviathan* from 1987 (a work widely read by students of history in southern Europe, but ignored elsewhere), has come as a vigorous reaction to a longstanding tradition of considering medieval Portugal as a precocious absolutist state.[45] And whilst

---

[45] António Manuel Hespanha, *As Vésperas do Leviathan. Instituições e poder político, Portugal—séc. XVII* (Coimbra: Livraria Almedina, 1994). See also the echoes of this stance across the reference multi-volume History of Portugal, José Mattoso, ed., *História de Portugal*, 8 vols. (Lisbon: Círculo de Leitores, 1993–4).

Hespanha's attempts at foraging into imperial history have remained less convincing, the relevance of his findings for imperial history is undeniable.[46]

How should a kingdom with such a fragile institutional backbone as Portugal have been able to build a solid, well-structured empire overseas? It is in the work of Luís Filipe Thomaz that this doubt comes most compellingly explored. Portuguese expansion, Thomaz has argued (perhaps at times excessively, but certainly driving home a key point), was deeply conditioned by internal factional divisions, especially between a 'commercialist' and a 'militarist' party at court. The rivalries played out globally, not just within the empire but also beyond its borders, through diplomatic and commercial rivalries reaching deep into Asian societies where Portuguese agents were active. This historiographical development resonates well with the emergence, especially in Cambridge, of studies into British imperial history exploring the fragilities of the body politic, and the empire's reliance on local collaborations. The Luso-Asianist approach has also delivered the most influential definition of Portugal's empire in Asia, re-branding it as a network, rather than a coherent imperial space.[47] Even critics of Thomaz agree that the old, nationalistic notion of a highly centralized empire cannot be revived.[48] Only recently have historians of the Spanish empire begun to follow an analogous, albeit more timid experiment, by exploring the notion of a 'polycentric monarchy'.[49]

The network paradigm deserves highlighting here in connection with changes in South Asian historiography.[50] Networks may be conveniently defined for our purpose, following the Indianist Monica L. Smith, as 'structures of interaction that include component parts linked not only to a single central point, but also to each other'. In a network, Smith adds, 'nodes and connectors are dependent upon each other, with a large potential number of combinations that enable those links to be sustained in a robust but flexible manner'.[51] Smith, perhaps the scholar who has most vigorously questioned the established notion of empire in pre-modern India, has suggested that we regard polities such as that of the Maurya as complex

---

[46] See António Manuel Hespanha and Catarina Madeira Santos, 'Os Poderes num Império Oceânico', in *História de Portugal*, edited by José Mattoso, vol. 4, pp. 395–413. Shortly after, an important multi-volume reference work was published: Francisco Bethencourt and Kirti Chaudhuri, eds., *História da Expansão Portuguesa*, 5 vols. (Lisbon: Círculo de Leitores, 1998).

[47] Luís Filipe F. R. Thomaz, *De Ceuta a Timor*, 2nd ed. (Lisbon: Difel, 1994), p. 210. This must be seen in connection with the second volume, titled *Les réseaux asiatiques* ('The Asian networks'), of Denys Lombard, *Le carrefour javanais. Essai d'histoire globale* (Paris: Éditions de l'École des Hautes Études en Sciences Sociales, 1990). Also see Anthony Disney, 'What was the Estado da Índia? Four Contrasting Images,' *Indica*, 38, 1–2 (2001), pp. 161–8.

[48] Francisco Bethencourt thus proposes the image of a 'nebula of power' in 'Political configurations and local powers', in *Portuguese Oceanic Expansion, 1400–1800*, edited by Francisco Bethencourt and Diogo Ramada Curto (Cambridge: Cambridge University Press, 2007), pp. 199 and 221. Again, *nébuleuse* is a concept that appears developed, albeit with a slightly different meaning, in Lombard, *Le Carrefour javanais*.

[49] Pedro Cardim, Tamar Herzog, José Javier Ruiz Ibáñez and Gaetano Sabatini, eds., *Polycentric Monarchies. How Did Early Modern Spain and Portugal Achieve and Maintain a Global Hegemony?* (Eastbourne: Sussex Academic Press, 2012).

[50] See Sanjay Subrahmanyam, 'State Formation and Transformation in Early Modern India and Southeast Asia', *Itinerario*, 12, 1 (1988), pp. 91–109.

[51] Monica L. Smith, 'Networks, Territories, and the Cartography of Ancient States', *Annals of the Association of American Geographers*, 95, 4 (2005), p. 838.

combinations of territories, corridors and networks, with a strong emphasis on the latter two components connecting imperial nodes across vast expanses of administratively empty space.[52] This is not to say that these polities were not 'proper' empires, but rather to enrich our understanding of pre-modern empires as polities built upon their own spatial, cultural, and communicational logics.

The challenge is in significant measure to think about imperial space as something different from territory. Whilst historians have learned to appreciate empires as a counterweight to the nation state, there is still some hesitation in accepting that imperial space is not just a larger or more complex variety of national space. The lack of distinction distorts our perception of early global encounters. As pointed out three decades ago by Eric Wolf, 'the habit of treating named entities such as Iroquois, Greece, Persia or the United States as fixed entities opposed to one another by stable internal and external boundaries interferes with our ability to understand their mutual encounter and confrontation'.[53] Most history books still come with maps to help situate the events they describe but, at the same time, also create a fundamental misunderstanding regarding the polities they portray.[54] Maps as we have come to use them tend to suggest the existence of territories in a sense borrowed from the modern nation state. Other constellations such as the hierarchically ordered, dynamically interacting networks of pulsating political centres, as we shall see them unfold in sixteenth-century Sri Lanka, are simply very difficult to describe cartographically. Because maps maintain the fiction of representing the spatial configurations of the world as it is, the territories they outline on paper then become powerful, quasi-natural entities to which historical polities seem to conform logically.[55] This is, intriguingly, not only a modern problem. Islands and peninsulas, of course, have for long served as the ultimate deceit offering the illusion of 'given' territories: they appear to have been drawn by nature itself. The idea that their outline somehow predisposes societies to fill them with a single polity has proven enormously influential both in Sri Lanka and in the Iberian Peninsula.[56] To overcome this problem and re-map what, with Lauren Benton, we could call the 'imperfect geographies' of the early modern imperial terrain, we need to un-map it first.[57]

Above all, we need to face the simple fact that the space in which interactions developed was *itself* unfolding as a meaningful setting during the period under

---

[52] Monica L. Smith, 'Territories, Corridors, and Networks: A Biological Model for the Premodern State', *Complexity*, 12, 4 (2005), pp. 28–35.

[53] Eric R. Wolf, *Europe and the People Without History* (Berkeley, CA: University of California Press, 1982), p. 7.

[54] This is indeed often the case for Sri Lanka, e.g. in Malyn Newitt, *A History of Portuguese Expansion, 1400–1668* (London/New York: Routledge, 2005).

[55] On the obsession of historians with the construction of national spaces, cf. John H. Elliott, 'A Europe of Composite Monarchies', in *Past and Present*, 137 (Nov. 1992), p. 50.

[56] On the role played by islands in the making of the European imagination of the Atlantic, see John R. Gillis, *Islands of the Mind: How the Human Imagination Created the Atlantic World* (New York: Palgrave Macmillan, 2004). Also see Juan Gil, 'As Ilhas Imaginárias', *Oceanos*, 46 (Abril/Junho 2001), pp. 11–24.

[57] Lauren Benton, *A Search for Sovereignty. Law and Geography in European Empires, 1400–1900* (Cambridge: Cambridge University Press, 2009), p. 4.

scrutiny. To study 'the Portuguese presence in Ceylon', we must first consider what 'Ceylon' and 'presence in' ought to signify. As Jean-Claude Waquet, Odile Goerg and Rebecca Rogers have put it, space in the historical narrative calls to be understood not as a pre-existing condition 'upstream' to history (*'en amont'*) but rather as something that results from it 'downstream' (*'en aval'*).[58] We need to venture into this study without assuming that Sri Lanka as a whole, or even the kingdom of Kōṭṭe as a part of it, meant anything at all to the Portuguese in 1506. We will have to listen to the words used at the time and infer the mental images hiding behind them to allow the picture to grow gradually, long before we even start creating our own, new maps.[59] This can only be done by exploring the complex cumulative effects of a myriad representational (and, as outlined above, communicational) acts. In the process, Lankan ideas about the insular space will necessarily be key.

## EMPIRES AS HIERARCHICAL BODIES: LAYERED SOVEREIGNTIES IN A GLOBAL PERSPECTIVE

What was it, then, that populated the mental maps of Lankan and Portuguese men and women interacting in the sixteenth century? If one of the aims of this book is to trace the history of the often subtle and transient images that communicating historical agents operated with at the intersection between two larger, porous and pulsating imperial spheres, then what building blocks can we expect to have been deployed in the first place? It seems important not to replace one methodological monster (the exposure of past polities to an anachronistic concept of territoriality) by another (a simplistic reduction of everything pre-modern to 'nodes', 'edges' and other concepts borrowed from network theory). The networks at play in the sixteenth century were traversed by very complex understandings of political hierarchy, power projection, scale, and political space. Even some embryonic form of modern territoriality was involved. But the crucial aspect is that everything was much less structured in space than has traditionally been assumed.

Perhaps the best way to come to grips with this is by beginning at the lower end of the scale, and approaching it through the so-called 'little kingdom' theory. As a scholarly concept, the little kingdom stems from the work of Bernard Cohn on North India.[60] It has been developed by Nicholas Dirks (on Tamil Nadu), Georg

---

[58] Jean-Claude Waquet, Odile Goerg and Rebecca Rogers, 'Introduction', in *Les espaces de l'historien. Études d'historiographie* (Strasbourg: Presses Universitaires de Strasbourg, 2000), p. 11. On the wider logics of the 'spatial turn' see Jürgen Osterhammel, 'Die Wiederkehr des Raumes. Geopolitik, Geohistorie und historische Geographie', *Neue Politische Literatur*, 43 (1998), pp. 374–97.

[59] On the importance and polyvalence of images cf. Sigrid Weigel, 'Bilder als Hauptakteure auf dem Schauplatz der Erkenntnis. Zur poiesis und episteme sprachlicher und visueller Bilder' in *Ästhetik Erfahrung*, edited by Jörg Huber (Zurich/Vienna/New York: Institut für Theorie der Gestaltung und Kunst/Voldemeer/Springer, 2004), pp. 191–212.

[60] See Georg Berkemer and Margret Frenz, 'Little Kingdoms or Princely States? Trajectories towards a (theoretical) conception', *Indian Historical Review*, 32, 2 (2005), pp. 104–21. The history of the concept is drafted in Bernhard Schnepel and Georg Berkemer, 'History of the Model', in *Sharing Sovereignty. The Little Kingdom in South Asia*, edited by G. Berkemer and Margret Frenz (Berlin: Klaus Schwarz, 2003), pp. 11–20.

Berkemer (on the multi-polity frameworks of medieval and early modern Kalinga) and Margret Frenz (on eighteenth-century Kerala), among others.[61] At the most basic level, a little kingdom is a small polity, often geographically marginal, near the bottom of a hierarchy descending from the imperial to the local.[62] What makes the concept most interesting for imperial historians is the fact that little kingdoms function as the units of a wider system based on a non-linear relationship between kingship and territory, allowing for flexible personal interactions between rulers in hierarchically complex, multi-polity networks. Whether the notion of a 'segmentary state', borrowed by Burton Stein from Africanists, describes such realities well, is far from clear.[63] A less polemic, more straightforward designation has taken hold among scholars of Sri Lanka, who now talk of 'tributary overlordship'.[64] Such systems contain a multitude of political centres, one of them tends to constitute their ritual apex at any given moment, and the others tend to be subject to it through forms of periodically renewed ritual submission. The rulers of the kingdoms set around the core of the system 'exercise actual sovereignty over their respective segments, while remaining ritually aligned to and dependent on an overlord.'[65] Crucially as well, the mechanism that allowed for the articulation between overlord and vassal could be replicated at more than one level and in various, often complicated combinations.[66]

In a virulent attack on the concept of 'little kingdom', the German Indianist Rahul Peter Das has argued that all such theorizing is pointless given the impossibility of giving an unambiguous translation of the word *rāja* itself. As a philologist, Das sees it best rendered by *rex* or *ruler*, rather than *king*. This, in his opinion, exposes the entire theory as untenable.[67] There is, to be sure, no doubt that translating any word constitutes a challenge, and that fully translating words referring to

[61] Bernard S. Cohn, 'Political Systems in Eighteenth-Century India: The Banaras Region', *Journal of the American Oriental Society*, 82, 3 (1962), pp. 312–20; Nicholas Dirks, 'The Structure and Meaning of Political Relations in a South Indian Little Kingdom', *Contributions to Indian Sociology* 13 (1979), pp. 169–206; Georg Berkemer, *Little Kingdoms in Kalinga. Ideologie, Legitimation und Politik regionaler Eliten* (Stuttgart: Franz Steiner, 1993); Margret Frenz, *Vom Herrscher zum Untertan. Spannungsverhältnis zwischen lokaler Herrschaftsstruktur und der Kolonialverwaltung zu Beginn der Britischen Herrschaft, 1790–1805* (Stuttgart: Franz Steiner, 2000).

[62] Barbara N. Ramusack, *The Indian Princes and their States* (Cambridge: Cambridge University Press, 2004), p. 5. Nicholas B. Dirks designates it as the 'lowest level of the late precolonial state'. *The Hollow Crown*, p. 5.

[63] See David Arnold, 'Introduction to Burton Stein's *History of India*', in Burton Stein, *A History of India*, 2nd edition, revised and edited by David Arnold (Oxford: Wiley-Blackwell, 2010), pp. xviii–xx.

[64] Michael Roberts, 'The Collective Consciousness of the Sinhalese During the Kandyan Era: Manichean Images, Associational Logic', *Asian Ethnicity*, 3, 1 (Mar. 2002), p. 32.

[65] Schnepel and Berkemer, 'History of the Model', p. 13.

[66] Cf. Charles Henry Alexandrowicz's famous classification of rulers as: (a) sovereigns who, in relation with other rulers, only figure as suzerains; (b) sovereigns who, whilst being suzerains towards some vassal rulers, were *also* themselves vassals of other suzerains; (c) sovereigns who were vassals of one or more suzerains and could shift their allegiance; and (d) vassals who functioned as 'quasi-sovereigns', attempting to access category (c). *An Introduction to the History of the Law of Nations (16th, 17th and 18th Centuries)* (Oxford: Clarendon Press, 1967), pp. 15–16.

[67] Rahul Peter Das, 'Little Kingdoms and Big Theories of History. Review of *Little Kingdoms in Kalinga: Ideologie, Legitimation und Politik regionaler Eliten* by Georg Berkemer', *Journal of the American Oriental Society*, 117, 1 (1997), pp. 127–34.

abstract concepts may ultimately be impossible. But it is rather startling how Das expects this universal dilemma to destabilize the little kingdom as an analytical tool, that is, a concept grounded precisely in the acceptance of the ultimate impossibility of fully translating anything from the past into the present.[68] Even more importantly, an essentialist critique fails to take into account the possibility of translation occurring, however imperfectly to the eyes of the modern philologist, in past historical contexts. Translation as such, describable in the widest sense as an 'act of mediation based on language', is a practice deeply steeped in history.[69] If one accepts the possibility of complex mediations based on a combination of verbal and visual or iconic forms (images, mental images and spatial representations at the intersection of writing, speaking, imagining and drawing), then a range of perspectives emerges where linguistically precise renderings are only a relatively small part of a much wider constellation of meanings. Translation operates in an intermediate space, somewhere in-between the source and the target culture, and this 'third space'—or whatever we may wish to call it—is an important subject of inquiry.

Whilst post-1750 developments suggest that Europeans may have begun to underline the differences between South Asian *rājas* and European *kings*—the British ditched those translations and went over to designating the former as 'chiefs' or 'princes' in the second half of the eighteenth century[70]—this was not the case in previous centuries. Both the Portuguese and the Dutch were quick to translate the term *rāja* as *rei* or *koning*, even in places such as Batticaloa or Wellassa in eastern Sri Lanka, where modern anthropologists would be inclined to speak of chiefdoms. The pervasiveness of this logic of understanding through imperfect translation has already been pointed out by Ivana Elbl in a little-noticed article on the Portuguese encounter with West Africa.[71] Whenever the word *rei* (king) or *reino* (kingdom) was used by the Portuguese to render a political situation in a different culture during the sixteenth century, this was because the institution and its symbolic space were perceived as being sufficiently well translated by the word. The category was not directly dependent on scale. Both Batticaloa and China could be seen as *reinos*.

Crucially, any king might head a kingdom and yet also pay tribute to another ruler further up in a dynamic constellation of powers. In fact, this not such a far cry from the complex hierarchies in place in Europe during the late medieval and part of the early modern period. Here, too, it was common for rulers to acknowledge the superiority of the Holy Empire and the Papacy, whilst acting as independent

---

[68] See Berkemer and Frenz, 'Little Kingdoms or Princely States?', p. 115.

[69] In German, a 'sprachbasierter Vermittlungsakt', as in Daniel G. König, 'Übersetzungen und Wissenstransfer. Zu einem Aspekt der Beziehungen zwischen lateinisch-christlicher und arabisch-islamischer Welt', *Trivium*, 8 (2011), p. 6 (http://trivium.revues.org/3875, last accessed 5 November 2017). Bibliography on the subject in Paula G. Rubel and Abraham Rosman, eds., *Translating Cultures. Perspectives on Translation and Anthropology* (London: Bloomsbury, 2003).

[70] Bernard S. Cohn, 'Political Systems in Eighteenth Century India: the Benares Region', *Journal of the American Oriental Society*, 82, 3 (1962), pp. 312–20.

[71] Ivana Elbl, 'Cross-Cultural Trade and Diplomacy: Portuguese Relations with West Africa, 1441–1521', *Journal of World History*, 3, 2 (1992), pp. 194–6.

kings (and even seeking to submit other, lesser rulers).[72] Although the word *imperium* came to be associated in Europe with an emerging idea of sovereignty as early as the twelfth century, it also remained imbued with the recognition that the late Roman Empire had become a complex body of which other kingdoms were 'dependencies' (Saint Isidore), the empire as a whole forming no longer 'a unitary and integrative territorial *imperium*, but rather an *imperium* in the form of a composite monarchy, linking disparate realms and territories under a single, supreme head'.[73]

Again, we need to pay attention to the small units that, together, allowed the system to work. Take for example Portugal. Its medieval embryo was a county known as *Condado Portucalense*, forming part of a wider Iberian system of small polities articulated through mechanisms of personal allegiance. As the Castilian monarchy expanded but struggled to exert direct control over lands conquered from Islamic powers in the south—which in fact constituted a complicated mosaic in its own right—they opted for indirect control based on personal allegiance. The first count of Portucale, Henry (r.1093–1112), was brought in from Burgundy to impose order in the area. Once in place, Henry acted independently within his fief, though he remained a vassal of Alphons VI, king of León, Castile, Galicia and Toledo. In fact, Alphons VI styled himself, between 1077 and 1109, as *Imperator totius Hispaniæ* precisely on grounds of various personal relations of overlordship. In significant measure, his emperorship was based on the perceived ability to secure the symbolic submission of other lords to the centre of the realm. To understand this empire, historians have had to accept the inadequacy of territoriality as an interpretive key.[74]

Later, under Henry's son Alphons (r.1112–1185), the county of Portucale broke loose and grew into an independent kingdom only to begin its own tradition of subjecting others.[75] It became, in the longer run, one of many cases where claims to *imperium* served as signs of a consolidated sovereignty in the broad sense of independence from former overlords.[76] In the mid-thirteenth century, the kings of Portugal conquered the Algarve, which maintained its formal status as a separate kingdom.[77] From the fifteenth century, rulers claimed dominion over parts of North Africa (the 'Algarve beyond the sea'), and then added other forms of lordship (*senhorio*) across West Africa, Ethiopia, Arabia, Persia and India to their title.[78]

---

[72] Cf. Garrett Mattingly, *Renaissance Diplomacy* (Boston, MA/Cambridge: Houghton Mifflin/Riverside Press, 1955), pp. 27–8 and Donald Matthew, *The Medieval European Community* (New York: St Martin's Press, 1977), pp. 255–7. Also see A. B. Bozeman, *Politics and Culture in International History* (Princeton, NJ: Princeton University Press, 1960), pp. 240–54.

[73] David Armitage, *The Ideological Origins of the British Empire* (Cambridge: Cambridge University Press, 2000), pp. 30 and 33.

[74] Cf. Richard Fletcher, 'The Early Middle Ages, 700–1250', in *Spain. A History*, edited by Raymond Carr (Oxford: Oxford University Press, 2000), pp. 63–89.

[75] A key exploration of early Portuguese History is José Mattoso, *Identificação de um país. Ensaio sobre As Origens de Portugal, 1096–1325*, 2 vols. (Lisbon: Estampa, 1985).

[76] Cf. Armitage, *The Ideological Origins*, p. 30.

[77] In fact, the formula 'king of the Algarve' was added to the royal title after the first conquest of the *taifa* capital Silves in 1189, and maintained even after the town was retaken by Muslim forces until 1242.

[78] The 'Algarve beyond the sea' was included in the title after various conquests in Morocco made between 1458 and 1471, and the 'lordship of Guinea' in 1486.

As soon as it crossed the sea, the expansionist process reverted to forcing foreign rulers into paying tribute rather than conquering lands. All this unfolded, of course, while the kings of Portugal remained vassals of the pope, whose authority in international matters they often accepted and to whom they offered periodical manifestations of allegiance. At the apogee of his imperial triumphs, Manuel I of Portugal (r.1495–1521) still showed his obedience to the Vatican. He sought legitimation through bulls and treaties to protect his realm from French and Castilian interference—whilst also doing everything in his reach to reduce the influence of the Roman Church within his own emerging empire.

None of this is easily translated into maps, and yet it was the spatially dynamic ground upon which Europeans could maintain dialogues about kingship and empire with other powers overseas. Recognizing each other's rulers as kings and emperors, even when there were evident differences in terms of power and courtly culture (and not necessarily to the advantage of the Portuguese), was a first and fundamental step in establishing a politically meaningful communication. It was the indispensable pre-condition for any kind of pact or agreement, even if it then led to symbolic submission of one part to the other. Kings could, once they recognized each other as such, engage in diplomatic exchanges on a notionally equal footing—and then negotiate their relation to each other within a complex hierarchical system such as that described above. This worked in part because kingship per se was seen as something that could bear qualification: a *mahārājan* or 'big king' could and would be designated by the Portuguese as a *'rei grande'*; a lesser ruler might, in contrast, come to be called a *'rei pequeno'*. A culturalist, historicist approach that pays attention to the symbolic forms negotiated by actors in the past is here not fundamentally incompatible with a more abstract hermeneutic stance grounded in modern ideal-types.[79] The two complement each other well, because the analytical concept of 'little king' can be made to refer back to historical uses of the words *rāja* and *rei*. Together, the two readings counteract essentialist approaches to the question of how to define kingship or empire 'as such'.

## ASTRAEA GOES GLOBAL: TOWARDS A CONNECTED HISTORY OF THE IMPERIAL THEME

As we move from observing the building blocks of imperial systems to appreciating the general principle of empire, the picture gains further coherence. Again, there needs to be a conceptual overture at the onset of our operations, and we are

---

[79] Cf. Justin Stagl, 'Szientistische, hermeneutische und phänomenologische Grundlagen der Ethnologie', in *Grundfragen der Ethnologie. Beiträge zur gegenwärtigen Theorie-Diskussion*, edited by J. Stagl and W. Schmied-Kowarzik (Berlin: Dietrich Reimer, 1993), pp. 18–42. On the threads that connect Weber to Geertz, see David N. Gellner, *The Anthropology of Buddhism and Hinduism. Weberian Themes* (New Delhi: Oxford University Press, 2001), pp. 62–9. On the polemic that opposed Weber and the phenomenologist Alfred Schütz (author of *Der sinnhafte Aufbau der sozialen Welt*, 1932), see John R. Hall, 'Cultural Meaning and Cultural Structures in Historical Explanation', *History and Theory*, 39, 3 (2000), pp. 335–40. The tensions are further explored in Stagl, 'Szientistische, hermeneutische und phänomenologische Grundlagen', pp. 15–49.

lucky today to have a vast literature that is very open-minded about what can be considered an empire. The complexities of the early modern European state system have received great attention especially thanks to historians interested in composite monarchies as the dominant political form of the early modern period. Frances Yates, Franz Bosbach, Helmut G. Koenigsberger, John H. Elliott, Anthony Pagden, James Muldoon, John M. Headley, and David Armitage have all emphasized the importance of empires or composite states as opposed to smaller, more compact polities announcing the nation state.[80] The number of political formations considered imperial has thus grown fast. It now includes, along with the Holy Roman Empire and León-Castile, Alfredian England and also sixteenth-century Britain as it confronted Ireland before venturing further into the Atlantic. At the intersection of the European system with the Islamic world, attention has turned to the Ottoman appropriation of Byzantine imperial symbols. In the southwestern and northeastern corners of the continent, remarkable materials have emerged regarding the imperial tradition of the Nasrid rulers of Granada, and the imperial ambitions of the kings of Lithuania.[81]

Beyond Europe, the proliferation of empires in recent scholarship reveals further overtures at the analytical level. In New World studies, the Aztec and Inca empires now share space with other imperial formations such as those of the Powhatan, the Comanche, the Iroquois, the Lakotas, or the Osages.[82] In West Africa, it has become possible to theorize about the empires of Ghana, Mali and Songhay.[83] What all these cases have in common is that the term 'imperial' builds on the analytical principle of suzerainty—or overlordship—as opposed to that of sovereignty, which carries a more narrow sense of undivided, unchecked direct control over a territory and its people. 'Imperial' here refers to what in Michael Doyle's

[80] Yates, *Astraea*; Franz Bosbach, *Monarchia Universalis. Ein politischer Leitbegriff der frühen Neuzeit* (Göttingen: Vandenhoek & Ruprecht, 1988); H. G. Koenigsberger, 'Dominium Regale or Dominium Politicum et Regale', in *Politicians and Virtuosi: Essays in Early Modern History* (London: Hambledon Press, 1986); John H. Elliott, 'A Europe of Composite Monarchies', *Past and Present*, 137 (Nov. 1992), pp. 48–71; Anthony Pagden, *Lords of all the World: Ideologies of Empire in Spain, Britain and France, c.1500–c.1800* (New Haven, CT: Yale University Press, 1995); James Muldoon, *Empire and Order. The Concept of Empire, 800–1800* (London/New York: MacMillan/St Martin's, 1999); John M. Headley, several pieces in *Church, Empire and World. The Quest for Universal Order, 1520–1640* (Aldershot: Ashgate Variorum, 1997); Armitage, *The Ideological Origins*.

[81] On the usage of the imperial title by the Ottomans in competition with Charles V, see Gülru Necipoğlu, 'Suleyman the Magnificent and the Representation of Power in the Context of Ottoman-Hapsburg-Papal Rivalry', *Art Bulletin*, 71 (1989), pp. 401–27. On the connections between the Nasrid imperial discourse especially in architecture, and its appropriation by Charles V, see Cammy Brothers, 'The Renaissance Reception of the Alhambra: The Letters of Andrea Navagero and the Palace of Charles V', *Muqarnas*, 11 (1994), pp. 79–102, especially p. 90. The connections between Roman and Islamic symbologies of universality in art and architecture have been highlighted by Oleg Grabar, 'From Dome of Heaven to Pleasure Dome', *Journal of the Society of Architectural Historians*, 49, 1 (1990), pp. 15–21 as well as in his classic *The Formation of Islamic Art* (New Haven, CT: Yale University Press, 1973), pp. 147–53. Also see the interesting recent discussion of empire as an etic concept in Zenonas Norkus, *An Unproclaimed Empire: The Grand Duchy of Lithuania from the viewpoint of Comparative Historical Sociology of Empires* (London/New York: Routledge, 2017).

[82] Pekka Hämäläinen, *The Comanche Empire* (New Haven, CT: Yale University Press, 2008), p. 3, note 3.

[83] David C. Conrad, *Empires of Medieval West Africa. Ghana, Mali and Songhay*, revised edition (New York: Chelsea House, 2010).

classificatory order of empires amounts to 'formal' but 'indirect' dominion, put into practice through the submission of local rulers to a distant overlord in a multi-layered system where the local is only tentatively integrated with the supra-local.[84] It is generally, as Schnepel and Berkemer have put it for the South Asian context, about building legitimacy and authority rather than power and command.[85]

There is no denying that suzerainty took very different forms in Sri Lanka as compared to the Portuguese empire (or indeed Virginia, or Mali), and it is naturally legitimate to emphasize those differences. But, as a concept that highlights the importance of indirect as opposed to more direct mechanisms of control, suzerainty resonates well with historical realities across the continents. Methodologically, this takes us a significant step forward in the evaluation of the supposed clash of early Portuguese (and, to some extent, European) imperialism with the political systems of Africa and Asia. If global history is about recognizing a nominally level playing field in a golden age of empires preceding the emergence of Hobsbawm's more narrowly defined 'Age of Empire', then the de-essentialization of our tools of analysis offers a chance for getting closer to how empire and imperial interactions worked in the sixteenth century.

Crucially, this is again not only a matter of re-thinking our analytical arsenal built around accommodating terms such as empire, kingdom or kingship.[86] Etic considerations open the door to emic contemplations of the usage of words in the past. The rulers of Kōṭṭe are a good example in this regard. Over the course of this study, they will greet us repeatedly as great kings (*mahārājan*), kings of kings (*mahārājadirājan*), and even imperial 'Turners of the Wheel' (*cakravarti*), a title carrying Universalist aspirations. As such they also appear in the Portuguese and Dutch texts of the period: they are *rei grande*, *emperador*, or *keijzer*. Similar hier-archizations can be observed elsewhere. Princess Matoaka was represented in seventeenth-century England as a 'daughter to the Mighty Prince Powhatan Emperour of Attanoughkomouck alias Virginia'?[87] Portuguese travellers to West Africa wrote about 'Mandimansa, emperor of all these kings' ('*Mandimansa, emperador de todos estes reis*'). And Italians spoke of '*lo Imperador de Meli [...] gran signor di negri*'?[88] Many more examples, suggesting the need for a systematic study of the historical nomenclature, can be found in the travel literature and geographical writings of the early modern period.[89]

Sixteenth-century Europeans went through a process of recognizing the imperial nature of numerous polities in Asia, Africa and America at the same time as imper-ial claims proliferated in Europe (in fact, we may still be far from understanding in

---

[84] Michael Doyle, *Empires* (Ithaca, NY: Cornell University Press, 1986).

[85] Schnepel and Berkemer, 'History of the Model', p. 13.

[86] Gardiner, *The Nature of Historical Explanation*, p. 60.

[87] 'FILIA POTENTISS: PRINC: POWHATANI IMP: VIRGINIÆ', translated into English below the medallion in a widely circulated engraving by Simon van de Passe, London, 1616.

[88] Both quoted in Elbl, 'Cross-Cultural Trade and Diplomacy', p. 195.

[89] Some are given in Giuseppe Marcocci, 'Too Much to Rule. States and Empires across the Early Modern World', *Journal of Early Modern History*, 20, 6 (2016), pp. 511–25.

which direction causality worked).[90] Frances Yates expounded in *Astraea* how the idea of empire circulated, and really grew in many directions, almost rhizomatically, throughout sixteenth-century Europe. The Imperial Theme contributed to the political performances of rulers in Germany, Italy, France, Britain and Spain. Charles V could have told a tale about imperial claims popping up, irritatingly, everywhere around him. Whilst it is possible to identify a genealogical tree for the imperial idea in earlier centuries, by the 1500s it was so ubiquitous that the common trunk, though still remembered, became less and less relevant. If one thing has come out of the countless attempts at pinning down what exactly an empire 'is' or 'was', then it is that no clear-cut definition can be found.[91] The imperial theme, however, offers us the possibility of tackling empire not as an entity but as a process or, to keep it closer to the vocabulary of the cultural history of the political, a performative act or stance grounded in the language and spatial perceptions of its time. In addition to anything that might *de facto* smack of imperial structures, it required something fundamental that the German historian Ulrich Leitner has called '*imperiale Selbstsicht*', that is, the way a polity sees itself as being imperial—which of course only works fully if others also recognize (or can be made to recognize) such claims.[92]

It is really only at this discursive, performative and self-reflexive level that we can come anywhere near a satisfying definition of empire. *Being imperial* in the sixteenth century was, in sum, a performative act—a carefully staged claim—it was usually particular rather than universal despite any Universalist echoes, and it was relational in nature.[93] Across Europe, it was not (or not just) about tracing back one's political genealogy to Rome anymore. It was most importantly about affirming oneself, and being perceived by others, as independent and as imperial in the European—and increasingly the global—theatres of diplomacy, trade and war. The same applies to the vast majority of interactions between polities around the globe. No empire was ever defined by its absolute size, or reach or complexity, but only by its ability to be accepted as being imperial by others.

Naturally, as anyone familiar with the sixteenth century will be aware, not all rulers with imperial ambitions effectively employed the words 'empire' and 'emperor'.

---

[90] See for the Portuguese side, António Vasconcelos de Saldanha, *Iustum Imperium. Dos tratados como fundamento do império dos portugueses no Oriente. Estudo de história do direito internacional e do direito português* (Lisbon/Macao: Fundação Oriente/Instituto Português do Oriente, 1997), pp. 309–17. On changes to imperial titulature in China under the Manchus, and what this may imply for the use of the word 'emperor', see Catherine Jami, 'Imperial Science Written in Manchu in Early Qing China: Does It Matter?', in *Looking at It from Asia: The Processes that Shaped the Sources of History of Science*, edited by F. Bretelle-Establet (Boston, MA: Springer, 2010), pp. 371–91.

[91] From the vast literature on the subject, see Susan Alcock et al., eds., *Empires. Perspectives from Archaeology and History* (Cambridge: Cambridge University Press, 2001), and the discussion on the Portuguese *Estado* in Sanjay Subrahmanyam, 'Written on Water: designs and dynamics in the Portuguese *Estado da Índia*', ibid., pp. 42–69, where the author suggests adopting a dynamic and 'minimalist' definition of empire.

[92] See the useful distinction between imperial 'structures' and 'processes' in Ulrich Leitner, 'Der imperiale Ordnungskomplex. Die theoretische Fiktion eines politischen Systems', in *Imperien und Reiche in der Weltgeschichte*, edited by Michael Gehler and Robert Rollinger (Wiesbaden: Harrassowitz, 2014), vol. II, pp. 1415–2.

[93] Cf. Armitage, *The Ideological Origins*, p. 31.

Is an emic perspective on empire possible at all in such cases? The answer is still affirmative. Rulers made their ambitions resonate through other words and gestures, widely understood and accepted as equivalents or quasi-equivalents. Most famously, Phillip II (r.1556–98) could not claim the imperial title once his father Charles (r.1516–56) had 'returned' it to Austria. He had to use the word 'Monarch' instead (while nurturing the thought of adopting the title 'Emperor of the Indies'), and yet rulers across the continents knew perfectly well that he was an imperial overlord, and recognized him as such.[94] As for Portugal, it would have been odd for John III (r.1521–57) explicitly to call himself an emperor, with Charles V being both his neighbour and brother-in-law. But the kings of the Avis dynasty did not refrain from boasting a royal title containing every indication that their dominion was imperial.[95] Manuel I not only surrounded himself with enormously expensive tapestries illustrating his global imperial reach.[96] He and his son John III were also 'By the Grace of God King of Portugal and the Algarves on this side of the Sea and beyond, Lord of the Conquest, Navigation and Commerce of Ethiopia, Arabia, Persia and India', a title adopted after the return of Pedro Álvares Cabral, the official discoverer of Brazil, from India in 1501.[97] In fact, in a letter to Manuel I from 1505, the first viceroy of India Francisco de Almeida wrote after having obtained tribute from some rulers in East Africa and India that 'Your Highness shall be [proclaimed] Emperor of this world here [i.e. the "Indies"]'. No other argument was given than the fact that Manuel had become king of kings. After the submission of the king of Hormuz in 1507, Almeida reiterated that 'Your Highness should not hesitate too much in calling Yourself *Imperador*, because never has a Prince had more justification to be [an emperor]'.[98]

The kings of Portugal never laid a claim to *imperium* by using the word as such, but they did, and systematically so, refer to themselves as 'kings of kings'[99] and as 'lords' (*senhores*) entitled to dominion over others along the shores of the Atlantic and Indian Oceans. This was widely understood as an imperial project, even if it was not *the* imperial project of Charles V. It was ultimately about claiming imperial status on the ground that they were overlords to a number of rulers.[100] During the second half of the century Manuel's grandson Sebastian (r.1568–78) began to style himself as 'Majesty' (*majestade*) precisely to underscore this imperial reach. Incidentally, the wider geopolitics of this will hardly come across as polemic. Whilst formally there was still only one imperial title in Europe, the Vatican had had to give its blessing in the late fifteenth century, well before the arrival of Charles V in Spain, to a division of the globe that was clearly imperial. It allowed for the legal

[94] Pagden, 'Fellow Citizens and Imperial Subjects. Conquest and sovereignty in Europe's overseas empires', *History and Theory*, 44, 4 (2005), p. 32.
[95] Luís Filipe F. R. Thomaz, 'L'idée impériale manuéline', in *La découverte, le Portugal et l'Europe, Actes du Colloque*, edited by Jean Aubin (Paris: Fondation Calouste Gulbenkian, 1990), pp. 35–103.
[96] Pedro Dias, *À Maneira de Portugal. Uma tapeçaria inédita* (Porto: VOC Antiguidades, 2007), pp. 24–7.
[97] Disney, *History of Portugal*, vol. 2, p. 127.
[98] Both letters quoted in Saldanha, *Iustum Imperium*, p. 321.
[99] On the Portuguese idea of being '*Rei de Reis*' see Saldanha, *Iustum Imperium*, pp. 321–31.
[100] Cf. Armitage, *The Ideological Origins*, p. 33.

pursuit of virtually unlimited direct or indirect dominion by the Portuguese and Castilian crowns in each of their hemispheres, and offered a basis for the justification of later military conquest. Ever since the complex negotiations leading up to the treaties of Alcáçovas (1479) and Tordesillas (1494) the Portuguese and the Castilian kings behaved as formally sanctioned, potential overlords on a global scale. While a fully-fledged occupation was not deemed feasible in the far-flung corners of the earth, the treaties allowed the Portuguese rulers to demand tribute from other rulers.[101]

Interestingly, it was in this function precisely that the Portuguese elite *also* began to see imperial constellations emerge on more distant horizons. Inevitably, decision-makers across the empire were drawn into the complex logics of inter-polity hierarchization in other continents.[102] Once they operated in Maritime Asia, the Portuguese not only developed an understanding of other regional hierarchies such as that involving the 'sultans' of Pasai, Malacca and Bengal and the many *rājas* surrounding them as minor rulers—they also became a part of those.[103] By 1519, the sultan of Ternate in the Moluccas, Abu Hayat, was writing to Manuel I addressing him as *Sultan Purtukal* precisely in this sense, recognizing him as a king superior to other kings along the lines of what *he* understood imperial hierarchies to be.[104] Incidentally, the word used for tribute, *páreas,* had earlier entered the Romance languages of Iberia from the Islamic tradition, through the practices of competing medieval *taifa* kingdoms in the south of the Iberian Peninsula paying tribute for military protection by Christian powers in the north. The rulers of those polities had been known in Castile as '*reyezuelos*'—literally, 'little kings'.[105]

The geographical movement built into the argument is deliberate: we are in no position at this point to decide on what paths exactly all these connectable notions of kingship and empire spread across the Eurasian ecumene. There are some signs, further to be investigated, that the diplomatic culture lubricating complex hierarchical systems such as those described here may have had deep roots in the Islamic world.[106] But at the very least, we can ascertain that the conceptual analogies prepared the ground for dialogues. In the sixteenth century, there was a critical mass of polities across the globe operating on grounds of analogous, or even homologous, strategies of power building, acting and soon interacting imperially, without conquering in the modern sense of the word—and understanding that they could measure forces and negotiate precisely on such grounds. This is what makes the encounter of the Portuguese with Asia particularly relevant to global

---

[101] Thomaz, *De Ceuta a Timor*, p. 219.

[102] See Biedermann, *The Portuguese in Sri Lanka and South India*, pp. 7–32.

[103] Tomé Pires, *Summa Oriental*, p. 398.

[104] Saldanha, *Iustum Imperium*, p. 323.

[105] Cf. Saldanha, *Iustum Imperium*, pp. 642–54, the classical study on Castile being Hilda Grassotti, 'Para la historia del botín y de las parias en León y Castilla', *Cuadernos de Historia de España*, 41–2 (1965), pp. 43–83.

[106] Zoltán Biedermann, Anne Gerritsen and Giorgio Riello, eds., *Global Gifts. The Material Culture of Diplomacy in Early Modern Eurasia* (New York: Cambridge University Press, 2018). A further parallel suggesting other, more complicated connections in the medieval period might be the 'great gifts' (*mahadanas*) practiced among Hindu rulers in South India. Cf. Dirks, *The Hollow Crown*, p. 37.

historians. In Sri Lanka, what unfolded was not simply the encounter of one people with another, but of one imperially minded society acting on the global stage with another, imperially minded society acting on a smaller, but conceptually commensurable, stage. The understanding of what it was to be a *rājadhirājan* in sixteenth-century Kōṭṭe converged with the Portuguese understanding of being *rei de reis* (king of kings). People understood this and acted upon it. The performance of styling oneself as *senhor da conquista*, *rei de reis* or *mahārājadirājan*, typically investing more in the staging of such claims than in the formation of well-structured territories, boundaries, or administrative apparatuses, were central to Lankan and Portuguese politics, as they were in many other parts of the globe.

Although the systems were far from identical—and we shall see many differences emerge over the following chapters—their interpersonal, non-territorial logics of power building made them notionally and practically interconnectable. Polities that, each in its own way, combined universalist ideas with a non-intrusionist, suzerainty-based stance on expansion, could meet and, effectively, talk to each other. This resulted in a precarious balance, but a balance nonetheless. With Portugal and Kōṭṭe, the polities chosen for the present study may strike the reader as small and, by some measures, insignificant in comparison to the empires of the Habsburgs, the Ottomans, the Mughals or the Ming. But in the way they inter-acted, in how they generated communicational flows connecting distant corners of the earth and feeding into political processes with a global impact in the longer run—namely, the first Habsburg conquest in South Asia, preparing the ground for Dutch and British interventions—they exemplify how global history is made at the intersection of distant societies structurally predisposed and willing to talk.

Each of the aspects touched upon in this introductory chapter points to the possi-bilities of connection and disconnection, convergence and divergence, diplomacy and conquest, not so much as mutually exclusive, but rather as profoundly intertwined aspects of the historical past. Ours is a task of observing how these aspects held each other in balance, fluctuating more or less intensively as cross-cultural interactions unfolded, until the dialogue broke down—temporarily at least, for we know little about what happened next. There is reason to assume that stories comparable to the one we are about to delve into abound across the globe.

# 2

# Lords of the Land, Lords of the Sea
## Establishing an Imperial Dialogue Against the Odds

To comprehend almost any conversation, it is key to know how it began. Yet in the story of European global expansion, initial or first encounters have widely served as sites of often unhelpful myth-making. Moments of early interaction, regularly associated with the liminal space of beaches, have been romanticized or maligned to the extent that conciliatory interpretations are often difficult to find.[1] Much of this has come down to how the sides involved are understood by historians in isolation from each other, describable as independent entities before being suddenly exposed to a face-to-face encounter. It seems reasonable that we attempt paying more attention to the relational logics at play, to the way that encounters are always more than just the sum of the parts involved.

In the case of Sri Lanka, the perception of the encounter with the Portuguese has been profoundly shaped by the notion that the newcomers arrived predisposed to conquer. Among South Asian nationalist historians, the resulting 'contact zone' has inevitably come to be seen, to use Marie-Louise Pratt's well-known formula, as a space dominated by 'conditions of coercion, radical inequality, and intractable conflict'—imposed by the Portuguese, of course.[2] To be clear, this has been in part down to the way later Lusitanian chroniclers wrote about Portuguese expansion. As Fernão de Queiroz put it in *The Temporal and Spiritual Conquest of Ceylon*, God sent unexpected winds and currents to show the Portuguese how 'He had brought them to India not as pirates, but conquerors'—conquerors, of course, of lands and souls, even though we shall see that they were for many years interested in neither.[3]

---

[1] See Greg Dening, *Islands and beaches: discourse on a silent land. Marquesas, 1774–1880* (Honolulu: University of Hawai'i Press, 1980). On the initial encounters of the Portuguese in the Atlantic and Indic, see Anthony Disney, 'Portuguese Expansion, 1400–1800: Encounters, Negotiations, and Interactions', in *Portuguese Oceanic Expansion, 1400–1800*, edited by Francisco Bethencourt and Diogo Ramada Curto (Cambridge: Cambridge University Press, 2007), pp. 283–90. On Sri Lanka, see Chandra Richard De Silva, 'Beyond the Cape: The Portuguese encounter with the peoples of South Asia', in *Implicit Understandings*, edited by Stuart Schwartz (Cambridge: Cambridge University Press, 1994), pp. 295–322. On the first encounter in Brazil, which falls close in time to the one in Sri Lanka and has elicited more debate, see Lisa Voigt, '"Por Andarmos Todos Casy Mesturados": The Politics of Intermingling in Caminha's "Carta" and Colonial American Anthologies', *Early American Literature*, 40, 3 (2005), pp. 407–39.

[2] Marie-Louise Pratt, *Imperial Eyes. Travel Writing and Transculturation* (London/New York: Routledge, 1992), p. 6.

[3] Fernão de Queiroz, *Conquista Temporal e Espiritual de Ceilão* (Colombo: Government Press, 1916), p. 138.

From such an epic enunciation, formulated over a century and a half after the events, the myth of a fatal first encounter preluding 450 years of colonial struggle arose effortlessly. It has been at the heart of the nationalist master narrative ever since.

How can we debunk this myth without playing into the equally pernicious notion that the earliest documented encounter in September 1506 was a harmless encounter, the beginning of an innocuous cross-cultural dialogue? To start with a clean sheet, it is worth highlighting two absences from which the colonial history of the region can only emerge gradually. The first is, unsurprisingly, an absence of Portuguese people from Sri Lanka. As far as we are able to ascertain, 1506 marked the beginning of what historians have generally designated the 'Portuguese presence in Ceylon'.[4] The second absence has been less noticed, yet it is instrumental for an understanding of how slowly the first was overcome. In 1506, it was not only the Portuguese who were absent from Sri Lanka. Sri Lanka was also largely absent from Portugal and Portuguese narratives. This absence is particularly striking in the early years of the century, when Sri Lanka—traditionally associated in the western geographic imagination with the fabulously rich island of Taprobane—rather than being embraced by Portuguese observers, was pushed to the margins. Whilst it would have been possible to sail from Cochin to Colombo in less than a week, it took the Portuguese more than seven years to do so.

This lack of interest played out on various fronts. One cannot but notice the lack of an evocative image of the island itself among early Portuguese writers and cartographers. Sri Lanka as a politically meaningful extension of land—a colonizable or explorable geographical unit producing rather than just exporting goods—is nowhere to be found in Portuguese texts or maps of the late fifteenth to early sixteenth centuries. To some extent, this may be down to the fact that the early protagonists of the encounter on the Portuguese side operated under a set of rules formulated by their crown which strongly discouraged them from venturing inland anywhere in Asia. The focus was to be, as we shall see, where the Portuguese had a technological advantage, on the sea. More decisively perhaps, South Asia—or even Asia as a whole—had a disconcerting effect on many Portuguese as it offered extremely tempting opportunities of trade and mercenary action, but very little space for the type of activities that had by the early 1500s become commonplace in Atlantic islands such as the Azores, Madeira, or Hispaniola. The Portuguese almost immediately developed an awareness that, whilst they had a chance to prevail militarily in the waters east of the Cape of Good Hope, the possibilities of dominion on the land were limited.[5]

---

[4] The date of the first official encounter is still generally held in Sri Lanka to be 1505, ironically on grounds of a mistake in Fernão Lopes de Castanheda's *History of the Portuguese Conquest of India*, one of the first sources to have been made widely available in English. The date of 1506 has been established beyond reasonable doubt by Donald Ferguson, 'The Discovery of Ceylon by the Portuguese in 1506', *Journal of the Ceylon Branch of the Royal Asiatic Society*, XIX, 59 (1907), pp. 284–400. The hypothesis of a first contact in 1501 has been explored by Geneviève Bouchon in 'A propos de l'inscription de Colombo (1501). Quelques observations sur le premier voyage de João da Nova dans l'Océan Indien', *Revista da Universidade de Coimbra*, 28 (1980), pp. 233–70, but no conclusive evidence is available. Cf. Jorge Flores, *Os Portugueses e o Mar de Ceilão, 1498–1543. Trato, Diplomacia e Guerra* (Lisbon: Cosmos, 1998), pp. 104–7.

[5] Flores, '"They have discovered us"'.

## NOT QUITE LIKE CIPANGO: THE VANISHING
## MYTH OF TAPROBANE

If Cipango, Cathay, and India, as described by Marco Polo, fired the imagination
of Columbus and enriched his early experience of what came to be known as the
Caribbean, why did the Taprobane of Strabo, Pliny, and Ptolemy not have a
comparable effect on the pioneers of Portuguese navigation to Asia?[6] The classical
topos of a fabulously rich island placed at the centre of the Indian Ocean, producing
endless amounts of precious stones and two harvests of crops every year, had
retained some importance in Europe during the medieval period. The resurgence
of Ptolemy's *Geography* after 1400 only invigorated the myth (Figure 2.1).[7] The
association between Taprobane and Sri Lanka was particularly strong in Italy,
where the Portuguese actively sought information on Asia before rounding the
Cape—it was indeed there that they picked up the name *Saylam*.[8] Though Polo in
particular had no Taprobane in the *Milione*, his fabulous island of *Seilla* (a name
derived from the Chinese *Hsi-lan* and related to the Arabic *Saylān*) was clearly
reminiscent of it.[9] Even as the myth of Taprobane began to shift eastwards to
Sumatra and Java, Ceylon retained an aura of exceptionality.[10] The mappamundi
of Fra Mauro, produced in Venice in the late 1450s at the request of Alphons V of
Portugal (r.1438–81), reproduced the classical image with only minor changes,
and thus perpetuated the idea of an island notable for its many marvels (*miraueie*).
It was not only *richissima* and *fertilissima*, distinguished from all other islands by its
enormous circumference of 3000 miles, but also blessed with such pure air and water
that its inhabitants lived *longissimamente* under the aegis of Adam, father of all men.[11]

---

[6] On the myth of Ταπροβάνη, see Albert Herrmann, 'Taprobane', in *Paulys Real-Encyclopädie der Classischen Altertumswissenschaft. Neue Bearbeitung begonnen von Georg Wissowa*, 2nd series, vol. IV (Stuttgart: Metzler, 1932), pp. 2260–72; D. P. M. Weerakoddy, 'Greek and Roman Notices of Sri Lanka and their historical Context', *Sri Lanka Journal of the Humanities*, 20 (1994), pp. 65–86; Jacques André and Jean Filliozat, *L'Inde vue de Rome. Textes latins de l'Antiquité relatifs à l'Inde* (Paris: Belles Lettres, 1986). On Columbus see Nicolas Wey Gómez, *Tropics of Empire: Why Columbus Sailed South to the Indies* (Cambridge, MA: MIT Press, 2008).

[7] Cf. Patrick Gautier Dalché, *La Géographie de Ptolémée en Occident (IVe–XVIe siècle)* (Turnhout: Brepols, 2009).

[8] Angelo Cattaneo, 'Venice, Florence, and Lisbon. Commercial routes and networks of knowledge, 1300–1550', in *Encompassing the Globe. Portugal and the World in the 16th and 17th centuries*, edited by Jay Levenson (Washington, DC: Freer and Sackler Galleries, 2007), vol. II, pp. 13–21.

[9] *Milione*, chs. 169 and 174. See Marco Polo, *Milione. Le divisament dou monde. Il Milione nelle redazioni toscana e franco-italiana*, edited by Gabriella Ronchi (Milan: Mondadori, 1982), pp. 233–4 and 253–6. 'Cipangu' is nearby in chs. 155–6, pp. 216–21.

[10] Poggio Bracciolini, *De l'Inde. Les voyages en Asie de Nicolò de' Conti. De varietate fortunae. Livre IV*, texte établi, traduit et commenté par Michèle Guéret-Laferté (Turnhout: Brepols, 2004), pp. 92–4. Note that the 'Catalan Atlas' of 1375, which drew on Polo, has '*Traprobana*' already displaced to the East, near Java.

[11] Caption taken from the facsimile in *Atlas du Vicomte de Santarem. Edition fac-similée des cartes définitives* (Lisbon: CNCDP, 1989), item 45. On Fra Mauro see Pietro Falchetta, *Fra Mauro's World Map, with a commentary and transcriptions of the inscriptions* (Turnhout: Brepols, 2006) and Angelo Cattaneo, *Fra Mauro's Mappamundi and Fifteenth-Century Venetian Culture* (Turnhout: Brepols, 2011). Polo and Conti were available in Portuguese in a print edition from 1502. *O livro de Marco Paulo—O livro de Nicolao Veneto*, edited by Francisco Maria Esteves Pereira (Lisbon: Biblioteca Nacional de Lisboa, 1922).

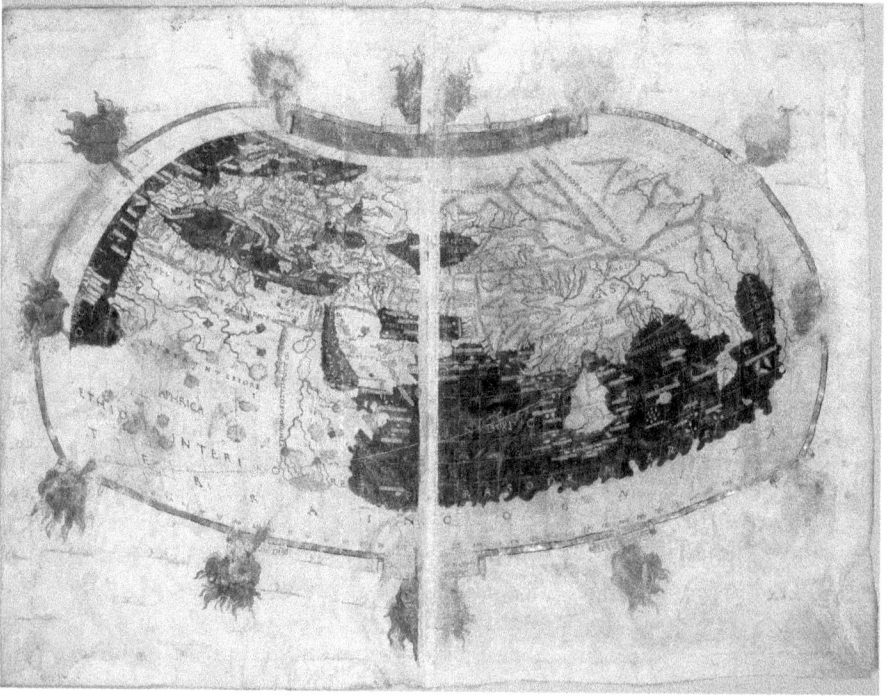

**Figure 2.1** Taprobane in the Geography of Ptolemy. Florence, late fifteenth century. The Huntington Library, San Marino, CA, Codex Wilton, HM 1092, fol. 53v–54.

In the aftermath of the voyage of Vasco da Gama to India, much of this imaginary vanished.[12] As the Portuguese arrived in Asian waters, they set out to produce new charts and texts, applying the techniques of maritime cartography developed in the Atlantic. Within less than four years, the contours of Maritime Asia underwent a profound transformation. A new subcontinent, yet unnamed but recognizable to the modern observer familiar with the concept of 'India', took central stage. As this new land appeared on the map, Lanka shrank and lost significance. In August 1499, the Portuguese monarch noted that 'the isle of Taprobane, which in those parts is called Ceylam', is 'not as large as we believed it to be'.[13] On the Cantino planisphere, a key chart finished in Lisbon in September 1502, the transformation was sealed (Figure 2.2).[14] In the shadow of the Indian subcontinent, a small, amorphous island of idolaters trading with Calicut found its place: *Seillam*. If maps are territories of the

---

[12] Most Portuguese maps of the sixteenth century are published in Armando Cortesão and Avelino Teixeira da Mota, *Portugaliae Monumenta Cartographica*, 5 vols. (Lisbon: PMC, 1960).

[13] Quoted in Carmen M. Radulet and Luís Filipe F. R. Thomaz, *Viagens portuguesas à Índia (1497–1513). Fontes italianas para a sua história* (Lisbon: CNCDP, 2002), p. 118, note 32.

[14] On Cantino see Ernesto Sabato, *La carta del cantino e la rappresentazione della Terra nei codici e nei libri a stampa della Biblioteca Estense e Universitaria* (Modena: Il Bulino, 1991).

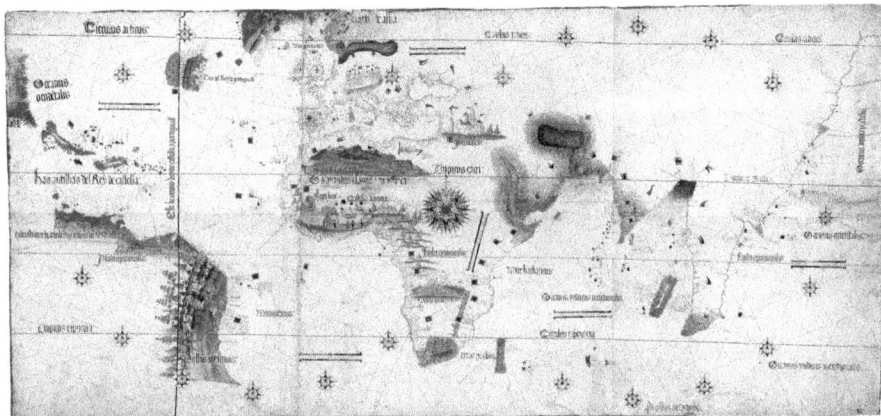

**Figure 2.2** *Seillam* in the shadow of the newly formed Indian subcontinent on the 'Cantino Planisphere', Lisbon, 1502. Biblioteca Estense Universitaria, Modena.

mind, then this new island was set to exert little oneiric appeal—lest it was reinvented in some way.[15] The reinvention, however, took almost a century to complete.

Whilst the myth of Taprobane was still occasionally mobilized in Portuguese texts produced for foreign audiences,[16] virtually no trace of that erudite fascination is to be found in the materials produced in Asia. Most Portuguese accounts strike a pragmatic tone explicitly detached from the classical tradition.[17] Epistemologically speaking, this was in tune with a wider shift to direct experience as a key criterion of truth.[18] It was broadly commented upon in Portugal that John II (r.1481–95) had rejected the proposals of 'a certain *Christóuam Colom*' not only because he was 'chatty and vainglorious', but also because he was 'full of phantasies about his island of Cypango', placing more trust in Marco Polo's *Milione* than in the scientific achievements of his time.[19]

The sobriety of maritime charts alone might, of course, not have stopped people from dreaming of treasure in *Seillam*. A new myth could have appeared in the place

[15] Cf. David Turnbull, *Maps are territories. Science is an atlas* (Chicago, IL/London: University of Chicago Press, 1993).

[16] Flores, 'A imagem do Oriente no Ocidente europeu: dos ecos da expansão mongol ao Portugal manuelino', *Revista da Biblioteca Nacional*, 2a série, 5, 2 (1990), pp. 30–1 and 'A Ilha de Ceilão e o Império Asiático Português', *Oceanos*, 46 (2001), pp. 102–3. Also see Donald F. Lach, *Asia in the Making of Europe*, vol. I (Chicago, IL/London: University of Chicago Press, 1965), pp. 3–30.

[17] José Sebastião da Silva Dias, *A política cultural da época de D. João III* (Coimbra: Universidade de Coimbra, 1969), vol. II, pp. 845–55.

[18] See Onésimo T. Almeida, 'Experiência a madre das cousas – experience, the mother of things – on the "revolution of experience" in 16th-century Portuguese maritime discoveries and its foundational role in the emergence of the scientific worldview', in *Portuguese Humanism and the Republic of Letters*, edited by M. Berbara and K. Enenkel (Leiden: Brill, 2011), pp. 381–400. Luís Filipe Barreto, *Descobrimentos e Renascimento. Formas de ser e pensar nos séculos XV e XVI* (Lisbon: IN-CM, 1983), p. 129.

[19] As pointed out by the chronicler João de Barros some decades later, in *Ásia de João de Barros*, edited by António Baião and Luís F. Lindley Sintra, reprint (Lisbon: IN-CM, 1988–2001), vol. I, book iii, chapter 11, p. 113. Cf. Luís Filipe F. R. Thomaz, 'Cipango', *Dicionário de História dos Descobrimentos Portugueses*, edited by Luís de Albuquerque (Lisbon: Caminho, 1994), vol. I, pp. 251–2.

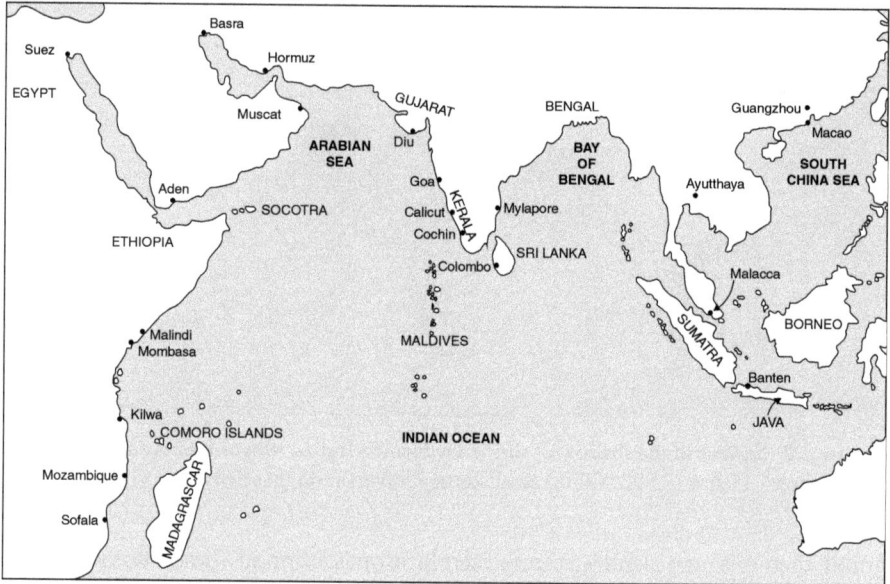

**Figure 2.3** Main ports of the Indian Ocean region.

of the old, as happened further East, where tales emerged about a fabulously wealthy land of gold, the *Aurea Chersoneso*. But generally speaking, the Portuguese did not experience the perceived lack of riches that prompted Columbus in the Caribbean to over-compensate rhetorically, claim the islands and start their colonization, thus reverting to a settling strategy that had proven successful in the Azores, Madeira or the Canaries.[20] Across Asia, the Portuguese were able to take part in commercial operations—fuelled, of course, by gold and silver from East Africa and the Far East—that became very complex very quickly (see Figure 2.3). The Cape Route was soon less important than intra-Asian trade, and the notion of extracting bullion to take home to Portugal lost relevance, until it reappeared in the 1560s. Nowhere in Asia or East Africa would switching the focus from high-profit trade to large-scale extractive and fiscal colonization make much sense in the early 1500s. If violence was to be used, it would be best employed to raid existing trade links or impose duties on the circulation, not the production of things.[21]

---

[20] Stephen Greenblatt, *Marvelous Possessions. The Wonder of the New World* (Chicago, IL: University of Chicago Press, 1991), pp. 52–85. This is of course a debatable explanation. A more straightforward argument is that Columbus played on two fronts simultaneously, hoping to trade with Asia, but also taking possession because, his being an expedition into the Atlantic, the contract with the Catholic kings involved laying claim to any islands found on the way. In any case, there is a discernible Atlantic model of colonization valid both in the Portuguese and the Spanish half of the ocean.

[21] As Anthony Disney put it in an oral presentation at the Institute of Historical Research in London, in 2007, the Portuguese faced three successive perspectives regarding Asian trade: loot it, tax it, or take part in it. Cf. Disney, *A History*, vol. II, pp. 145–59.

Nor was there much of a grand plan for expansion across the Indic. Manuel I may have dreamt of going through the Arabian Sea to reconquer Jerusalem, but centrifugal forces interacting with Asian pull factors in commerce and diplomacy undermined attempts at centralizing the expansionist process.[22] Before the governorship of Afonso de Albuquerque began in 1509, Portuguese strongholds and trading posts (*feitorias*) sprang up as parts of various successive, often short-lived projects with little coherence. Whilst some of the outposts proved resilient (for example Cochin and Cannanore, where forts established in the early 1500s survived until the 1660s, and of course Goa, which remained under Portuguese rule from 1510 to 1961), others were abject failures (for example, the forts set up in the islands of Angediva and Soqotra in 1506 and 1507, and even a brief official presence in the hostile port of Calicut).[23] In 1505, when Francisco de Almeida was dispatched from Lisbon with orders to establish a series of forts and then proclaim himself viceroy (he eventually chose Sofala, Kilwa, Angediva, Cochin, and Cannanore), Ceylon was mentioned only cursorily. It was one among several secondary objectives to which the king ordered some caravels to be dispatched, but only if 'dispensable'.[24] And indeed, why target this island when 'in the Indies there are so many things to discover'?[25] The main exports of Lanka in particular—cinnamon, elephants, and precious stones—were all to be had in Indian ports at competitive prices.

If there was pressure to carve out an imperial sphere of interest in Asia, then this was due only to the ghost of Spanish competition—and here indeed a grand imperial vision does creep into the picture, but built around a concept of *conquista* aiming not at conquest, but at the collection of tribute from local rulers. Manuel I wanted to plant as many *padrões* as possible along the shores of Asia: stone pillars indicating that Portuguese navigators had at least briefly set their foot on the land, creating an aura of precedence should any other European fleets intrude.[26] There were, at the time, concrete fears of Spanish but also French interloping, and it is indeed remarkable how Portugal maintained an exclusive grip over the Cape Route for much of the sixteenth century. In significant measure, European nations felt discouraged from venturing into the dangerous waters of the South Atlantic and South Indic as Asian goods were available in Lisbon and (from 1508 to 1549) at the Portuguese royal warehouse in Antwerp, at relatively competitive prices. The Dutch only chose to invest in the Cape Route after the closure of the Portuguese ports under the Iberian Union of crowns, late in the 1580s. But Spanish westward voyages were deemed a danger early on by the Portuguese in Asia.

---

[22] Cf. Thomaz, 'L'idée impériale manuéline'.

[23] On the various constellations of forts in the Indian Ocean region between 1503 and 1509, see João Paulo Oliveira e Costa and Vítor Luís Gaspar Rodrigues, *Portugal y Oriente: El proyecto indiano del Rey Juan* (Madrid: Fundación Mapfre, 1992), pp. 63–85.

[24] Royal orders (*regimento*) to Francisco de Almeida, Lisbon, 5 March 1505, *Cartas de Afonso de Albuquerque, seguidas de documentos que as elucidam*, edited by Raimundo António de Bulhão Pato (Lisbon: Academia Real das Ciências, 1884–1935), vol. II, pp. 327–8.

[25] *Regimento* for Francisco de Almeida, *Cartas de Afonso de Albuquerque*, vol. II, p. 327.

[26] *Regimento* for Francisco de Almeida, *Cartas de Afonso de Albuquerque*, vol. II, p. 328.

The practice of setting up stone pillars illustrates the Portuguese approach to exploration and *conquista* well. It began along the African coast in the mid-fifteenth century, and inspired Castilians to do the same with wooden crosses in the hemisphere they considered as theirs. Once planted, a *padrão* helped establish, from an Iberian perspective, a certain right over an area, complementing the general entitlement deriving from the division of the globe into two spheres under the treaty of Tordesillas (1494).[27] In the words of Manuel I, it was important to set up these stone columns to show 'that we were first in taking possession'. It meant, to be more precise, the perfecting of the general right of conquest with concrete explorations on the ground.[28] The position of each *padrão* would be noted on maps and in texts which bore testimony to the global surveying efforts. At a time when much more land was being surveyed than could possibly be conquered and colonized in a foreseeable future, the expanding web of *padrões* expressed the Portuguese crown's latent right of conquest and reinforced it by signalling a material capability of reaching distant places.[29]

It is worth insisting on the specific signification of the word *conquista* in this context. The *conquista* mandate gave the Portuguese a potential right to claim parts of the globe rather than an effective right of possession, a *ius ad rem* rather than a *ius in re*, as Luís Filipe Thomaz has put it. As a concept, it had its roots in the medieval Iberian tradition. It could be invoked to extort tribute (*páreas*) from rulers whilst their territories were not conquered, and it was indeed what justified, from a Portuguese perspective, tributes claimed by Francisco de Almeida in East Africa (Kilwa) and India (Chaul).[30] The first royal plan specifically regarding Ceylon took shape in 1506 precisely within this logic. Informed of a Castilian armada that was purportedly being set up to search for Malacca, the monarch reacted and insisted that the waters extending between India and Southeast Asia be explored. For a brief moment, the monarch even mentioned that Ceylon might serve as an operational hub for Portuguese activities—but nothing happened.[31]

There can be little doubt that the concept as such of *conquista*, even in its softer sense, was inherently aggressive, an ominous sign of confrontations to come, both on the Portuguese and the Spanish side of the globe. It was, however, clearly a very abstract notion, carrying both the potential for future, armed conquest, and for more pragmatic strategies of diplomacy and trade. To entice his viceroy to act,

---

[27] On Tordesillas see Luís de Albuquerque, *O Tratado de Tordesilhas e as dificuldades técnicas da sua aplicação rigorosa* (Coimbra: Universidade de Coimbra, 1973); Luís Adão da Fonseca and Maria Cristina da Cunha, eds., *O Tratado de Tordesilhas e a diplomacia luso-castelhana no século XV* (Lisbon: INAPA, 1991), offers a large bibliography on the topic.

[28] Manuel I to Francisco de Almeida, s.l., [1506], *Cartas de Afonso de Albuquerque*, vol. III, p. 270.

[29] On *padrões* see Avelino Teixeira da Mota, 'Padrões dos Descobrimentos', in *Mar, Além-Mar. Estudos e ensaios de História e Geografia*, vol. I (Lisbon: JIU, 1972), pp. 43–51; Barros, *Ásia*, vol. I, book iv, chapter 11, p. 160.

[30] Thomaz, 'L'idée impérial manuéline', pp. 38–41.

[31] Manuel I to Francisco de Almeida, s.l., [1506], in *Cartas de Afonso de Albuquerque*, vol. III, p. 270 and 275. On the shifting centres of the *Estado*, see Catarina Madeira Santos, '*Goa é a chave de toda a Índia*'. *Perfil político da capital do Estado da Índia (1505–1570)* (Lisbon: CNCDP, 1999), pp. 89–91 and *Entre Velha Goa e Pangim: a capital do Estado da Índia e as reformulações da política ultramarina* (Lisbon: CEHCA, 2001), pp. 3–5.

Manuel I had to paint a picture of commercial profit, not military glory or settler utopianism. Cinnamon, pearls, and 'many other goods and things of great value' were what mattered to people like Almeida.[32] The viceroy finally dispatched his son Lourenço to explore the sea between South India and Ceylon, but motivation ran low. In one of the accounts of the events of 1506, we are told that the young Almeida's arrival in the island was unintended, the result of a storm that hit the armada while exploring the Maldives.[33]

## AN ENCOUNTER OF LITTLE SIGNIFICANCE: THE PORTUGUESE AT COLOMBO IN 1506

Upon entering the bay of Kolambā, the most important port of Sri Lanka due to its proximity to the capital city of Kōṭṭe, Lourenço de Almeida signalled the aggressivity inherent to the Portuguese mandate by looting a number of Muslim-owned ships. The act as such was a brutal affirmation of a deep-seated desire for wider supremacy, translatable into a superior position in trade. This act of privateering was also seen, however, as clearly pertaining to the maritime sphere, a part of the conflict that opposed the Portuguese to the Mappilas, Muslim traders of the Malabar Coast of South India. The physical violence was not to be carried inland. Almeida dispatched an emissary to Kōṭṭe, a city established in the early 1400s some miles further southeast, with a conciliatory message.[34] According to one chronicler, Almeida sent word that he had arrived in the island as a merchant, with some goods to trade 'in good peace and friendship'. The king of Kōṭṭe, Dharma Parākramabāhu IX (r.1489–1513), responded by dispatching a courtier carrying a ring as a sign of trust.[35] The two parties appear to have engaged in a constructive dialogue, quite possibly at the expense of the third party, the Mappilas, left out of the conversation. Unfortunately, we have no further details about the messages exchanged.[36]

---

[32] Manuel I to Almeida, *Cartas de Afonso de Albuquerque*, vol. II, p. 275. For a helpful though outdated overview of the Portuguese cinnamon trade, see *Os Descobrimentos e a Economia Mundial. 2a edição correcta e ampliada*, 4 vols. (Lisbon: Presença, 1981–83), vol. II, pp. 191–4.

[33] Flores, *Os Portugueses*, p. 124.

[34] Gaspar Correia, *Lendas da Índia*, edited by M. Lopes de Almeida (Porto: Lello & Irmão, 1975), vol. I, p. 647. On the ruins of old Kōṭṭe see E. W. Perera, 'Alakeswara: His Life and Times', *Journal of the Ceylon Branch of the Royal Asiatic Society*, 18 (1904), pp. 281–312 and 'The Age of Sri Parākrama Bāhu VI', *Journal of the Ceylon Branch of the Royal Asiatic Society*, 22 (1910), pp. 6–45. A summary description is in Georg Schurhammer, *Francis Xavier. His Life, His Times*, vol. II, Rome, 1977, pp. 414–20. For a plan, see Strathern, *Kingship and Conversion*, p. xvii.

[35] Correia, *Lendas*, vol. I, pp. 647–8.

[36] Cf. Saldanha, *Iustum Imperium*, p. 527. On Dharma Parākramabāhu IX see Bouchon, 'Les rois de Kotte au début du XVIᵉ siècle', *Mare Luso-Indicum*, 1 (1971), pp. 65–96 and 163–8, which is not disproven by Mendis Rohandeera, 'Dharma Parakramabahu IX: The False King of Ceylon Inflated by the Portuguese Historians – A Historiographical Perspective', *Vidyodaya Journal of Social Sciences*, 8 (1996), pp. 13–45. The Portuguese request or *requerimento* should not be mistaken for a *requerimiento* in the Spanish sense of the word. The latter, a legally binding text that played a major role in the legitimation of conquest in the New World, was created in 1510.

What we do know is that during these negotiations Almeida never set a foot on land. He followed the royal orders that his father had received the previous year. No person was to leave the ships in Asia 'at any time' unless they were to enter a Portuguese fort. The only exception would be the *feitores* (trade delegates) and their scribes when doing business, and very occasionally other people such as emissaries. Core diplomatic activities were to be conducted onboard Portuguese vessels.[37] In fact, the unease of the earliest Portuguese visitors to Kōṭṭe is recorded in the Lusitanian chronicles. The envoys were 'led through such dense forests that they could not see the sun', along trails so tortuous that it 'seemed more of a labyrinth than a path leading anywhere'.[38] In the Portuguese version of the tale, the only thing that kept the envoys aware of the proximity of the sea were the cannon fired from a ship at regular intervals.[39] In the Sinhalese tradition, the expression '*Parangiya Kōṭṭeta vage*', which translates as 'leading the Franks to Kōṭṭe', is still taken to mean something like 'going along tortuous paths' or 'wandering around without orientation'.[40] True or not, the story is illustrative of the unease with which the Portuguese left the element that had carried them across the globe.

No permanent, official Portuguese presence originated from the first encounter.[41] An agreement was reached regarding the delivery of a substantial amount of cinnamon to the fleet, and the promise that more could be had in subsequent years. Not much else happened on the Portuguese side—except naturally the planting of a *padrão* near the harbour of Colombo, as a 'sign that this land was at peace with the Portuguese'.[42] According to one chronicler, the king of Kōṭṭe suggested that the Portuguese place *padrões* in all his ports along the southwestern Lankan coast, but the latter replied 'that this one in particular sufficed for all'.[43] In describing Colombo to Manuel I, the Almeidas underlined that they had found a peninsula 'like that of Cannanore [in South India], where a fort could be built, abundant in water and with a good port [and] on the way to Malacca'.[44] But nothing was done. As for the comparison with the South Indian outpost at Cannanore— where a fortified *feitoria* had been created in 1501 on a peninsula separated from the mainland by an artificial trench—it is significant not so much as a sign of engagement with the land, but quite precisely the opposite.[45] Colombo was

[37] *Cartas de Afonso de Albuquerque*, vol. II, pp. 307 and 314.

[38] Fernão Lopes de Castanheda, *História do Descobrimento e Conquista da Índia pelos Portugueses*, edited by M. Lopes de Almeida (Porto: Lello & Irmão, 1979), vol. I, p. 264. Barros, *Ásia*, vol. I, book x, chapter 5, p. 396.

[39] Queiroz, *Conquista*, p. 139.

[40] Cf. Ferguson, 'The Discovery of Ceylon by the Portuguese in 1506', p. 310.

[41] Bouchon, 'Les rois de Kotte', p. 75. Flores, *Os Portugueses*, p. 125.

[42] Castanheda, *História*, vol. I, p. 264; cf. Correia, *Lendas*, vol. I, p. 654. This original *padrão* was probably destroyed before 1518. Cf. Correia, *Lendas*, vol. II, p. 540.

[43] Correia, *Lendas*, vol. I, pp. 654–5.

[44] Francisco de Almeida to Manuel I, s.l., 27 December 1506, *Cartas de Afonso de Albuquerque*, vol. II, p. 393. The same argument appears in a second letter dated 5 December 1508, copied by Correia in *Lendas*, vol. I, p. 917.

[45] See Biedermann, 'Colombo versus Cannanore: Contrasting Structures of Two Early Colonial Port Cities in South Asia', *Journal of the Economic and Social History of the Orient*, 53, 2 (2009), pp. 413–59. A revised version is in *The Portuguese in Sri Lanka and South India. Studies in the History of Empire, Diplomacy and Trade, 1500–1650* (Wiesbaden: Harrassowitz, 2014), pp. 103–48.

deemed interesting because it might allow the Portuguese to create a fortifiable, artificial island off the larger island of Ceylon. The only other text resulting from the encounter that contained some sort of geographical information was produced by a nobleman, António Real, who had earlier been to Italy serving Charles VIII of France. He fleetingly compared Ceylon with Sicily. But here, too, the main aspect carrying the text was the variety of goods to be had in Ceylon, and how easily they could be taken to India. No words were lost regarding the land itself.[46]

Everything converges to suggest that the protagonists of the first encounter on the Portuguese side saw Ceylon essentially as a place of transit. If they expressed a moderate interest, it was in tradable goods. The Portuguese sought at the time to take part in the circulation of things, as in other parts of Asia, not their direct extraction or production. According to one account of the events, the king of Kōṭṭe declared toward the end of the diplomatic exchange that 'whilst the Portuguese were lords of the sea, he was lord of the land'.[47] Having presented himself as a merchant from the onset, Almeida must have felt contented. His was a family of maritime traders and occasional privateers, not conquistadors.

## ON THE OTHER SIDE: LANKAN POLITICAL FRAGMENTATION AS A PULL FACTOR

To ask how the elite of Kōṭṭe dealt with the newcomers is another, very different matter. If we can gain an understanding of what politically relevant meanings may have been generated during the encounter of 1506 on the Lankan side, we stand a chance of filling the relative void on the Portuguese side. We may, along the way, 'provincialize' a European nation in the sense of deconstructing it as a dominant knowing subject and making it into an object of Lankan knowledge.[48] It is a central contention of this book that the Portuguese were pulled into Sri Lanka by local elites because of the latter's powerful interest in foreign diplomatic and military cooperations—that the pull factors were at least as important as, if not more important than, the push factors, and that trade was only one part of the equation in Kōṭṭe.[49] The paucity of Lankan sources giving specific evidence about what happened in 1506 may seem disheartening at first—there is indeed very little written in Sinhala or Tamil for much of the sixteenth century.[50] Yet the contextual evidence

---

[46] António Real, s.l., s.d., in *As Gavetas da Torre do Tombo* (Lisbon: CEHU, 1960–77), vol. X, pp. 365–6.

[47] Valentim Fernandes to Stephan Gabler, Lisbon, 26 June 1510, published with a slightly flawed Portuguese translation by Albin Beau in António Brásio, 'Uma carta inédita de Valentim Fernandes', *Boletim da Biblioteca da Universidade de Coimbra*, 24 (1960), pp. 344 and 352. Cf. Correia, *Lendas*, vol. I, p. 649.

[48] David Washbrook, 'Problems in global history', in *Writing the History of the Global. Challenges for the 21st century*, edited by Maxine Berg (Oxford: Oxford University Press, 2013), pp. 25–6.

[49] Much of the argument here draws inspiration from Strathern, *Kingship and Conversion*.

[50] The closest written accounts are two almost identical, but ambiguous passages in the *Rājāvaliya* and the *Alakeśvara Yuddhaya*, two Lankan chronicles written decades later. *The Rājāvaliya or a Historical Narrative of the Sinhalese Kings from Vijaya to Vimala Dharmasuriya II*, edited by B. Gunasekara, reprint (New Delhi: Asian Educational Service, 1995). *Alakesvara Yuddhaya*,

is both abundant and compelling. In 1506, entering into a positive relationship with the Portuguese appeared as a suitable strategy (and not just a short-term tactical move) to the ruling elite of Kōṭṭe for a variety of reasons. It is worth dwelling upon three of these—the internal political fragmentation of the island; the existing regional networks of power; and the mechanisms articulating the former with the latter—with some emphasis on the *longue durée* before we proceed.[51]

Centrifugal forces left a deep imprint on the Lankan system from the end of the Anurādhapura period, in the late first millennium AD, if not earlier. No Lankan ruler could fully unify the island into a single, directly controlled realm until the modern era. A considerable number of polities shared the island space, each of them structured around its own centre claiming to possess certain attributes of royal dignity—ideally, a set of seven features known as '*satta rājjaṇgāni*' (translatable as the 'seven elements of sovereignty' or '*rāja*-ship') and a court with a series of dignitaries in charge of political, ritual, and administrative matters.[52] Even in those rare moments when the symbolic centre of the system—the 'first and most stable king' at Kōṭṭe, as an early Portuguese observer put it—claimed to control the entire island, the authority thus exerted was fundamentally reliant on the tributary submission of other kings and warlords who, naturally, did all they could to evade obligations (Figure 2.4).[53] Tribute also structured relations between ruling figures further down the hierarchy, with the lords of remote areas like the Vanni and the eastern woodlands, for example, paying tribute to Kandy or Jaffna. Tributary overlordship as a system relied on periodical renewal at all levels, ideally in annual *däkum* ceremonies, which replicated at an inter-ruler level the offerings practised

---

edited by A. V. Suravira (Colombo: Ratan Book Publishers, 1965). Cf. Chandra Richard De Silva, 'Beyond the Cape: The Portuguese encounter with the peoples of South Asia', in *Implicit Understandings*, edited by Stuart Schwartz (Cambridge: Cambride University Press, 1994), pp. 295–322 (with a translation by De Silva of the relevant passage on pp. 311–12); Michael Roberts, 'A Tale of Resistance: The Story of the Arrival of the Portuguese in Sri Lanka', *Ethnos*, 54, 1–2 (1989), pp. 69–82; C. R. De Silva, 'Islands and Beaches: Indigenous Relations with the Portuguese in Sri Lanka after Vasco da Gama', in *Vasco da Gama and the Linking of Europe and Asia*, edited by Anthony Disney and Emily Booth (New Delhi: Oxford University Press, 2000), pp. 280–94.

[51] The panorama of Lankan sources for the period studied in this book is—unless one includes documents written in Portuguese—very poor. Few materials survive beyond the *Rājāvaliya* and the *Sītāvaka Hatana (The Sītāvaka War)*, edited by Rohini Paranavitana (Colombo: Ministry of Cultural Affairs, 1999); see Strathern, *Kingship and Conversion* for some additional materials, none of which have had much to offer on the story explored in this book. In the longer *durée*, see however *Mahāvamsa or the Great Chronicle of Ceylon*, translated into English by Wilhelm Geiger (London: Oxford University Press for the Pali Text Society, 1912) and *Cūlavamsa, being the more recent part of the Mahāvamsa*, transl. into German by W. Geiger and from the German into English by C. R. Rickmers, 2 vols. (London: n. p., 1929). The seventeenth century offers considerably more.

[52] These included at Kōṭṭe, originally, the Tooth of the Buddha (kept in the Temple of the Tooth, the *Dalada Maligawa*), the most important royal treasure of the island (the *rajasādhana, rajabhaṇda* or *kosa*), plus the paraphernalia of the throne (*āsana* or *pallanka*), the crown with the great stone *cūlāmaṇi*, the white umbrella *seta-chatta*, the fly-whisk *cāmara*, the royal dagger *acchijja-cchurikkā*, the elephants and horses, the harem, the court. Wilhelm Geiger, *Culture of Ceylon in Medieval Times*, edited by Heinz Bechert (Wiesbaden: Harrassowitz, 1960), pp. 124–36.

[53] The expression is taken from Barros, *Ásia*, vol. III, book ii, chapter 1, fol. 28. On tribute, see Tikiri Abeyasinghe, 'The kingdom of Kandy: foundations and foreign relations to 1638', in *University of Peradeniya History of Sri Lanka*, edited by K. M. De Silva (Peradeniya: University of Peradeniya, 1995), vol. II, pp. 139–61.

**Figure 2.4**  Sri Lanka in the sixteenth century.

by villagers to village-holders.[54] Many different things could be transacted as tribute, from elephants and precious stones to princesses and, more prosaically, coinage.

Such a political order was inevitably unstable. Whenever a lesser ruler refused to pay tribute to the overlord, the relationship had to be re-established by force.

[54] Cf. Ralph Pieris, *Sinhalese Social Organization* (Colombo: Ceylon University Press, 1956). Gananath Obeyesekere, *Land Tenure in Village Ceylon* (Cambridge: Cambridge University Press, 1967). Roberts, 'The Collective Consciousness', pp. 31–2. Also see Gananath Obeyesekere, *The Cult of the Goddess Pattini* (Chicago, IL/London: University of Chicago Press, 1984).

For example, when a warlord in the central highlands refused, towards the end of the reign of Parākramabāhu VI of Kōṭṭe (r. *c*.1411–66[55]) to pay his tribute, the great king dispatched an army and authorized its leader to take control of the area to pay the tribute himself.[56] In the 1540s, the king of Sītāvaka rebelled and a warlord was sent from Uva in the Kandyan highlands to besiege him in the name of Bhuvanekabāhu VII of Kōṭṭe. Significantly, this only occurred after several years of breach of agreement, during which no one in the centre felt capable of re-establishing the order.[57]

The primary operative aim of power-building was not the demarcation of territories, but the negotiation (imposition, disruption) of tributary relations between rulers.[58] To put it bluntly, the power of kings rested primarily on the control of people (or groups of people, through key individuals), not lands—an aspect to bear in mind as it will resurface time and again. Occupying a village tended to have little effect if the local leaders were not willing to acknowledge the occupiers' authority. Populations could otherwise vanish into the woods and leave no one to be ruled over. This disconcerting state of affairs still worried the British in the early nineteenth century, when Robert Brownrigg noted that 'they hide their Property and Families in the Woods, take up Arms [...] and abandoning their dwellings follow their Leaders through the Country, hiding in Caves or any other Places of concealment when closely pressed'.[59] In an environment where land—much of it unused—was more abundant than people, most peasants were subjects of the greater rulers at Kōṭṭe or Kandy only indirectly, by obeying someone who in turn obeyed a leader further up—or could be diverted to offer tribute elsewhere. The imposition of a *rāja*'s judicial authority was usually limited to bi-annual visits of envoys wandering through the realm to judge capital crimes, somewhat like royal judges (*juízes de fora*) did in Portugal, but in an even more unstable environment.[60]

From 1489 onwards, even the core areas of the kingdom of Kōṭṭe, where the *rājas* of Kōṭṭe had acted as sovereigns, not just suzerains, began to fall apart. Shortly before his death, Vira Parākramabāhu (r.1477–89) ordered the partition of his realm among five princes: Dharma Parākramabāhu retained the dignity of *mahārājan* at Kōṭṭe; Rājasiṃha was made *rāja* in Menikkaddawara; Vijayabāhu *rāja* in Rayigama; Sakalakalāvallaba *rāja* in Udugampola; and Taniyavallabāhu *rāja* in Katupiti Madampe, all relatively close to Kōṭṭe.[61] Whilst the title of *rājadhirājan*

---

[55] Dates taken from G. P. V. Somaratne, 'Rules of succession to the Throne of Kotte', *Aquinas Journal*, 7 (1991), pp. 17–32.

[56] *Rājāvaliya*, p. 69.       [57] Queiroz, *Conquista*, pp. 208–11.

[58] The practice of keeping 'boundary books' to register divisions of land might be pointed out as potentially contradicting this idea, but such texts operate at a distinct level, defining the extension of village lands, not of kingdoms. Cf. H. A. P. Abhayawardana, *Boundary Books of Mediaeval Sri Lanka* (Colombo: Academy of Sri Lankan Culture, 1999).

[59] Despatch dated 19 February 1818, from Robert Brownrigg to the Earl Bathurst, quoted in Sujit Sivasunderam, 'Cosmopolitanism and indigeneity in four violent years: the fall of the kingdom of Kandy and the Great Rebellion revisited', in *Sri Lanka at the Crossroads of History*, edited by Zoltán Biedermann and Alan Strathern (London: UCL Press, 2017), p. 196.

[60] Cf. Geiger, *Culture of Ceylon*, p. 139.       [61] G. P. V. Somaratne, 'Rules of succession', p. 19.

or 'king of kings' was beyond anyone's reach during these years, Dharma Parākramabāhu in Kōṭṭe kept his prominence and the title of *mahārājan* ('great king').[62] Hence the appearance, in the earliest Portuguese sources, of the designation of '*rei grande*'. According to the *Rājāvaliya*, Dharma Parākramabāhu consulted with his brothers, the *rājas* of the southwestern lowlands, as he ruled.[63]

The partition was more hierarchical than some historians have assumed.[64] Kōṭṭe kept the imperial regalia and retained a symbolic prominence that proved meaningful during much of the sixteenth and seventeenth century. Whilst the classical 'galactic polity' of Southeast Asia, as analyzed by Stanley Tambiah, lacked a stable centre, the Sri Lankan constellation tended to maintain, throughout the period studied in this book, its fixation on at least one symbolic centre at Kōṭṭe.[65] Dom Filipe Botelho, a Sinhalese Catholic noble writing in the 1630s, thus emphasized the role of Kōṭṭe at the apex of the Lankan imperial system.[66] But this is not just what emerges from Portuguese sources, which in this regard could be held accountable for some bias given that Kōṭṭe was the polity that eventually fell into the hands of the *Estado*. The distinctive status of Kōṭṭe is enunciated in an inscription dating to the reign of Jayavīra Parākramabāhu (r.1466–9)[67] in terms that are very similar to those appearing in documents produced during the dealings of the king of Kandy with the Dutch in the 1680s, suggesting a strong continuity in this regard.[68] Over two centuries after the order established by Parākramabāhu VI fell apart, Kōṭṭe was still referred to as the symbolic centre of Lanka, the crucible of overlordship that the king of Kandy, Rājasiṃha II, needed to conquer to legitimately carry the Lankan imperial title. This ruler, whilst appearing as *keijser* in Dutch documents, remained reluctant to proclaim himself *cakravarti* in the Sinhalese version of the same papers while the Kōṭṭe throne escaped his control.[69] The system, whilst subjected to centrifugal forces of a feudal kind, was also deeply imbued with a centripetal ideal reminiscent of the Aśōkan imperial model.[70]

---

[62] Cf. Geiger, *Culture of Ceylon*, p. 111.     [63] *The Rājāvaliya*, p. 73.

[64] Cf. G. P. V. Somaratne, *The Political History of the Kingdom of Kotte* (Colombo: Godage and Brothers, 1975), pp. 186–8 and Abeyasinghe, *Portuguese Rule*, pp. 9–10.

[65] Alan Strathern, *Kingship and Conversion*, pp. 27–30. Cf. Stanley J. Tambiah, 'The Galactic Polity in Southeast Asia', *Culture, Thought, and Social Action. An Anthropological Perspective* (Cambridge, MA: Harvard University Press, 1985).

[66] Jorge Flores and Maria Augusta Lima Cruz, 'A "Tale of two Cities", a "Veteran Soldier", or the struggle for endangered nobilities: The two *Jornadas de Huva* (1633, 1635) revisited', in *Re-exploring the Links. History and Constructed histories between Portugal and Sri Lanka*, edited by Jorge Flores (Wiesbaden: Harrassowitz, 2007), pp. 95–123.

[67] Stele of Gadaladeniya, erected under Jayavīra Parākramabāhu (1466–1469), *Epigraphia Zeylanica: being lithic and other inscriptions of Ceylon*, edited by Don Martino de Zilva Wickremasinghe, Senarat Paranavitana and Humphrey William Codrington, vol. IV, 3 (London: Henry Frowde, 1933), pp. 21–4.

[68] Especially the impressive document 'Secreete Conferentie tusschen den Heere Gouverneur Laurens Pijl en den Gannebandaer off den gesant van Sijn Keijserlijke Maijesteit van Candia', 18–21 March 1686, Nationalarchief The Hague, Codex 1309, fols. 503ss.

[69] K. W. Goonewardena, 'Kingship in XVIIth Century Sri Lanka: Some Concepts, ceremonies and other practices', *Sri Lanka Journal of the Humanities*, 3 (1977), pp. 9–16.

[70] Cf. Éric Meyer, 'Comment caractériser les royaumes sri lankais anciens? Remarque critique sur les concepts de féodalisme et de société hydraulique', in *De la royauté à l'état, anthropologie et histoire du politique dans le monde indien*, edited by Jacques Pouchepadasse and Henri Stern (Paris: EHESS,

The term *cakravarti* may, in such an unstable context, strike the reader familiar with South Asian history as a wild exaggeration. Could any Lankan *rāja* or *mahārājan* really aspire to being a *cakravarti* in a way even vaguely approaching the glorified models of the Indian past? The key to answering this question resides in not taking an essentialist approach. Much like '*imperator*' in the European tradition, the Universalistic term '*cakravarti*' in the South and Southeast Asian tradition went through centuries of interpretations and reinterpretations as it was appropriated and adapted in startlingly diverse contexts.[71] By the late medieval period, it makes sense to talk about a '*Cakravarti* Theme' comparable to the 'Imperial Theme' identified for Europe by Frances Yates.[72] The analogy with European imperial claims is not limited to the appropriation of a title by ambitious individuals on the periphery of an older imperial heartland. Like the Latin West, South Asia went through a process of political fragmentation and vernacularization that, in the end, allowed imperial claims to proliferate in a polycentric environment, making Universalist claims in a geographically limited context.[73] These appropriations made the semantics of *cakravarti*-ness increasingly complex as they were adapted to specific regional settings. In fact, the concept of *cakravarti* was itself a composite, predestined to generate further variations, carrying as it did a spiritual side, reflecting the Buddha's path to illumination, and a secular side, geared towards the conquest of the world and its submission to a single just ruler serving as 'Universal Monarch'.[74] As Tambiah put it, the *cakravarti* was as much a 'World Conqueror' as he was a 'World Renouncer'.[75]

---

1991), p. 212. On the Aśōkan model in Sri Lanka, cf. Bardwell L. Smith, 'The Ideal Social Order as Portrayed in the Chronicles of Ceylon', in *The Two Wheels of Dhamma. Essays in the Theravada Tradition in India and Ceylon*, edited by Gananath Obeyesekere, Frank Reynolds and Bardwell L. Smith (Chambersburg, PA: American Academy of Religion, 1972), pp. 31–57.

[71] Originally meaning 'Turner of the Wheel' or 'World Conqueror' in the classical Buddhist ideology of kingship—see Stanley J. Tambiah, *World Conqueror and World Renouncer: a study of Buddhism and polity in Thailand against a historical background* (Cambridge: Cambridge University Press, 1976)—this term was increasingly used again in Sri Lanka from the thirteenth century, reflecting an influx of more markedly Hinduized South Indian conceptions where the military might of the ruler gained importance, thus connoting a 'supreme overlord' ruling primarily by power (*danda*) rather than through claims to the virtuous path (*dhamma*); see John C. Holt, *The Buddhist Visnu: Religious Transformation, Politics and Culture* (New York: Columbia University Press, 2004), p. 42.

[72] Frances Yates, *Astraea. The Imperial Theme in the sixteenth century* (London: Routledge and Kegan Paul, 1975). See Chapter 1 of this volume.

[73] Sheldon Pollock, 'India in the Vernacular Millennium: Literary Culture and Polity, 1000–1500', *Daedalus*, 127, 3 (1998), pp. 41–74.

[74] Reynolds, 'The Two Wheels of Dhamma: A Study of Early Buddhism', in *The Two Wheels of Dhamma. Essays in the Theravada Tradition in India and Ceylon*, edited by Gananath Obeyesekere, Frank Reynolds and Bardwell L. Smith (Chambersburg, PA: American Academy of Religion, 1972), pp. 6–30.

[75] Tambiah, *World Conqueror, World Renouncer*. In the case of Sri Lanka, the two aspects have been argued to be strictly complementary. Each side of the double-edged *cakravarti* concept derives from a pair of contrasting, but also deeply interdependent notions: *laukika* for military and political conquest, and *lokottara* for spiritual progress: see John C. Holt, *Buddha in the Crown. Avalokiteśvara in the Buddhist Traditions of Sri Lanka* (Oxford: Oxford University Press, 1991), pp. 24–5.

The *cakravarti* title was first used by Sri Lankan rulers in the late twelfth century, at a time when military expansion into South India appeared possible.[76] The act of taking a fleet overseas to invade the subcontinent from which the Sinhalese and their religion originated marked a moment of great symbolic significance.[77] Once these overseas interventions were over, the word *cakravarti* remained in use with a more specific sense relating to the island itself.[78] Hence the emergence of expressions such as *dīpa sakviti* (the '*cakravarti* of the island') or *Lankeśvara* (the '*cakreśvara* of Lanka'). These terms came to overlap semantically with the notion of a ruler being *Trisinhaladhiśvara*, the 'lord of the three Sinhala countries'.[79] Significantly, *Trisinhaladhiśvara* is the Lankan imperial term that found its way into Chinese imperial texts in the early fifteenth century.[80]

The appropriation of such words, their political utterance, was achieved through ritualized gestures. Jayavīra Parākramabāhu (r.1466–9), for example, a grandson of Parākramabāhu VI, performed a specific ritual to signal his position at the top of the hierarchical ladder, a superior kind of annointment known as *svarnābhiṣeka*.[81] The expression '*svarnābhiśeka mangalyayaṭa paḷamuva kaḷa dik-vijayehidi*' designated a political ritual in direct connection with the idea of the 'conquest of the [four] quarters' of the island—the 'conquest' being, crucially for our argument, a reference to overlordship, not direct control. This imaginary, Goonewardena has argued, was linked with the notion that the *cakravarti* acted as a *Bōdhisattva*, whilst more common matters of governance could be left to *rājas*.[82] With the benefit of hindsight, we can say that the claim proved unsustainable, Jayavīra Parākramabāhu

[76] *University of Ceylon History of Ceylon*, vol. I, part 2 (Colombo: Ceylon University Press, 1960), p. 529 and Jonathan Walters, 'Buddhist History: the Sri Lankan Pali *Vamsas* and their Commentary', in *Querying the Medieval. Texts and the History of Practices in South Asia*, edited by Ronald Inden, Jonathan Walters and Daud Ali (Oxford: Oxford University Press, 2000), pp. 125–54.

[77] On the ambiguous relationship with the polities of South India, namely the Cōḷas, see W. I. Siriweera, *History of Sri Lanka from earliest times up to the sixteenth century* (Colombo: Dayawansa Jayakody, 2002), pp. 40–4. It remains to be discussed to what extent the successive Cōḷa invasions of Lanka (993, 1017, 1215, 1287) may or may not be compared to the Portuguese occupation. See *University of Ceylon History of Ceylon*, vol. I, part 1 (Colombo: Ceylon University Press, 1959), pp. 45–7, 60, 80. Also see Wilhelm Geiger, 'Army and War in Mediaeval Ceylon', *Ceylon Historical Journal* 4 (1954–55), pp. 153–68.

[78] Jonathan Walters, 'Buddhist History: the Sri Lankan Pali *Vamsas* and their Commentary', in *Querying the Medieval*, pp. 132–45. K. W. Goonewardena, 'Kingship', pp. 1–32. Alan Strathern, 'Sri Lanka in the long Early Modern Period: Its Place in a Comparative Theory of Second Millenium Eurasian History', *Modern Asian Studies* 43, 4 (2009), pp. 828–30.

[79] Goonewardena, 'Kingship', p. 13. These being Rajarata, Malayarata and Rohana until the thirteenth century; Pihitirata, Māyārata and Ruhuna in the following period; and possibly Kōṭṭe, Kandy and Jaffna in the sixteenth century. Alan Strathern, 'The Royal "We". A Review of *Sinhala Consciousness in the Kandyan Period 1590s to 1815* by Michael Roberts', *Modern Asian Studies* 39, 4 (2005), pp. 1013–26 has alerted to the possibility of other configurations in later periods. In a more speculative vein, Roberts, *Sinhala Consciousness*, pp. 56–7 has suggested a parallel between the 'three parts' and the three gems (*tunsarana* or *tisarana*) of Buddhism, the Buddha, the *Dhamma* and the *Sangha*.

[80] K. M. M. Werake, 'A re-examination of Chinese Relations with Sri Lanka during the 15th century A. D.', in *Modern Sri Lanka Studies* II, 1–2 (1987), pp. 96–7.

[81] Senarat Paranavitana, 'Civilisation of the Period: Economic, Political and Social Conditions', in *University of Ceylon History of Ceylon*, vol. 1, part 2 (Colombo: Ceylon University Press, 1960), p. 731.

[82] Goonewardena, 'Kingship', pp. 7 and 10.

being incapable of resisting the rebellion of his brother, who took the throne as
Bhuvanekabāhu VI. Ironically, as well, Jayavīra Parākramabāhu's proclamation of
imperial status led to further fragmentation, in the midst of which the Portuguese
arrived. Whilst relying on ritual performance to enunciate imperial claims, the
system called for concrete military power to work.[83] The Portuguese, in 1506,
understood none of this.

## SRI LANKAN POLITICS AND THE RATIONALE
## OF CO-OPTING FOREIGNERS

As one might expect, the instability at the inter-polity level of Lankan politics resonated with a great intra-polity volatility. The latter reached a high point around the
turn of the sixteenth century. Within each of the royal courts of Sri Lanka, factional rivalries led to frequent outbursts of violence.[84] In theory, there were some
rules dictating the succession of deceased rulers, but in practice succession was
open to complicated mechanisms of renegotiation through diplomacy and blunt
force.[85] Given the tentacular nature of the Sri Lankan 'royal family',[86] it was common for individuals from one court to lay claim to a throne at another court or, if
a throne was not vacant, to use family ties to destabilize rivals. This is how, as we
shall see, women often came into the frame as powerful political agents. In Kōṭṭe,
the picture resulted in a series of short-lived reigns, especially between 1466 and
1521. Only four out of eight kings ruling between 1411 and 1551 died of a natural
cause, and only once was the death of a ruler not followed by a major outburst of
violence. This one occasion occurred in 1489, when bloodshed was avoided by the
partition of the realm itself.[87]

It was of relatively little use that, in theory, kings saw themselves as the primordial lords of the land, keeping the right to give and take villages[88] along with the
entitlement to do justice on a superior level, thus contributing to the overall order

---

[83] At one point during these years the first autonomous ruler of the central highlands, Senasammata Vikramabāhu (r. c.1469–c.1511), adopted the titles *cakravarti* and *trisimhaladhisvara*. Abeyasinghe, 'The kingdom of Kandy', pp. 139 and 143. This is most likely to have been a momentary gesture to underline his defiance of Kōṭṭe, and simultaneously impose overlordship on surrounding warlords.

[84] Cf. Somaratne, 'Rules of succession to the Throne of Kotte'.

[85] On the similarities between the Sri Lankan and the Indian systems of succession, see Heinz Bechert, 'Mother Right and Succession to the Throne in Malabar and Ceylon', in *The Ceylon Journal of Historical and Social Studies*, 6 (1962), pp. 25–40.

[86] On the 'solar' and 'lunar' dynasties and their links with India, see Geiger, *Culture of Ceylon*, pp. 111–13.

[87] Somaratne, 'Rules of Succession', pp. 17–32.

[88] On the long debate in Sri Lankan historiography regarding the effectiveness of the royal rights over the land, see W. I. Siriweera, 'The Theory of the King's Ownership of Land in Ancient Ceylon: an Essay in Historical Revision', *The Ceylon Journal of Historical and Social Studies*, New Series, 1 (1971), pp. 48–61, 'Land Tenure and Revenue in Medieval Ceylon (AD 1000–1500)', *The Ceylon Journal of Historical and Social Studies*, New Series, 2 (1972), pp. 1–49, and *History of Ceylon*, pp. 146–67, with copious bibliography. See also H. W. Codrington, *Ancient Land Tenure and Revenue in Ceylon*, Colombo, 1938.

of the world.[89] Whilst the lordship over land as such was certainly in connection with the ruler's role as protector of the Buddhist *Sangha* and the Temple of the Tooth, the *Dalada Maligawa*,[90] it was also in practice deeply dependent on the contingencies of court factionalism, inter-polity competition, and political tensions on the ground. A contractualist tradition further limited royal discretion both conceptually and practically.[91] Ideally, a Buddhist *rāja* possessed a power to 'make real the wishes of people' (*iddhi*) vaguely relatable to the—equally debatable—thaumaturgical powers of kings in Europe.[92] But this, along with the more general responsibility attached to kingship of maintaining justice, order, and prosperity in the realm through the cultivation of certain exclusively royal virtues (*dasarājadharma*), also entailed a crucial element of accountability.[93] Regicide was a legitimate option, and it was practised with assiduity.

Standing at the centre of such an unstable system, the kings of Kōṭṭe found solace not just in performances of ritual supremacy, but also, more prosaically, in military activities and, closely connected to those, in the cultivation of diplomatic ties with powers overseas. For a significant part of the fifteenth century, Parākramabāhu VI maintained his leadership in the island while acting as a tributary of the Chinese Son of Heaven. The memory of the *cakravarti*-ship of Parākramabāhu VI was well alive in 1506 and, along with it, the memory of how it had been imposed in the first place.[94] The beginning of Parākramabāhu's reign had been marked by two decisive interventions led by Zheng He, in 1406 and 1411.[95] True, there is considerable debate regarding the details of those events, but the key elements at the core of the story sustain this line of thought.[96] Parākramabāhu and his faction ended up imposing themselves in a field cleansed of their most powerful rivals by foreign intervention. The Chinese, in their turn, accepted the new status quo and thus tacitly protected it.[97] Over the following decades, Parākramabāhu VI sent a number of tributary missions to the Middle

[89] John C. Holt, *Buddha in the Crown* and *The Religious World of Kirti Srī: Buddhism, Art and Politics in Late Medieval Sri Lanka* (Oxford: Oxford University Press, 1996).

[90] H. L. Seneviratne, *Rituals of the Kandyan State* (Cambridge: Cambridge University Press, 1978), pp. 89–98.

[91] This is one of the main contentions of Tambiah, *World Conqueror*, where the ruler's responsibility for the maintenance of the cosmic order is underlined. Such a responsibility naturally entailed accountability, an aspect flagged up repeatedly in Strathern, *Kingship and Conversion*.

[92] This appears in a fifteenth-century text, the *Lovāda Saṅgarāva*. Roberts, *Sinhala Consciousness*, p. 44.

[93] Roberts, *Sinhala Consciousness*, p. 45.

[94] Both Dharma Parākramabāhu IX (r.1489–1513) and Vijayabāhu VI (r.1513–1521) were grandsons of Parākramabāhu VI. Somaratne, 'Rules of succession', p. 18.

[95] See Roderich Ptak, 'China and Portugal at Sea. The Early Ming Trading System and the *Estado da Índia* Compared', *Revista de Cultura*, 13–14 (1991), pp. 21–8.

[96] The events are in Senarat Paranavitana, 'The Kotte Kingdom up to 1505', in *University of Ceylon History of Ceylon*, edited H. C. Ray, vol. I, part 2 (Colombo: Ceylon University Press, 1960), pp. 663–83, attacked by G. P. V. Somaratne in 'Grand Eunuch Ho and Ceylon', *Journal of the Ceylon Branch of the Royal Asiatic Society*, New Series, 15 (1971), pp. 36–47 over a number of details. The latter then attracted criticism from Werake, 'A re-examination'.

[97] Paranavitana, 'The Kotte Kingdom up to 1505', pp. 667–8 and Goonewardena, 'Kingship', pp. 7–8.

Kingdom, some under the leadership of central figures of his court. Embassies are documented for 1416, 1432, 1433, 1435, 1436, 1445, and 1459.[98]

The fifteenth century thus saw the consolidation of a political imagination where the tributary submission of the most important ruler of Lanka to a foreign empire was not just seen as possible, but also desirable. After the Chinese hegemony evaporated, smaller, if also less respectable overlords, could be found in closer proximity, on the Indian mainland. Whilst the symbolic dimension of such exchanges was certainly not the same as with China, the practicalities proved comparable. Towards the end of the fifteenth century, the *rāja* of Kōṭṭe entered a tributary relationship with the *rāja* of Kollam-Venad. The latter was a relatively minor player in South India in comparison with Calicut, but geographically proximate and engaged in the maintenance of a powerful, militarily viable network of trade in the Sea of Ceylon. An early Portuguese source states that the 'main king' (*rei primçipall*) of Lanka was a vassal of the king of Kollam and payed a tribute of forty elephants a year.[99]

This was not primarily—or not just—a matter of trade. Through Kollam, the rulers of Kōṭṭe affirmed their grip on diplomatic relations overseas. And from Kollam, they received a most vital good: Karāva troops.[100] In exchange for elephants and possibly some monetary tribute, the rulers of Kōṭṭe obtained the human resource necessary for making war against other *rājas* in the island, and also for protecting themselves. Whether such troops are perfectly described as 'mercenaries' (the Sinhala word is *ayudhia*) is debatable, but the principle is clear: by importing men from abroad (*desantaranivasino yodha*) capable of serving in the army and in the palace guards, Sri Lankan rulers attempted to consolidate their position in an unstable political landscape. Whoever had access to such imports had an advantage. Hence the practical and not only symbolic importance, in the early sixteenth century, of securing privileged relations with foreign powers. Paying tribute was not an objective in itself, and indeed as soon as the *rāja* of Kōṭṭe felt able to throw off the overlordship of Kollam with Portuguese assistance, he did.[101] But tributary relations were perceived as a manageable necessity, a potentially valuable source of political advantage.

While Kōṭṭe claimed a monopoly over external tributary relations, rulers elsewhere in the island attempted to obtain similar deals. Although it is the foreign diplomacy of Kōṭṭe with southwestern Indian polities (including the *Estado*) that catches the historian's eye, other, less well-documented ties clearly did develop

---

[98] Somaratne, 'Grand Eunuch Ho', pp. 45–6.

[99] Pires, *A Suma Oriental de Tomé Pires e o Livro de Francisco Rodrigues*, edited by Armando Cortesão (Coimbra: Imprensa da Universidade, 1978), p. 188. Also see Brás de Albuquerque, *Comentários de Afonso de Albuquerque, 5a edição, conforme à 2a edição, de 1576*, edited by Joaquim Veríssimo Serrão (Lisbon: IN-CM, 1973), p. 14, which mentions tribute to Kollam in 1503.

[100] M. D. Raghavan, *The Karava of Ceylon. Society and Culture* (Colombo: K.V.G. de Silva & Sons, 1961), pp. 5–14. Cf. Strathern, *Kingship and Conversion*, p. 22.

[101] For example, the economic exploitation of the Gampola kingdom by Jaffna in the fourteenth century must have been resented—it was imposed by military force, and involved having 'tribute' collectors in various places. I thank John Rogers for this remark, which sits well with the swiftness of Kōṭṭe's distantiation from Kollam.

across the strait. The kings of Sītāvaka came to maintain, as we shall see, alliances with South Indian Muslim powers, namely the Mappilas of Cannanore. The *rāja* of Jaffna payed tribute to the Nāyak of Thanjavur in 1548,[102] receiving Badaga troops in exchange.[103] According to the Italian traveler Lodovico Vartema, the 'four kings' of Ceylon (either a concrete reference to four rulers, or a distant echo of the four satrapies of Pliny's Taprobane)[104] were tributaries of the king of Vijayanagara, receiving much-needed rice in exchange for their allegiance.[105] It is imaginable that Jaffna in particular maintained such a relationship in the early 1500s, before it switched to Thanjavur, while Kōṭṭe went with Kollam and later the Portuguese *Estado*.

Perhaps the most intriguing aspect is how straightforwardly the expanding Portuguese *Estado* fitted into the existing system regionally and locally, at once defying the status quo and playing into the perpetuation of the logic sustaining it. Whilst the Portuguese faced consistent opposition at Calicut, the apex of Kerala's multi-polity hierarchy, they found allies in smaller kingdoms that saw the new-comers as an opportunity to break free from their existing tributary ties. Hindu *rājas* in Cochin, Kollam, and Cannanore entered agreements with the Portuguese.[106] What these new deals promised was not only an acceptable alternative to the overlordship previously exercised by the *Samudri Rāja* of Calicut, but a solution that was eminently readable because analogous tributary arrangements had been commonplace.[107] That this involved violence is beyond discussion. The Portuguese accounts are as explicit in this regard as those produced by Muslims, the most vigorously targeted group.[108] But tributary relations based on a periodical meas-urement of forces had been an integral part of South Indian and Sri Lankan politics for centuries. It was down to South Asian rulers to either confront the Portuguese—as some did—or make use of them.[109]

---

[102] Queiroz, *Conquista*, p. 225.    [103] Queiroz, *Conquista*, p. 211.

[104] Pliny, *Naturalis Historia*, VI, 25.

[105] 'Itinerario di Lodovico Barthema', in Giovanni Battista Ramusio, *Navigazioni e Viaggi*, edited by Marica Milanesi (Turin: Giulio Einaudi, 1978), vol. I, p. 846.

[106] On Cochin and Cannanore see Costa and Rodrigues, *El proyecto indiano*, pp. 63–9 and, above all, the detailed study of events in Aubin, 'L'apprentissage de l'Inde'. On Cannanore's strategy of seek-ing Portuguese assistance against Calicut see Geneviève Bouchon, *Mamale de Cananor. Un adversaire de l'Inde portugaise (1507–1528)* (Genève/Paris: Librairie Droz, 1975), pp. 57–8. On the short-lived peace talks in Calicut see Biedermann, 'A última carta de Francisco de Albuquerque (Cochim, 31 de Dezembro de 1503)', *Anais de História de Além-Mar* 3 (2002), pp. 123–53. On the naval techniques used by the Portuguese see Vítor Luís Gaspar Rodrigues, 'A evolução da arte da Guerra dos Portugueses no Oriente (1498–1622)' (PhD dissertation, Insituto de Investigação Científica Tropical, Lisbon, 1998). Also see A. J. R. Russell-Wood, 'For God, King and Mammon: The Portuguese Outside of Empire, 1480–1580', in *Vasco da Gama and the Linking of Europe and Asia*, edited by Anthony Disney and Emily Booth (New Delhi: Oxford University Press, 2000), pp. 261–79.

[107] António Vasconcelos de Saldanha, *Iustum Imperium. Dos tratados como fundamento do império dos portugueses no Oriente. Estudo de história do direito internacional e do direito português* (Lisbon/ Macao: Fundação Oriente/Instituto Português do Oriente, 1997), pp. 356–66 and 394–5.

[108] Namely the Tuhfat al-Mujahidin Fi Ba'd Ahual al-Burtukaliyyin by Zainuddin Makhdoom. *História dos Portugueses no Malabar por Zinadím. Manuscrito árabe do século XVI traduzido e anotado*, edited by David Lopes, 2nd ed. (Lisbon: Edições Antígona, 1998).

[109] Strathern, *Kingship and Conversion*, pp. 21–3.

## DISCOVERING THE PORTUGUESE: THE
## LANKAN PERSPECTIVE IN 1506

Once all this information is on the table, the initial encounter of 1506 acquires a new dimension. The pull factors that began to act upon the Portuguese when they first visited Colombo were substantial. To maintain its status within Sri Lanka, Kōṭṭe needed to secure privileged access to external trade and military resources through the tributary submission to an overseas polity. And with Portuguese power growing in South India, there was no reason not to turn to these newcomers for a deal. At the very least, the king of Kōṭṭe needed to make sure that the Portuguese were not co-opted by his own rivals.

The emerging picture is rather different from traditional interpretations of the 1506 events. It has been said that the exchange of gifts, and principally the concession of a large amount of cinnamon to the Portuguese, was a relatively innocent expression of friendliness. This interpretation has indeed been useful in overcoming the triumphalism of the chronicles (one Baroque chronicler spoke of Kōṭṭe's 'capitulation' and a great naval parade to celebrate its subjection into Portuguese imperial dominion).[110] But it has also thrown out the baby with the bath water, leading to depoliticized interpretations of the concession as a somewhat naïve gesture of goodwill paving the way for trade.[111] Whilst there can be no doubt that uncertainties surrounded words such as 'gift', 'friendship', and 'tribute' in 1506, there is now scope to argue that it was precisely this ambiguity that helped establish a platform for further interactions. What Dharma Parākramabāhu IX was after was an alliance that would secure him, in exchange for payments he was willing to make, the military and commercial support of the Portuguese. To him, this was a strategic gesture made with a view to building a lasting bond. He may not have been fully understood, but his actions were coherent and forward-looking. Whilst the exact words employed are lost to us, the notion that he was a 'lord of the land' with a friendly rapport to the Portuguese 'lords of the sea' became the bedrock of a century-long relationship.

It was indeed Dharma Parākramabāhu IX who made the next move. Shortly after the first encounter, he defied his former overlord, the king of Kollam, by not paying the agreed annual tribute. To add weight to his stance, he also began to coin his own currency, soon known as the *fanams* of Kōṭṭe. According to one observer, he was met with disapproval by the *rāja* of Cannanore and other rulers on the Malabar Coast, and soon engaged in military actions against them (presumably against their ships in Lankan ports).[112] From the perspective of Kōṭṭe, this was a powerful sign that the encounter of 1506 had been a success. The new 'friendship' could be hoped to yield lasting benefits. In the rough world of South Asian

---

[110] Queiroz, *Conquista*, p. 142.
[111] Cf. C. R. De Silva, 'Beyond the Cape: The Portuguese encounter with the peoples of South Asia', in *Implicit Understandings*, edited by Stuart Schwartz (Cambridge: Cambridge University Press, 1994), pp. 295–322. Jorge Flores, *Os Portugueses*, p. 125.
[112] Pires, *A Suma Oriental*, pp. 184–5.

inter-polity competition, the ruling elite of Kōṭṭe had shown that it was well prepared to take a new challenge as an opportunity.

On the Portuguese side, the Almeidas briefly considered setting up a fort at
Colombo, but did nothing further. In 1507, the viceroy simply dispatched two
vessels to fetch the tributary cinnamon.[113] Whilst Manuel I reacted positively to
the news of the first encounter,[114] resources on the ground remained scarce. When
tensions around Chaul, Dabul, and Diu in the north led to armed confrontation
that same year, India was once again prioritized.[115] Consequently, Parākramabāhu
IX refused to pay. The vessels dispatched to collect cinnamon in 1508 came back
empty, and the king of Kōṭṭe imported Karāva troops from South India again.[116]
It comes as no surprise that once Goa was conquered in 1510 and emerged as a
possible new headquarters situated further north than Cochin, the island was
pushed even deeper into the corner.[117]

## GREAT EXPECTATIONS: NEGOTIATING THE FIRST
## FORT AT COLOMBO, 1513–1519

The gulf between Lankan ambition and Portuguese indifference widened further
during the governorship of Afonso de Albuquerque (gv.1509–15). Albuquerque,
generally closer to Manuel I than Almeida had been, received an explicit request
from Sri Lanka in 1513 to set up a garrison in the island. The new king, Vijayabāhu
VI (r.1513–21), was under pressure from a brother competing for the throne. He
offered the Portuguese a piece of land for the construction of a fort which might
help secure his position.[118] However, Albuquerque's reach was limited. Around the
ports of Kerala and Sri Lanka, the so-called 'Cochin group' of private merchants
weary of crown control dominated Portuguese activities.[119] Ironically, the new
Sinhalese king had sent word of his intentions precisely to Cochin, where reactions
were bound to be tepid. The captain of Cochin, Lourenço Moreno, had in fact
proposed the previous year that the authorities send vessels to Ceylon only once
every year.[120]

When a fervent advocate of free trade succeeded Afonso de Albuquerque as
governor, the prospect of an official presence in Ceylon became even more remote.

---

[113] Correia, *Lendas*, vol. I, p. 718.

[114] Manuel I to Diogo Lopes de Sequeira, Almeirim, 13 February 1508, *CAA*, vol. II, pp. 413–14.

[115] Flores, *Os Portugueses*, pp. 127–9.

[116] *Mandado* by Francisco de Almeida, Cochin, 25 September 1508, in Flores, *Os Portugueses*,
doc. 1. Correia, *Lendas*, vol. I, p. 899. On the return to Cochin see Castanheda, *História*, vol. I,
pp. 412–22 and Barros, *Ásia*, vol. II, book iii, chapter 1, p. 99.

[117] Flores, *Os Portugueses*, p. 130.

[118] Albuquerque to Manuel I, Cannanore, 30 November 1513, *Cartas de Afonso de Albuquerque*,
vol. I, p. 138.

[119] See Inácio Guerreiro and Vítor Gaspar Rodrigues, 'O "grupo de Cochim" e a oposição a Afonso
de Albuquerque', in *Studia*, 51 (1992), pp. 119–44.

[120] António Real to Manuel I, Cochin, 15 December 1512, *Cartas de Afonso de Albuquerque*,
vol. III, p. 349.

Lopo Soares de Albergaria (gv.1515–18) is generally credited with deregulating whatever trade Albuquerque had brought under official control, and allowing hundreds, if not thousands of Portuguese men to leave their ships and forts and try their luck elsewhere. New, independent merchant colonies sprang up especially around the Gulf of Bengal, forming the so-called 'shadow empire'.[121] No such colony is documented for Ceylon for the 1510s, although it may have existed.[122] Ironically, however, Lopo Soares ended up building the fort that Manuel I demanded.[123] This apparently counterintuitive move may have been down to a very pragmatic realization. Creating a garrison would be ultimately more advantageous for Soares and his followers than leaving the task to a more centralistically minded successor. The governor decided to sail to Ceylon in the last year of his term.[124]

When the fleet arrived in Colombo in early November 1518, the Portuguese were given formal permission by Vijayabāhu VI to set up quarters.[125] The building Soares wished to create was, essentially, a fortified trading post, a '*feitoria-fortaleza*'.[126] Once the Portuguese disembarked to start construction, they met with some resistance, but crucially the opposition came from the king's own rivals.[127] Sakalakalāvallaba, *rāja* of Udugampola, an heir of Vira Parākramabāhu in 1489 and ever since a rival to Vijayabāhu, was at the heart of local resistance to the building of a Portuguese fort.[128] His move was not about ridding the island of foreigners, but making sure that their presence would not benefit the current ruler. Ingeniously enough, Sakalakalāvallaba whipped up tensions and then encouraged Vijayabāhu to attack the Portuguese—only to eventually make peace with the governor himself, 'offering cinnamon, elephants, and whatever else he wanted, if only [the governor] agreed to make *him* king of Ceylon'.[129]

The Portuguese knew by now, from experience gathered in India, the basics of how to play the military and diplomatic game with fragmented, multi-centric polities. In this case, they prevailed militarily and used their position to negotiate, eventually refusing Sakalakalāvallaba's offer and obtaining a better deal from Vijayabāhu.[130] The new agreement expressed more clearly than before a relation of hierarchical submission. An annual tribute was set at 400 *bahars* of cinnamon, ten elephants, and some high-end jewellery.[131] Vijayabāhu also agreed to sell any

---

[121] Sanjay Subrahmanyam, *The Portuguese Empire in Asia 1500–1700. A political and economic history* (London: Longman, 1993).

[122] Flores, *Os Portugueses*, p. 136.      [123] Barros, *Ásia*, vol. III, book ii, chapter 2, fol. 28.

[124] See Flores, *Os Portugueses*, pp. 138–9.

[125] Barros, *Ásia*, vol. III, book ii, chapter 2, fol. 28v mentions 700 armed Portuguese men ('homens de armas portugueses'). Castanheda, *História*, vol. I, p. 939 has 900. Correia, *Lendas*, vol. II, p. 540 speaks of a thousand, along with 200 'Malabars'.

[126] Correia, *Lendas*, vol. II, p. 540. Castanheda, *História*, vol. I, p. 940.

[127] Castanheda, *História*, vol. I, pp. 940–2. Queiroz paints a particularly sinister portrait of Lopo Soares as a prolific killer of Muslims in *Conquista*, pp. 144–6.

[128] Correia, *Lendas*, vol. II, pp. 541–2.      [129] Correia, *Lendas*, vol. II, p. 543. Emphasis added.

[130] Correia, *Lendas*, vol. II, pp. 543–4.      [131] Castanheda, *História*, vol. I, p. 942.

remaining cinnamon to the Portuguese below market value.[132] This was then, formally, the beginning of Portuguese overlordship in Sri Lanka. But if tensions arose subsequently, it was not out of resistance to tributary overlordship or to the foreign presence as such. Vijayabāhu, like any Lankan king looking back on a long tradition of tributary arrangements, would have been willing to pay if the Portuguese gave him the military support he needed on the land. The problem was to become the lack of engagement shown by the Portuguese.

The new fort was built on the tip of a peninsula protecting the bay of Colombo from the ocean, an isolated piece of land known as *Galboka*, the 'rocky shore'. This was in fact the spot that had caught the Almeidas' attention in 1506, when they compared the site to Cannanore.[133] It was at a comfortable distance from Colombo, separated from the town by a creek and a wasteland roughly equivalent to what later, in the Dutch period, became the Fort District. As if this was not enough, the Portuguese also dug a deep trench separating the fortified area from the land, creating an artificial island comparable to that of Cannanore. All this was done 'whilst the governor remained on the ships with all his captains'.[134] A wall was built from waterfront to waterfront, and two further walls erected to form a triangular fort (Figure 2.5). None of these walls is likely to have measured much more than 50 metres. Between the small fort and the trench, a stretch of land about a stone's throw wide was used to provide additional dwellings for the soldiers.[135] The garrison comprised a little less than 200 men.[136]

The compound was a trading fort ('*fortaleza de trato*'), an almost perfect expression of how Portuguese maritime power worked when forced onto the land in the early 1500s, and indeed the sort of outpost that Columbus may have imagined setting up to trade with Asia.[137] These were structures built to feed local trade goods into the maritime network whilst keeping a clear distance from the societies that produced them. The soldiers and administrators were in theory allowed to cross the bridge over the trench, but strongly discouraged from going further

---

[132] One *português de ouro* per *bahar*. Correia, *Lendas*, II, p. 545. Castanheda, *História*, vol. I, p. 942.

[133] On the fort, see Biedermann, 'Colombo versus Cannanore'.

[134] Correia, *Lendas*, vol. II, p. 541.

[135] Correia, *Lendas*, vol. II, p. 541.

[136] Cf. *infra*. The figure of 200 soldiers is in Correia, *Lendas*, vol. II, p. 546. Cf. Flores, *Os Portugueses*, p. 139, who argues for a smaller number. The name was *Santa Bárbara*, cf. Bouchon, 'Les rois de Kotte', p. 260.

[137] The expression is used in *O livro de Duarte Barbosa*, vol. II, p. 279. Cf. Virgínia Rau, *Feitores e Feitorias. "Instrumentos" do Comércio Internacional Português no Século XVI* (Lisbon: Brotéria, 1966), p. 18. Cf. Maria Emília Madeira Santos and Vítor Luís Gaspar Rodrigues, 'A feitoria-fortaleza e o comércio transcontinental da coroa portuguesa no século XVI', in *Portugal no Mundo*, edited by Luís de Albuquerque, reprint (Lisbon: Alfa, 1993), vol. II, pp. 557–70 and Godinho, *Os descobrimentos e a economia mundial*, vol. II, pp. 64–70. Also see Artur Teodoro de Matos, *O Estado da Índia nos anos de 1581–1588: Estrutura Administrativa e Económica. Alguns elementos para o seu estudo* (Ponta Delgada: Universidade dos Açores, 1982), pp. 17–20.

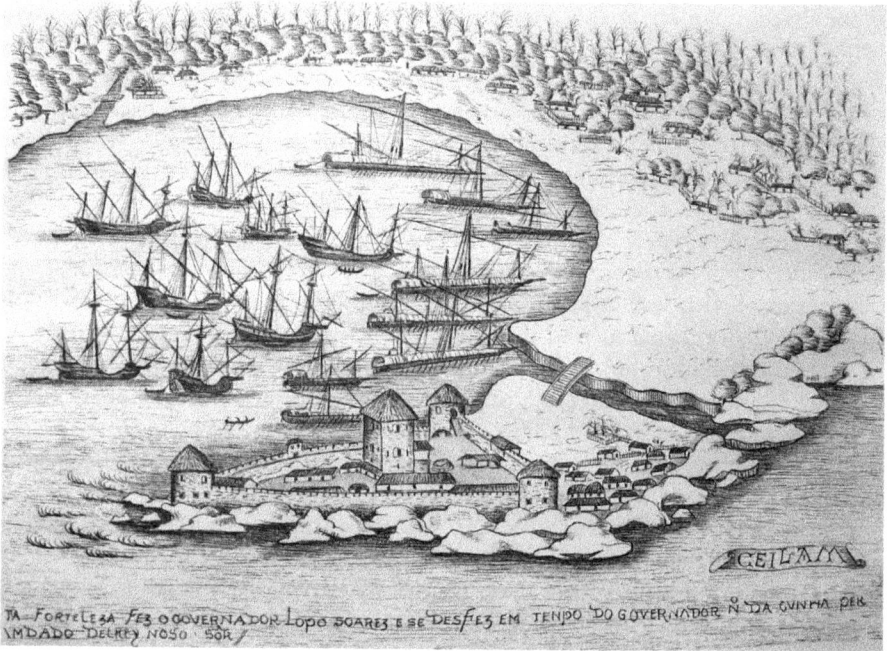

**Figure 2.5** The Portuguese fort built near Colombo in 1518. Hand-drawn copy of the original contained in the manuscript of Gaspar Correia's *Lendas da Índia*, mid-sixteenth century. Copy published in the first printed edition of the *Lendas*, Lisbon, 1858. Image in the public domain.

inland. Deserters were severely punished.[138] The problem for the Kōṭṭe elite was not an excess of Portuguese power projected into the land, but a manifest lack of engagement with it. *Santa Bárbara de Columbo*, as the fort was called, was established to feed the trading networks of the Portuguese, not to serve as a bridgehead for military action in Sri Lanka.

## HUMBLE RESULTS: THALASSOCRACY AND MARGINALITY, 1519–1524

The first Portuguese fort in Sri Lanka highlights the contradictions of early Portuguese polity building in Asia, the obstacles faced by the elite of Kōṭṭe in harnessing Portuguese power under such murky circumstances, and the historiographical challenges resulting from this. Historians have learned to appreciate the network

---

[138] João da Silveira to Manuel I, Colombo, 27 October 1519, in Bouchon, *Mamale de Cannanore*, p. 186.

model as it helps counter narratives that were used to overemphasize the imperial ambitions of Portugal on the Asian continent. Everything we have seen so far seems to confirm the notion that the *Estado* was built around the water without ambitions to control lands. Yet it would also be imprudent to take the theory too far. The network metaphor has its limitations. Even as the Portuguese *Estado* refrained from fomenting conquests, it began to expose its resources to local political matters. Had there only been little depots on islands that no one dared to leave, one might agree that the system would have come close to being purely a maritime network. But because there were people looking at each other across the trenches, some coming and going, and in particular a Sinhalese ruler with a persistent interest in using Portuguese troops for his own purposes, the fort was bound to become more than just a neutral 'dot' on the map. It was a seed from which something else could start to grow.

The *first* fort at Colombo was an ephemeral affair though. Its fundamental defect was that it had been established by a faction of Portuguese society that wished to keep royal involvement in the region to a minimum. When Diogo Lopes de Sequeira (gv.1518–22), again a closer ally of Manuel I, arrived in India, he made a vigorous attempt at re-establishing the royal trade monopoly.[139] But all he could do over the following years was to attempt imposing maritime control, and even this was largely in vain.[140] Increasingly disconnected from the complex realities of the Indic, the ageing monarch developed a vision of royal power emanating from the fort at Colombo that was in stark contrast with the realities on the ground. In December 1519, 400 soldiers had been sent to replace the garrison established the previous year, and the fort structures consolidated.[141] A complete set of crown officials was now in place, including a *feitor*, two scribes, and three *almoxarifes* in charge of the logistics of feeding the garrison.[142] All Lankan trade was expected to go through Colombo and be duly taxed. But isolationism and mistrust remained the dominant note on the ground.[143] In its battle for a tighter regulation of trade, the *Estado* had to confront not only the Mappilas, but also private Portuguese entrepreneurs. The largest capture of 'illegal' cinnamon by a royal patrol during these years was made not on an 'enemy' vessel, but on a Portuguese ship going privately to Diu, from where the cargo would have gone straight into the traditional Middle Eastern networks.[144] One of the last orders issued by Manuel I before his death in 1521 was for an inquiry into the poor quality of the tributary cinnamon arriving from Kōṭṭe.[145] The monarch felt that the best of the spice was being diverted, a suspicion confirmed by recent research that

---

[139] Barros, *Ásia*, vol. III, book iii, chapter 1, fol. 56v.
[140] See Flores, *Os Portugueses*, pp. 143–6 on the role of the Coromandel fleet.
[141] Flores, *Os Portugueses*, p. 144. Barros, *Ásia*, vol. III, book iv, chapter 6, fol. 104v.
[142] Flores, *Os Portugueses*, pp. 322–3.
[143] Cristóvão Lourenço Caracão to Manuel I, Cochin, 13 February 1522, in Bouchon, 'Les rois de Kotte', p. 167.
[144] Flores, *Os Portugueses*, p. 147.
[145] 'Inquirição que tirou Lopo de Brito', in Bouchon, *Mamale de Cananor*, pp. 190–205.

shows how cinnamon reappeared in large quantities in the Levantine ports, en route to Istanbul and Venice, a little before 1520.[146]

Imposing power on the land by patrolling the sea may have seemed a viable strategy from a distance, but was impossible to achieve on the ground. Some men tried to alert the monarch about this. In 1518 already, a captain patrolling the Sea of Ceylon expressed how he felt overstretched in his efforts to force vessels to visit Colombo for taxation.[147] A little later, in 1522, a man called Cristóvão Lourenço Caracão felt the need to explain to the king how centralizing the Lankan elephant and cinnamon trade in Colombo was impossible because it was also conducted in many smaller ports.[148] The rulers of Kōṭṭe themselves tended to refer to Colombo in conjunction with other coastal towns in the island's southwest.[149] At a time of scarce and scattered Portuguese resources, controlling the area proved a task far beyond the means of the Colombo garrison. Soon after the idea was floated of pressuring 'kings and lords' across Sri Lanka by cutting their rice supplies, the garrison itself became dependent on external support. The walls crumbled, and the only way of getting deserters back from Kōṭṭe, where they were well received despite a clause in the agreement of vassalage forbidding such practices, was to take local individuals hostage around the fort.[150]

Relations with Kōṭṭe deteriorated, until on a Friday afternoon the Portuguese attacked Colombo in a brutal surprise attack.[151] This random attempt at projecting power beyond the perimeter of the fort produced a violent reaction. The fort was besieged.[152] A little settlement that had sprung up next to the fort with mixed Luso-Lankan households was destroyed.[153] Only thanks to the unexpected arrival of a Portuguese galley was the garrison saved, and the Lankan troops defeated.[154] Humiliated by his own allies, Vijayabāhu VI saw his fragility exposed. At the end of 1521, three of the king's sons joined efforts to kill their father. Partition was, again, the solution found.[155] Bhuvanekabāhu VII (r.1521–51) proclaimed himself *mahārājan* of Kōṭṭe, retaining the largest number of villages (around 2800 at that moment). Substantial parts of the kingdom went to the brothers who assisted him in the regicide: roughly 1200 villages to the new *rāja* of Sītāvaka, Māyādunnē (r.1521–81) and 600 to the *rāja* of Rayigama, Pararājasiṃha (r.1521–38).[156]

---

[146] Cf. Godinho, *Os descobrimentos*, vol. II, p. 29. Also see C. R. De Silva, 'Trade in Ceylon Cinnamon in the Sixteenth Century', *The Ceylon Journal of Historical and Social Studies*, New Series, 3, 2 (1973), p. 17and Sanjay Subrahmanyam, 'The birth-pangs of Portuguese Asia: revisiting the fateful "long decade" 1498–1509', *Journal of Global History*, 2, 3 (2007), pp. 261–80.

[147] António Miranda de Azevedo to Manuel I, Colombo, 8 November 1519, *Gavetas*, vol. IV, p. 140.

[148] Caracão to Manuel I, Bouchon, 'Les rois de Kotte', pp. 165–6.

[149] On the multitude of ports in the area see Flores, *Os Portugueses*, pp. 31–76.

[150] João da Silveira to Manuel I, [Colombo], 27 October 1519, in Bouchon, *Mamale*, pp. 186–8.

[151] Bouchon, 'Les rois de Kotte', pp. 261–3. Barros, *Asia*, vol. III, book iv, chapter 6, fol. 104v.

[152] C. R. De Silva, 'Sri Lanka in the Early Sixteenth Century: Political Conditions', in *University of Peradeniya History of Sri* Lanka, vol. II, edited by K. M. De Silva (Peradeniya: University of Peradeniya, 1995), vol. II, p. 23.

[153] Cristóvão Lourenço Caracão to Manuel I, Cochin, 13 January 1522, in Bouchon, 'Les rois de Kotte', pp. 164 and 166.

[154] Barros, *Asia*, vol. III, book iv, chapter 6, fol. 106.

[155] On the regicide and partition see De Silva, 'Sri Lanka in the Early Sixteenth Century', pp. 23–4.

[156] De Silva, 'Sri Lanka in the Early Sixteenth Century', pp. 62–3.

The Portuguese stood by as the kingdom of Kōṭṭe was dismembered and when, soon after the regicide, some members of the defeated court faction took refuge in the fort, the captain refused to cooperate in a plot designed to regain power. According to a certain João Garcês, who was present during the negotiations, 'the prince of Chilaw [who had been appointed by Vijayabāhu as his successor] and the regents and captains [who supported him] all came to the fort, handing themselves in to Fernão Gomes de Lemos, drawing his attention to the riches of the island and how large the [royal] treasure was, and [saying] that they would give it to him if he helped them'.[157] Garcês suggested accepting the offer and putting troops at the disposal of the dislodged fraction, thus engaging in an exchange that would have been workable on both sides. But the principle of non-intervention prevailed.

The next governor, Duarte de Meneses (gv.1522–4) further neglected the fort. The new king, Bhuvanekabāhu VII, also did little to collaborate. On the one hand, he had witnessed—and benefitted from—the indifference of the Portuguese. On the other, he may have felt powerful enough after the patricide to govern without the military assistance of the *Estado*. When a revolt erupted under the leadership of an influential ex-minister and nephew of Vijayabāhu VI who had probably been among those seeking assistance from the Portuguese, the latter remained neutral again, and the rebels were defeated. Strengthened in his position, Bhuvanekabāhu decided to turn the cinnamon tap.[158] While private trade continued to flow, the official tributary payments were delayed and reduced.[159] In such an atmosphere, those in the *Estado* who advocated abandoning Colombo gained the upper hand. Their vision was now in tune with a larger plan formulated in 1519 by Aires da Gama, a figurehead of the Portuguese commercialist lobby, against Manuel's imperial vision.[160] Under the pretext of a cost-effective demilitarization and in the face of what he expounded as an impossibility of making any conquests on the lands, Gama had proposed that the permanent official position in Ceylon be abandoned.[161] In 1524, the fort was dismantled, and most of the remaining men transferred to other outposts in the Indic.

The first official establishment in Ceylon was a failure, the result of a conjugation of factors on the Portuguese side that barred the newcomers from engaging fully with the Lankan political realities. A connection had been established, but with an important disjunction at its core impeding the full flow of communications. To the Portuguese in particular, the notion of abandoning the water and getting involved on the land remained uncomfortable. This was of course unfortunate in a context where making that move was exactly what the Kōṭṭe elite expected from them. And yet, this eerily dysfunctional setup left its imprint on Luso-Lankan

[157] João Garcês to John III, Cochin, 2 January 1529, in Luís de Albuquerque and José Pereira da Costa, 'Cartas de "serviços" da Índia (1500–1530)', *Mare Liberum*, 1 (1990), p. 329.

[158] De Silva, 'Sri Lanka in the early sixteenth century', pp. 63–4. This minister was a certain Virasūriya or Pilässe Vīdiyē Baṇḍāra.

[159] Correia, *Lendas*, vol. II, pp. 832, 853.

[160] Analysed in detail in Sanjay Subrahmanyam, 'Making India Gama: The Project of Dom Aires da Gama (1519) and Its Meaning', *Mare Liberum*, 16 (1998), pp. 43–7. Also see Flores, *Os Portugueses*, pp. 152–3.

[161] Gama to Manuel I, Cannanore, 19 January 1519, *Gavetas*, vol. IV, p. 215.

relations. It stood at the intersection, even if it was only briefly, between the imperial imagination of Kōṭṭe and the haphazard empire building of the Portuguese. Lankan nobles had started to come to the fort to tell the Portuguese about local riches and military opportunities. When the fort disappeared, the flow of people did not cease. In fact, as we shall see in the next chapter, the dismantling of the fort paved the way for new, more effective forms of interaction. People could now come and go unrestrained, the Lankan elite could talk with increasing conviction about their own ideas of empire to fire up Portuguese individuals, and *Ceilão* could begin to take on new meanings, albeit at a gentle pace, in the Portuguese imagination.

# 3

# The Matrioshka Principle
# and Its Discontents

## Connecting Imperial Ideas Across the Continents

How could an imperial dialogue start to unfold after two rather unpromising decades of early contacts? Where—geographically, culturally, and socially speaking—could connections appear, gain traction, and become robust enough to have a larger historical impact? With the abandonment of the Colombo fort in 1524, mentioned at the end of the previous chapter, Goa declared its unwillingness to invest resources in Sri Lanka. At Kōṭṭe, Bhuvanekabāhu VII was free to look for viable allies in South India again. Both sides stood at a crossroads, not unusual in a world where early contacts—from Hispaniola to Virginia to China—were often marked by discontinuity. In 1524, the Portuguese presence in the island could have sunk into obscurity again, and an entirely informal colony like others that sprang up in the Bay of Bengal might have developed. However, things took a different turn. The decisive event for the survival of official Luso-Lankan relations occurred right after the demolition of the fort, as a tiny group of Portuguese men remained in the island and became active as soldiers—not serving the king of Portugal, but the king of Kōṭṭe.

## DISPERSAL AND A NEW BEGINNING: GO-BETWEENS AT KŌṬṬE AND COLOMBO, 1524–1527

Go-betweens have seen their historiographical fortunes revived, their role now being widely acknowledged as having been crucial for the making of early modern empires.[1] In 1524, the Portuguese retreat from Colombo was not a complete withdrawal, and it was the *Estado* itself that dropped the seed from which a group of go-betweens would grow. A *feitor* and a scribe were left in the island along with about fifteen soldiers to guard them.[2] John III (r.1521–57), the new monarch who

---

[1] On 'Portuguese' go-betweens see Dejanirah Couto, 'Quelques observations sur les renégats portugais en Asie au XVIeme siècle', *Mare Liberum*, 16 (1998), pp. 57–85; Maria Augusta Lima Cruz, 'Exiles and renegades in early sixteenth century Portuguese India', *Indian Economic and Social History Review*, 23, 3 (July–Sept. 1986), pp. 249–62; Alida Metcalf, *Go-betweens and the colonization of Brazil, 1500–1600* (Austin, TX: University of Texas Press, 2005).

[2] Fernão Lopes de Castanheda, *História do Descobrimento e Conquista da Índia pelos Portugueses*, edited by M. Lopes de Almeida (Porto: Lello & Irmão, 1979), vol. II, p. 299. According to Fernão de Queiroz, *Conquista Temporal e Espiritual de Ceilão* (Colombo: Government Press, 1916), p. 163, the number went down to eight soon after.

had agreed to cut expenses by closing the fort, hoped that a low-maintenance trading post (*feitoria*) might support the crown's commercial interests.[3] But precisely during the mid 1520s official fleets ceased entirely to patrol the area, thus leaving the Portuguese *feitor* and his men largely at the mercy of local forces. When threatened, they had to seek refuge in Kōṭṭe.[4]

Interestingly, the disconnection of these men from the *Estado*, and with it the prospect of new connections to Kōṭṭe, was precisely what encouraged Bhuvanekabāhu VII to offer tributary payments again. To be sure, the Portuguese were a miniscule group of little more than a dozen or two.[5] But many of these men were originally soldiers, and that is what made them most interesting to Bhuvanekabāhu VII. Left alone by the *Estado*, they became dependent in practice on the 'lord of the land', more than on the 'lord of the sea'. Kōṭṭe was one of many mercenary-hungry Asian capitals at the time.[6] Now, at last, an actual transfer of soldiers seemed to be taking shape. They may have been on the *Estado* payroll officially, but by offering tribute Bhuvanekabāhu could style himself as the one keeping up the arrangement. The situation came close, in practice, to what the late Vijayabāhu VI had originally intended. Portuguese men were available in the island, but without the impediments resulting from their attachment to a full garrison.

Why the Portuguese should have been so coveted across Asia as military specialists is not entirely clear. Their success in Asian armies may have been exaggerated by Portuguese sources in the first place, but military training on the battlefields of Morocco and subsequent experiences in far-flung corners of the globe may have given them an advantage. Firearms may have been part of the equation, though their effectiveness in wet climates was low and many specialists in this field were Flemings and Germans rather than Portuguese— not to mention the fact, of course, that others in Asia knew how to use them. Under certain circumstances, and especially in confrontation with Muslim enemies, the Portuguese seem to have organized themselves well, fought ferociously, and thus helped galvanize other troops.[7] This tactical capability may have been their main asset.

A key episode from 1525 illustrates this. When a Mappila merchant-warlord from Kerala appeared in Colombo with a large fleet to regain control of the port,

[3] John III to Henrique de Meneses, s.l., [1526], in Jorge Flores, *Os Portugueses e o Mar de Ceilão, 1498–1543. Trato, Diplomacia e Guerra* (Lisbon: Cosmos, 1998), p. 338.

[4] Cristóvão Lourenço Caracão to Manuel I, Cochin, 13 January 1522, in Bouchon, 'Les rois de Kotte', pp. 65–96 and 163–8.

[5] Even a decade and a half later, only about thirty Portuguese individuals were known to be operating in the kingdom of Kōṭṭe. On the incoherence of the group, Gaspar Correia, *Lendas da Índia*, edited by M. Lopes de Almeida (Porto: Lello & Irmão, 1975), vol. II, p. 519.

[6] See for example the many instances of Portuguese mercenaries in Fernão Mendes Pinto's *Peregrination*, written in the second half of the sixteenth century and printed in 1614. *The Travels of Mendes Pinto*, edited and translated by Rebecca Catz (London/Chicago, IL: University of Chicago Press, 1989).

[7] On maritime warfare see Vítor Rodrigues, 'A evolução da arte da Guerra dos Portugueses no Oriente (1498–1622)' (PhD dissertation, Insituto de Investigação Científica Tropical, Lisbon, 1998). For a more detailed exploration of the problem of the military revolution in Maritime Asia, see André Murteira, 'A navegação portuguesa na Ásia e na rota do Cabo e o corso neerlandês, 1595–1625' (PhD dissertation, Universidade Nova de Lisboa, 2016).

he demanded that all Portuguese individuals living in the kingdom be handed over to him.[8] The Mappilas were, after all, openly at war with the Portuguese. Bhuvanekabāhu VII, however, offered the little group of men refuge in Kōṭṭe.[9] The ensuing events made them into a cohesive, militarily viable body. They participated in an expeditionary force that defeated the Mappilas at Colombo.[10] The episode, soon talked about in the *Estado* as a miracle, contains a crucial detail that was properly acknowledged neither by chroniclers nor by later historians. The small group of Portuguese soldiers sent to Colombo was part of a much larger fighting force of 600 men led by a Lankan *ārachchi*, a high-ranking military leader.[11] The victory over the Mappilas is significant above all because it shows a first instance of Luso-Lankan military collaboration that was in accordance with older South Asian practices, where foreign mercenaries would assist local troops. Effectively, the Portuguese men fought for and under the authority of Bhuvanekabāhu VII, a heathen king in a heathen land.

In 1525, there was no other option available to these men than to intertwine their destinies with Lankan royal authority. On the day before the battle, the fighters entrusted Bhuvanekabāhu VII with their last wills and belongings, asking him to submit those to the next representative of the *Estado* arriving in Colombo if they died.[12] The Lankan ruler thus effectively performed a role that would normally have been played by a Portuguese *provedor dos defuntos*, an administrator of goods for subjects deceased far from their relatives. None of the men died, but the bonds established proved durable. The following year, when an armada brought orders for the *feitor* to be replaced, the latter protested by presenting two documents, not one: on the one hand, he produced an official document of support issued by the Portuguese governor. On the other, he gave evidence that 'the king of *Çeilam* wanted him to stay'. This overlap of hierarchies at the intersection of two spheres of authority set the tone for years to come. The official Portuguese response, to be sure, was unambiguous on this occasion. Both *feitor* candidates were removed from Bhuvanekabāhu's sphere of authority and reincorporated physically into the *Estado*, at Cochin.[13]

The prospect of cooperation that emerged, however problematically, in the eyes of the Kōṭṭe elite is crucial for an understanding of the subsequent decades. The arrangement of 1525 came close in practice to what the kings of Kōṭṭe had expected from the very beginning, and was to be invoked as an ideal time and again. The king of Portugal would make troops available in exchange for tribute. These men would act directly under the orders of the Sinhalese ruler. In fact, Bhuvanekabāhu VII, encouraged by his rival brothers' relative fragility, felt in a position to propose a new, overarching agreement with the Lusitanian crown. He now spoke of 'the friendship of Your Highness', rather than resorting to the word 'vassalage'. Sometime in 1526, he declared that Portuguese crown officials should leave the island precisely

---

[8] On this man, 'Balia Hacem', see Flores, *Os Portugueses*, p. 161.
[9] Castanheda, *História*, vol. II, p. 300.
[10] Correia, *Lendas*, vol. II, pp. 521–2 and 547–8. Queiroz, *Conquista*, p. 163.
[11] Queiroz, *Conquista*, pp. 163–4. Castanheda, *História*, vol. II, p. 300.
[12] Correia, *Lendas*, vol. II, p. 521.
[13] Afonso Mexia to John III, Cochin, 20 January 1526, in Flores, *Os Portugueses*, pp. 344–5.

on grounds of this friendship.[14] The plan was that some of the men—namely the soldiers—would stay, be formally detached from the *Estado* and, crucially, re-attached as subjects to the ruler of Kōṭṭe. This amounts to a strikingly straightforward act of localization as identified by scholars in other contexts.[15] Kōṭṭe was attempting not only to attract foreigners to its shores, but also digest them and transform them into a local asset.

The idea was presented to the Portuguese crown by a man familiar enough with the structures of the *Estado*, but also sufficiently distant from them, to serve as an intermediary: a certain Nuno Álvares Pereira, a petty noble who had served in the Colombo fort and subsequently entered the entourage of Bhuvanekabāhu VII.[16] Pereira affirmed that 'because he [Bhuvanekabāhu] himself maintains that the friendship of Your Highness does not oblige him to keep a *feitor* nor anyone else [representing the Portuguese crown]' in the island, any such officials could simply be done away with. And the *feitor* would not be the only one to go:

> [T]he king of *Çeilam* states that it is not necessary to have a *recebedor* ['receiver'] of yours to collect the cinnamon and [other] things that [he] gives to you, because in order for this [activity of] collecting [to work] there is no need for more than a black man of yours simply living here to remind him when to get the cinnamon ready.[17]

The 'black man of yours' ('*hum negro voso*') is an interesting formula not only because preference seems to be given to someone born in Asia. It is above all crucial because, whilst the word 'yours' suggests a service to John III, the ensuing formula '*somente estar aly hum homem*' strips this figure of exogenous authority. It emphasizes how this individual's main function would be to 'be there' and remind Bhuvanekabāhu of his obligations without projecting exogenous authority into the island. Men with no strings attached—this was the kind of Portuguese presence Bhuvanekabāhu expected. The plan was not devised to purge the kingdom of foreigners. The point was to get rid of foreigners not subjected to the Lankan king. Once a clean slate was created, a new elite corps of men drawn and withdrawn from the *Estado* could gradually be built up, which would then take orders in Kōṭṭe:

> Your Highness should order the governor to send them to [Bhuvanekabāhu], and [the king] should have them under his own orders, because they will be safer if handed over to him, rather than [being there] on account of the governor.[18]

---

[14] Nuno Álvares Pereira to John III, Goa, 15 November 1527, in Albuquerque and Costa, 'Cartas de "serviços"', p. 315. According to this letter, Bhuvanekabāhu had made a similar request between 1524 and 1526.

[15] O. W. Wolters, *History, Culture, and Region in Southeast Asian Perspectives*, revised edition (Ithaca, NY: Cornell University Press, 1999). A number of mostly literary examples of localization are given on pp. 58–67.

[16] See Georg Schurhammer's proposed identification of Nuno Álvares Pereira in *Ceylon zur Zeit des Königs Bhuvaneka Bahu und Franz Xavers 1539–1552* (Leipzig: Verlag der Asia Major, 1928), p. 148.

[17] Pereira to John III, Goa, 15 November 1527, in Albuquerque and Costa, 'Cartas de "serviços"', p. 315.

[18] Pereira to John III, Goa, 15 November 1527, in Albuquerque and Costa, 'Cartas de "serviços"', p. 315.

This brief passage offers an early snapshot of what Bhuvanekabāhu VII wished his tributary relationship with the Portuguese king to be. John's overlordship would find an expression in the island of Lanka *through* the person of Bhuvanekabāhu. As for the salaries, an almost identical proposal from 1541 (where the annual number of troops rose to fifty) suggests that they would have been paid by the Lankan ruler. This was, in fact, the way military specialists from South India had been integrated into the fabric of Lankan society in earlier centuries.

## ELITE TROOPS FROM FOREIGN LANDS: THE LANKAN LOGICS OF INCORPORATION

It is worth at this point emphasizing, once more, how firmly rooted such proposals were in the Lankan political tradition, and how much of the ongoing effort to attract Portuguese troops was down to Lankan agency. Kōṭṭe had a long tradition of integrating foreign military specialists.[19] Historically, military migrants were often given land grants, or positions in close proximity to the ruler, or both.[20] Generally, such troops came from South India—the classical Lankan chronicles already mention *damilas*, *keralas*, and *kannatas*[21]—and their integration into Lankan society tended to occur at a relatively high level.[22] In the eleventh century, under Cōḷa rule, the royal court had begun to import elite troops from India known specifically as *vēlaikkāra*. These were destined for the personal protection of the ruler from internal enemies. The habit of keeping a personal guard consisting of foreigners was then adopted by Sinhalese rulers, namely Vijayabāhu I (r.1070–1110), the 'liberator' of the island, and Parākramabāhu I (r.1153–86).[23] During the period studied in this book, Māyādunnē, *rāja* of Sītāvaka and a rival of Kōṭṭe between 1521 and 1578, made, according to the *Rajvaliya*, 'many *Vaddakaru*' come from Kollakā/Kollam, in Kerala.[24]

Military specialists were also imported as *agampadi* or *akampadiyar*, a term sometimes establishing a subtle distinction from *vēlaikkāra*.[25] This was in response to wider (demographic, social) deficiencies in the recruitment of Lankan men for warfare.[26] In late medieval Sri Lanka, the word *agampada* designated a set of mercenaries, usually of foreign origin, supplementing the less well-trained rural troops

[19] Geiger, *Culture of Ceylon*, p. 151.
[20] Lorna Dewaraja, *The Kandyan Kingdom of Sri Lanka 1707–1782*, second revised edition (Colombo: Lake House, 1988), pp. 53–9.
[21] Geiger, *Culture of Ceylon*, p. 151.    [22] Dewaraja, *The Kandyan Kingdom*, pp. 53–66.
[23] Siriweera, *History of Sri Lanka*, pp. 48, 52, 56–7, 87.    [24] *The Rājāvaliya*, p. 78.
[25] On the etymology see H. W. Codrington, 'Medieval Mercenary Forces in Ceylon', *Ceylon Literary Register*, Third Series, III, 9 (1934), pp. 387–90. On the *agampadi* as a caste in the north of the island, p. 388. On the intricacies of using the concept of caste, see Jackie Assayag, 'La caste entre histoire et anthropologie. Le "grand jeu" interprétatif', *Annales HSS*, 58, 4 (2003), pp. 815–30, with abundant bibliography.
[26] Siriweera, *History of Sri Lanka*, p. 88.

recruited 'in the country' (*ratthavāsika senā*), the *lekamas* or *hevavasam*.[27] According to an early Portuguese observer, 'the people [of *Ceilão*] are very weak', and among the fighting men employed by the kings of Kōṭṭe and Sītāvaka 'the best are these [men] from Kollam who serve them for a salary'.[28] Later on, Portuguese texts generally designated these foreign-born troops as *atapata*, and whilst the etymological relation with *agampada* is not quite clear (there may have been a phonetic convergence with a military title, *attapattu*) some sources clearly identify them as elite soldiers employed beyond the limits of palatial compounds.

Sixteenth-century examples abound. In 1582, Māyādunnē's successor Rājasiṃha I was said to have 2,000 'men of *atapata*', incidentally under the command of a Portuguese renegade.[29] The *Rājāvaliya* affirms that in 1593 the 'great guard' (*maha atapatta*) of Sītāvaka, commanded by an *atapattu arachchi*, had twelve companies on payroll.[30] In the kingdom of Kandy this tradition lived on until at least the middle of the eighteenth century.[31] In Kōṭṭe, too, Bhuvanekabāhu VII kept recruiting both Indian mercenaries and other military specialists whom he attempted to bind to his person by having them settle and marry into select Lankan families.[32] The 'services' performed by these groups were diverse. *Agampadis* served as elite troops in war (*netti agampadi*), and at times in the royal guards (*rāja agampadi*), but they could also be employed in the collection of agrarian taxes (*muhukala agampadi*).[33]

To obtain such people from India, it was necessary to maintain diplomatic relations. To integrate them efficiently, it was important to find a balance between segregation and assimilation. The extent to which identities in sixteenth-century Sri Lanka were more complex than nationalist historians assume has been revealed most impressively in the work of Alan Strathern, who has gone to great lengths to identify the characteristics of Sri Lankan 'indigenism' during this period. If indigenist feelings existed at all, then they were based only partly on the notion of Sinhalaness. The geographical notion of 'Lankaness' played a significant role; the Lankan indigenism combined a certain cosmopolitan vein with a 'selective' and 'spasmodic' type of xenophobia; it may be associated with Buddhist revivals, but not necessarily dissociated from other religious traditions; it had no strong unitary state to fall back upon; it remained open to the selective import of foreign elements into Lankan society; and whilst it stipulated a strong bond between the people and their rulers, neither the former not the latter had to be Sinhalese.[34]

---

[27] On the perceived lack of military skill, see 'Itinerario di Lodovico Barthema', in Giovanni Battista Ramusio, *Navigazioni e Viaggi*, ed. by Marica Milanesi (Turin: Giulio Einaudi, 1978), vol. I, p. 846 and *O Livro de Duarte Barbosa, edição crítica e anotada*, edited by Maria Augusta da Veiga e Sousa, vol. II (Lisbon: IICT, 2000), p. 280. Cf. Siriweera, *History of Sri Lanka*, p. 89 and Geiger, *Culture of Ceylon*, p. 153.

[28] Caracão to Manuel I, Cochin, 13 January 1522, in Bouchon, 'Les rois de Kotte', p. 167.

[29] Queiroz, *Conquista*, pp. 356 and 349.        [30] *The Rājāvaliya*, p. 96.

[31] Codrington, 'Medieval Mercenary Forces', p. 385.

[32] According to two seventeenth-century Sinhala documents, the *Kandure Bandaravaliya* and the *Kiravelle Rajamula*, both at the British Library, cited in Strathern, *Kingship and Conversion*, pp. 29 and 32.

[33] Codrington, 'Medieval Mercenary Forces', pp. 389–90.

[34] Strathern, *Kingship and Conversion*, pp. 236–47. Cf. for example S. Paranavitana, 'Aryan Settlement: the Sinhalese', in *University of Ceylon History of Ceylon*, edited by H. C. Ray, vol. I, part 1 (Colombo: Ceylon University Press, 1959), pp. 82–97, a critique of which can also be found in

There was, to be sure, some sense of indigenousness as a backdrop against which foreignness could be pitched—in fact, Strathern and the Sri Lankan historian Michael Roberts have both advocated for a nuanced reading of indigeneity, which goes against the grain of simplistic nationalist narratives but still traces the roots of a proto-national Lankan identity into a distant past. The Sinhalese word '*raṭa*' (country) seems to have played an important role. The expression *Pita raṭe aye*, a 'person from a foreign country', could generate in its plural form (*raṭṭu*) a meaning translatable as 'foreigners' or 'strangers'. The word *raṭa* also generated the expression *raṭavesiya*, meaning 'our country', and even something like 'subjects'.[35] The complex semantic fields of words such as *para* ('other', 'enemy', 'person from abroad') and *rupu* ('enemy', 'stranger') point in a similar direction, where the main distinction between 'us' and 'them' is one based in the belonging to a land or an area associated with a particular ruler, more than to a particular ethnic group. In fact, nowhere in the *Rājāvaliya*, for example, would a Lankan ruler be accused of bringing foreigners into the island. What was criticized was the excessive proximity and subservience of the Kōṭṭe rulers to the Portuguese, which naturally implies also the reverse problem: the lack of interest shown by the Portuguese in following the Sinhalese monarch's orders.[36] Whilst all this did not exclude the existence of xenophobic sentiment, or at least a wariness regarding people coming from the outside, the guiding principles allowing for the integration of foreigners into Lankan society were firmly in place, capable of driving diplomatic interactions and giving Lankan rulers a strong sense of what they wished to achieve.[37]

## A STRANGE CONVERGENCE: KŌṬṬE AND A PLAN TO DEMILITARIZE THE ESTADO

An intriguing interjection is due at this point, because the plan formulated by Bhuvanekabāhu VII and presented by Nuno Álvares Pereira came very close to a plan cooked up during those same years under the aegis of the Duke of Bragança, the most powerful advocate of a non-interventionist strategy in the Portuguese empire. It had been in part due to him that the fort of Colombo was dismantled in 1524, and in 1529 he was still insisting that all fortresses in India except Goa and Cochin be abandoned. The radical proposal was part of a larger offensive against the positions of the crown. Malacca and Hormuz were to be sold to Asian rulers and even in Morocco, where it all had begun, only two fortresses were to be kept at Safi and Azemmour.[38] In another proposal, from 1528, the Duke argued

---

R. A. L. H. Gunawardana, 'The People of the Lion. The Sinhala Identity and Ideology in History and Historiography', *Sri Lanka Journal of the Humanities*, V, 1–2 (1979), pp. 1–36.

[35] Roberts, *Sinhala Consciousness*, pp. 31–2.     [36] *The Rājāvaliya*, pp. 78–9.

[37] Cf. Roberts, *Sinhala Consciousness*, p. 34 contending that this logic was later transformed under the weight of conflicts with the Portuguese: 'the impact of exogenous forces had the capacity to render specific *para saturan* into a more awesome "outsider" than the *pitagankarayo* next door'.

[38] Bragança to John III, Vila Viçosa, 12 February 1529, *As Gavetas da Torre do Tombo* (Lisbon: CEHU, 1960–77), vol. IX, p. 539. Cf. Luís Filipe Thomaz, 'O "testamento político" de Diogo Pereira, o Malabar, e o projecto oriental dos Gamas', *Anais de História de Além-Mar*, 5 (2004), p. 131.

against the official presence in the Moluccas and against an establishment in the Sunda Strait.[39] This was a global vision of commercial expansion only to be vaguely supported, but not regulated, by the crown.

Bhuvanekabāhu's proposal was thus in tune, superficially at least, with the radical commercialism of a sector of Portuguese society involving the Braganças, the Gamas, and the traders of Cochin. This is interesting because Nuno Álvares Pereira—whose full name invokes that of the founder of the House of Bragança— may have had an affiliation with the network. Whilst Bhuvanekabāhu is likely to have hoped that even after decommissioning its officials in the island the Portuguese crown would still patrol the sea, Pereira watered down the latter element. The armada to be used was the already overstretched Coromandel fleet, and it would only spend a limited amount of time near Colombo, during the southwestern monsoon.[40] For much of the season when winds were favourable to trade, from mid-October to January, the doors would stand wide open for private enterprise.

It would not be surprising if Pereira turned out to be a Bragança agent. We would here be speaking of a causal link—obscure but significant—rather than just a convergence. But whatever his original personal status was, what seems most significant is how Pereira already served in two functions at the same time: he may have been a covert representative of the Portuguese commercialist lobby in Kōṭṭe, but he also became a key figure in Bhuvanekabāhu's efforts to reach a new deal with the Portuguese crown. Indeed, he was a little of both and effectively acted as a go-between serving more than one lord at the same time. None of this would have been possible while the Portuguese were confined to the fort at Colombo. Everything seemed possible now.

## CONNECTING CONFLICTS: THE REGIONALIZATION OF THE SRI LANKAN WARS, 1528–1537

Unfortunately for Bhuvanekabāhu VII, what had appeared tangible around 1525 proved difficult to achieve soon after. Towards 1528, the balance of powers in the southwestern lowlands began to tilt in favour of his younger brother Māyādunnē, the *rāja* of Sītāvaka.[41] Sītāvaka, a city situated less than 50 kilometres inland from Colombo on the Kelani River, had entered the post-Vijayabāhu era with a significantly smaller pool of villages than Kōṭṭe. But under Māyādunnē it challenged the status quo. The fragility of Kōṭṭe may have seemed conjunctural at first, but it soon became structural. For six full decades, until the implosion of the Sītāvaka polity

---

[39] Bragança to John III, Vila Viçosa, 3 September 1528, in Luís Filipe Thomaz, 'O malogrado estabelecimento oficial dos portugueses em Sunda e a islamização de Java', in *Aquém e Além da Taprobana. Estudos luso-orientais à memória de Jean Aubin e Denys Lombard*, edited by Luís Filipe Thomaz (Lisbon: CHAM, 2002), pp. 553–5.

[40] Pereira to John III, in Albuquerque and Costa, 'Cartas de "serviços"', p. 315.

[41] See Chandra Richard De Silva, 'The Rise and Fall of the Kingdom of Sitawaka (1521–1593)', *The Ceylon Journal of Historical and Social Studies*, 7, 1 (1977), pp. 1–43.

in the early 1590s, the rulers of Kōṭṭe saw themselves challenged by the restless efforts of a neighbouring kingdom attempting to occupy the old imperial centre.

Crucially, this development was not only local. The conflict took on regional proportions as the two chief rulers of the Lankan southwest began to compete diplomatically for foreign military resources. Whilst Bhuvanekabāhu VII concentrated on the Portuguese, Māyādunnē placed his hopes on the Muslim ports of Kerala, including Calicut—though as we shall see, he had no fundamental objection to courting the Portuguese either. The Mappila option was a logical one for Sītāvaka, a city that had offered refuge to Muslims when they were expelled from Colombo in the turmoil of 1525.[42] Very soon after that event, Māyādunnē sent an embassy to the *Samudri Rāja* of Calicut, offering him not only to trade in 'some ports in the island', but also 'to become his tributary'.[43] Empire, hegemony, and tributary overlordship were not areas where the Portuguese could act unchallenged as 'lords of the sea'. An intense competition developed, soon dragging the Portuguese into unexpected theatres of war.

Māyādunnē offered Calicut gifts and money in exchange for a fleet.[44] He was actively building a network of alliances in South India following the fundamental logics of tributary diplomacy, and happy to explore the Portuguese among other options. His move inaugurated a period that soon saw an increasing involvement of both rival maritime powers—the Portuguese and the Mappilas—on the Lankan land. It would have been difficult indeed, militarily, to keep the two elements apart, be it only for the simple reason that no centre of political power was located directly on the Lankan seashore, but all were sufficiently close to the ocean to be affected by naval operations. As soon as the Calicut-sponsored, Muslim-led fleet arrived in Lankan waters around the end of 1527, Māyādunnē laid siege on Kōṭṭe. Bhuvanekabāhu VII and his Portuguese mercenaries had to wait for external support. Soon the matter was discussed in Goa, and eventually in Portugal, and it was agreed that help should be sent to Bhuvanekabāhu VII whenever possible because 'he is a vassal of the king of Portugal'.[45] For the first time, an explicit verbal connection appears between Bhuvanekabāhu's vassalage and an obligation of the Portuguese crown to intervene.

Apart from the return of 'vassalage' into the language of inter-imperial communication, things still seemed to move in an overall acceptable direction for Bhuvanekabāhu VII. The mere rumour of the imminent arrival of a fleet of eight vessels in the early months of 1528 sufficed to discourage the Calicut fleet and prompted Māyādunnē to lift his siege.[46] But the damage to Bhuvanekabāhu's reputation was done. Just a year after he had formulated his bold proposals, Bhuvanekabāhu had suffered the first in

---

[42] Queiroz, *Conquista*, p. 164. Cf. De Silva, 'Portuguese policy towards the Muslims'.

[43] *Conquista*, p. 165.

[44] Diogo do Couto, *Da Asia* (Lisbon: Livraria de São Carlos, 1973–1975), vol. V, book i, chapter 6, p. 61.

[45] João de Barros, *Ásia*, edited by António Baião and Luís F. Lindley Sintra, reprint (Lisbon: IN-CM, 1988–2001), vol. IV, book ii, chapter 7, p. 87.

[46] Queiroz, *Conquista*, p. 166; Barros, *Ásia*, vol. IV, book ii, chapter 7, pp. 87–8. On the armada and its context, see Luís Filipe Thomaz, 'O malogrado estabelecimento', pp. 463–6.

a series of humiliating attacks by a younger brother who in the 1521 partition had clearly been a junior partner. By December 1528, it was rumoured in Cochin that 'this year already [Bhuvanekabāhu] submitted himself with all his treasure [...] to the *feitor* during an attack launched against him by his brothers, and is [now] so inclined towards us that he is expected [...] to become a Christian'. Whilst the promise of conversion—an aspect to which we shall return—may at this point not have been more than a piece of gossip generated in India, the most important aspect was that Bhuvanekabāhu recognized his military dependence on the *Estado*. Far from demanding the removal of the *feitor* and his men, Bhuvanekabāhu VII now went back to 'requesting that a tower be built [by the Portuguese] where the fort once stood'. He was a more assiduous vassal than ever, delivering 800 quintals of 'very good cinnamon'.[47] But the conjuncture pointed in a direction that was quite different from what Bhuvanekabāhu had imagined only two or three years before.

Ironically, in a blatant repetition of Afonso de Albuquerque's refusal to build a fort in 1513, the Portuguese authorities, worried about the resources available to the *Estado*, declined. Whilst the documentation is scarce for these years, it has been shown that the backdrop for the Luso-Lankan interactions between 1525 and 1539 was increasingly an open war against the Mappilas.[48] This was primarily a maritime conflict, although it did involve numerous actions on the land. The larger dynamics of the war were now beyond Bhuvanekabāhu's control, and by October 1533 the king was sufficiently intimidated to sign a new agreement with the *feitor* António Pessoa, who was by then also serving as *alcaide-mor*, a title possibly indicating some military powers although the men at his disposal were not formally recognized as a military corps by the *Estado*. This new treaty allowed the Portuguese to purchase cinnamon at even more advantageous conditions than before, without a need for other investments.[49]

The rise of Sītāvaka was in many ways typical of the Lankan political system. As Māyādunnĕ's influence grew, Bhuvanekabāhu lost the ability to control villages and revenues in the lowlands. But Māyādunnĕ wanted more. He ultimately coveted the throne of Kōṭṭe, the key to 'the Monarchy of that entire island'.[50] This could be achieved, on the one hand, through military action—an abundance of which occurred in the late 1530s. On the other hand, Māyādunnĕ resorted to dynastic strategy. He was, after all, a brother and legitimate heir to Bhuvanekabāhu. When he worked towards a marriage with Bhuvanekabāhu's daughter Samudrā Dēvi, the courtly faction supporting Bhuvanekabāhu at Kōṭṭe began to support an alternative line of succession to the throne. As the divide deepened, the anti-Māyādunnĕ faction pressed Bhuvanekabāhu into offering Samudrā Dēvi's hand to

---

[47] Afonso Mexia to John III, Cochin, 30 December 1528, in Flores, *Os Portugueses*, pp. 347–9.
[48] Flores, *Os Portugueses*, pp. 160–83.
[49] Chandra Richard De Silva, 'Colonialism and Trade: The Cinnamon Contract of 1533 between Bhuvanekabāhu, King of Kotte and António Pereira, Portuguese Factor in Sri Lanka', *University of Colombo Review*, 10 (1991), pp. 27–34. The Portuguese text of the treaty is in Flores, *Os Portugueses*, pp. 350–1.
[50] Couto, *Da Asia*, vol. V, book ii, chapter 4, p. 163.

a military leader known as Vīdiyē Baṇḍāra, a grandson of Sakalakalāvallaba, the once powerful rival brother of Vijayabāhu VI.[51]

An attack launched by Māyādunnē in 1536 may well have had to do with this decision. In 1538, further clouds appeared above Māyādunnē's head as Samudrā Dēvi gave birth, in Kōṭṭe, to a royal prince, Dharmapāla.[52] It must have been clear to anyone in the old capital that as the possibility of a settlement with Māyādunnē waned, the necessity of securing Portuguese assistance became more vital than ever: the only alternative to dynastic string-pulling was war. Crucially, this otherwise relatively minor conjuncture of southwest Lankan factional strife now became linked up with the ongoing larger conflict around Ceylon. Once it was clear that Kōṭṭe sought Portuguese assistance and Sītāvaka found allies in the Mappila network and in Calicut, the internal war became intertwined with the fight for supremacy in the South Indian sea—a conflict that then, over the years, came to involve an even vaster constellation opposing the Portuguese and their Asian and African allies to Muslim powers all over Maritime Asia.[53]

The increasing intertwinement of local and regional conflicts becomes apparent in three major attacks launched by Māyādunnē with Mappila assistance against Kōṭṭe at the end of 1536, the end of 1537, and the end of 1538. Whilst potentially tedious, the details of this conjuncture are worth spelling out as they throw light on the shifting characteristics of the new warfare. The first siege was laid in October 1536 and prompted the dispatch from Cochin of an armada commanded by Martim Afonso de Sousa, a member of one of Portugal's most powerful families and a key military leader of the *Estado*, in early February 1537. As had happened earlier, Māyādunnē quickly reached a deal with Bhuvanekabahau and abandoned the siege. Sousa still disembarked and marched triumphantly to Kōṭṭe where, having obtained generous monetary compensation, he offered future assistance.[54]

A similar series of events unfolded again in February–March 1538. Martim Afonso de Sousa may have had orders of 'waging crude war' against Māyādunnē, but again, the Portuguese had little interest in getting much involved.[55] True, Sousa proceeded to Ceylon after defeating a large Mappila force at Vēdālai, off the Indian littoral, and seemed determined to fight the Sītāvaka army.[56] But he was not surprised when Māyādunnē's forces dispersed as they had before. Again, the Portuguese marched to Kōṭṭe, where Sousa received ample rewards, including a hefty 'loan' of 20,000 *cruzados* 'to help pay the salary of his troops'. All this was

---

[51] De Silva, 'The rise and fall of the Kingdom of Sitawaka', p. 9. Sakalakalāvallaba had been a rival brother of king Vijayabāhu VI and expressed worries about the latter's alliance with the Portuguese in 1518.

[52] On the complicated princely titles in the Lankan tradition (*rajaputtā, ādipāda, mahādipāda, uparaja, yuvaraja*) see Geiger, *Culture of Ceylon*, pp. 119–23. Princesses usually appear as *rajini*, though the higher honor of *devi* was given to queens and at times to the daughters of rulers.

[53] Cf. Flores, *Os Portugueses*, p. 181.

[54] Couto, *Da Asia*, vol. V, book i, chapter 6, p. 61. Queiroz, *Conquista*, pp. 167–8. Barros, *Ásia*, vol. IV, book vii, chapter 22, pp. 485–6.

[55] Queiroz, *Conquista*, p. 172.

[56] Couto, *Da Asia*, vol. V, book ii, chapter 4, pp. 163–75. Barros, *Ásia*, vol. IV, book viii, chapter 13, p. 541.

offered by Bhuvanekabāhu VII 'with many words of great obligation', thus combining monetary support with symbolic submission.[57] In a time of great financial distress for the *Estado*, the ease with which the Sinhalese monarch kept offering money in exchange for military assistance, prompting high-ranking Portuguese leaders to come and go between India and the island, is remarkable. In fact, it amounted again to a practice that was very much in line with earlier arrangements. And similar deals were being done between Māyādunnē and the Mappilas.

Māyādunnē's sieges were, along with the Portuguese maritime expeditions launched in reaction to them as relief campaigns (*socorros*), in the process of becoming routine operations. Bhuvanekabāhu does not seem to have been entirely unhappy with this state of affairs, in which he still had the resources to play a relatively active role, as long as he could remain in control of the imperial centre of Kōṭṭe, the best cinnamon-producing areas nearby, and the port of Colombo. But it also became clear during these years of radicalization (the Mappila-Portuguese maritime conflict was reaching its peak and the relations between Bhuvanekabāhu and Māyādunnē were at their lowest) that new solutions had to be found. In Kōṭṭe, the need for a properly formalized submission to the Portuguese crown and a clearer definition of the terms of the vassalage became increasingly evident.

## A FAILED CONNECTION: (MIS)UNDERSTANDINGS IN THE MILITARY SEASON OF 1538

Had Sītāvaka not exerted such pressure, and had this not been done in part with the assistance of the Mappilas, then the need for Kōṭṭe to get more involved with the Portuguese would probably not have been the same. The Portuguese now sensed that a defeat of Kōṭṭe at the hands of Māyādunnē could shift the cinnamon trade to the Mappilas. As the decade drew to its end, this preoccupation ceased to be limited to the two or three dozen Portuguese individuals residing in the island. It began to be felt and discussed in Goa, Cochin, and even in the informal colonies on the Coromandel Coast.[58] Year after year of relief campaigns to Colombo and Kōṭṭe, together with the fear of losing access to the ports of the island, drove these otherwise deficiently interconnected, often disengaged, Lusophone communities into taking a more active and strategic interest in Lankan affairs.

As we begin to see the formation of an intricate regional web involving political, military, and communicational connections, it is important not to lose sight of how unstable the environment was and how easily misunderstandings could occur. A dramatic episode from 1538–9 illustrates this well. The triggering event occurred when, shortly after Martim Afonso de Sousa left Colombo, yet again with substantial rewards in his pocket, Pararājasiṃha, a little king who had ruled the Rayigama area since the regicide of 1521, died. Before Bhuvanekabāhu could regain control

---

[57] Barros, *Ásia*, vol. IV, book viii, chapter 13, p. 541. Cf. Couto, *Da Asia*, vol. V, book ii, chapter 5, pp. 179–80.
[58] Flores, *Os Portugueses*, pp. 172–4.

over this area south of Kōṭṭe, Māyādunnē moved in, secured the submission of several hundred villages, took possession of the royal treasure and other paraphernalia at Rayigama, and thus became structurally 'more powerful' (albeit still commanding less authority) than the king of Kōṭṭe. Simultaneously, Māyādunnē secured sufficient support within the Kōṭṭe court to impede Bhuvanekabāhu from attacking. He then dispatched ambassadors to Calicut to organize a final siege against the Lankan capital.[59] Everything was on track for a showdown that would require substantially more from the *Estado* than just a relief armada. Around the middle of 1538 the outgoing governor Nuno da Cunha (gv.1529–38), who had never shown much interest in the island, issued a request to the Portuguese community on the Coromandel Coast for assistance in Ceylon.[60] In Mylapore (São Tomé de Meliapor), Miguel Ferreira, an oligarch operating on the fringes of the *Estado* and involved in Lankan trade, agreed to assemble a force of 400 men to combat the Mappilas in the island.[61] However, when Ferreira arrived near Chilaw on the west coast of Lanka he received orders from the new viceroy, Garcia de Noronha (vr.1538–40), who had assumed functions in mid-September, prompting him to sail north to Diu. News of the second Turkish-led siege of this port in Gujarat, the greatest military challenge to the *Estado* in a decade, had reached Goa on 3 October.

Though the siege at Diu was lifted in early November, Ferreira was still in north Indian waters when a renewed call for assistance came from Bhuvanekabāhu VII. When Ferreira arrived at Colombo, two messages reached him on board his ship. On the one hand, Bhuvanekabāhu 'had nothing left but Kōṭṭe'. On the other hand, the Mappila leaders and 'many other principal Moors from Calicut' were in the nearby port of Negombo, or possibly Puttalam.[62] As Ferreira attacked, the Mappilas dispersed inland.[63] Crucially though, this was followed by a terrestrial regrouping that the Portuguese did not expect. The Mappila forces joined those of Māyādunnē further inland. Predictably, Ferreira first avoided pursuing them. But as he sailed on to Colombo in the hope of hearing that the siege might have been lifted as in previous years, he received a final urgent request from Bhuvanekabāhu to march to Kōṭṭe.[64] The Sinhalese monarch was in acute danger not only externally, but also internally. He now kept himself surrounded by a personal guard of about forty Portuguese men, and he 'did not allow them to leave the fort to fight because he was afraid that his own people would betray him'.[65] Finally, as Ferreira

---

[59] Couto, *Da Asia*, vol. V, book ii, chapter 10, p. 207.

[60] Miguel Ferreira to John III, Goa, 26 November 1539, in Georg Schurhammer and Ernst August Voretzsch, *Ceylon zur Zeit des Königs Bhuvaneka Bahu und Franz Xavers 1539–1552* (Leipzig: Verlag der Asia Major, 1928), pp. 81–93 (henceforth cited as '*Ceylon*'). Cf. De Silva, 'The rise and fall of the Kingdom of Sitawaka', pp. 9–11.

[61] On Ferreira see Jorge Flores, '"Um homem que tem muito crédito naquelas partes": Miguel Ferreira, os "alevantados" do Coromandel e o Estado da Índia', *Mare Liberum*, 5 (1993), pp. 21–37.

[62] Ferreira to John III, *Ceylon*, pp. 82–4. Couto, *Da Asia*, vol. V, book v, chapter 8, p. 472. Correia, *Lendas*, vol. IV, p. 80.

[63] Ferreira to John III, pp. 84–5. Cf. Correia, *Lendas*, vol. IV, p. 80 and Couto, *Da Asia*, vol. V, book v, chapter 8, p. 472.

[64] Ferreira to John III, *Ceylon*, p. 85.     [65] Correia, *Lendas*, vol. IV, p. 80.

disembarked, the siege was lifted. The Portuguese marched to Kōṭṭe once more to collect their rewards.

In a way, Bhuvanekabāhu had again obtained what his alliance made him feel entitled to. Things could have ended here as they usually did, but they did not. Some days after his arrival, Miguel Ferreira suddenly left Kōṭṭe with about 300 musketeers, not for Colombo, but for Sītāvaka. This Portuguese force was accompanied by a much larger Lankan force commanded by Bhuvanekabāhu VII in person, a very unusual occurrence. For the first time, a joint Luso-Lankan army marched up the Kelani valley towards the foothills of the mountainous interior. There were considerable logistic and military challenges as Māyādunnē had built various temporary fortifications along the way. Thus Ferreira was forced to fight several skirmishes along the way, three of them on open battlefields. After the fourth clash, something entirely unexpected happened again. Bhuvanekabāhu took the lead and pushed ahead to Sītāvaka, arriving before Ferreira. A final battle took place near Māyādunnē's capital, involving thousands of troops, numerous war elephants, and many deaths.[66] Bhuvanekabāhu and Ferreira won and entered Sītāvaka, but the campaign was still not over. From here, the two leaders pursued the fleeing Māyādunnē further inland. After a long and rather confusing series of events, Ferreira made an ultimatum that was entirely out of tune with the habitual practices of Lankan warfare. He asked Māyādunnē to send him the heads of his allies, the Mappila leaders. The details of the episode are telling. When Māyādunnē rather understandably hesitated, Ferreira sent word that 'if any of them happened to escape [...] we have no agreement whatsoever'. Māyādunnē, in contrast, replied that it would be a 'great shame' for him to do so, and attempted to negotiate a safe passage for the Mappilas.[67] Ferreira remained uncompromising, adding that he would rather 'enter his palace and burn it down with his women and children inside' than tolerate a further refusal. Only when Ferreira received the heads did he retreat to Kōṭṭe.[68]

Ferreira's intransigence points to the first major misunderstanding between Portuguese and Lankan leaders about how to conduct war and practise imperial expansion. Bhuvanekabāhu's interest was to re-establish the political order in the island's southwest. His hope upon Ferreira's arrival was that, as in previous years, everything would go back to normality within a few days. Once Māyādunnē retreated, Bhuvanekabāhu had no interest in further military activities. The talks he conducted with Ferreira touched upon internal matters such as the removal of the current *feitor*. Ferreira, in contrast, momentarily defied one of the fundamental mechanisms of Lankan politics, the periodical renegotiation of relations between kings. Bhuvanekabāhu did what he could to control him—hence his participation in the campaign—but the gap only widened. Ferreira himself later described how the two Sinhalese kings kept negotiating even after the Portuguese were not interested in talks any more. They attempted, for example, to arrange for the

---

[66] Correia, *Lendas*, vol. IV, p. 81. Ferreira to John III, *Ceylon*, p. 86.
[67] Ferreira to John III, *Ceylon*, pp. 87–8.
[68] Correia, *Lendas*, vol. IV, p. 82. Ferreira to John III, *Ceylon*, pp. 86–8. Cf. Couto, *Da Asia*, vol. V, book v, chapter 8, pp. 473–5.

handing over of some family members by the younger to the elder brother, a practice traditionally associated with tributary submission.[69]

In a sign of troubles to come, Ferreira overlooked—or chose to ignore—that it was not a part of Bhuvanekabāhu's mandate to annihilate Māyādunnē, but only to force him back into subordination. A chronicler would later write that Ferreira had wanted to put Bhuvabekabahu 'in possession of the entire kingdom' ('*de posse do inteyro Reyno*'). From the description of the events, one gathers that Ferreira effectively attempted to turn back the clock on post-1521 fragmentation.[70] Instead of restoring a temporarily broken relation of suzerainty, Ferreira overshot and attempted to impose the control of Kōṭṭe over a larger, unified realm. This could be a potentially dramatic moment for our narrative, as it anticipates by decades a similar misunderstanding that changed the course of history at the end of the century. This time around, however, the rupture was temporary, and the Portuguese had no clear idea about what to do next. It could well be that Ferreira's principal aim was not so much to get rid of Māyādunnē, but of the Mappila leaders. Once this was achieved, his duty was done.

For all this to happen at that moment precisely, the dragging on of the Mappila wars throughout the 1530s played perhaps the most significant role. After years of fierce fighting on the seas and along the shores of South India and Sri Lanka, some Portuguese leaders began to think of definitive 'solutions' to the conflict. Beheading the Muslim network appeared as a viable alternative to the ongoing war of attrition. In this sense, the expedition to Sītāvaka can be seen as a collateral extension on the land of a conflict that was being fought on the sea. Terrestrial realities could thus also begin, inversely, to creep into the geographical imagination of some Portuguese formerly fixated on the oceans. Ferreira is an interesting case in that, after many years of building up a maritime trade network on the fringes of the *Estado*, he may have started to think about 'going terrestrial'. In a letter addressed to John III in November 1539, he asked for an official monopoly on Luso-Lankan trade.[71] Some years later, in 1546, Ferreira obtained from the crown a land grant in Mannār and the adjacent mainland area of Mantota, following what may well have been an attempt to attain further respectability and economic stability as an owner of lands, and not just a trader on the sea.[72]

Whilst it might thus be tempting to interpret the events of 1538–9 as reflecting a wider, increasing appetite among Portuguese nobles for agrarian and other landborne revenues in the empire, the evidence in this regard is rather slim.[73] It would be premature to see the Ferreira campaign as a first instance of Portuguese *conquistadorism* in Ceylon. Despite its geographical depth, the campaign is comparable to other actions against the Mappilas at the time, for example at Vilinjam and Kayalpatnam in India.[74] It preludes the most famous planned pillaging expedition of those years, the failed '*jornada*' of Martim Afonso de Sousa to the Tirumala-Tirupati

---

[69] Ferreira to John III, *Ceylon*, pp. 85–8.    [70] Queiroz, *Conquista*, p. 178.
[71] Ferreira to John III, *Ceylon*, p. 92.
[72] João de Castro to Miguel Ferreira, Goa, 15 January 1546, *Ceylon*, p. 279.
[73] Cf. Sanjay Subrahmanyam, 'Holding the World in Balance: The Connected Histories of the Iberian Empires, 1500–1640', *American Historical Review*, 112, 5 (2007), p. 1370.
[74] On Vilinjam and Kayalpatnam, see Flores, *Os Portugueses*, p. 165.

temple complex in South India in 1543.[75] Such actions were short-term temporary conquests of sorts, which amounts to saying that they were conquests only in a very limited sense of the word. They were not designed to create a stable terrestrial extension of Portuguese power, but simply to inflict damage on enemies—and of course, tragically, wreak havoc among the local population by looting temples and towns, the details of which are only rarely given in the sources for these years. The campaign of Miguel Ferreira did not inaugurate an epoch of Portuguese territorial appropriation in Sri Lanka, even though it was an early instance of extreme and unadapted, politically indigestible brutality in the island. Most importantly for the purpose of our story, it was a step in the ongoing apprenticeship that revealed, gradually, a land which had practically not appeared in earlier texts, and now began to open up geographically and politically before the eyes of some Portuguese.

## EXPLAINING THE MATRIOSHKA PRINCIPLE: KŌṬṬE'S DIPLOMATIC OFFENSIVE, 1541–1543

Even after news of the expedition of 1538–9 arrived in Lisbon, the Portuguese crown showed little political interest in Sri Lanka. Bhuvanekabāhu's vassalage remained associated in Lisbon primarily with trade. In 1526, John III had written to Goa that if Bhuvanekabāhu had any complaints, they should be filed *there* and then forwarded to Lisbon. Diplomatic impulses were to be transformed by the *Estado* into administrative ones. Direct correspondence between Kōṭṭe and the Portuguese court was to be avoided.[76] The treaty of 1533, with its detailed discussion of cinnamon prices and trading conditions, is a clear expression of how much the Portuguese crown was interested in milking Kōṭṭe commercially, and how little it wished to do to support it militarily.

At one crucial moment in 1541, Bhuvanekabāhu VII decided to take a more assertive stance and explain his vision of the inter-imperial deal to the Portuguese in a clearer and louder voice than before. Encouraged perhaps by the blow that had been dealt to Sītāvaka and its Mappila allies in 1539, the king of Kōṭṭe had decided to marry off his daughter to a loyal aristocrat rather than, as promised earlier, to Māyādunnē. Once his grandson Dharmapāla was born, Bhuvanekabāhu designated him as his heir, thus effectively excluding Māyādunnē from the succession to the throne. To seal this move, the king then sent an embassy to Lisbon. The ensuing reception, in 1542, of Bhuvanekabāhu's ambassador at the Portuguese court was a

---

[75] See Sanjay Subrahmanyam, 'An Eastern El-Dorado: The Tirumala-Tirupati Temple complex in early European views and ambitions, 1540–1660', in *Syllables of Sky: Studies in South Indian Civilization in Honour of Velcheru Narayana Rao*, edited by David Shulman (New Delhi: Oxford University Press, 1995), pp. 338–90 and Alexandra Pelúcia, *Martim Afonso de Sousa e a sua Linhagem. Trajectórias de uma Elite no Império de D. João III e de D. Sebastião* (Lisbon: CHAM, 2009), p. 231.

[76] John III to Henrique de Meneses, [1526], in Flores, *Os Portugueses*, p. 338. On the political changes of the 1520s see Vitorino Magalhães Godinho, 'A viragem mundial de 1517–1524 e o Império português', in *Ensaios* (Lisbon: Sá da Costa, 1978), vol. II, pp. 205–21. João Paulo Oliveira e Costa, 'Do sonho manuelino ao realismo joanino. Novos documentos sobre as relações luso-chinesas na terceira década do século XVI', *Studia*, 50 (1991), pp. 121–56 and 'O império português em meados do século XVI', *Anais de História da Além-Mar*, 3 (2002), pp. 87–121.

splendid instance of Asian diplomacy in Europe, and indeed one with few parallels in the sixteenth century.[77] It is a mystery how so little has since been written about it, especially since a detailed corpus of archival documents survives to complement the visual imagery offered by the so-called 'coronation casket' mentioned in the introduction to this book (see Figures 0.2 and 0.3).[78] Perhaps this has to do with the fact that, at the time, and despite the pomp with which the Lankan embassy was received, John III showed no interest in publicizing the events any further. Where his father would have been most likely to commission a richly illustrated, printed account of the reception, John simply went silent. It could also be that the lack of interest shown by historians has to do with the apparent lack of grandeur— one might even be tempted to say, the outright disorder—of the written documents surviving in the Portuguese national archive. On the other hand, it is difficult not to feel compelled by the magnificent casket that was sent along with the ambassador, already introduced at the beginning of this book, to attempt a re-reading of the events in the light of the developments observed over the past chapters.

Perhaps the most remarkable aspect of the embassy is how the memory of the events remains today shaped by the material produced in Kōṭṭe, not in Portugal. The 'coronation casket' itself shows how carefully and effectively the entire narrative was crafted even before the embassy left the Lankan shore. A single detail suffices to prove the point: according to the Portuguese chronicles, the ceremony was performed 'in the Portuguese manner'—but kings in Portugal were usually acclaimed, not crowned. Yet on the casket, the act of placing a crown upon the Sinhalese prince's head is a key motif. Either the Lankan embassy managed to convince John III to perform a foreign ritual, which would be remarkable—or it did not, but then it is still the image of a coronation as imagined in Sri Lanka that has survived to this day.[79] Bhuvanekabāhu's choice of ambassador was even more prescient. Śrī Rāmarakṣa was the Sinhalese monarch's *purohita*, a high-ranking, very skilled and charismatic Brahmin minister, an alter ego of the king, and a guarantor of the ritual appropriateness of courtly rituals such as coronations. Śrī Rāmarakṣa was certainly involved in the preparation of the embassy, including the making and the display of the casket at Kōṭṭe; he may have carried it into the presence of the Portuguese monarch and certainly did present it; he probably held the opening speech asking for Dharmapāla to be accepted as a future vassal in a proxy coronation ritual depicted already on the casket; he was part of the coronation itself; and he spent several months

---

[77] Accounts in Queiroz, *Conquista*, pp. 184–5, Correia, *Lendas*, vol. IV, pp. 306–70 and Paulo da Trindade, *Conquista Espiritual do Oriente*, edited by Félix Lopes (Lisbon: CEHU, 1962–1967), vol. III, pp. 24–5.

[78] Strathern, *Kingship and Conversion* is the exception and offers valuable insights. The wider context is explored in Zoltán Biedermann, 'Diplomatic Ivories: Sri Lankan Caskets and the European-Asian Diplomatic Exchange, 1500–1600', in *Global Gifts. The Material Culture of Diplomacy in Early Modern Eurasia*, edited by Zoltán Biedermann, Anne Gerritsen and Giorgio Riello (New York: Cambridge University Press, 2018), pp. 88–118. There is an abundant art historical literature on the caskets as such, a recent summary of which can be found in Sujatha Arundathi Meegama, 'The local and the global: the multiple visual worlds of ivory carvers in early modern Sri Lanka,' in *Sri Lanka at the Crossroads of History*, edited by Zoltán Biedermann and Alan Strathern (London: UCL Press, 2018), pp. 113–40.

[79] Saldanha, *Iustum Imperium*, p. 584.

at the Portuguese court after the reception, networking inside the royal family, and gaining a social capital that proved decisive for Kōṭṭe over the following decade.[80]

Let us have a second glance, then, at the casket presented to John III by Śrī Rāmarakṣa, before we explore the written corpus that comes along with it. In the introduction, I highlighted the vignettes narrating the coronation as such: they emphasize the mutuality of the bond created between overlord and future vassal. I also mentioned how Bhuvanekabāhu had himself represented in full majesty on the two side panels of the casket. Crucially, the references to transcontinental vassalage constituted only a relatively small part of the visual programme of the casket. All the other parts, which would have struck the viewer once they turned the casket, or indeed moved around it (the side panels would have been the ones most visible to much of the audience as the casket was carried towards John III), emphasized Bhuvanekabāhu's supremacy in the Lankan political theatre. On one of these side panels, the monarch was represented in full imperial glory, sitting on the lion throne, wearing the multi-tiered Lankan crown, and holding a lotus flower, an emblem of the Buddha.[81] He soared confidently above his two inferior brothers, the *rājas* of Sītāvaka and Rayigama, leaving no doubt about his pre-eminent position in the island.[82] On the opposite end of the casket, the representation of the great king alone, riding an elephant amidst emblems such as flywhisks and a parasol, offered a further, eminently readable declaration of military and political glory.

This was obviously an attempt at presenting power relations around Bhuvanekabāhu as more stable and unambiguously hierarchical than they were. It also amounts to the closest evidence we have, along with an undated copper plate inscription and some scattered Portuguese comments, that Bhuvanekabāhu VII did see himself as an imperial figure of the highest order. In the copper plate inscription, which may have originated during his early days as a monarch, but would also make sense in the context of the early 1540s, his title was given as 'His Majesty the sovereign Lord Sri Bhuvanaika Bahu [...] sovereign Lord of Tri Sinhala and Lord of the nine gems'.[83] It was a fleeting glory, as a letter written in 1546 by a Franciscan friar already noted that Bhuvanekabāhu *'used to be emperor'* (*'amtigamemte era Emperador'*).[84] By 1552, Bhuvanekabāhu's successor Dharmapāla presented himself as 'great king, like his grandfather' (*'Rey gramde como seu avoo'*)— a formula that appears to render the title of *mahārāja*, not *cakravarti*.[85] But the point to retain is that in 1541–2 Bhuvanekabāhu engaged in the imperial dialogue with John III styling himself as a majestic figure standing at the apex of the Lankan imperial system, a monarch aspiring to the highest ritual honours, hovering far

---

[80] I give some more details on his long diplomatic career in 'Cosmopolitan Converts. The Politics of Lankan Exile in the Portuguese Empire', in *Sri Lanka at the Crossroads of History*, edited by Zoltán Biedermann and Alan Strathern (London: UCL Press, 2017), pp. 141–60.

[81] Jaffer and Schwabe, 'A Group of Sixteenth-Century Ivory Caskets', pp. 3–14.

[82] Strathern, *Kingship and Conversion*, p. 27.

[83] *Epigraphia Zeylanica: being lithic and other inscriptions of Ceylon*, edited by Don Martino de Zilva Wickremasinghe, Senarat Paranavitana, and Humphrey William Codrington, vol. III (London: Henry Frowde, 1933), pp. 244–7. The word 'sovereign' was introduced by the translator and should be taken in its widest sense, including elements of suzerainty. On the symbolism of 'Trisinhala', see chapter 2 above.

[84] Simão de Coimbra to John III, Goa, 25 December 1546, *Ceylon*, p. 420. Emphasis added.

[85] Noronha to John III, Cochin, 27 January 1552, *Ceylon*, p. 587.

above any lesser rulers and serving as the sole legitimate interlocutor of the Portuguese. He was, it can be added, still objectively a rich and reliable vassal overall, capable of paying tribute regularly and willing to supply additional services, including generous loans and elaborate luxury objects such as the very casket on which these scenes were shown.[86] Everything proclaimed the self-evident rationality of perpetuating this particular overlord-vassal relationship, the only viable one in Lanka. The emphasis was, as one would expect, on mutuality and commensurability in the inter-imperial relationship, rather than on its hierarchical aspects. Visually, the link between the image of Bhuvanekabāhu sitting on the lion throne and the physical presence of John III sitting on the Portuguese throne must have been striking during the reception.

The iconographic programme of the 'coronation casket' can help us interpret Bhuvanekabāhu's written complaints and requests, some of which seem at odds with its magnificence. Following a solemn opening oration, a number of subsequent points refer to apparently minor issues, threatening to drown the grand diplomatic message in petty details. And yet an attentive reading of this corpus offers a remarkably comprehensive picture of what the elite of Kōṭṭe imagined its vassalage to the distant Portuguese monarch to be. The following summary of Bhuvanekabāhu's 'notes' (*apontamentos*) from 1541 amounts to a textual map—albeit not an easily readable one—of a complex political vision. The official Portuguese responses from 1543, including some blatant lacunae examined further below, demonstrate the limits of that very dialogue.[87]

| Complaints and requests presented by Bhuvanekabāhu VII (Kōṭṭe, 1541) | Concessions made to Bhuvanekabāhu VII by John III (Almeirim, 1543) |
| --- | --- |
| 0. [Lost petition, possibly an oration performed in Portuguese, Tamil and/or Sinhala by the chief ambassador Śrī Rāmarakṣa, with or without the assistance of a translator, to ask for support to be given to Dharmapāla as successor to the Kōṭṭe throne.] | John III agrees that Dharmapāla shall succeed on the throne of Kōṭṭe and expresses the hope that he may reign without opposition or interference. All officials of the *Estado* shall be notified. |
| 1. Māyādunnē has taken over some **ports** that belonged to Bhuvanekabāhu. To safeguard the integrity of his domains and his revenue, Bhuvanekabāhu asks that the following **complaints** be heard. | Conceded. |
| 2. Bhuvanekabāhu has the obligation to pay *páreas*, but is not allowed to sell the remaining **cinnamon** and is instead forced to burn it. A request is made to obtain authorization for the sale of 100 *bahars* of cinnamon per year to the East of Cape Comorin. | Not mentioned. |

*(continued)*

[86] On the vast legacy of ivories sent to Portugal during the 1540s, see Annemarie Jordan Gschwend and Johannes Beltz, *Elfenbeine aus Ceylon: Luxusgüter für Katharina von Habsburg (1507–1578)* (Zurich: Museum Rietberg, 2010).
[87] *Ceylon*, pp. 99–106 and 110–21.

**Continued**

| Complaints and requests presented by Bhuvanekabāhu VII (Kōṭṭe, 1541) | Concessions made to Bhuvanekabāhu VII by John III (Almeirim, 1543) |
|---|---|
| 3. The **cinnamon** is kept in a warehouse, the keys to which are with the *feitor* and a servant of Bhuvanekabāhu. But the *feitor* manages to steal cinnamon and leaves only the worst behind. | Not mentioned. |
| 4. Portuguese private **traders** force people into selling their goods at low prices and buying their own merchandise, including things people do not need, at high prices. | The subjects of Bhuvanekabāhu should not suffer humiliations or loss of property. No Portuguese subject should sell goods in the kingdom of Kōṭṭe if it is not for a just price and in **conformity** with the customs of the land. Infractions will be punished by the confiscation of those goods, to be handed over to the people of the land. |
| 5. There are about thirty Portuguese Christians in the kingdom of Bhuvanekabāhu, both married and unmarried, who are forcefully buying **lands**. No-one should be allowed to purchase lands without the authorization of Bhuvanekabāhu, without paying a fair price, and without performing the obligations and services associated in Ceylon with the ownership of land. | Taking into consideration the **friendship** [*sic*] that exists between the two kings, John III orders that no Portuguese person should be able to acquire lands or gardens without the authorization of Bhuvanekabāhu, and only under the condition of paying a fair price and performing the **services** to which the owners of the said lands and gardens are by custom obliged. Infringing any of these rules will lead to the loss of the land, to be handed back to Bhuvanekabāhu. |
| 6. The Portuguese **lend money** to local people, but they falsify the records of such deeds and force the subjects of Bhuvanekabāhu to pay back more than they agreed to. People who protest have been taken captive and at times sold as slaves in Cochin. | John III wishes to **protect** all the subjects of Bhuvanekabāhu and will not tolerate such offenses. It shall be forbidden to the Portuguese to lend money in Ceylon, under threat of losing the said money and, furthermore, of having to pay an equal amount to the *Misericórdia* of Cochin. |
| 7. No **vessels** should leave the port of Colombo without the authorization of Bhuvanekabāhu, who should be able to have them controlled and see whether they have on board abducted people, criminals, or undeclared cinnamon. | Bhuvanekabāhu shall be informed about any vessel departing Colombo, so that he can order **inspections** and emit a certificate. Otherwise the entire cargo is to be handed over to the *Misericórdia* of Cochin. |
| 8. Many **slaves** in Ceylon convert to Catholicism to gain freedom. They should pay an indemnity to their owners. As for free persons converting to Catholicism, they should keep paying their taxes on lands and gardens, and should not see their debts pardoned. | The slaves who convert should be sold to Christians, rather than freed. Whoever owns lands and gardens and does convert should **continue** to perform the services to which they are obliged by custom. |
| 9. There are nine ports in the kingdom of Kōṭṭe, where the **feitor** has placed his own men of trust. They are **corrupt**, practise extortions and manipulate prices. When a heathen is condemned to pay a fine in agreement with traditional law, it is sufficient for him to pay a bribe to one of the *feitor's* men, who will confirm that the fined person is in his service. The king of Kōṭṭe thus loses out on fines. The *feitor* should deal with nothing but the cinnamon of John III. | John III orders that all his Portuguese subjects pay the **taxes** due to Bhuvanekabāhu VII, as anyone else going to the country to do business, under threat of losing to Bhuvanekabāhu all the goods they bring to the country. |

10. The **feitor** should be forbidden from sending men to the lands of **Māyādunnē**, in order to avoid rebellions and other disorderly behaviour.

Not mentioned.

11. The ports of Kalpitiya and Chilaw belong to Bhuvanekabāhu, and according to custom the revenue of one out of every five days of the **pearl fishery** belongs to the king (one out of every twelve in bad years), independently from what the fishers pay to the Portuguese captain of the Fishery Coast.

Not mentioned.

12. Christians cut down people's **trees** in the villages for the construction of boats, causing great damage. They should be compelled to cut trees deeper in the forest.

The trees for the making of ships should be cut in the forest, and no vessel should be built without the **authorization** of Bhuvanekabāhu and the governor.

13. To avoid various problems (offensive behaviour and thefts that also concern John III; the rebellious attitudes of the kings of Sītāvaka and Jaffna; the misdeeds of the *feitor* in these lands; the losses of land to rival kingdoms), **fifty armed men** should be sent to Kōṭṭe every three years to secure peace. They may be paid by John III, but will receive additional incentives from Bhuvanekabāhu VII. They **shall not obey the *feitor***, but only the king of Kōṭṭe, who will command them to defend the interests of the king of Portugal.

Not mentioned.

14. [Illegible]

Tammiṭa Sūriya Baṇḍāra Senadhipati, the younger brother of Vīdiyē Baṇḍāra, head of the army, shall be **chief chamberlain** [*camareiro-mor*] of Dharmapāla after the death of Bhuvanekabāhu VII, and the office shall remain in his family after his death.

António Pereira, **interpreter** [*língua*] of Bhuvanekabāhu VII and assistant to the ambassador Śrī Rāmarakṣa, is nominated officially as *língua* until the end of his life.

15. Bhuvanekabāhu requests that, in addition to his annual export allowance of **cinnamon** agreed upon in the past, another 30 *bahars* be conceded.

Not mentioned.

16. Bhuvanekabāhu asks that Duarte Teixeira, who is accompanying the ambassador to Lisbon, be nominated as *feitor* indefinitely, as long as he serves John III well, under the condition that he never places a man of his retinue [*apaniguado*] in any port and that he deals exclusively with the cinnamon pertaining to the Portuguese king.

Not mentioned.

Once the casket and, with it, Śrī Rāmarakṣa stood in the presence of John III, the ambassador performed a solemn opening oration, possibly given in Sinhala or Tamil and then translated into Portuguese by the interpreter (*língua*) mentioned in one of the later decrees. Whether '*Imperador da Taprobana*' was the expression used to designate Bhuvanekabāhu whilst the Portuguese monarch was called '*Rey dos Reys*', as the later chronicler Queiroz has it, is not certain. It is plausible though in the light of the casket's iconography. In this opening speech, Bhuvanekabāhu demanded the recognition of Dharmapāla as the sole legitimate successor to the Lankan imperial throne, along with a commitment to his defence. Then, the tone changes. The register of the requests makes it doubtful whether they would have been presented in public at all, rather suggesting an exchange of a less pompous nature, quite possibly extended over several days or weeks of negotiations. However, it remains important to acknowledge how the complaints were drawn up in Kōṭṭe as a single, coherent statement of intentions. A careful reading does indeed suggest that the two dimensions—the pompous and the petty—were skilfully intertwined for presentation to the Portuguese king.

Bhuvanekabāhu VII excelled at exploring the personal logics of power building. His list of requests competently explores a series of people-based, easily understandable, even apparently banal complaints, only to then link them up with the wider, more idiosyncratic but politically crucial principles of the vassalage imagined. The key problems experienced by Bhuvanekabāhu VII as a vassal of John III are introduced through the figures of the bullying go-between and the dishonest royal official. These were easily readable on both sides. Go-betweens were a threat when they moved back and forth with too much self-confidence, claiming to be protected by whichever legal system suited them best in each given moment. They effectively defied Lankan *and* Portuguese crown authority, undermining that key characteristic of kingship shared by Bhuvanekabāhu and John, the ability to judge and to punish. The corrupt administrator required no further explanations: he (personified by the cunning *feitor* who steels the best of the tributary cinnamon) was a well-known, widely detested figure. Whilst some forms of corruption were common and indeed part of the system, an excessive drive for self-enrichment was perceived as undermining not only the monarch's authority but also his financial capability across the empire.

Crucially, the Lankan monarch was not just asking John III to support him in controlling rogue traders and a corrupt *feitor*. He also wished to obtain Portuguese military personnel for his own service. This particular request was, I believe, the most important aspect of the diplomatic mission along with the acceptance of Dharmapāla as successor to the throne. Obtaining Portuguese soldiers for Lankan warfare had been at the heart of earlier diplomatic efforts, but always proved difficult to achieve. Now, Bhuvanekabāhu upped his game by offering a long-term plan. He requested fifty armed men to be dispatched to Ceylon every three years. But that in itself was not enough. The men, he asked, should then be placed under his own command. They would not come from Goa or Cochin as a regiment, led by a captain or any other official on the payroll of the *Estado*, and they would not take any orders from inside the Portuguese empire. 'Those men', the monarch explained, 'shall not be obliged to do what your *feitor* orders them, but only what I tell them with a view to serving Your Highness.'[88] The troops that Kōṭṭe hoped to receive were to be a malleable raw material without a juridical identity or exogenous mandate of their own, ready to be integrated and deployed locally as had been the case with Indian military specialists before. They were to be localized specifically and directly into the service of the Lankan monarch.

It is interesting to note how this key request pertaining to the management of people contained a spatial aspect of great significance. To be sure, Bhuvanekabāhu did not offer a map of his realm other than the diagrammatic image on the right end of the casket, where he could be seen sitting between and above his two brothers. It was the hierarchical logic of the partition that stood at the centre of his preoccupations, not the precise spatial configuration of the kingdoms. But as a whole these apparently loose spatial aspects point to a very coherent notion of what the Lankan imperial polity needed to be, and of *where* it stood in relation to the Portuguese empire. Key to Bhuvanekabāhu's diplomatic effort was that 'naturally' given receptacle of empire, the island of Lanka itself, referred to time and again as *Ceilão*. Foreigners, including the Portuguese, were welcome to cross its beaches and settle as traders or soldiers inside it. They could even keep their language and religion. But once on Lankan soil, they needed to shed their allegiance to John III and accept the authority of Bhuvanekabāhu VII. In this sense, the inter-personal logics of the Lankan imperial imagination did take on a remarkably strong spatial form. Outside the island, John III was expected to patrol the seas and maintain resources that might be deployed to protect Kōṭṭe, for example from the Mappilas. Inside the island, he was expected to let go of his resources and place them under the authority of the ruler of Kōṭṭe. This was how Bhuvanekabāhu VII expected his insular empire to thrive: it was to nest inside the larger empire of John III, huddling within it as if contained in a bubble, paying tribute to a distant overlord but remaining protected from that lord's global realm by a membrane running along the littoral of Lanka itself. That membrane, crucially, needed to be kept intact for the vassalage to function according to Lankan expectations. It was the most important element of an idea that I have described elsewhere as the 'Matrioshka Principle'.[89]

Under such a light, the Lankan imagination appears as both cosmopolitan *and* obsessed with its attachment to a single, symbolically laden place. The island of Lanka appeared remarkably porous to the circulation and integration of people, yet also intransigent and impermeable when it came to monarchical authority. However unstraightforward, multi-layered and complex the polity's internal configuration, it still coalesced around a very clear sense that Kōṭṭe, standing at the apex of the insular imperial realm, had the prerogative of extending its imperial umbrella over all Lanka *without* leaving space for an exogenous authority to radiate

[88] Bhuvanekabāhu VII to John III, *Ceylon*, p. 105. Translation taken from Vito Perniola, *The Catholic Church in Sri Lanka. The Portuguese Period. Original Documents translated into English* (Dehiwala: Tisara Prakasakayo, 1989–1991), vol. I, p. 20.

[89] Zoltán Biedermann, 'The Matrioshka Principle and How It Was Overcome: Portuguese and Habsburg Attitudes toward Imperial Authority in Sri Lanka and the Responses of the Rulers of Kōṭṭe (1506–1656)', *Journal of Early Modern History*, 13, 4 (2009), pp. 265–310.

into the island. The local—the island—would ideally inhabit the global as a part protected *by and from* the whole. It would draw strength from Portuguese imperial resources, but would deploy them in the island only after detaching them from their original context and 'localizing' them: allowing them, in the sense proposed by O. W. Wolters, to become part, locally, of a new cultural whole, rather than expressing an exogenous interference.[90] Inevitably, the question arises whether the principle of nesting empires could ever be fully understood, let alone accepted, by John III in the way the Lankan elite imagined it.

## THE LIMITS OF CONNECTABILITY: EMERGING DISJUNCTIONS

In part—and this is the interpretation that classic connected history would highlight—the vision of nesting empires could be made readable to the Portuguese elite on grounds of the simple fact that it rested upon a logic of empire building analogous on the two sides involved: the logics of indirect rule, of imperial expansion based on the personal submission of lesser kings to tribute-demanding overlords. This was what had allowed a conversation to unfold over the decades. But to what extent could this principle be fully translated, or indeed made to work? The Lankan notion of the island as a shell for Kōṭṭe's imperial authority was one thing, the reception of this idea among the Portuguese another. Imperfect translations may not be an absolute obstacle to communication, but they do inflect meanings and, once the receiving side acts in accordance with those modified meanings, the consequences can end up creating considerable tensions. The answers given by John III to Bhuvanekabāhu show precisely the extent to which an inter-imperial understanding remained difficult even as Luso-Lankan diplomacy reached its zenith.

In the first of the responses dispatched by John III between 12 and 16 March 1543,[91] the monarch confirmed the legitimate succession of Dharmapāla to the throne of Kōṭṭe and underlined the interest of the *Estado* in defending Bhuvanekabāhu's heir.[92] As a matter of fact, the birth of Dharmapāla, which had exacerbated the rivalry between Bhuvanekabāhu and Māyādunnē, had already been known in Goa and Lisbon in 1539,[93] and at least some people had shown an awareness of the importance of supporting the young prince.[94] Through this fundamental concession, John III demonstrated that he understood the basic dynastic issues at stake in Kōṭṭe, and that his empire was willing to support one faction of

[90] O. W. Wolters, *History, Culture, and Region in Southeast Asian Perspectives*, 2nd revised edition (Ithaca, NY: Cornell University Press, 1999), p. 55.
[91] One decree on 12 March 1543, four on 13, three on 14 and two on 16 March, all issued in Almeirim near Lisbon, and preserved at the Arquivo Nacional Torre do Tombo. *Chancelaria de D. João III—Doações*, 6, fols. 43v–46v, *Ceylon*, pp. 110–21.
[92] Royal decree (*alvará*), 12 March 1543, *Ceylon*, p. 111.
[93] Cf. De Silva, 'The Rise and Fall of the Kingdom of Sitawaka', p. 12.
[94] Estêvão da Gama to John III, Goa, 11 November 1540, *Ceylon*, p. 95.

the Lankan elite to stabilize the little empire nesting within the sphere of influence of the *Estado*.

Regarding the private traders, John III made a drastic and indeed surprising concession. On 13 March 1543, it was decided that any Portuguese individual purchasing land in Ceylon would be obliged not only to pay a fair price for the transaction, but also to carry out for Bhuvanekabāhu the services traditionally attached to the usage of that land.[95] In theory this could have included military services to a Buddhist ruler, and it is legitimate to ask whether the Portuguese court lawyers understood this.[96] The main rationale for signing this decree would have had to do with a wish to control the private traders by giving Bhuvanekabāhu VII authority over them. The royal secretary Pero de Alcáçova Carneiro proposed at the time that 'no Portuguese [man] should be allowed to reside [be a *morador*] in Ceylon without the permission of the governor and the agreement of the king'. Unauthorized settlers could have been expelled from the island under this proposal.[97] It may indeed be argued that the idea of controlling the private settlers with the help of the Lankan monarch was not in complete contradiction with the Portuguese juridical setting. Bhuvanekabāhu could formally be conceived of as an entity extending the powers of John III. The latter was, as a king, entitled to delegate some of his authority. This was the basis, among other things, for the governorship that existed in Goa since 1510, an institution grounded, like the late medieval Aragonian viceroyalty (developed in the Mediterranean and extended to the New World in 1535), in formal arrangements between the king and the parliaments representing society at large.[98] Bhuvanekabāhu himself does seem to have referred to something of the sort when, in a later letter, he expounded his own role as a sort of re-transmitter of Portuguese royal authority into Sri Lanka. There he encouraged the Portuguese crown to pass decrees valid in the island as if they were destined for a kingdom of their own, on grounds that he as a loyal vassal would then put them into practice locally (*'como em seu Reyno, pois tem em mym hum tam leall vasalo e seruidor'*).[99]

The fundamental problem remained, however, the same: whose authority should any troops dispatched from Goa (that is, not *moradores*, but *soldados*) abide by once they were active in the island? In practice, Bhuvanekabāhu wished Portuguese soldiers to be stationed in the island, but John III remained reluctant to strip them of all exogenous authority when they moved into the 'nesting' realm. An entire section of the *apontamentos* dedicated specifically to this matter was left unanswered. At the end of the day, the decrees of 1543 were signed by a ruler who, as one would expect, had his own political realities in mind more than those of his vassal. He had

---

[95] Royal decree, 13 March 1543, *Ceylon*, p. 114.

[96] Strathern, *Kingship and* Conversion, pp. 99–101.

[97] Arquivo Nacional Torre do Tombo, *Cartas dos Vice-reis*, n° 100. The marginal notes are mentioned in Strathern, *Kingship and Conversion*, p. 56.

[98] José Adelino Maltez, 'O Estado e as Instituições', in *Nova História de Portugal*, edited by Joel Serrão and A. H. Oliveira Marques, vol. V (Lisbon: Presença, 1998), pp. 372–3. On viceroyalty in the Spanish empire, see Alejandro Cañeque, *The King's Living Image: The Culture and Politics of Viceregal Power in Colonial Mexico* (New York: Routledge, 2004).

[99] Bhuvanekabāhu to Queen Catherine, Kōṭṭe, 11 December 1549, *Ceylon*, p. 538.

been open to parts of what the Kōṭṭe elite envisaged, but on certain points the dialogue reached its limits. Some of the Portuguese crown's silences must have been deliberate, namely the refusal—another glaring omission in the 1543 decrees—to make concessions on the cinnamon trade.

At a deeper level, though, it may also be the case that John III effectively failed to understand the full complexity of the situation. There is a cultural argument to be made here: by the 1540s, John III may simply have lacked the mental tools to grasp the full extent to which his vassal was an embattled ruler who desperately needed Portuguese troops *and* an intact authority. Only half a century earlier, a Portuguese monarch like John II (r.1481–95) might have been better equipped to empathize. In the 1480s, John II had been confronted with severe internal opposition, namely by Ferdinand II, Duke of Bragança, to a series of centralizing reforms.[100] He had presided in person over the trial of the Duke, which ended in a death sentence proclaimed in 1483. The monarch killed another of his rivals, the Duke of Viseu, self-handedly in 1484. That was still a time when the king's body, and with it the integrity of the realm (the last Luso-Castilian war had been fought in the 1470s), faced the palpable threat of dismemberment. John II never travelled through his kingdom lightheartedly, not even around Lisbon. He invested in his personal guards much in the way that Lankan monarchs did.[101] But the climate of conspiracy surrounding the Portuguese monarchs was attenuated under Manuel I at the turn of the century, when the Bragnças were rehabilitated. Further centralizing reforms met with a much less dramatic resistance. The Portuguese royal guards increasingly took on courtly functions that had little to do with the personal security of the king.[102] John III was born into an environment where royal bodies were not exposed to existential threats anymore. By the time he ascended the throne in 1521, his younger brother, Luís, was a tamed and politically inoffensive man. It is striking that Bhuvanekabāhu, reacting to the decrees passed in 1543, wrote precisely to Luís with the following words: 'I beg Your Highness to send me support because I assure you that I live in constant fear, and I do not know who might guard my person, my brother [Māyādunnē] being my worst enemy and traitor.'[103]

Ironically, John III may also have been misled by the image of royal magnificence that Bhuvanekabāhu transmitted especially during the Śrī Rāmarakṣa embassy. The iconographic programme of the 'coronation casket' may have been misread as reflecting a kind of royal power that was by then under construction in Portugal, but not in Sri Lanka. Things were shifting in the Iberian kingdom. On the one hand, sovereignty as a concept was still associated here with the topos of 'preeminent power' and the idea that the king acted as supreme judge in his kingdom,

---

[100] On John II, see João José Alves Dias, Isabel Drumond Braga and Paulo Drumond Braga, 'A conjuntura', in *Nova História de Portugal*, edited by Joel Serrão and A. H. Oliveira Marques, vol. V (Lisbon: Presença, 1998), pp. 701–3.

[101] Augusto Cardoso Pinto, *A guarda del rei Dom João II: notas para a história das guardas reais portuguesas* (Lisbon: Centro Tipográfico Colonial, 1930), pp. 13–15.

[102] Pinto, *A guarda del rei*, pp. 13–15. Dias, Braga and Braga, 'A conjuntura', pp. 703 and 713. On the guards of Manuel I, see António Francisco Barata, 'Regimento da Gente da Ordenança e das vinte lanças da Guarda', *Archivo Histórico Portuguez*, I (1903), p. 83.

[103] Bhuvanekabāhu VII to Dom Luís, Kōṭṭe, 28 November 1543, *Ceylon*, p. 123.

rather than, as Jean Bodin would later theorize, as supreme legislator.[104] In this regard, an understanding of Lankan-type royal authority was possible. On the other hand, however, Portugal had already begun to go down the path of incipient territorialization, as we shall explore in more detail soon. Under John III, the borders of the realm in the Peninsula had been redrawn with a meticulousness unheard of before, the kingdom subjected to a first systematic cartographical survey—one of the earliest of its kind in Europe—and pockets of aristocratic power began to be regarded as anomalies rather than the rule. The internal heterogeneities of Portugal, whilst still in the process of being addressed, were already far less dramatic than those of Sri Lanka. None of this can be currently theorized in more detail as we await a fully fledged study of the concept of sovereignty in Renaissance Portugal. Yet everything points to a very unsettling environment of Luso-Lankan matches and mismatches, analogies and incompatibilities, adding up to a picture where disconnection was as much a reality as connection.

Was the embassy a success, then? It was, in that it strengthened the personal attachment of the Kōṭṭe elite to the Portuguese royal family, including John III, his wife Catherine and his brother Luís, for years to come. This proved of great importance the turmoil of the following decades. On the other hand, the concrete results were minimal. Even as Śrī Rāmarakṣa was paraded through Lisbon, Kōṭṭe suffered another siege at the hands of Māyādunnē. Bhuvanekabāhu remained caught in a local and regional conflict that global diplomacy could not quite resolve. His reach across the Lankan lowlands was severely curtailed precisely in 1542–3.[105] It is not that dialogue was impossible between the two monarchs. At one level the two men were well-positioned to talk to each other. But the mutual compatibility of their political imaginations was only one part of the equation, and as time went by the incompatibilities gained weight. At the end of the day, John III remained not only unwilling to invest the resources needed for the military consolidation of Bhuvanekabāhu's rule, but perhaps incapable of appreciating the differences between the Portuguese and the Lankan political landscape and the need for a more forthcoming attitude. At the level of high diplomacy, where for a moment anything seemed possible, substantial obstacles had appeared. To understand how Luso-Lankan relations came out of this impasse, we need to return to the murky grounds of Lankan politics and observe diplomacy operating at a slightly lower level than the grand encounter of 1542.

[104] See Pablo Fernández-Albaladejo, *Fragmentos de Monarquía* (Madrid: Alianza Editorial, 1992), pp. 73–5.
[105] Cf. De Silva, 'The rise and fall of the kingdom of Sitawaka', p. 12.

# 4

## Conversion Diplomacy
### Lankan Imperial Projects and the Politics
### of Catholic Universalism

As the Lankan monarchy struggled to get its message across, and the Portuguese crown failed to understand what exactly was expected from it, communication began to prove more effective in a different social and geographical context. At some distance from the courts of Kōṭṭe and Lisbon, conversations got underway in the 1540s between a range of Lankan kings, princes and aristocrats, on the one hand, and a series of individuals standing on the middle to lower echelons of the Portuguese imperial hierarchy, on the other. Whilst the geographical imagination in Lisbon remained patchy with regard to Sri Lanka even after the 1542 embassy, we shall now see the first inklings of a territorial vision of the island appear—on the margins, in close proximity to Lankan imperial dynamics, and with an important new element thrown into the picture: the prospect of converting Lankans to Catholicism.[1]

The fact that 'peripheral' initiatives should play a role in our story is unsurprising, given the Portuguese empire's propensity to, as Sanjay Subrahmanyam famously put it, allow the tail to wag the dog.[2] The most compelling alternative for Bhuvanekabāhu VII and other Lankan rulers to high diplomacy with Lisbon and Goa was to interact with and co-opt individuals on the fringes of the *Estado* who were ready to reach out across cultural and political borders and intertwine their own lives with those of Asian elites, but also in a position to shake the centres of the Lusitanian realm by sending word from the margins. We have seen already how the pool of potential go-betweens had begun to grow after the dismantlement of the Colombo fort 1524. The following decades saw the emergence in Sri Lanka and South India of new political projects that, gradually, began to drag the *Estado* down a path quite different from that set out by John III. To understand the

---

[1] To be sure, territorialization as we shall encounter it further below was still a distant reality. See Michael Biggs, 'Putting the State on the Map: Cartography, Territory, and European State Formation', *Comparative Studies in Society and History*, 41, 2 (1999), pp. 374–405.

[2] Cf. Subrahmanyam, 'The Tail Wags the Dog: Sub-Imperialism and the *Estado da Índia*, 1570–1600', in *Improvising Empire: Portuguese Trade and Settlement in the Bay of Bengal* (New Delhi: Oxford University Press, 1990), pp. 137–60. This is not to be confounded with the overall peripheral status of the *Estado* as a whole in relation to the kingdom of Portugal, incisively described in George D. Winius, 'Few Thanks to the King: The Building of Portuguese India', in *Vasco da Gama and the Linking of Europe and Asia*, edited by Anthony Disney and Emily Booth (New Delhi: Oxford University Press, 2000), pp. 484–95.

unfolding of such plans, it is necessary to take just a brief step back in time before we leap forward to the extraordinary final decade of Bhuvanekabāhu's reign.

## OPPORTUNITY CRISIS IN THE *ESTADO* AND LANKAN POLITICAL PROJECTS

Manuel I had cultivated an image of military and religious engagement with Asia, but he had also faced the opposition of a lobby that saw expansion as a purely commercial affair. The constellation had then shifted under John III, whose administration proved unwilling to invest substantial military resources in Ceylon, while it was now individuals from the lower and intermediate ranks of the social spectrum who began to push for political change. But why? The shift is best seen in connection with developments in the opportunity structure of the empire, something historians have only recently begun to look into. Being a soldier or a petty officer in the nascent *Estado* had been one thing while the system expanded, but became another when, in the 1520s, growth stalled. Whilst commercial opportunities kept mushrooming especially beyond the edges of the empire, in the realms of other rulers,[3] the pool of opportunities for men aiming to build a career in the *Estado* began to dwindle. Although it is difficult to say precisely when the lack of official positions became an overwhelming reality—the chronology varies for different types of positions[4]— the pressure seems to have mounted significantly just after 1520. In such a context, the dismantlement of even a single fort such as that of Colombo meant not only a considerable number of positions lost, but also the prospect of longer and more conflict-laden waiting lists for remunerated occupations elsewhere.

A lack of opportunities is often a key factor in the generation of new projects among those who are not part of the fully established elite, and the Portuguese empire was no exception.[5] One way forward for a petty or mid-ranking noble incapable of securing a lucrative post and yet unwilling to cross the line into the informal empire or beyond, was to propose new fields of action to the crown. Proposals would, ideally, serve to generate military activity and create new payroll positions. They would also draw the administration's attention to particular individuals and increase the chances of a royal grant. The first sign of an inflection in the way Portuguese men in Asia thought about Ceylon appears as early as 1522. A man called Cristóvão Lourenço Caracão wrote from Cochin to the king in Lisbon claiming that the governor needed to be forced to go to Ceylon 'with all the power of India'. The author of the letter suggested to 'invade the land and take the kingdom away from this king [Bhuvanekabāhu VII] and put a king

---

[3] Jorge Flores, 'Portuguese entrepreneurs in the Sea of Ceylon (mid-sixteenth century)', in *Maritime Asia. Profit Maximization, Ethics and Trade Structure, c. 1300–1800*, edited by Karl Anton Sprengard and Roderich Ptak (Wiesbaden: Harrassowitz, 1994), pp. 125–50.

[4] João Paulo Oliveira e Costa, 'A nobreza e a expansão. Particularidades de um fenómeno complexo', in *A Nobreza e a Expansão. Estudos biográficos* (Cascais: Patrimonia Historica, 2000), pp. 13–51.

[5] Alan G. Johnson, 'Opportunity structure, deviance', in *The Blackwell Dictionnary of Sociology. A User's Guide to Sociological Language, Second Edition* (Oxford: Blackwell, 2000), pp. 214–15.

[in place] on behalf of Your Highness'—a puppet king, that is, who would govern the island in conformity with Portuguese interests. The letter also proposed the collection of taxes at all Lankan sea ports. The new king would be able to pay a much higher tribute than Bhuvanekabāhu VII, and peace would reign across 'the land'.[6]

The proposal may seem audacious and could be read as an early sign of conquistadorism in South Asia. But we need to be careful not to project later experiences of conquest, or experiences of conquest made elsewhere, into it. Conflating ideas of conquest into a single concept echoing the Spanish enterprise in the New World does not take us far. Like many other projects that we shall encounter, Caracão's was vague with regard to operational details. Where he does reveal a concrete plan is in the way he places the verb *tomar* ('to take') in proximity to the idea of placing a new king on the throne, rather than taking over the throne as such. This, along with a proposal that the new arrangement would allow for the coinage of money in the island—a practice that had played a strong symbolic role before the arrival of the Portuguese—should make us suspicious.[7] For who was Caracão's source of inspiration? It is certainly significant that the actual travails of imposing order in the island would, in this proposal, be left to others than the Portuguese. A suitable leader could, according to Caracão, be taken from a coastal polity in South India to participate in the invasion and then serve as king in Kōṭṭe. This new ruler would bring Indian troops and rely on them to consolidate his position over the years—the verb *senhorear* ('to dominate') being employed in its gerundive form as '*ir senhoreando*', indicating a clear sense that dominion, and perhaps eventually domination, would be a work in progress. Whoever planted such ideas in Caracão's mind—and it does seem to have been someone in Sri Lanka with close ties to South India—was certainly thinking of the Portuguese as an instrument to achieve a goal other than Portuguese colonization. It is also telling that Caracão remained largely in the dark about the geography of Sri Lanka. He may have had personal ambitions, but his knowledge of the physical realities of the island was poor. His understanding of the 1521 partition was muddled at best, and his description of the kingdom of Kōṭṭe suggests that he saw it essentially as a maritime polity, the interior being insalubrious and of no particular economic or other interest to him. Towards the end of the text, a distant king living in the mountains is vaguely alluded to. The image that Caracão had of Ceylon was blurry, to say the least.

Some years later, in 1529, another Portuguese official of relatively low social standing presented his plans to John III, again writing from Cochin. João Garcês had come to Asia around 1505 and acquired sufficient linguistic skills to serve as an official interpreter—a *língua*—in the fortress at Colombo when it was established in 1518.[8] In 1529 he still described himself as a man with no financial resources or connections—a 'poor foot soldier'—battling in solitude for his distant king. Garcês was a man with a declared interest in what was usually termed as the 'matters of the land' ('*cousas da terra*'). In 1521 already, while still serving in Colombo, he had attempted to convince his captain to intervene in Kōṭṭe and seize the royal

---

[6] Lourenço Caracão to Manuel I, Cochin, 13 January 1522, in Bouchon, 'Les rois de Kotte', p. 167.
[7] See Chapter 2.          [8] Flores, *Os Portugueses*, p. 133.

treasure. This, he himself admitted, was a plan that had emerged from conversations with Lankan nobles in the wake of the assassination of Vijayabāhu VI. After the regicide, a group of local leaders had taken refuge in the fortress and attempted to convince the Portuguese to take sides. Garcês was there and listened. Clearly, the *língua* was a man of little influence in the imperial apparatus, subalternized by the captain of Colombo and later capable of naming as his patrons only a long-gone earlier captain, and an ex-*feitor*. He had every reason to look out for career alternatives, and it must have made much sense to him to propose an extension of the geographical scope of the crown's activities. Kōṭṭe appeared as a possible stage for such a move, and other parts of the region seemed equally in reach. 'Past the island of *Çeyllam*', he wrote, 'there are many ports [...] that will pay many *pareas* to Your Highness if someone was just to go there and collect them.' Garcês even claimed to have 'discovered' the pearl fisheries in the Strait of Mannār, during a captivity he endured near Cape Comorin—yet another instance of local agency in the production of 'Portuguese' knowledge on Asia.[9]

In comparison with the proposal made at the same time by the Duke of Bragança who, as we have seen, argued for an abandonment of most official positions in Asia, Garcês's plans were ambitious, muscular, and forward-looking. What made his proposal most original was that it presented an opportunity for expansion *into* the island. Again, though, the pull factors prove to be key. Garcês's letter relies heavily on information obtained from local interlocutors, and it is here that the driving force of the argument lies:

> This very island is now in such a state that, if the captains so wish, they can take it, because the [royal] brothers are fighting among themselves and the people of the land are all frightened of them and very much desire to see them dead, saying that those who have not respected the law with regard to their father will not respect it with regard to [the people] either.[10]

The 'people of the land' were of course the nobles who had attempted to convince the Portuguese to take sides in 1521 already. Theirs was a mission of awakening Portuguese interest in striking militarily in a moment of crisis. It seems plausible to say that the verb 'taking' (*tomar*) offered a semantically open-ended notion of somehow extending imperial dominion, without going into the details of how this might be handled by the two sides involved. But the cherry on top of the cake presented by Garcês functions at a slightly different discursive level. It consists of a rather extraordinary personal conversation that the *língua* affirms to have had in Kōṭṭe with none other than the old Vijayabāhu VI himself. A monarch who, despite his untimely death, floats majestically above the agitated waters of the *courte durée* as an ultimate source of legitimacy with regard to visions of Lanka as a whole. This is what Garcês writes about him and his dominion:

> of this land I do not wish to say more than what the old king used to say: God gave him a better share [of the world] than to any other king [...] his land was full of precious

⁹ João Garcês to John III, Cochin, 2 January 1529, in Luís de Albuquerque and José Pereira da Costa, 'Cartas de "serviços" da Índia (1500–1530)', *Mare Liberum*, 1 (1990), p. 329.
¹⁰ Garcês to John III, in Albuquerque and Costa, 'Cartas de "serviços"', p. 329.

stones, and the mountains full of elephants, and the hills full of cinnamon and the sea full of pearls, and all this was, he said, thanks to Adam our father having been there, and his footprint being there, and to confirm the truth of this [the king suggested that] I looked at all the other mountains [and how] the said [mountain of Adam] is the highest of them all, and all the others in all four parts [or all four directions of the island] are inclined towards it, and the same [can be seen with] the woods and palm trees, and to hear the truth [about this] I [was told to] ask Franciso Pais, *feitor* of Quilon, because he had seen it.[11]

This is the earliest text written in Portuguese to draw the reader's attention to the interior of the island. The riches produced are in tangible connection with the quasi-mythical land that produces them. Both Garcês and Pais had been exposed, over the years, to much South Indian and Sri Lankan geographical lore. The idea of Lanka as a rich, beautiful, and blessed island thus made its comeback to the Portuguese geographical imagination, from where it had so dramatically been expelled by the cartographers around 1500. This was knowledge transfused directly into and resonnating with the Portuguese system, but not generated by it.

Later developments shall further substantiate this impression, but a caveat is due at this point: no linear increase in the degree of exposure Portuguese individuals had from Lankan and South Indian narratives can be observed. Caracão in 1521 had been less exposed to Lankan lore than Garcês in 1529, but in an anonymous letter from 1530 addressed to John III the Lankan footprint appears again reduced. The author here suggests that Ceylon be handed over 'along with its islands surrounding it' to some Portuguese man of a good lineage, on grounds that they were all lands 'of Your Highness' situated within his nominal sphere of conquest.[12] A first reading of this sketchy formula could suggest that the author was attempting to transfer the Atlantic model of donatary captaincies to Asia, and thus complete the mental operation that Columbus had undergone in the Caribbean in 1492–3, shifting from a project of trade to one of colonization. The Azores and the island of Madeira, where a regime of colonization and economic development had been successfully developed, are mentioned nearby in the letter. There is also reference to how the proposed occupation would limit the 'domination'—*senhorear* is the verb employed, once again—of the island by Muslims. The latter points to an atavistic reflex among many Portuguese nobles, whose ideas for Asia often resonated with the Iberian *reconquista* tradition and its echoes in North Africa, where many had their earliest battlefield experiences.[13] In other words, there are signs here of a rare amalgamation of settling and crusading ideas.

But does this really mean that the author of the 1530 letter imagined Ceylon to be conquered and sliced up for colonization in a hard-hitting combination of the Moroccan (crusading) and the Atlantic islands (colonizing) models? When the letter

[11] Garcês to John III, in Albuquerque and Costa, 'Cartas de "serviços"', p. 329.

[12] Anonymous to John III, s.l. [1530], *Documentos sobre os Portugueses em Moçambique e na África Central, 1497–1840*, vol. VI (Lisbon: CEHU, 1969), p. 298.

[13] See Maria de Lourdes Rosa, 'Velhos, novos e mutáveis sagrados... um olhar antropológico sobre formas "religiosas" de percepção e interpretação da conquista africana (1415–1521)', *Lusitania Sacra*, 2a série, 18 (2006), pp. 13–85.

was written, it must have been abundantly clear to anyone that the prospect of raising cattle or planting sugar cane in Sri Lanka made little sense in comparison with the possibility of trading in cinnamon, elephants, and precious stones. Nor was there any precedent for large territorial conquests anywhere else in the *Estado* at the time. The anonymous proposal was, in fact, not for hundreds of colonists to come and settle, but for one or two *fidalgos* to be allowed to extract revenues and conduct trade (Madagascar, the other island mentioned, was expected to feed three or four). Unsuprisingly, the letter gives away the factional sympathies of the author: it mentions as a potential candidate for the tenure of Lankan revenues the Cochin-based merchant Francisco Pereira, a staunch free trader with interests across the South Indian region. Pereira seems to have been close to Martim Afonso de Sousa, a later governor who during these early years showed no interest whatsoever in building up a land-bound sphere of influence for the crown.[14] Seen under such a light, the 1530 proposal appears in a rather stark contrast with the proposal made by Garcês. It slices up Sri Lanka into generous chunks of territory only to remove these spaces from crown control. It stood closer to the maritime commercial creed of the Cochin traders than to the militarism of certain petty nobles, not to mention the more complex visions of the Lankan elite.

## IMAGINING CONQUEST IN THE EAST:
## THE BOUNDS OF AN IDEA

The construction of the Portuguese image of Ceylon as a surface onto which plans of conquest and other ideas of extended control could later be projected was a process that unfolded tortuously over the 1520s to 1540s. Any ideas of conquering the island as it began to appear in the imagination would depend on variables inherent to the word *conquista* itself. Until well into the fourth decade of the sixteenth century, no Portuguese possession in the Asian sphere of nominal Iberian conquest extended beyond the immediate surroundings of a seaport. Even the ports themselves were rarely the result of a military invasion: with the exception of Goa, Malacca, and Hormuz, most footholds resulted from concessions negotiated with Asian and African rulers. The first Portuguese experience of extensive control over lands in Asia occurred in the so-called 'northern province' (*Província do Norte*) in the mid 1530s, but remains poorly understood. This sizeable stretch of land extending for about 100 km along the littoral between Bassein (occupied in 1534) and Daman (occupied in 1531 and formally ceded to the Portuguese in 1539) resulted from a concession made by Sultan Bahadur in exchange for Portuguese military assistance in Gujarat.[15] It yielded considerable revenues in taxes levied on

[14] On Pereira, see Flores, *Os Portugueses*, pp. 112 and 115.
[15] Dejanirah Couto, 'Em torno da concessão da fortaleza de Baçaim (1529–1546)', *Mare Liberum*, 9 (1995), pp. 117–32. André Teixeira, 'Os primórdios da presença portuguesa em Baçaim— 1534–1554: notas sobre a situação financeira e político-militar do primeiro "território" do Estado da Índia', in *D. João III e o Império. Actas do Congresso Internacional*, edited by Roberto Carneiro and Artur Teodoro de Matos (Lisbon: CHAM/CEPCEP, 2004), pp. 337–65.

agricultural production on the basis of a pre-existing model of prebendal concessions (based on the Indo-Persian *iqṭāʿ*), which the Goan elite and some families residing more closely were quick to appropriate.[16] Yet its administrative and political integration into the *Estado* was tentative, and whilst it has been suggested that there may have been a connection with the push for territorial captaincies in Brazil, which began around 1534, the links seem rather tenuous so far.[17] As we have just seen, an attention to terrestrial revenue does not amount to a fully fledged territorial project. Around Goa itself, the Portuguese only achieved control over the territories of Bardez and Salcete (the so-called 'old conquests') in the late 1540s, under circumstances that are yet to be fully understood.[18]

The incipient, tenuous territorialization of imperial discourses in the *Estado* was complicated at a deeper level by the ambiguities underlying the kind of onto which the idea of conquest might be projected. When it comes to Sri Lanka, we are dealing with territories of the mind construed at the junction between two commensurable and communicating, yet in some ways already quite distinct, cultures of politicizing space. The above-quoted passage from the letter of João Garcês illustrates the conundrum.[19] At first sight, the references to a marvellously rich natural environment resonate with earlier Iberian descriptions of the Caribbean and Brazil. The landscape is lush and fertile. It exudes a primordial, quasi-paradisiac quality reinforced by references to Adam. And yet, in contrast with Brazil, Lanka was *known* not to be void of political powers. If the Portuguese were to gain control here, they knew it had to be against the background of existing political—indeed, imperial—structures and, to be realistically feasible, inevitably in cooperation with the very elite that transmitted such topoi. João Garcês did not even attempt to twist his wording to fit a concept of space more in tune with the emerging European idea of territory, to which we shall come later. In his Lanka, everything converges to pay homage to a single sacred centre. Adam's Peak stands here not only for the mountain as such, but also for the very nature of the Lankan polity: a space revolving centripetally around the figure of the Kōṭṭe monarch and his personal ability to control other rulers around him. This was, again, an expression of power over people, rather than power over lands. The parallel with earlier conceptions of space prevalent in Medieval Europe, fast receding in the Renaissance, are striking.[20]

---

[16] See Luís Frederico Antunes, 'Algumas considerações sobre os prazos de Baçaim e Damão', *Anais de História de Além-Mar*, 3 (2002), pp. 231–57.

[17] Cf. Sanjay Subrahmanyam, 'Holding the World in Balance: The Connected Histories of the Iberian Empires, 1500–1640', *American Historical Review*, 112, 5 (2007), p. 1370.

[18] Cf. Saldanha, *Iustum Imperium*, p. 228 and Ângela Barreto Xavier, *A invenção de Goa: poder imperial e conversões culturais nos séculos XVI e XVII* (Lisbon: ICS, 2008), pp. 74–5. Also see Inácio Guerreiro and Luís de Albuquerque, 'A política de Portugal no Oriente e as suas flutuações', in *Portugal no Mundo*, edited by Luís de Albuquerque, reprint (Lisbon: Alfa, 1993), vol. II, pp. 460–3. It is far from clear to what extent crown policy played a decisive role in these conquests at all.

[19] Garcês to John III, in Albuquerque and Costa, 'Cartas de "serviços"', p. 329.

[20] David Woodward, 'Reality, Symbolism, Time, and Space in Medieval World Maps', *Annals of the Association of American Geographers*, 75, 4 (1985), pp. 510–21 and 'Cartography and the Renaissance: Continuity and Change', in *The History of Cartography*, vol. III, *Cartography in the European Renaissance*, edited by David Woodward (Chicago, IL/London: University of Chicago Press,

We have seen this theme flare up earlier and shall come back to it again, but it seems useful at this point to emphasize how the Lankan notion of a space ordered through personal power relations with a focus on a vertical imperial axis left a heavy imprint on the ways in which early Portuguese individuals attracted by the system came to understand it. It was within the spatial logics of tributary overlordship that much of the opening up of Portuguese minds to Lankan space began, and it would take a long time until this logic was overcome. The very idea of controlling 'all Lanka' as it appears in the projects formulated by Portuguese men from the 1520s onwards, and especially in the 1540s, takes its roots in the Lankan imagination more than in a transplant of the *reconquista* and *povoamento* (settling) ideals from the Atlantic to the Indic. It is in Lanka, more than anywhere else, that we ought to seek the roots of the emerging geographical imagination.

## FROM LUNACY TO POLICY: INTERVENTIONISM AND RELIGIOUS LEGITIMATION

The written record is relatively scarce for the 1530s, but by the time we are able to pick up the thread again, in the early 1540s, ideas for a muscular political and military approach to Ceylon were moving upwards on the social ladder of the *Estado*. How did this happen? How could men such as Caracão and Garcês, petty officials operating with limited reach and struggling to make themselves heard, begin to influence the course of events in an empire with global ambitions?

Personal connections between the men on the ground and some more powerful individuals further up in the hierarchy of the *Estado* (but below the level of governorship) seem to have played a key role. Take Martim Afonso de Sousa, a representative of one of Portugal's most powerful families and a man bound to become governor of India a few years later. Known originally for his interest in keeping government small and independent trade big, Sousa's take on Ceylon and South India started to shift as he was exposed to men operating on the ground—men with whom he conversed especially during his journeys to Lanka in 1537 and 1538. One official who may have had an impact on Sousa is a man called Nuno Freire de Andrade, a *feitor* and *alcaide-mor* who had led Bhuvanekabāhu's Portuguese guard through two sieges.[21] Another connector was a Franciscan commissary who, at the end of the campaign of Miguel Ferreira in 1539, showed up in Colombo on his way from Goa or Cochin to the Coromandel Coast. This friar—probably António Padrão—participated in an ad hoc council that decided to remove another *feitor*, Pero Vaz Travassos, from his post on grounds that he had offended Bhuvanekabāhu. The said council also included a certain Lopo Vaz de Sequeira (possibly a son of Diogo

2007), pp. 3–24. See chapter 8 for a more detailed exploration of the transition to early modern spatiality.

[21] Diogo do Couto, *Da Asia* (Lisbon: Livraria de São Carlos, 1973–1975), vol. V, book i, chapter 6, p. 62. Cf. Fernão de Queiroz, *Conquista Temporal e Espiritual de Ceilão* (Colombo: Government Press, 1916), pp. 161–70.

Lopes de Sequeira) and a man called André de Sousa, who would soon emerge as one of the chief protagonists of the Lankan project patronized by Martim Afonso de Sousa, when the latter became governor.[22] Beyond the well-established and documented decision-makers such as Sousa, these other names signal an increasing number of individuals operating at a clear distance from Lisbon and Goa and willing to explore personal contacts with parts of the Lankan elite. Some may have married into local families, and many more are probably lost to us as they have left no trace in the record. Some became known in Sri Lanka as *Pidalgus*, a pompous designation based on the word *fidalgo*, more often than not at odds with their low social status in the *Estado*.[23] Together, they created the fertile ground upon which Lankan political ideas could fall to then be directed to official decision-makers in the *Estado*.

But what about the receiving end, the highest echelons of Portuguese society in India and Europe? Conversations and epistolary connections alone would not have sufficed to transform a set of ideas unloved by John III into topics of political discussion at the highest level. For the emerging projects to be heard, there needed to be an increased receptiveness at or at least near the top of the hierarchy. In this regard, the cultural history of the reign of John III, stretching from 1521 to 1557 and usually seen as a period of military and financial consolidation in the Asian empire, is key. The period is significantly better understood today than it was a decade or two ago, but its cultural transformations remain poorly appreciated by political historians. Some thus still see the changes of the Joanine period primarily through the prism of the monarch's personal history and 'strategic vision'.[24] In reality, the most interesting hypotheses are clearly those focusing on wider social, cultural, and even aesthetic transformations.[25] Two aspects stand out from the new picture: first, this period saw a significant growth in the emphasis on religion in political discourse; second, there was an increased conflation of the deeds of the Portuguese with those of imperial Rome. The religious inflection appears in the record for Sri Lanka right at the beginning of the decade. In March 1541, the Jesuit Francis Xavier reported how Martim Afonso de Sousa

> told me the other day how in [ . . . ] an island inhabited by Pagans [*gentios*] only, [and] free of Moors or Jews, we shall reap a rich harvest, and he [Sousa] sees no difficulty in [having] the king of that island [of Ceylon] become a Christian along with all the people [of his kingdom].[26]

There are various ideas at work in this brief passage pointing to a complex, ongoing process of connection and incipient intertwinement at the intersection between Lankan *cakravartism* and Catholic Universalism. The motif of a single Lankan

---

[22] Miguel Ferreira to John III, Goa, 26 November 1539, in Georg Schurhammer and Ernst August Voretzsch, *Ceylon zur Zeit des Königs Bhuvaneka Bahu und Franz Xavers 1539–1552* (Leipzig: Verlag der Asia Major, 1928) (henceforth cited as '*Ceylon*'), p. 89.

[23] Cf. *Rājāvaliya*, p. 80.

[24] Cf. João Paulo Oliveira e Costa, 'O Império português em meados do século XVI', in *Anais de História de Além-Mar*, 3 (2002), pp. 107, 110–11.

[25] Cf. Luís Filipe Thomaz, 'Estrutura política e administrativa do Estado da Índia', in *De Ceuta a Timor*, 2nd edition (Lisbon: Difel, 1998), pp. 207–43.

[26] Francis Xavier to Ignacio de Loyola and Jean Codure, Lisbon, 18 March 1541, *Ceylon*, p. 98.

monarch ruling over the island and taking with him its 'entire population' on the path to conversion is so perfectly in tune with both traditions that even contemporaries failed to realize how the formula combined two very different strands of thought into one fabulously plausible idea. Suddenly the old topos of militarily unifying Lanka under one overlord appeared bathed in a new light that was bound, in the specific conjuncture of the 1540s, to facilitate its reception on the higher echelons of Portuguese society. The theme of 'spiritual conquest' began to move into Portuguese hearts and minds.

Historians have been tempted to see the religious surge in Portugal and its empire under John III as a result of the appearance of the Jesuits in the early 1540s. This, along with an anachronistic take on the confessional inflection resulting from the Counter-reform (the Council of Trent only began in 1545), has considerably fraught the understanding of the processes involved.[27] Recent findings leave little doubt that the beginnings of the dynamic go back to the 1530s and that it is best understood as a combination of closely intertwined political, social, and aesthetic developments.[28] Well before the Jesuits could even think of establishing themselves in Ceylon, a division of the Franciscans known as *Piedosos* or *Capuchos* was observing the island and making plans to settle there. These discalced friars, only recently identified as key players for Ceylon by Alan Strathern, played an important role in giving the Portuguese interactions with Lankan elites a religious dimension.[29] They were protégés of the Dukes of Bragança, who had welcomed them in their lands around 1500, and as such a logical presence in a region traditionally placed in the sphere of influence of the commercialist lobby and its sub-imperialists supporters in South India. Ironically, however, they soon began to engage in the formulation of plans for the island that involved a more substantial crown-sponsored intervention.

The new religious fervour came, it must be added, wrapped in sober clothes. After the death of Manuel I, prophecies about the imminent arrival of the messianic

[27] For a thorough introduction to the matter, Federico Palomo, *A Contra-Reforma em Portugal, 1540–1700* (Lisbon: Livros Horizonte, 2006). Some useful additional notes on the problem of confessionalization in Portugal can be found in Maria Helena Queirós, 'A Contra-Reforma em Portugal 1540–1700, Federico Palomo, Lisboa, Livros Horizonte, 2006, 130 p. Nota crítica à obra', in *Via Spiritus*, 16 (2009), pp. 175–86.

[28] See Ângela Barreto Xavier, '"Aparejo y disposición para se reformar y criar outro nuevo mundo." A evangelização dos indianos e a política imperial joanina', in *D. João III e o Império. Actas do Congresso Internacional*, edited by Roberto Carneiro and Artur Teodoro de Matos (Lisbon: CHAM/CEPCEP, 2004), pp. 783–805. Alan Strathern, '*Os Piedosos* and the Mission in India and Sri Lanka in the 1540s', ibid., pp. 855–64; Biedermann, 'De regresso ao Quarto Império', ibid., pp. 103–20. For a more conventional approach see João Paulo Oliveira e Costa, 'A diáspora missionária', in *História Religiosa de Portugal*, edited by Carlos Moreira Azevedo (Lisbon: Círculo de Leitores, 2000), vol. II, pp. 273–8. Giuseppe Marcocci, *L'invenzione di un impero. Politica e cultura nel mondo portoghese (1450–1600)* (Rome: Carocci, 2010), p. 60 has argued that the acknowledgement of the small number of Christians in Asia by Pedro Margalho in his *Phisices Compendium* (1520) may already be a sign announcing this dynamic.

[29] Strathern, 'Os Piedosos'. On their first patron, see Maria de Lurdes Rosa, 'D. Jaime, duque de Bragança: entre a cortina e a vidraça', in *O tempo de Vasco da Gama*, edited by Diogo Ramada Curto (Lisbon: Difel, 1998), pp. 319–32.

Fifth Empire were branded as heterodox.[30] Conversion, the authorities now contended, would take time and much hard work to happen globally. Rather than looking forward in exaltation to the end of time, the elites began to refer to the Roman empire again.[31] There was a vigorous re-introduction of the Renaissance style in art and literature through royal and aristocratic patronage from the mid 1520s, and most markedly from the 1530s.[32] In contrast with the flamboyant excesses of Manueline art, the reign of John III brought the adoption, first, of a simplified Italianate style, and second, of a more elaborate, but remarkably stripped-down version of mature Renaissance architectural fashions, giving birth to the so-called 'Portuguese plain style'.[33]

The new *Pax Lusitana* resonated with the world of Constantine more than that of Augustus, its subjects fantasizing about an empire that would engage in (re)Christianizing itself to then Christianize, with method, the rest of the world.[34] In other words, the renewed emphasis on religion came with a heightened attention to *Romanitas*, which in its turn required a renewed attention to imperial space in two ways: on the one hand, because the memory of Rome was inherently one of territorial conquest and sweeping Romanization, the material heritage of which was being rediscovered across Portugal precisely at this time; and on the other hand, because Portugal itself, and then its overseas possessions, began to transmute in the minds of many into a receptacle for a religiously homogenous society.[35] The Joanine period saw the unfolding of anxieties about religious diversity in Portuguese society, and increasingly the imposition of a new, vigorously normative kind of social discipline through religion.[36]

---

[30]  Luís Filipe Thomaz, 'L'idée impériale manuéline', p. 100.

[31]  Rafael Moreira, 'Cultura Material e Visual', in *História da Expansão Portuguesa*, edited by Francisco Bethencourt and Kirti Chaudhuri (Lisbon: Temas e Debates, 1998), vol. I, p. 480.

[32]  Moreira, *A Arquitectura do Renascimento no Sul de Portugal*. Ana Maria Alves, *As Entradas Régias Portuguesas. Uma Visão de Conjunto* (Lisbon: Livros Horizonte, 1986), pp. 36–49 and *Iconologia do poder real no período manuelino. À procura de uma linguagem perdida* (Lisbon: IN-CM, 1985). Also see *História da Arte Portuguesa*, vol. II, *Do 'Modo' Gótico ao Maneirismo*, edited by Paulo Pereira (Lisbon: Temas e Debates, 1995) and Jorge Muchagato, 'Os valores artísticos. A arquitectura', in *Nova História de Portugal*, vol. V, edited by João José Alves Dias (Lisbon: Presença, 1998), pp. 505–42.

[33]  George Kubler, *A Arquitectura Portuguesa Chã. Entre as Especiarias e os Diamantes (1521–1706)*, 2nd ed. (Lisbon: Nova Vega, 2005), pp. 42–3. Also see Sylvie Deswartes, *Les enluminures de la Leitura Nova 1504–1552. Etude sur la culture artistique au Portugal au temps de l'Humanisme* (Paris: Fondation Calouste Gulbenkian, 1977), pp. 184–95.

[34]  Portuguese historians have weighted the various components of the process differently. Francisco Bethencourt, 'A Inquisição', in *Portugal: Mitos Revisitados*, edited by Yvette K. Centeno *et al.* (Lisbon: Edições Salamandra, 1993), pp. 99–138 has highlighted the penetration of the Inquisition tribunals by royal power. José Pedro Paiva, 'A Igreja e o Poder: Interpenetração da Igreja e do Estado', in *História Religiosa de Portugal*, vol. II, p. 139 has emphasized, inversely, the 'clericalization' of government.

[35]  Xavier, 'Aparejo y disposición'. Strathern, 'Os Piedosos'. Biedermann, 'De regresso ao Quarto Império'. On *romanitas* also see Anthony Pagden, *Lords of All the World: Ideologies of Empire in Spain, Britain and France, c. 1500–1800* (New Haven, CT/London: Yale University Press, 1995).

[36]  Cf. António José Saraiva, *História da Cultura em Portugal*, reedited in collaboration with Óscar Lopes and Luís de Albuquerque (Lisbon: Gradiva, 2000), vol. II, pp. 161–240. Francisco Bethencourt, *História das Inquisições. Portugal, Espanha e Itália* (Lisbon: Temas e Debates, 1996). Also see Xavier, 'Aparejo y disposición', pp. 787–8 for a critique of the simplistic division of John's reign into one 'cosmopolitan' and another more zealous 'phase', a theory largely due to José Sebastião da Silva Dias, *A política cultural da época de D. João III*.

Because the peoples of Asia were mostly beyond the reach of Portuguese secular and religious authorities, the effects of the confessional and classicist turns occurred in substantial measure in the imagination. A good example of this is the creation of the bishopric of Goa in the 1530s, soon followed by ideas of creating an episcopate for Ceylon. As a political act it reflects a conscious attempt by the crown to add symbolic value to Goa as an administrative centre that had only recently taken over from Cochin.[37] The transfer, begun under the viceroy Nuno da Cunha in 1529, prepared the ground for the making of Goa into a 'Rome of the East'.[38] It was through a combination of political and religious functions that the city assumed its full imperial status and could begin to radiate across South Asia as a whole. Most interestingly, the creation of the episcopate implied the drawing of borders well beyond the bounds of the *Estado*. Vast stretches of the continent were sliced up for potential spiritual conquest—but of course none of this tended to be in tune with existing political boundaries, let alone any military capabilities of the *Estado*.

This mental reorganization is reflected in a little-noticed piece of written advice submitted by a body of court lawyers (*letrados*) to John III around November 1545. A central theme of the paper was that dioceses and provinces should be created with clear borders to improve the spreading of the Catholic faith.[39] That this was not just a lofty idea becomes evident from a letter written by Francis Xavier to Ignacio de Loyola a little earlier, in 1542. There already, Xavier talked enthusiastically about plans to regroup scattered Christian populations from South India and make them settle in Mannār, an island off the Lankan coast, creating clearly delimited confessional territories and consolidating Portuguese power in the straits. The Christians, Xavier suggested, would need to be placed under Portuguese jurisdiction and religious control—in all likelihood a process to be led by missionaries, though the deployment of military officials to protect the Catholic colony was probably considered as well.[40] The area originally covered by the bishop of Goa—essentially, all Asia—thus began to be subdivided into new virtual territories. These became powerful vehicles for imaginary territorialization at the higher levels of society,[41] precisely where Joanine caution also dictated material austerity:[42] a paradox

---

[37] See José Pedro Paiva, 'Dioceses e organização eclesiástica', in *História Religiosa de Portugal*, vol. II (Lisbon: Círculo de Leitores, 2000), pp. 187–99 and Costa, 'A diáspora missionária: os bispados ultramarinos', ibid., pp. 281–4, with a comprehensive analysis of the creation of dioceses.

[38] Catarina Madeira Santos, '*Goa é a chave de toda a Índia*. *Perfil político da capital do Estado da Índia (1505–1570)* (Lisbon: CNCDP, 1999), pp. 201–78.

[39] Advisory paper (*parecer*), [Évora], [November 1545?], *Ceylon*, p. 261.

[40] Xavier to Loyola, Tuticorin, 28 October 1542, in *Epistolae S. Francisci Xaverii aliaque eius scripta, nova editio ex integro refecta*, edited by Georg Schurhammer and Joseph Wicki, vol. I (Rome: IHSI, 1944), pp. 150–1.

[41] Sanjay Subrahmanyam, 'Du Tage au Gange au XVIe siècle: une conjoncture millénariste à l'échelle eurasiatique', in *Annales HSS*, 56, 1 (2001), pp. 51–84 sees territorialization at play for the first time in the activities of Martim Afonso de Sousa. A more cautious approach appears in Xavier, 'Aparejo y disposición', pp. 794–5.

[42] Cf. Roger Chartier, 'Construção do Estado Moderno e formas culturais. Perspectivas e questões', in *A História Cultural entre Práticas e Representações*, edited by Roger Chartier (Lisbon: Difel, 1988), pp. 215–29. On the spatial and social structures in Portugal and attempts to reform them see João José Alves Dias, *Gentes e espaços (em torno da população portuguesa na primeira metade do século XVI)* (Lisbon: JNICT, 1996).

breaching the consolidative logics of crown politics, but also playing into them by shifting attention from military and commercial to religious expansion—the third and last facet of Portuguese expansionism to take shape in Asia, after the official *Estado* and the shadow empire.

Reading the letters of Francis Xavier in particular, one can see how the notion of spiritual conquest was taking shape as a militant enterprise with its own incipient territoriality.[43] Importantly here—in contrast with the vast space of the Indian subcontinent—the island itself as a geographical form predisposed to host a single coherent society was gaining some power over Portuguese minds. In other words, a new 'diocese of Ceylon' could be seen to coincide 'naturally' with the whole of the island. It is important, however, to keep this surge in connection with everything we have said before. However freshly the Jesuits may have come from Rome to Ceylon, they still absorbed old Lankan topoi. When the Ignatians were allowed, for a brief moment in the early 1550s, to plan their own missions in the island otherwise seen as a Franciscan field of action, the Jesuit Baltasar Gago fantasized not only how Sri Lankans would be easy to convert; he also wrote that

> this land is the best there is in the world. The woods are of cinnamon in many parts, and other parts yield oranges, *sidrões*, and lemons; it has a great many rivers and sources and is very rich and fertile.[44]

Such words could have come straight out of the mouth of a Lankan ruler—and indeed, as we shall see, they probably did. It makes sense to argue that political Catholicism allowed for topoi with a religious-territorial potential to gain respectability at the interface between Lankan and Lusitanian imperial discourses. The following sub-chapters consolidate this impression. They explore the process with reference to various parts of Sri Lanka, in an attempt to order the often devilishly complicated political and diplomatic connections of the mid-sixteenth century geographically.[45] Ideally, they should then be drawn together in one vast tableau, as I shall attempt further below.

## A NEW LAND IN THE STRAITS: MILITARY PLANS FOR JAFFNA (1540–1545)

Jaffna in the North of Sri Lanka was one of the earliest foci of Portuguese diplomatic activity to see the intertwinement of religious and military arguments. The beginnings of this process may well be in closer connection to South Indian developments than to Kōṭṭe politics. Whilst no single polity controlled the straits in the sixteenth

---

[43] See for example, on South India and Ceylon, Xavier to Company, Cochin, 27 January 1545, in *Monumenta Xaveriana* (Madrid: Typis Augustini Aurial, 1899–1912), vol. I, pp. 365–72 and, with critical notes, in *Ceylon*, pp. 141–4.

[44] Baltasar Gago to the Company in Portugal, Cochin, 20 January 1552, *Ceylon*, pp. 575–6.

[45] See C. R. De Silva, 'The Rise and Fall of the Kingdom of Sitawaka (1521–1593)', *The Ceylon Journal of Historical and Social Studies*, 7, 1 (1977), pp. 1–43 and Tikiri Abeyasinghe, 'The Politics of Survival: Aspects of Kandyan External Relations in the Mid-Sixteenth Century', in *Journal of the Royal Asiatic Society of Sri Lanka*, New Series, XVII (1973), pp. 11–21.

century, Indian hegemonic claims over the area were still in the air. Both Vijayanagara and Travancore had claimed overlordship over the kingdom of Jaffna in the early years of the century. Like the rulers of Kōṭṭe, those of Jaffna were used to paying tribute—mostly in the form of elephants—in return for military assistance and, at times, Indian-born troops. Caṅkili, king of Jaffna (r.1519–61), relied largely on Telugu-speaking warriors who settled in Lankan villages in exchange for their military services. He had every reason to be worried after his likely involvement in the assassination of king Pararājasekaran, his father, and in the destitution of his own older brother, the chosen successor to the throne, in 1519.[46]

This brother, known as Varothaya, spent much of his life in exile in the Kayalpatnam area of modern Tamil Nadu aspiring to regain power. As a junior prince his position was comparable to that of Māyādunnē, but unlike the latter, he did not have a 'real' power basis in the form of villages, let alone a capital such as Sītāvaka. At some point, perhaps as early as the 1520s, he understood that Portuguese support might be of use to him in his project of overthrowing Caṅkili. But only around 1540 does he reappear in the written record. At that point—and we can only imagine how many unsuccessful attempts at lobbying the *Estado* Varothaya had made in the meantime—he finally convinced the viceroy Garcia de Noronha (gv.1538–40) to examine his claims, resulting in orders to the Portuguese captain of the Fishery Coast, João Fernandes Correia, to mount an expedition to Jaffna. This plan failed due to Correia's blatant lack of interest, but Varothaya did not relent. In 1543, we see him travelling to Cow Island near Jaffna on board a fleet commanded by governor Martim Afonso de Sousa (gv.1542–5), having paid the latter the sizeable sum of 4000 *pardaus*. Again, he was to be disappointed. Sousa accepted an offer of tribute by Caṅkili amounting to 5000 *pardaus* and abandoned the campaign.[47]

Finally, in 1544, the prince upped his bid. He proposed nothing less than to be baptized. And whilst we do not know when exactly he first made this proposal, it did happen roughly at the same time as another Lankan prince, Jugo Baṇḍāra, whom we shall meet again soon, took baptism in Colombo from André de Sousa—a man who had been in close contact with Martim Afonso de Sousa before. The web was tightening. In January 1545, Francis Xavier had an encounter with Varothaya in the South of India, during which the two conversed about the recent massacre of Christians perpetrated by Caṅkili in the island of Mannār.[48] Xavier did not hesitate to report back to Europe that

---

[46] Cf. C. R. De Silva and S. Pathmanathan, 'The Kingdom of Jaffna up to 1620', in *University of Peradeniya History of Sri Lanka*, vol. II, edited by K. M. de Silva (Peradeniya: University of Peradeniya, 1995), pp. 106–7.

[47] Queiroz, *Conquista*, p. 144. Miguel Ferreira to João de Castro, São Tomé de Meliapor, 28 March 1546, *Ceylon*, pp. 346–7. Gaspar Correia, *Lendas da Índia*, edited by M. Lopes de Almeida (Porto: Lello & Irmão, 1975), vol. IV, p. 325.

[48] In 1544, several thousand fishing folks in Mannār were converted within little more than a month. When Xavier left, Caṅkili had around 600 neophytes killed. The massacre is described in detail, though with considerable exaggeration, in A. J. B. Antoninus, *The Martyrs of Mannar. Second enlarged edition* (Colombo: St Joseph Press, 1945). Cf. Schurhammer, *Francis Xavier*, vol. II, pp. 470–1.

The king who killed these Christians [of Mannār] has a brother who is the true heir of the kingdom [...] This brother says [...] that if the [Portuguese] governor can put him in possession of the kingdom, he shall become a Christian with the principal [men] of his kingdom. The governor is thus ordering his captains that, if this brother of the king becomes a Christian along with his people, they should hand over the kingdom to him, and kill the king who killed the Christians, or do whatever I request on behalf of the governor.[49]

According to Xavier, Caṇkili's brother Varothaya was the favourite candidate in Goa for controlling Jaffna. Yet the expedition never took off, and for a very prosaic reason: a Portuguese ship coming from Pegu was stranded near Jaffna and the influential owner, hoping to regain his merchandise, put pressure on the authorities not to meddle in local affairs.[50] But the Jaffna question remained open, as is further illustrated by an episode from early 1546, when the new viceroy João de Castro (vr.1545–8) ordered Varothaya to be contacted again. Miguel Ferreira—who had led the 1538–9 expedition against Māyādunnē—found the prince residing three leagues from Kayalpatnam, in India, with 'his son, his grandchildren and many of his relatives and friends', still hoping someday to sit on the throne in Jaffna.[51] Ferreira promised Varothaya that he would do everything 'to put him in possession of the kingdom' and sailed to Mannār, where he discussed the options with the new captain of the Fishery Coast, Aires de Figueiredo. The decision was made to organize an expedition against Jaffna in September 1546. Back home in São Tomé de Meliapor, on the Coromandel Coast, Ferreira—the very man who had gone after Māyādunnē and his Muslim allies without even mentioning the Catholic faith in 1539—wrote to the governor:

> Believe me, Your Lordship, that if you order Jafanapatão to be taken, you will make over two hundred thousand Christian souls, and I say this on grounds of what I have seen and what I know [...] Just consider the greatness of this service to God, and whether the King Our Lord will be contented or not, Your Lordship shall know.[52]

However opportunistic Ferreira and Varothaya may come across here, their letters matter because, increasingly, people further up began to listen. In the background, an image of Sri Lanka began to emerge that was far more comprehensive than before. Jaffna had, in earlier decades, been seen primarily as a place facing the strait, rather than a part of Lanka. Now, Jaffna was not only becoming a little territory—to be controlled through a vassal ruler, to be conquered through mass conversions—in the imagination of some. It also began to grow together with the rest of Lanka into the larger geographical unit designated as *Ceilão*. 'This island of Jafanapatão', one observer notes in November 1545, 'is not an island of its own but the very same island as Ceilão.'[53] The change may seem subtle because the documentation

---

[49] Xavier to the Company in Rome, Cochin, 27 January 1545, *Ceylon*, p. 143.
[50] Xavier to Diogo de Borba and Misser Paulo, São Tomé de Meliapor, 8 May 1545, *Ceylon*, pp. 146–7.
[51] Miguel Ferreira to João de Castro, São Tomé de Meliapor, 28 March 1546, *Ceylon*, p. 347.
[52] Ferreira to Castro, São Tomé de Meliapor, 28 March 1546, *Ceylon*, p. 348.
[53] André de Sousa to John III, Goa, 15 November, *Ceylon*, p. 214.

is scarce, but from the 1540s onwards Jaffna assumed an increasingly important role in the Portuguese imagination not only as a key piece in the South Indian great game, but also as a potential launching pad for expeditions into the rest of Lanka.

## BETWEEN THALASSOCRACY AND 'CAKRAVARTISM': THE PRINCES OF KŌṬṬE, 1543–1545

Where Jaffna offers us sketchy impressions at best, Kōṭṭe allows for a more comprehensive analysis. The new conjuncture appears to have been ignited by the appearance of the discalced Franciscans from Portugal in the wake of the embassy of Śrī Rāmarakṣa. The little group of friars arrived in 1543 following what some at the court of John III had interpreted as a hint that Bhuvanekabāhu VII might be willing to convert.[54] Logically, the friars insisted that such a promise be kept, preaching to the king and organizing debates on religious matters.[55] The important point for this study is that the news about the friars and their insistence on conversion spread fast. In 1544 alone, three potential heirs to the throne of Kōṭṭe, all young men sidelined by Bhuvanekabāhu, were baptized.

The first of these neophytes was Jugo Baṇḍāra, a disgruntled son of Bhuvanekabāhu. Jugo had enjoyed his father's support as an heir until 1539,[56] when the birth of Dharmapāla, Bhuvanekabāhu's daughter's son, left him empty-handed. He survived as a member of a faction hostile to the king at Kōṭṭe and became attached to a Portuguese middleman who was beginning to act as a lobbyist for Lankan matters in the *Estado*, André de Sousa.[57] When he converted in 1544 and made plans to leave for Goa, Bhuvanekabāhu VII had him assassinated.[58] It is certainly significant that the task of killing Jugo was given to Vīdiyē Baṇḍāra, the father of Dharmapāla. But Jugo's supporters did not stand by idly. They developed their own microdiplomacy with the Franciscans, who soon saw to it that Jugo's death was followed by news of miraculous signs. The earth was rumoured to have quaked, and the Holy Cross to have appeared in the sky above Kōṭṭe. The soil of the island opened up in the shape of the cross where the prince had been martyred. Such tales spread quickly to the Portuguese possessions in India and contributed to a wider atmosphere of religious exaltation.[59]

[54] The promise, accompanied by an equally controversial note on the supposed conversion of Śrī Rāmarakṣa, is included in the Latin summary of the Jesuitic letters that arrived at Rome in 1543, *Ceylon*, pp. 107–8. Also see the account in Francisco Gonzaga, *De origine seraphicae religionis* (Rome, 1587), probably taken from a report written in the island in 1543 or 1544, reproduced with annotations in *Ceylon*, pp. 125–34. According to this document, Bhuvanekabāhu made it clear in 1543 already that this was a misunderstanding, and Śrī Rāmarakṣa is reported to have declared not to have made any promise either.

[55] See Strathern, 'Os Piedosos'.

[56] Jugo Baṇḍāra may have been one of two sons of Bhuvanekabāhu who had received Miguel Ferreira at Colombo in 1539. *Ceylon*, p. 85.

[57] Sousa to Prince Henry, Goa, 15 November 1545, *Ceylon*, p. 203.

[58] Xavier to Company, Cochin, 27 January 1545, *Ceylon*, p. 143. Sousa to Dom Henrique, *Ceylon*, p. 203.

[59] Sousa to Prince Henry, Goa, 15 November 1545, *Ceylon*, p. 203.

Following this first sacrifice in the name of Christ, a new culture of religiously flavoured diplomacy began to grow. Briefly after the death of Jugo, two other disgruntled princes contacted Sousa. Both were taken by Portuguese soldiers to the Franciscan church at Colombo for baptism and, much to the distress of Bhuvanekabāhu, managed to escape to India.[60] It is telling that around the same time another source mentions how the Sinhalese ruler had lost trust in his Portuguese guard and hired men of other origins.[61] The Sinhalese king's opponents retreated to India only to escalate their attack and, in their communications, go global. The elder of the princes, who had taken the name Dom João in honour of the Portuguese monarch,[62] arrived at Cochin with his entourage, accompanied by André de Sousa, on 27 January 1545. On the same day, the prince signed a letter addressed to the Queen of Portugal, which was immediately dispatched to Lisbon.[63] He also met Francis Xavier, who described the encounter with no further delays in another letter. There, the Jesuit affirmed confidently that 'before long many [people] of that kingdom [of Ceilão] will convert to our Holy Faith' because the people were 'deeply moved' by the miracles that occurred at Jugo's funeral and, perhaps most importantly, because 'the prince [...] is the heir to the kingdom'.[64] The lucky coincidence of the party's arrival from Colombo with the departure of an official fleet from Cochin to Lisbon, along with André de Sousa's evident managerial skills, ensured that the cause of Dom João, cast in a Catholic frame, could receive proper diffusion.

The princes then moved to Goa. Dom João and his younger brother, who had taken the name of Dom Luís in honour of the Portuguese king's junior sibling, set up quarters in a property owned by André de Sousa. They were not alone: with them were 'many honoured people' determined to accompany them in the quest for power in Sri Lanka.[65] Sousa covered their expenses and kept a keen eye on their education and public relations. The future of a Lankan political faction hostile to Bhuvanekabāhu VII began to take shape between the house of a private individual involved in Lankan affairs and a governor increasingly interested in South Indian matters, at a time when the crown itself remained incapable of formulating a compelling new policy for Ceylon. Martim Afonso de Sousa (gv.1542–5) received the princes well and, although he had no official mandate to do so, granted Dom João the Lankan villages that had belonged to Jugo Baṇḍāra. Decisions and symbolic gestures were beginning to be made in Goa about affairs pertaining strictly to the Lankan monarchy—without a word from Lisbon. The grant even included

---

[60] Sousa to Prince Henry, Goa, 15 November 1545, *Ceylon*, p. 203.

[61] João de Vila do Conde to João de Castro [Kōṭṭe], 17 November 1545, *Ceylon*, p. 224.

[62] Xavier to Company, Cochin, 27 January 1545, *Ceylon*, p. 143.

[63] Dom João wrote at least one letter to Queen Catherine that day, cf. *Ceylon*, p. 185. For the date see p. 202. The younger Dom Luís came a week later. Dom João to John III, Goa, November 1545, *Ceylon*, p. 216.

[64] Francis Xavier to Rome, Cochin, 27 January 1545, *Ceylon*, p. 144. In May 1545, Xavier was already writing that he hoped to see Jesuits accompanying the princes to Ceylon. Xavier to Mestre Diogo de Borba and Misser Paulo, São Tomé de Meliapor, 8 May 1545, *Ceylon*, pp. 146–7.

[65] Dom João to Queen Catherine, Goa, 15 October 1545, *Ceylon*, p. 187.

a seaport which, evidently, the prince, his mentor, and the governor saw as a potential alternative to Colombo.[66]

But why did the governor back a plan brought to Goa from the periphery of the empire at a time when John III was nominally committed to Bhuvanekabāhu VII as his sole Lankan vassal? The governor had led a tentative pillaging expedition to the South of India in 1543 and may have been looking for other opportunities nearby.[67] In terms of image management, the timing was perfect because a campaign in the Sea of Ceylon could be styled as revenge for the Jaffna king Caṅkili's massacre of the Christians of Mannār, a little island off the Lankan northwestern littoral, in 1544.[68] Amidst the haze of personal ambition, greed, and political cunning, a larger strategic horizon also began to emerge which attracted interest. An armed strike against Jaffna now came to be seen as a step forward in the creation of a Christian vassal kingdom in the straits, and a matter connected with the future of Kōṭṭe. In July 1545, Goa saw the arrival of an embassy precisely from Jaffna, with nobles expressing their support for Dom João and Dom Luís as candidates to the throne in Kōṭṭe. As we have seen already, the enemies of Caṅkili, some of whom were exiled in India, had themselves started to target the Portuguese as a potential ally. In fact, the 1545 Jaffna delegation to Goa *also* proclaimed that Dom João was the legitimate heir to the throne of Jaffna. The argument put forward was curiously twisted: because the people of Jaffna had 'formerly been vassals of the king of *Ceilão*', Dom João was, as a legitimate heir of Bhuvanekabāhu, entitled to the throne of Jaffna.[69] This is ironic because Jaffna had been among the first to cease paying tribute to Kōṭṭe in the late fifteenth century, and because the delegates invoked the potential of Bhuvanekabāhu VII to be *cakravarti* over all Lanka in an attempt to legitimize a candidate anxious to undermine precisely the latter's authority. But such contradictions were not perceived as obstacles in Goa. Martim Afonso de Sousa ordered a fleet to be put together to place Dom João on the Jaffna throne.

The initiative only came to a halt due to the arrival of a new viceroy, João de Castro, in early September 1545.[70] Castro (vr. 1545-48) arrived in Asia as a man of caution, disinclined to military action on the land. He famously wrote:

Under no circumstances should the Portuguese enter as much as a handspan into the interior of India, because nothing keeps the peace and conserves our friendship with the kings and lords of India, except that they believe and consider it most certain that we are content with the sea, and that we have no plans for, nor do we imagine that we will ever come to desire, their lands.[71]

---

[66] Dom João to John III, Goa, 15 November 1545, *Ceylon*, p. 217.

[67] Georg Schurhammer, *Francis Xavier: His Life, His Times*, 4 vols. (Rome: IHSI, 1973–1982), vol. II, pp. 360–80. Sanjay Subrahmanyam, 'An Eastern El-Dorado'. Cf. Flores, *Os Portugueses*, pp. 191–3 and Queiroz, *Conquista*, pp. 197–201.

[68] Dom João to John III, Goa, 15 November 1545, *Ceylon*, pp. 217–18.

[69] André de Sousa to John III, Goa, 15 November 1545, *Ceylon*, p. 213.

[70] Dom João to John III, Goa, 15 November 1545, *Ceylon*, p. 217.

[71] *Cartas de D. João de Castro a D. João III*, edited by Luís de Albuquerque (Lisbon, 1989), p. 12, quoted and translated in Subrahmanyam, 'Holding the World in Balance', p. 1373.

Whilst the new viceroy paid due respect to the Sinhalese princes, he put the campaign planned under Sousa on hold and attempted to gain a clearer picture by dispatching two men of his own trust, Duarte Barbudo and the Franciscan *Piedoso* friar João de Vila do Conde, to Kōṭṭe.[72] Ironically though, Castro's cautions led to an increase in unfavourable news about Bhuvanekabāhu VII. Barbudo's arrival in Kōṭṭe coincided with what must have been the lowest point in the long story of Lankan vassalage to John III. The Sinhalese king felt upset about the breaking, not only by dispersed individuals, but also by the head of the *Estado*, of the central clause agreed upon in Lisbon in 1542: that his grandson Dharmapāla shall be considered the only legitimate heir to his throne. News about Martim Afonso de Sousa's preparations for an expedition had reached Kōṭṭe fast: when the first vessels of the cinnamon fleet arrived at Colombo in September 1545, Bhuvanekabāhu was already aware that the princes were to be brought home to challenge him.[73] He was also worried, as always, about rival Lankan nobles gaining access to Portuguese communicational channels.

Palace intrigues in Kōṭṭe were at their most complicated. Now, a hostile queen consort gave signs of wishing to convert and encouraged the Goan authorities to support Dom João and Dom Luís against her husband.[74] Such activities at the heart of the Lankan court, threatening enough per se, had increased chances of resonating across the Portuguese apparatus up to the highest echelons, where Bhuvanekabāhu had hitherto felt his position to be relatively secure. In October 1545, Dom João wrote directly to Queen Catherine in Lisbon, urging her to remind her husband of how his mother was awaiting him in Kōṭṭe, ready to rise against Bhuvanekabāhu and support him as a Christian king. Inevitably, the prince concluded that 'the entire island of Ceilão will become Christian, and God Our Lord shall be praised'.[75] The author of another letter sent from Goa to Europe around the same time repeated the idea that 'the majority' of people in Ceylon wanted to become Christians seven times on a single sheet of paper.[76]

For such reasons alone Bhuvanekabāhu had much to fear. But the official exploratory mission of Duarte Barbudo and frei João de Vila do Conde also coincided with the arrival of another piece of rather spectacular news: the king of Kandy was promising to convert. We shall see the details of this proposal, which opened up a whole new front for plans of military intervention, further below. The consequences for Bhuvanekabāhu were dramatic. Pressure was mounting against him on various fronts, and he was being beaten where he always thought he had the decisive edge, in his privileged personal relationship with the Portuguese royal family. New throne candidates and rival kings were managing to transmit their messages across the globe, into the highest echelons of Portuguese society, promising the one thing that Bhuvanekabāhu was not willing to do: to convert to

---

[72] Sousa to John III, Goa, 15 November 1545, *Ceylon*, p. 213. Dom João to John III, Goa, 15 November 1545, *Ceylon*, p. 218.
[73] Francisco Álvares to João de Castro, Kōṭṭe, 6 October 1545, *Ceylon*, p. 170.
[74] Álvares to João de Castro, Kōṭṭe, 6 October 1545, *Ceylon*, pp. 171–2.
[75] Dom João to Catherine, Goa, 15 October 1545, *Ceylon*, p. 186.
[76] Juan de Beira to Martín de Santa Cruz, Goa, 20 November 1545, *Ceylon*, pp. 226–7.

the Christian faith. In fact, the news from Kandy even put pressure on Dom João and Dom Luís. The promise of conversion formulated in the hitherto untalked of kingdom of Kandy quickly generated interest. As even André de Sousa, the Kōṭṭe princes' mentor, showed signs of being enthused by the Kandyan project towards the end of 1545, Dom João and Dom Luís had to up their game. And so they did.

## THE 'MATRIOSHKA PRINCIPLE' STOLEN: DOM JOÃO PROPOSES TO JOHN III

In November 1545, Dom João and his Franciscan counselor Mestre Diogo, certainly still with some assistance by André de Sousa, put into writing one of the most ambitious political plans proposed for Ceylon in the sixteenth century. What they produced in Goa was an explosive amalgamation of Portuguese and Lankan ideas of kingship, empire, conversion, and conquest, skillfully intertwined and adapted to the political needs of the moment. The project survives in a letter addressed to the royal prince and cardinal of Lisbon, Henry, and was to be presented by him personally to the monarch. There were three main points to be discussed, along with some other topics to be mentioned.

First, Dom João asked for the confirmation by John III of his right to be considered the legitimate heir of '*Ceilão*', and also king of Jaffna. Second, the prince asked for 'jurisdiction over all the Christians on this side of Cape Comorin, in civil and criminal matters, and that judges shall be appointed by myself, and the proclamation of sentences [shall be] in my name'. This meant that 'they [shall] all come to live in my land, because they are dispersed across Gentile kingdoms and are judged as if they were [Gentiles]'.[77] The Lankan ideal of kingship, resonating with Portuguese notions of the king as supreme judge, is here projected into a space with strategic implications, where the Portuguese geographical imagination was in the process of creating new territories of the mind—on grounds of, but also gradually departing from, Lankan notions of space and authority. The proposal clearly links up with a plan we have already heard of to regroup Christian populations dispersed around the Palk Strait and create a politically viable Christian territory on one side only of the water, in northern Sri Lanka.[78] But in Dom João's proposal this was also embedded in a vision of Lanka as a whole, a topos of relevance on two fronts: first, as an obvious echo of the old Lankan idea of the unity of the island, now with an explicit inclusion of Jaffna; and second, because this would mean the transfer of people converted in India by the Jesuits into a land controlled by the Franciscans. The friars believed all Lanka to be theirs, even though this was essentially based on their historical relationship precisely with the monarch whom they now threatened to undermine: Bhuvanekabāhu VII.

[77] Dom João to Prince Henry, Goa, 15 November 1545, *Ceylon*, p. 209.
[78] Francis Xavier to Inácio de Loyola, Tuticorin, 28 October 1542, *Epistolae S. Francisci Xaverii aliaque eius scripta, nova editio ex integro refecta*, edited by Georg Schurhammer and Joseph Wicki (Rome: IHSI, 1944–5), vol. I, pp. 150–1.

Third, Dom João asked for something that could have come straight out of the *apontamentos* of Bhuvanekabāhu himself. Following a reflex we have come to appreciate already, the prince demanded the power to make appointments for all official positions in his realm without interference from Goa. Amidst the turmoil of the mid 1540s, the old idea was very much alive that tribute could be paid to an overlord in exchange for military support, but the nesting empire that was Lanka would need to remain intact, impervious to any urge of Lisbon and Goa to project power into it. Other requests followed: the throne candidate asked that the lands in Kōṭṭe once promised to prince Jugo, and later confirmed to be Dom João's, be handed over to Dom Luís, the younger of the princes. This is significant because it shows how, whilst the project postulates Lanka as a realm to be kept free of Portuguese administrative and judicial powers, it simultaneously proceeds to organize its lands and populations along the principles of layered suzerainty, and hand over some of them to a younger prince. This would likely have been a scheme of tributary overlordship, and possibly a scheme inspired by the partition of 1521. Logically, the fifth point of the letter was that in the case of Dom João dying, Dom Luís should be confirmed as his heir, thus neutralizing other candidates. Some other objectives were also voiced which may seem less significant in terms of political theory, but could have had considerable impact in practice. There was talk about the new king's ability to build ships, conduct trade with 'all the lands of our friends', to decide over war and peace 'on the sea and on the land against all kings and lords who are against Christians and the service of Your Highness', and secure revenue from the pearl fishery which was claimed to belong to Kōṭṭe by ancient custom.[79] Under each of these headings, the proposals underline the importance of allowing the Lankan vassal king to act without the interference of the governors or any other Portuguese officials—but always with the military resources of the *Estado* at hand.

Inevitably, John III would need to make one contribution. It shall not come as a surprise to us by now that the monarch was expected to send troops for the personal guard of his new Sinhalese vassal. The project mentions 100 Portuguese men, married or not, to start with. To leave no space for misunderstandings, it is clarified that this guard would function exclusively at the expenses of Kōṭṭe and with no interference from Goa. Dom João even asked for permission to force any Portuguese individuals coming to Ceylon into serving him and receiving a salary from him. Finally, as had also been the case in the 1541 *apontamentos*, there were references to particular Portuguese individuals involved in the plan and hoping to reap some benefits. André de Sousa was to be the new king's perpetual 'captain and governor', replacing Bhuvanakebahu's favourite Vīdiyē Baṇḍāra. The Franciscan Diogo de Borba, in his turn, was to head the new bishopric of Ceylon, a freshly imagined territory extending through 'all the dominions' (*domínios*) of the Sinhalese ruler: in other words, the island as a whole.[80]

---

[79] Dom João to Prince Henry, Goa, 15 November 1545, *Ceylon*, pp. 209–10.

[80] Dom João to Prince Henry, Goa, 15 November 1545, *Ceylon*, p. 210. Cf. Diogo de Borba to Simão Rodrigues, Goa, 18 November 1545, *Documenta Indica*, edited by Joseph Wicki (Rome: Monumenta Historica Societatis Iesu, 1948–), vol. I, p. 50.

Much of what the anxious prince put on the paper was not new, often even resonating with the great diplomatic dialogue of 1541–3. But in the way it blended all that with the religious promise, it turned out to have a much increased oneiric potential. Indeed, the proposal—which could not be kept secret—was so potent that, almost simultaneously with Dom João, Bhuvanekabāhu himself made a renewed attempt in November 1545 to explain his vision of vassalage directly to the new viceroy of India, João de Castro. In this letter, Bhuvanekabāhu VII tried to clarify that the conversion of people in Ceylon was not a problem in itself, but only inasmuch as it produced legal and fiscal ambivalence. 'From ancient times up to now', he wrote, Lankan kings 'have given these lands to whom they wanted, and [...] could take the said lands away from them, which I cannot do once they become Christians'. And: 'the [Christians] with whom I am happy are those who become [Christians] because they understand the faith *and* pay me my dues [*direitos* and *foros*]'.[81] Bhuvanekabāhu himself remained deeply reluctant to convert, and for good reasons. As Alan Strathern has argued, he needed to remain an active patron of the Buddhist *Sangha* for the maintenance of royal authority, an aspect that the monarch could not expound in much detail to his Portuguese overlord in a time of heightened Catholic zeal.[82]

The princes, in contrast, had nothing to lose, and thus no qualms about promising whatever might move hearts in Goa.[83] Not surprisingly, Bhuvanekabāhu came to complain bitterly about how the Portuguese encouraged Lankan individuals with political ambitions and no respect for the rules of the game to come forward and destabilize the situation.[84] A few years earlier the proposal of Dom João would not have stood the slightest chance of being taken seriously in Goa, let alone in Lisbon. Even as the project was being written up, some voices in Portugal remained cautious. But the potential legality of an invasion of Jaffna was now discussed, and some argued that John III had a 'licence' to wage war on Caṅkili to avenge the massacre of Mannār.

It is not that religious and military arguments were naturally destined to go hand in hand in the Portuguese sphere. In reality, they had often been at odds and pitched against each other with passion by different groups of interest. Yet in the 1540s the convergence of the two strategies created a potent mix. In fact, even commerce, that old enemy of faith, was added to the picture by the most calculating zealots. At the end of 1545, the vicar Miguel Vaz, one of the most vociferous defenders of the religious regeneration of the empire, presented a long list of proposals for Ceylon. A series of marginal notes written by the powerful secretary of state, Pero de Alcáçova Carneiro, reveal how the document was read with care in the highest sphere. Vaz presented the large-scale Christianization of Ceylon as a

---

[81] Bhuvanekabāhu VII to John III, Kōṭṭe, 12 November 1545, *Ceylon*, pp. 194–6. Emphasis added.

[82] Strathern, *Kingship and Conversion*, pp. 130 and 146.

[83] Dom João to John III, Goa, 15 November 1545, p. 219.

[84] See friar João de Vila do Conde to João de Castro, [Colombo], 17 November 1545, *Ceylon*, p. 224.

key objective of crown policy.[85] Interestingly as well, he justified the religious enterprise in connection with a reinforcement of the crown's cinnamon allowance. Forty *bahars* of the spice were to be set aside to finance the new mission, which was in turn hoped to help stabilize local political conditions.[86]

The question by late 1545 was not *whether* the Portuguese should intervene militarily in Ceylon anymore, but where, how, and supporting whom. Whilst the Portuguese royal family did remain formally faithful to their vassal, the project of intervening militarily in a more decided manner became less and less preposterous from a moral *and* economic point of view—the latter being of great importance at a time of stress on royal finances. In such a conjuncture, Dom João began to emerge as a viable alternative to Cankili in Jaffna in the short term, but ultimately also to Bhuvanekabāhu in Kōṭṭe. Vaz invested all his influence in having the Jaffna project recommended to Goa by the monarch. As we shall see, John III conceded precisely this—even though, ever faithful to his cautious character, he also ended up maintaining Bhuvanekabāhu VII under his personal protection. In December 1545, the Portuguese monarch dispatched orders to Goa for the Jaffna project to go ahead.[87]

## AN ELDORADO IN THE HIGH MOUNTAINS OF CEYLON: KANDY, 1542–1545

As if all this was not complicated enough, a third focus of attention emerged during the 1540s in the kingdom of Udaraṭa, generally known as *Candea* or, later on, Kandy.[88] The local rulers had once paid tribute to Kōṭṭe, but behaved as independent *rājas* from the last quarter of the fifteenth century. Their autonomy was consolidated while Māyādunnē fought with Bhuvanekabāhu in the 1520s and 1530s. Whether this process can be seen as one of state formation is discussable. Numerous episodes in the sixteenth century suggest that Kandy was a rather loose set of smaller lordships often proving impossible to rule over as a whole.[89] Whilst the Sri Lankan historian Tikiri Abeyasinghe has emphasized the relative stability of the kingdom in the longer run, a series of crises in the sixteenth century remind us of the frailty of its power structures. As anywhere else in the island, rulers dearly needed foreign support. On the other hand, Kandy's first independent ruler had managed to impose suzerainty over minor lords in the Four Korales, in Uva, and

---

[85] Miguel Vaz to John III, [Évora?] [November 1545?], *Ceylon*, pp. 229–60. On the marginal notes see the introductory commentary by Schurhammer on p. 229.

[86] Vaz to John III [Évora?], [November 1545?], *Ceylon*, p. 247.

[87] John III to João de Castro, Évora, 1 December 1545, *Ceylon*, pp. 266–7.

[88] The name *Kandy* (in Dutch and English) or *Candea/Cândia* (in Portuguese), derived from *kanda*, Sinhala for mountain. The central town of the realm, now generally also called Kandy, was known as Senkadagala and, later, Mahanuvara. Abeyasinghe, 'The kingdom of Kandy', pp. 139–40.

[89] The political independence of Kandy from Kōṭṭe had its roots in the 1470s, when Senasammata Vikramabāhu (r.1469–1510) took advantage of the difficulties that Bhuvanekabāhu VI experienced in imposing order through the lowlands. C. R. De Silva, 'Sri Lanka in the early sixteenth century', in *University of Peradeniya History of Sri Lanka*, vol. II, edited by K. M. de Silva (Peradeniya: University of Peradeniya, 1995), vol. II, p. 14. In 1521, the king of Kandy supported the regicide at Kōṭṭe.

in the eastern lowlands between Trincomalee and the Menik Ganga.[90] It was common for the ruler of Kandy to seek matrimonial alliances in the Southwest, namely in Kōṭṭe, especially to protect themselves from the expansion of Sītāvaka. Finally, Kandy's 'politics of survival'—a term coined by Abeyasinghe himself[91]—included a constant quest for allies in South India (and later with the Dutch and the Danish). In other words, Kandy was a particularly unstable polity at the beginning, but went on nevertheless to participate powerfully in the ordering of the Lankan space. It played a role locally and regionally, and saw no hindrance to taking up global communications either. In the early 1540s, Jayavīra Baṇḍāra, the ruler of Kandy, felt capable of entering the diplomatic game unfolding around him.[92] His first documented initiative is symptomatic of the atmosphere of diplomatic experimentation in the island. Sometime in mid 1542, an obscure Portuguese petty noble with a pompous name—Nuno Álvares Pereira, not necessarily identical with the homonymous author of the 1527 letter[93]—heard a rumour in Negombo that the king of Kandy sought for a diplomatic mediator:

> Being in Negombo I heard about the desire of this king [of Kandy] to have the friendship of the king our lord, and that he was not [our king's friend] only because he had no one to negotiate on his behalf. I wrote to him that if he had such [a desire] as I was told he had, I would make this known to the Lord Governor and the Captain Major. As soon as he received my message, he sent some men to fetch me. This is what has brought me here [to Kandy] and nothing else. I arrived in July 1542.[94]

Once in Kandy, Pereira did what he had been hired to do. He wrote an elaborate letter in Portuguese on behalf of the Kandyan ruler and prepared a diplomatic mission to the governor Martim Afonso de Sousa in Goa. How the translation of the Kandyan proposal into Portuguese was managed exactly is unclear, though Pereira appears to have had some language skills. A first emissary left Kandy with the letter and a set of precious stones—a sensible diplomatic gift in times of uncertainty, as they were easy to hide—on 14 August 1542.[95]

To lure Portuguese forces to the island, the letter offered the Portuguese a *feitoria* at Trincomalee, a large natural harbour facing the Bay of Bengal. There would be an annual tribute of 15 tuskers and 300 oars for galleys, a much valued good that was

---

[90] Tikiri Abeyasinghe, 'The kingdom of Kandy: foundations and foreign relations to 1638', in *University of Peradeniya History of Sri Lanka*, vol. II, edited by K. M. de Silva (Peradeniya: University of Peradeniya, 1995), vol. II (1995), pp. 140–2.

[91] Tikiri Abeyasinghe, 'The Politics of Survival: Aspects of Kandyan External Relations in the Mid-Sixteenth Century', *Journal of the Royal Asiatic Society of Sri Lanka*, New Series, XVII (1973), pp. 11–21.

[92] There are doubts about the identity of this ruler, which Pieris and Fitzler see as being Vikramabāhu, a man referred in the *Rājāvaliya* as ruling from 1542. *Ceylon and Portugal*, part I, *Kings and Christians 1539–1552* (Leipzig: Asia Maior, 1927), p. 5.

[93] This obscure figure has been identified by Schurhammer as an illegitimate son of the Count of Feira. Three sons of the count did indeed travel to India with Martim Afonso de Sousa in 1541, but Álvares Pereira is not mentioned in the fleet register. Contemporaries referred to him as 'a Portuguese [...] who claims to be a person of honour', 'a certain Nuno Álvares Pereira', or even 'a poor practical soldier'. *Ceylon*, p. 148.

[94] Nuno Álvares Pereira to João de Castro, Kandy, 13 October 1545, *Ceylon*, p. 175.

[95] Pereira to João de Castro, Kandy, 13 October 1545, *Ceylon*, p. 175.

talked about with some preoccupation in the *Estado* during those years due to the difficulties of finding adequate wood in India. It was also proposed to pay the salaries of the *feitor* and of twenty well-armed Portuguese soldiers. Once again, the boundaries between 'friendship' and 'tributary submission' were somewhat blurry. The reaction to Jayavīra's proposals in India was cautious, but positive. An anonymous Flemish trader (a *casado*) from the southern port of Quilon arrived in Kandy in early 1543, accompanied by an interpreter (*topaz*), to establish the trading post at Trincomalee.[96] They brought letters announcing that Miguel Ferreira, the protagonist of the 1538–9 campaign, was readying himself at Nagapattinam with a partner, a certain Amaro Mendes, to come to Trincomalee. According to Nuno Álvares Pereira, the king was enthused and sent a large company to receive the announced troops.

Historians invested in proving the patriotic credentials of Kandy have emphasized the commercial rationale of the original request, and the separation of political heartland from maritime rim.[97] In practice, however, the document suggests that Jayavīra planned precisely to employ the men where we would by now suspect them to have been most wanted: in the centre of the realm, serving in his royal guard.[98] It is certainly no coincidence that the ruler was facing, at that exact moment, a challenge to his authority involving a discussion around throne succession.[99]

Because Nuno Álvares Pereira was a part of the Kandyan reception committee, we can reconstruct not only how it proceeded, but also what obstacles it faced on the periphery of Kandy's sphere of influence. We are venturing into new terrain geographically and communicationally. When the Kandyans arrived near Trincomalee, their passage was barred by a local chief, giving us a clear sense of the limited influence of the Kandyan overlord on local affairs. On the other side, the Portuguese grew impatient. From the seventy or eighty men participating initially, only about twenty to thirty remained in place by the time the Kandyans got through to Trincomalee. Pereira then suggested approaching Kandy by taking a more westerly route, through lands falling under the influence of Jaffna. But the party inadvertently entered an area temporarily obeying Sītāvaka. The men were forced to march about 200 km to the south. In Sītāvaka, Pereira was not punished, but simply asked to serve as a diplomatic mediator for king Māyādunnē himself. He had to write yet another letter to Goa, this time expounding Māyādunnē's interest in becoming an ally of the Portuguese. Clearly, there was a gap between the demand for diplomatic scribes and the supply. Only then could the committee march back to Kandy, where it arrived on 15 July 1543. Instead of the expected ten days, their journey had taken four and a half months.[100]

These and some other wanderings constitute the first directly documented instances of Portuguese travels through the interior of Ceylon. For the first time,

---

[96] Pereira to João de Castro, Kandy, 13 October 1545, *Ceylon*, pp. 175–6.

[97] Abeyasinghe, 'The politics of survival', p. 15. Cf. Nuno Álvares Pereira to João de Castro, Kandy, 13 October 1545, *Ceylon*, p. 183.

[98] Pereira to Castro, Kandy, 13 October 1545, *Ceylon*, p. 183. Cf. De Silva, 'The rise and fall of the kingdom of Sitawaka', p. 17 and Abeyasinghe, 'The politics of survival', p. 17.

[99] De Silva, 'The rise and fall of the kingdom of Sitawaka', p. 16.

[100] Pereira to Castro, Kandy, 13 October 1545, *Ceylon*, pp. 176–8.

we know positively that Portuguese individuals marched through vast stretches of land in areas subjected to Kandy, Jaffna, and Sītāvaka, and even other parts of the island controlled by none of the three. Communication was definitely not a simple business during these years, and the stories surviving in the record illustrate rather colourfully how the capacity to dispatch emissaries and get them safely to their destination with small items such as letters, gems, and jewels was what determined the success or failure of diplomatic initiatives. Military activities—precisely what these letters were intended to intensify—would often hinder the circulation of people and news. As someone put it in late 1545, 'without war it takes [from Kandy to Kōṭṭe] five or six days, and now [letters only arrive] with much luck'.[101]

After several failed attempts at establishing a conversation with Portuguese decision-makers in India, king Jayavīra of Kandy felt desperately isolated in his mountain kingdom. Māyādunnē of Sītāvaka was getting ready to attack him, and tensions also mounted on the Jaffna front. In March 1545, Jayavīra made a final attempt at sending letters to the *Estado*. He chose a Brahmin and a Gujarati man to carry the letters, and told them to go to Colombo through Kōṭṭe. He asked for forty Portuguese soldiers to defend Kandy—and added one final promise. On 3 April 1545, Jayavīra Baṇḍāra, supported by Nuno Álvares Pereira, dispatched a set of palm leaf documents (*olas*) and paper letters in which Jayavīra of Kandy not only placed himself politically 'in the hands' of the Portuguese governor, but also offered to embrace the Catholic faith. Still awaiting a reply in October, Jayavīra decided to send an ambassador directly to the new viceroy, João de Castro. He promised again to be baptized, and to have his son and chosen successor, Karaliyaddē Kumara Baṇḍāra, educated in the Catholic religion. Inevitably, he added that 'many' in his kingdom would take baptism if only the governor came in person.[102]

How did Jayavīra in the Kandyan highlands get the idea that by promising his conversion he might receive the support he had otherwise failed to secure? The events described unfolded in 1545 while in Kōṭṭe the Franciscans were, as we have seen already, attempting to convert Bhuvanekabāhu VII and exploring other potential avenues of proselytizing the Kōṭṭe elite. We have seen how violently Bhuvanekabāhu reacted when Jugo Baṇḍāra was baptized, causing Dom João and Dom Luís to go into exile. As it happens, the mother of Dom João was Jayavīra's sister-in-law: a sister of the Kandyan queen consort, the mother of Karaliyaddē Baṇḍāra, chosen by Jayavīra to succeed on the throne.[103] There can be little doubt that political strategies were being actively discussed between various members of the tentacular Lankan royal family, including very active female members, and that in the process ideas crossed cultural borders, connecting Lankan royalty, Franciscan

[101] Francisco Álvares to João de Castro, Kōṭṭe, 6 October 1545, *Ceylon*, p. 173.
[102] Pereira to Castro, Kandy, 13 October 1545, *Ceylon*, pp. 178–83. Nuno Álvares Pereira to Francisco Álvares, Kandy, 12 September 1545, *Ceylon*, pp. 150–3. The name of the prince can be deduced from *Rājāvaliya*, p. 82. Cf. 'Caralea Bandar' in Couto, *Da Asia*, vol. VI, book viii, chapter 4 and Queiroz, *Conquista*, p. 574. Also see the notes by Schurhammer in *Ceylon*, p. 152.
[103] Cf. Pereira to Álvares, Kandy, 12 September 1545, *Ceylon*, p. 153. Karaliyaddē's mother was from the so-called Kirawella lineage and was said to have been educated by Sakalakalāvallaba, the man who had incited Vijayabāhu in 1518 to attack the Portuguese. Cf. *Rājāvaliya*, p. 82.

missionaries, Portuguese mercenaries, and various other players. Indeed, Nuno Álvares Pereira confirms that some of the ideas in the letters were directly inspired by conversations held through the internal communicational channels of the royal family, about which we know nothing else.[104]

Friar João de Vila do Conde, whose understanding of the political geography of Lanka remained sketchy,[105] wrote a note in October 1545 stating that 'once this king [of Kandy] becomes a Christian, this is the best way for all the kings and people of this land to convert to our faith'.[106] Within days, a number of individuals in Kōṭṭe and Colombo also voiced their opinion towards Goa. Duarte Teixeira, who had nourished high hopes only a few years earlier when he co-authored the Lisbon petitions of Bhuvanekabāhu VII, found new hope in the prospect of a Kandyan conversion.[107] Francisco Álvares, a newly appointed royal overseer of justice and finance in the Estado, expressed his sympathy for Jayavīra, from whom he had received a letter in Portuguese.[108] Jorge Velho, an emissary who had carried some of these letters, recommended that the viceroy take his armada to Trincomalee and march from there to Kandy. 'For the love of God', he begged,

> come and assist this king, which would equal to saving this entire island, so many men, so many women, so many children, so much treasure.[109]

Clearly, the mental horizons of these men, who felt encouraged to write as Lankan princes mounted one diplomatic offensive after another and the governors in Goa requested additional information to see through the confusing picture, started to widen. It was finally opening up to the 'mountains of Camdia, in the interior without a port on the sea', a key area formerly absent from written transactions.[110] Incidentally, Bhuvanekabāhu himself, who found some temporary solace in a pragmatic alliance with Māyādunnē against Jayavīra, rediscovered the appeal of attempting to dominate the highlands—not only on grounds of the old cakravarti ideology, but also because Kandy might then offer him a place to retreat if a Portuguese fleet arrived at Colombo with hostile intentions. To my knowledge, this is the earliest documented sign that a sense may have been forming in Lanka of how the highlands could become a vast fortress against the newcomers (an asset rather than a liability)—but ironically it appears in a letter written in Kōṭṭe.[111]

That none of this was simple or straightforward and that we are witnesses to a moment of great strategic, tactical, and emotional turmoil among the Portuguese and their Lankan interlocutors, is particularly evident from a little note attached by the acting feitor of Colombo, António Ferreira, to one of his letters from October 1545. Like so many others, Ferreira was giving his expert advice on grand

---

[104] Pereira to Francisco Álvares, Kandy, 12 September 1545, Ceylon, p. 152.
[105] João de Vila do Conde to João de Castro, Kōṭṭe, 17 November 1545, Ceylon, p. 225. Cf. Jorge Velho to João de Castro, Colombo, 13 November 1545, Ceylon, p. 200.
[106] João de Vila do Conde to João de Castro, Kōṭṭe, 4 October 1545, Ceylon, p. 159.
[107] Duarte Teixeira to João de Castro, Kōṭṭe, 5 October 1545, Ceylon, p. 167.
[108] Francisco Álvares to João de Castro, Kōṭṭe, 6 October 1545, Ceylon, p. 172.
[109] Jorge Velho to João de Castro, Colombo, 13 November 1545, Ceylon, p. 200.
[110] António Ferreira to João de Castro, Kōṭṭe, 5 October 1545, Ceylon, p. 161.
[111] Duarte Teixeira to João de Castro, Kōṭṭe, 5 October 1545, Ceylon, pp. 165–6.

strategic issues at the same time as he was pursuing a more personal interest in obtaining royal grants. On the one hand, he insisted, the Portuguese needed more military resources in the island. In the same letter, however, he also opened a little door for his own retreat to where he felt the Portuguese remained at their best, the sea: 'I remind Your Lordship, given that you have granted me the voyage of Coromandel, not to forget having it confirmed by His Highness, because, *Senhor*, the profits of this land are, it seems to me, in a bad conjunction.'[112]

The 1540s saw a sometimes disconcerting intertwinement of matters local, regional, and global. With local political objectives in mind, Lankan rulers and princes reached out to an empire operating across the region as part of its global interests. They appealed specifically to the most global aspect of its ideology, Catholic Universalism, to convince its authorities to invest resources in the resolution of unquestionably local matters. This produced a spectacular multiplication of letter-writing agents, a well-documented intensification of communications, and signs of a widening of geographical horizons on both sides. Political ideas, however unrealistic they may now seem, were flowing at remarkable speeds, and they were beginning to make an impact. For this to happen, it was crucial that people along the way felt strongly about some particular aspect of the message itself—and religion proved to be the ingredient that had been missing earlier. A fertile environment emerged in which dreams of military action, supported by religious arguments, could gain influence in the *Estado*. Clearly, the net was tightening around Bhuvanekabāhu VII. Yet we have still not witnessed a single military campaign in the island responding to direct royal orders from Lisbon. For a concerted intervention to happen, the pressure needed to mount much further.

---

[112] António Ferreira do João de Castro, Kōṭṭe, 5 October 1545, *Ceylon*, p. 162.

# 5

# Moving into the Native Ground
## Turmoil and Diplomatic Diversification
## in the Middle of the Century

It is worth halting for a moment at this point and asking ourselves about possible parallels, in other parts of the world, to the transformations under way in mid-sixteenth century Sri Lanka. When historians of the Portuguese and Spanish empires talk about the power of the periphery and of sub-imperial processes, agency is most commonly attributed to groups that may be on the fringes of the system, but originated from Iberia. The elites of Cochin, Bahia, Mexico, Luanda or Macao are acknowledged to have made their impact, in often peculiar ways, on the creation of new structures of trade, social, and political power in many parts of the world.[1] Powerful groups have been identified in places that are even further in the shadows, such as the colonies around the Bay of Bengal and the South China Sea. But what we have begun to observe in the Lankan case goes quite clearly beyond those instances of peripheral 'tails' wagging the imperial 'dog'.[2] In our story, the power to influence decisions in Lisbon and Goa emanates from historical actors with roots entirely outside the official realm, operating out of places far beyond the reach of the Portuguese crown with their own imperial theme. How can we then describe the space in which this inter-imperial encounter took place?

## BETWEEN MIDDLE AND NATIVE GROUND: SRI LANKA'S PLACE IN BORDERLAND HISTORY

Borderlands and contact zones are everywhere in early modern studies, and thus potentially nowhere at all.[3] To make them historiographically relevant, we need to examine how they functioned as conduits for the transmission of ideas and thus

---

[1] See e.g. C. R. Boxer, *Portuguese Society in the Tropics. The Municipal Councils of Goa, Macao, Bahia, and Luanda, 1510–1800* (Madison/Milwaukee, WI: University of Wisconsin Press, 1965).

[2] Sanjay Subrahmanyam, 'The Tail Wags the Dog: Sub-Imperialism and the *Estado da Índia*, 1570–1600', in *Improvising Empire: Portuguese Trade and Settlement in the Bay of Bengal* (New Delhi: Oxford University Press, 1990), pp. 137–60.

[3] See Pekka Hämäläinen and Samuel Truett, 'On Borderlands', *Journal of American History*, 98, 2 (2011), pp. 338–61. On the semantics of these terms also see Michel Baud and Willem Van Schendel, 'Toward a Comparative History of Borderlands', *Journal of World History*, 8, 2 (1997), p. 213 and Jeremy Adelman and Stephen Aron, 'From Borderlands to Borders: Empires, Nation-States, and the Peoples in Between in North American History', *American Historical Review*, 104 (1999), pp. 814–15.

contributed to configurations of power that ultimately helped form the world we live in. Much of this book resonates with recent scholarship on borderlands, contact zones, and early interactions in the New World, and because we are engaging with one of many imperial encounters of the global sixteenth century, it is worth spelling out where global historians may build new bridges.[4]

Key to the new historiography of the New World has been a preoccupation with how to redistribute agency. The challenge remains to avoid 'the irony that, in the very act of criticizing western domination, one often ends up reifying the power of the dominator to a degree that the agency of non-Western cultures is reduced to a single possibility: resistance'?[5] Attempts at integrating the two sides of early modern encounters in the Atlantic have often come at the cost of either exoticizing 'the Natives' (an accusation typically wielded against Tzvetan Todorov, for his semiotic approach to the Spanish-Mexican encounter), or making their existence irrelevant beyond the realm of European discourse (as in Stephen Greenblatt's reading of Columbus' Caribbean activities), or rendering non-European agency intelligible primarily 'by endowing all actors with Western ways of making sense' (arguably the most widespread problem of all).[6] What can historians of European expansion in Asia learn from such challenges and from the rich historiography that has arisen in response to them?[7] And might lessons flow in the inverse direction, too?

Peru in particular has seen the emergence of a vibrant revisionist historiography. Most spectacularly perhaps, Gonzalo Lamana has described the Andean conquest as an extended process where domination long preceded Spanish dominance. This has involved, quite appropriately, experimenting with chronologies that challenge those created by early imperial chroniclers, and rethinking agency. The objective of the revision is not so much to negate the impact caused by Spanish imperialism in Peru, but to detach the analysis thereof from the discursive structures created during the colonial period itself. In a less theoretically elaborate vein and, one suspects, with the spectre of depoliticization looming large, Gauvin Bailey's fresh take on the 'Andean Hybrid Baroque' has emphasized how an understanding of 'Mestizo Art' entails a deconstruction of the 'local' and the 'imperial' as analytical categories. Most usefully, Bailey argues that the resulting culture can be adequately explained through the lens of neither of the sides involved, but only as an intermediate construct resulting from the encounter as such.[8] Heidi Scott, in a study of the Andean colony as a 'Contested Territory', has emphasized the importance of opposition and negotiation in the establishment of the colonial order—not to trivialize the

---

[4] For an overview on the topic, see Hämäläinen and Truett, 'On Borderlands'.

[5] Lydia H. Liu, *Translingual Practice: Literature, National Culture and Translated Modernity* (Stanford, CA: Stanford University Press, 1995), quoted in Douglas Howland, 'The Predicament of Ideas in Culture: Translation and Historiography', *History and Theory*, 42 (2003), p. 53.

[6] See Gonzalo Lamana, *Domination without Dominance: Inca-Spanish Encounters in Early Colonial Peru* (Durham, NC: Duke University Press, 2008), p. 2.

[7] On some of the most relevant trends in Spanish American historiography, see Steve J. Stern, 'Paradigms of Conquest: History, Historiography, and Politics', *Journal of Latin American Studies*, 24 (1992), pp. 1–34.

[8] Gauvin Alexander Bailey, *The Andean Hybrid Baroque: Converging Cultures in the Churches of Colonial Peru* (Notre Dame, IN: University of Notre Dame Press, 2010).

violence involved, but to highlight complex 'conditions of contingency, compromise, and modification' in the new space under construction.[9] Much of this scholarship builds on the questioning of the very notion of conquest, as preluded three decades ago in Inga Clendinnen's *Ambivalent Conquest* and developed in Stephanie Wood's *Transcending Conquest*.[10]

One fundamental difference between Peru and Sri Lanka in the mid-sixteenth century persists, however: whilst military victory and formal incorporation (and indeed the official planning thereof) were a point of departure for interactions in Mexico and the Andes, this was not the case in the Indian Ocean island. Here is an aspect that New World historians may wish to take into consideration when questioning, with an at times extreme revisionist enthusiasm, the notion of conquest trauma: in comparison with the Lankan case, the Mexican and Peruvian panoramas remain grim because, before most of the 'negotiations' now highlighted by historians could unfold, one party did set out to crush the other in a swift succession of devastating military victories. The chronology may be different in Peru from the one in Mexico, but in comparison to Sri Lanka it is still fairly compact and, despite all its complications, takes a much more straightforward course than anything we witness in Ceylon. The three 'paradigms' of conquistadorism described by Steve Stern (the utopias of wealth, religion, and social precedence) could explode into the New World almost at once, wreaking havoc in a way that would have been unimaginable in any of the Portuguese areas of interest in the East, let alone in Sri Lanka. Naturally, there were soon responses, 'entanglements' and 'ambiguities' across the Spanish colonies, and for many Spanish settlers the 'utopias vanished', the conquest remained unfinished.[11] But it is striking for a historian of Asia how the mainstream in New World historiography seems to have become *so* prone to downplay the nominal moment of conquest, the comparatively quick move from experimenting with tributary vassalage to beheading native states and placing them under Spanish governorship. Is it not worth underlining, even in a nuanced revision of the materials, how Spanish expeditions tended to involve the leadership of 'prospective governors' from the onset?[12] The recent work of Jeremy Mumford may bring some welcome clarification regarding the depth of the rupture (especially the Spanish resettlement of Andean populations), but even here one senses a hesitation to embrace what Serge Gruzinski rightly described, in a now distant historiographical past, as the 'shock of conquest'.[13]

---

[9] Heidi V. Scott, *Contested Territory. Mapping Peru in the Sixteenth and Seventeenth Centuries* (Notre Dame, IN: University of Notre Dame Press, 2009).

[10] Inga Clendinnen, *Ambivalent Conquest. Maya and Spaniard in Yucatan, 1517–1570* (Cambridge: Cambridge University Press, 1989). Stephanie Wood, *Transcending Conquest. Nahua Views of Spanish Colonial Mexico* (Norman, OK: University of Oklahoma Press, 2003).

[11] Stern, 'Paradigms of Conquest', pp. 18 and 21.

[12] Karen Spalding, *Huarochirí: an Andean Society under Inca and Spanish rule* (Stanford, CA: Stanford University Press, 1984), p. 116.

[13] Jeremy Ravi Mumford, *Vertical Empire: The General Resettlement of Indians in the Colonial Andes* (Durham, NC: Duke University Press, 2012). Serge Gruzinski, *The Mestizo Mind. The Intellectual Dynamics of Colonization and Globalization* (New York/London: Routledge, 2002), p. 33. Originally published in 1999.

This is an obvious contrast worth spelling out, then: whilst Peru and Mexico were quickly added, nominally at least, to the possessions of the Castilian crown, Sri Lanka, like much of Maritime Asia, remained formally outside the body politic of Portuguese crown possessions. Ceylon was a potential *conquista*, as we have seen already, but not legally a possession that had gone—or was expected to go—through *conquista* as a military act.[14] Expeditions dispatched to the island were not organized in a way that could have led to a formal incorporation until late in the sixteenth century. Their fundamental rationale (if there was a rationale at all on the Portuguese side) was to maintain the regime of tributary overlordship. The island thus *hosted* a colony of Portuguese individuals seeking local opportunities. Mexico and Peru *became* colonies, however much we may then wish to question who was really in charge.

What are, then, the possible parallels between Sri Lanka and the New World? Perhaps the most interesting terms of comparison are not the core areas of Mexico and Peru, nor even the more peripheral Spanish conquests such as Yucatán. What comes to mind most powerfully are large parts of America not coveted by the Spanish crown at all. Seventeenth-century Chesapeake and New England offer themselves as templates, where tiny European communities depended very largely upon their Native American surroundings to survive.[15] The 'Middle Ground' described by Richard White in his classic study of the Great Plains emerges as another, possible parallel. But there are some differences, too, regarding the concrete political and military realities on the ground. White's Midwest served as a space that all parties involved agreed gradually to transform into a new playground for mutual observations, interactions and, to some extent, an understanding and recognition of each other's codes of behaviour and thought.[16] This space was physical, not just metaphorical, and has no clear parallel in mid-sixteenth century Ceylon. All things considered, Sri Lanka may come closest to what Kathleen DuVal has identified, in a key study of the Arkansas Valley, as 'the Native Ground': a space occupied by a strong Native American polity needing 'neither accommodation nor resistance' to thrive, and exerting significant pressure on newcomers to let themselves be 'incorporated' into existing power structures. When Europeans arrived, DuVal argues, 'they found themselves recruited by those who were already there, who sought to teach the newcomers their interpretation of the history, customs, and peoples of the region'.[17] Similar processes prevailed in the 'Comanche Empire' studied by Pekka Hämäläinen, where early European settlers had to subject to native authority to survive.[18] It is here, in areas not claimed by any European crown during the sixteenth century, that we find the most potent parallels to our Lankan story.

[14] See Chapter 2.

[15] See James Horn, *Adapting to a New World. English Society in the Seventeenth-Century Chesapeake* (Chapel Hill, NC/London: University of North Carolina Press, 1996).

[16] Richard White, *The Middle Ground: Indians, Empires, and Republics in the Great Lakes Region, 1650–1815* (Cambridge: Cambridge University Press, 1991).

[17] Kathleen DuVal, *The Native Ground. Indians and Colonists in the Heart of the Continent* (Philadelphia, PA: University of Pennsylvania Press, 2006), pp. 4–5.

[18] Pekka Hämäläinen, *The Comanche Empire* (New Haven, CT: Yale University Press, 2008). For a selection from the vast literature on comparable, though not necessarily similar, cases from North American history, see p. 367, note 7.

We can venture that politically, Sri Lanka in the mid sixteenth century was still largely a place dominated by local power-building processes, to which the Portuguese were summoned to contribute by the local elites. Disruptions of the logics of tributary overlordship, namely in 1539 and, as we shall see, 1551, did occur. But the Portuguese were still largely responding to local processes and initiatives, and had no coherent plan of their own for the island. Culturally, in contrast, Lanka had started to become a place of increasingly important amalgamations and cross-fertilizations. Perhaps the way to put it is that it was largely as a political Native Ground that Lanka sent its imperial ideas into the global communicational system connecting it with Goa, Lisbon, and Rome. But not everyone stood as firmly behind the old notion of vassalage as Bhuvanekabāhu VII did: as other rulers and princes began to add a Christian element to their projects, cultural hybrids began to form. These hybrids began to ascend the social ladder of the Portuguese imperial apparatus, appealing increasingly not just to the lower and middle, but also the upper echelons. Thus, they paved the way for the transformation of Lanka into a more ambiguous political space—and eventually, further down the line, a space imaginable and manageable as an object of conquest. The permeation of the Lankan realm by global forces and ideas occurred gradually *as the Lankan elite* launched its own local ideas into the global communicational space over the years, contributing to the transformation of the latter, and making the global empire more prone to think about its own future in a local political theatre.

Even as conversions were added to the deal, the notion that promises of vassalage could be made to the benefit of local political projects remained remarkably firm on the Lankan side. Infiltrations—the global starting to seep into the local—began to occur precisely because Lankan royalty fought so proactively for access to the resources of the Portuguese empire. And perhaps—but we are still a long way from seeing the *dénouement* of our story—it was precisely because the Native Ground felt so solid to Lankan rulers and princes that, imperceptibly, the cultural ground rock of Lankan politics, and with it the Lankan ability to digest the global into the local, started to erode.

## A TIME FOR HAWKS: MOUNTING PRESSURES FOR AN INTERVENTION IN CEYLON

Because the picture of new connections springing up across the island is so extraordinary, it is well worth insisting on the gradual, often disconcerting, historical emergence of new political and geographical perspectives. In 1545, two unlikely allies, Bhuvanekabāhu and Māyādunnē, ganged up on Jayavīra, lord of Kandy. News of this perplexing rearrangement, which drove home to all the complication of Lankan politics, arrived in Goa in December. It was simply not clear who would stand on whose side anymore.[19] Yet the setback also coincided with the arrival of

---

[19] André de Sousa to John III, Goa, 20 December 1545, in Georg Schurhammer and Ernst August Voretzsch, *Ceylon zur Zeit des Königs Bhuvaneka Bahu und Franz Xavers 1539–1552* (Leipzig: Verlag der Asia Major, 1928) (henceforth cited as '*Ceylon*'), pp. 274–5.

yet more letters and gifts from Kandy.[20] From these letters, the picture emerged of a fresh, straight-talking candidate carrying all the promise one could dream of. André de Sousa, originally the mentor of the princes of Kōṭṭe, embraced the idea of a campaign in the highlands. He was undergoing a cognitive shift of his own, and starting to think of Lanka in a way that was less focused on Kōṭṭe and Jaffna than before. Some of what happened, to be sure, was simply a transfer of Lankan geo-political topoi from Kōṭṭe to Kandy. In the minds of men like Sousa, the wondrous qualities of Lanka condensed again around Kandy. A new country began to appear to the Portuguese in the island's mountainous interior:

> This Kingdom of *Camdia* is in the middle of the island of *Ceilão*. It measures thirty leagues in any direction [...] It is a fertile land abundant in food [...] elephants and wax and areca nuts and [precious] stones; it also has much cinnamon. It is reasonably rich treasure-wise [...] It is a much populated kingdom [...] All this I know truly and very well from a number of people who have been there. And I myself have also been there once. There are some very large mountains wherever one enters the kingdom, with great [mountain] passes which they can easily defend [...] Inside the land is very flat.[21]

The author of these lines, André de Sousa, was not alone in hearing about the mountain kingdom as a new land of opportunity. Goa in December 1545 was already bustling with plans for expeditions to Ceylon's promising interior. Letters were coming and going, and discussions 'heating up the matter' as people talked.[22] Finally, on Christmas Eve, the viceroy decided that, whilst the planned grand campaign had to wait, a smaller expedition of thirty to forty men and two Franciscan friars could be sent to Kandy.[23]

The ensuing expedition to the mountain kingdom was about as inglorious as one can imagine. A party of fifteen men led by André de Sousa left Goa in January 1546. It grew to about forty men over the course of an almost comically troublesome voyage.[24] In the meantime, Jayavīra was besieged by Māyādunnē and pressed into paying a heavy tribute, but also desperate enough secretly to be baptized as 'Dom Manuel'.[25] News of this event soon reached Sousa in Colombo, prompting him to sail to Galle, where he purchased an additional vessel to carry the local mercenaries ('*negros*') he recruited. When the boat leaked, the party was forced to make landfall on a deserted beach in the Yāla region. Tellingly enough, Sousa

[20] New letters and gifts arrived in Goa on 18 December. Pero Fernandes to John III, Goa, 20 December 1545, *Ceylon*, p. 273. Some jewellery had arrived before by way of a Franciscan friar. Receipt, Goa, 13 December 1545, *Ceylon*, p. 268. André de Sousa also mentions the arrival of 'letters and *olas*' from Kandy. Sousa to John III, Goa, 20 December 1545, *Ceylon*, p. 275.

[21] Sousa to John III, Goa, 20 December 1545, *Ceylon*, pp. 276–7.

[22] Letters were also exchanged between Kōṭṭe and Kandy. Nuno Álvares Pereira to Dom João de Castro, Kandy, 29 May 1546, *Ceylon*, pp. 362–3. A certain Pero Fernandes Sardinha, for example, wrote directly to John III about the viceroy's plan to go to Ceylon. Goa, 20 December 1545, *Ceylon*, p. 273.

[23] João de Castro to John III, Goa, 24 December 1545, *Ceylon*, p. 278.

[24] On the journey, see André de Sousa to João de Castro, Kandy, 27 May 1546, *Ceylon*, pp. 358–9. António Padrão to João de Castro, Kandy, 7 June 1546, *Ceylon*, pp. 371–6. Nuno Álvares Pereira to João de Castro, Kandy, 29 May 1546, *Ceylon*, pp. 362–70.

[25] Pereira to Castro, Kandy, 29 May 1546, *Ceylon*, p. 363.

dispatched the remaining functioning vessel to the Coromandel Coast, where it had always been destined, with a cargo of merchandise. The men, now finally reduced to a party with a purely military mission, made the remarkably unfortunate choice of trying to reach Kandy by foot.[26] The region of Yāla and the southern fringes of the central mountains are to this day among the most unhospitable parts of the country. Sousa later admitted that he had thought Kandy was 'nearer and less troublesome' to reach than it turned out to be. If there was any sense of direction, it must have come from one of the Lankan mercenaries in the group, but not someone familiar with the actual terrain. The men walked, as one of them put it, 'forty leagues through mountains and woods so rough that I have never in my life seen anything alike, nor do I hope I will ever again'.[27]

Despite the difficulties, Sousa was received jubilantly in the highland capital, because Māyādunnē had abandoned the siege after hearing of his arrival.[28] King Jayavīra's baptism was, one letter suggests, made public.[29] In May, five Kandyan aristocrats converted, ostentatiously intertwining the kingdom's destinies with those of the *Estado*: a nephew of the king became 'Dom João de Crasto' (as the viceroy). A certain *Canaca Modeliar* took the name of 'Martim Afonso' (as Martim Afonso de Sousa). Three other *mudaliyārs* became 'Nuno Álvares' (as Nuno Álvares Pereira, who remained active as a secretary and advisor); 'Pero Vaz' (possibly supported by Pero Vaz Travassos, an ex-*feitor* who had fallen out with Bhuvanekabāhu at Kōṭṭe a few years earlier); and, of course, 'André de Sousa'.[30]

Everything seemed to be falling into place, but in reality all this was just the beginning of yet another series of disappointments. The three Portuguese leaders— friar António Padrão, Nuno Álvares Pereira, and André de Sousa—failed to get along with each other.[31] Jayavīra offered generous compensation for their services, but immediately the bickering began.[32] Sousa nominated officials, ordered a prison to be set up, and walked around holding up a Portuguese banner.[33] In other words, he began to create what he imagined were the signs of a new centre of Portuguese authority. He wrote to Goa assuring the viceroy that the conversion of the people of Kandy was only a matter of time.[34] Yet soon his men rebelled.[35] He still wrote to

---

[26] Sousa to Castro, Kandy, 27 May 1546, *Ceylon*, pp. 359–60. Simão de Coimbra to John III, Goa, 25 December 1546, *Ceylon*, p. 421.

[27] Padrão to Castro, Kandy, 7 June 1546, *Ceylon*, p. 372. Regarding the itinerary, cf. Vito Perniola, *The Catholic Church in Sri Lanka. The Portuguese Period. Original Documents translated into English* (Dehiwala: Tisara Prakasakayo, 1989–1991), vol. I, p. 156. On Lankan roads and footpaths see R. Manukulasooriya, 'Transport in Sri Lanka in Ancient and Mediaeval Times', *Journal of the Royal Asiatic Society of Sri Lanka*, New Series, 24 (1978–79), pp. 49–85.

[28] Padrão to Castro, Kandy, 7 June 1546, *Ceylon*, p. 372.

[29] Sousa to Castro, Kandy, 27 May 1546, *Ceylon*, p. 355.

[30] Pereira to Castro, Kandy, 29 May 1546, *Ceylon*, p. 365. Note however that the king refused to have his sons baptized lest the viceroy came from Goa with a larger force. Sousa to Castro, Kandy, 27 May 1546, *Ceylon*, pp. 356–7.

[31] Sousa to Castro, Kandy, 27 May 1546, *Ceylon*, p. 360. Padrão to Castro, Kandy, 7 June 1546, *Ceylon*, pp. 372–3.

[32] João de Castro to John III, Diu, 16 December 1546, *Ceylon*, p. 414.

[33] Padrão to Castro, Kandy, 7 June 1546, *Ceylon*, p. 373.

[34] Sousa to Castro, Kandy, 27 May 1546, *Ceylon*, p. 357.

[35] André de Sousa to João de Castro, Kandy, 10 June 1546, *Ceylon*, pp. 377–8.

Goa in an optimistic tone, but blamed friar António for being out of touch with Lankan realities.[36] The friar, in his turn, depicted Sousa as a false captain and Jayavīra as a false Christian 'who does not even know how to make the sign of the Cross'. For the pessimistic Franciscan, the landscape itself now came into stark contrast with the paradisiac image that had been painted in Goa:

> The land is very rugged. One cannot reach it from the sea in less than thirty leagues, or twenty through [the lands of] Māyādunnē. The people are weak, the food is poor, the waters cold. Few people live in it, [and they are] melancholic due to being surrounded by mountains. Everything is in the hands of the king, and the people are poor. I cannot put it all into words.[37]

Whilst some Portuguese were behaving as if theirs was a mission of imperial expansion, others felt how the situation was indeed far beyond their control. Theirs was a tiny group of men tossed onto the stage in a notoriously complex highland realm, where practically all political agency remained firmly in the hands of a Lankan king and numerous competing warlords.

Not everything was lost, to be sure. Bhuvanekabāhu VII offered to cooperate with Jayavīra and the Portuguese against Māyādunnē again, and proposed to marry prince Dharmapāla (crowned in Lisbon) to a daughter of Jayavīra. This was a direct offence to Māyādunnē, who had just sought a dynastic match in Kandy. Encouraged by the new alliance, Jayavīra now threatened Māyādunnē and asked him to repay the tribute he had just received.[38] In this confusing conjuncture, one of the most extraordinary claims to Catholic 'cakravartiship' came to the surface. It was formulated not by the king, but by an anxious prince fearful of being sidelined by a sister. This young man had diplomatic talent. As friar António felt increasingly gloomy about Jayavīra, the 'old dog', he displaced his desire to the king's son, a prince 'robust with the arms, quiet and stern', and of course willing to make his conversion public if the viceroy decided to come.[39] The plans and hopes of the candidate were put into writing, and the prince himself addressed a letter to João de Castro at Goa. Therein, he stated that:

> I do not lie as other kings [do]. Your Lordship should know that, whilst my father has become a Christian in secret, I will never become [a Christian] in such a manner. Because I shall be a sun shining over all my people and thus [over] this whole island [of Sri Lanka].[40]

Out of the darkness of friar António's despair, and out of the cold and rugged mountains of Ceylon, shines a formula that is startling even by the standards of our corpus. A Sinhalese prince has resorted to the solar metaphor, a central element of Lankan thought about kingship *and* an eminently readable political and

---

[36] Sousa to Castro, Kandy, 27 May 1546, *Ceylon*, p. 356.
[37] Padrão to Castro, Kandy, 7 June 1546, *Ceylon*, pp. 374–5.
[38] Pereira to Castro, Kandy, 29 May 1546, *Ceylon*, pp. 367–8.
[39] Padrão to Castro, Kandy, 7 June 1546, *Ceylon*, p. 374.
[40] Prince of Kandy to João de Castro, copy in Simão de Coimbra to John III, Goa, 25 December 1546, *Ceylon*, p. 428.

religious topos on the Portuguese side, to facilitate the combination of two distinctly connectable imperial imaginaries. Despite all the frictions and contradictions, high hopes were placed again in the coming of the viceroy, now expected for September 1546. It is quite remarkable how the Portuguese stationed in Kandy, having experienced the sheer physical difficulty of reaching the city, continued to be so invested in planning the expedition of a viceroy (an alter ego of John III) who had never ventured far inland anywhere else in Asia. In early June, another bundle of letters was dispatched to Goa through Batticaloa, the Coromandel Coast and the southern parts of Vijayanagara, to keep up the momentum.[41] But by the time they arrived in Goa, precisely in September, the *Estado* was once again in crisis. Faced with a set of Turkish-inspired attacks at Diu, Chaul, and Bassein, João de Castro could only promise to engage in a campaign, or indeed send his son Álvaro, once the war in India was over.[42]

In reality, Castro was very much in doubt about Sri Lanka. The princes of Kōṭṭe residing in Goa had died of disease earlier in 1546. A relatively level-headed report brought back from Kōṭṭe by Duarte Barbudo, along with the frankly confusing news from Kandy, had left Castro wondering. In a letter to John III, he confessed: 'this Kandy business is obscure, and the letters I get from Ceylon about [Jayavīra's] conversion [...] are so contradictory that I truly cannot decide'. Visibly tired of being put under pressure, Castro added a recommendation for John III to lay Lankan matters to rest for some time: 'this project, it seems, shall be completed by God in due time, but not by force, nor through the pressure of friars'.[43] And, in a more playful letter to his son, the viceroy commented how, should the Castros be accused of not being zealous enough, they could always go and serve Charles V for a proper salary. Distressed by the idiosyncrasies of Lusitanian empire building in South Asia, Castro longed for the clarity of policy reigning in the realm of the one and only true emperor, the one who was also king of Rome.[44]

## TO ROME, WITH LOVE: ASCENDING POLITICAL IDEAS IN THE *COURTE DURÉE*

But Rome was to return to Castro with a vengeance. True, the viceroy's evasive attitude was in consonance with the tone of some royal letters of the time. John III could not quite make up his mind either about what to do.[45] But in reality, João de Castro was, by the beginning of 1547, cornered. Bhuvanekabāhu's diplomatic monopoly was gone; Portuguese soldiers and friars were traversing some of

---

[41] Coimbra to John III, Goa, 25 December 1546, *Ceylon*, p. 427. On the road that led across the Ghats through Kumily Pass, see Pius Malekandathil, *Portuguese Cochin and the Maritime Trade of India, 1500–1663* (New Delhi: Manohar, 2001), p. 203.

[42] João de Castro to John III, Diu, 16 December 1546, fragments put together in *Ceylon*, p. 412.

[43] Castro to John III, Diu, 16 December 1546, *Ceylon*, p. 411 and 414.

[44] João de Castro to Álvaro de Castro, Diu, 14 January 1547, *Ceylon*, pp. 440–1.

[45] John III to João de Castro, Almeirim, 8 March 1546 (second letter), reconstructed in *Ceylon*, pp. 337–9. The quoted copy is from c.1564.

the most remote areas of the island, drawn in by self-proclaimed local allies of the empire; members of the Lankan elite in every one of the island's main kingdoms were actively lobbying for support through a variety of communicational channels. The increased flow of written, and sometimes oral, often idiosyncratic information and imperial imagery left its mark on the system. Opinions about Ceylon were now being given everywhere, and in a pre-bureaucratic system of decision-making, the constant murmur became the new tune. Like an electric current that forms a magnetic field around the conductor, the letters and their carriers had begun to create their own field of power.

The cautious John III himself had at one point, in February 1546, become carried away for a moment and announced to Pope Paul III that Portuguese troops were about to invade Ceylon. The news in Rome, which made it into print before the end of the year, was that Varothaya, the candidate to the Jaffnan throne, 'offered to become a Christian with all his people'. And the prospects of Dom João, whose death was not yet known in Europe, were said to be even brighter: 'if it pleases God that he should come to reign [...] the entire kingdom of Ceilão and the entire land of Malabar [!] will soon receive the Christian faith'.[46] This Roman proclamation is the crowning moment of an extraordinary success story for an idea so outlandish that only a few years earlier it had been simply ignored. The idea of converting a whole country grounded in millennia of Buddhist and Hindu traditions was, thanks to a complex set of communications and miscommunications, connections, reflections, resonances, and coincidences, propelled to the symbolic summit of all hierarchies in Europe. There is certainly a case to argue that sometimes the history of ideas happens in the *courte durée*.

In Goa, a multitude of voices kept insisting that their plans for Ceylon were in the best of interests to the crown because they would contribute to the spreading of the Catholic faith. Invoking that 'all those people' in Ceylon were ready for baptism, the bishop Juan de Albuquerque declared emphatically that, 'for the love of Jesus Christ I [wish] to be one of those going to baptize the king of Kandy [...]. And I shall seek the alms to pay for the voyage myself.' When he received some less encouraging news from Kandy in December 1546, the bishop passed it on to Castro, but added that this was 'not to cool down his good intentions, but rather to ignite them'.[47] As he would insist in another letter, written to the viceroy's son Álvaro in January 1547, 'one cannot take away from the king of Kandy that he has been baptized [...] the mouth now standing open to allow [us to] enter the river. I believe [that we can enter] his kingdom carrying the banner of our faith.'[48]

High-ranking men from Iberia were talking about fighting in an island that, only five years earlier, had been little more than an amorphous blot on the map, an appendix at best to a string of South Asian seaports considered much more important, and an object of generally obscure squabbles between peripheral groups of

---

[46] John III to Paul III, Almeirim, 19 February 1546, Italian translation printed in Rome in 1546 (*Copia de vna littera di noue delle Indie Orientali...*), *Ceylon*, p. 289.
[47] Juan de Albuquerque to João de Castro, Goa, 28 December 1546, *Ceylon*, p. 436.
[48] Juan de Albuquerque to Álvaro de Castro, Goa, 22 January 1547, *Ceylon*, pp. 442–3.

interest. The banners of Christ and the banners of the king were to be planted in a mountain kingdom that had barely been known three years before. As it happened, the temporary suspension of the project due to the Turkish attack on Diu only served to further encourage the enthusiasts. Even with the viceroy still busy at Diu in early 1547, the bishop of Goa asked for permission to dispatch 150 men and proposed to accompany them in person with some mercenaries hired at his own expense.[49] Put under such pressure, João de Castro conceded that a new expedition be led to Kandy under the command of an experienced captain, António Moniz Barreto.[50]

## DIPLOMATIC FRAGMENTATION, 1546–1547

Before we begin to imagine a major invasion of Sri Lanka getting under way in 1547, however, let us ask that single, most basic question again: what *was* Ceylon in the imagination of those making decisions in the *Estado*? Speaking in terms of political space, what most intensely fuelled Juan de Albuquerque's imagination was the sense that, against a backdrop of a deeply fragmented and unintelligible island, the notion of its unity, now voiced most audibly by a prince in Kandy, could be tied up with the Catholic Universalist project. As seems to be the case time and again in human history, an excess of complexity prompted some to embrace straightforward, crude answers. The increasing amount of often disconcerting information about the Native Ground began to pave the way for Portuguese decision-makers to think of it as a potential ground for something approaching military conquest.

In the realm of facts, complexity still dominated, and indeed it increased. On the fringes of Kōṭṭe, Sītāvaka, Kandy, and Jaffna, a further set of polities playing the intricate game of tributary overlordship began to surface. In 1546 already, the Franciscan letter-carrier friar Simão had been intercepted in the Sri Lankan east by a local warlord claiming the title of 'king of Batticaloa'. Everything in the micro-diplomatic offensive of this local lord will sound familiar to us by now. The king acknowledged the suzerainty of Kandy but needed external support to keep a lid on his own unruly subjects. Having attempted to impose his 12-year-old son as successor, he had run into some internal opposition, and showed great interest in the Portuguese when they marched through his realm. He asked to be recognized as a 'vassal and friend in arms' ('*vasalo, e amigo em armas del-Rey de Portugal*'—a rather quirky combination of three different terms used in Portuguese high diplomacy to designate different types of allies: vassals, friends, and brothers-in-arms).[51]

---

[49] Juan de Albuquerque to Álvaro de Castro, Goa, 22 January 1547, *Ceylon*, pp. 442–3.
[50] António Moniz Barreto, whom João de Castro trusted (*Ceylon*, p. 408), had come from Portugal in 1529, fought at the side of Martim Afonso de Sousa in 1535, and been in the battle of Diu in 1546. A later letter underlines his proximity to the Castros. Álvaro de Castro to André Soares, Sintra, 5 August [1549?], *Ceylon*, pp. 535–7.
[51] See António Vasconcelos de Saldanha, *Iustum Imperium. Dos tratados como fundamento do império dos portugueses no Oriente. Estudo de história do direito internacional e do direito português* (Lisbon/Macao: Fundação Oriente/Instituto Português do Oriente, 1997).

He also requested a pair of hunting dogs as a sign of his new alliance, and declared that he would be willing to convert. And he explained that from now on John III could consider the kingdom of Batticaloa as if it was his own: the Portuguese could, for example, build ships there as he would happily provide the necessary wood.[52]

Once António Moniz Barreto reached Sri Lanka in 1547, the first local ruler he ran into was the said king of Batticaloa, who had no intention of letting his potential allies slip through his fingers again.[53] Barreto had Kandy on his mind and eventually managed to leave this little known polity behind—not even in his wildest dreams would he imagine that it might later become the first Dutch foothold in Ceylon. But the march to Kandy was, again, long and difficult. Along the way Barreto became aware of yet another set of smaller 'kingdoms' that functioned as subsidiaries of Kandy in the eastern part of the island. Local leaders came out to meet him as he marched on for three weeks, asking Barreto 'to make them Christians'. First there was the 'King of the land of *Vylaçem*' (Wellassa) with a retinue of local notables. Then came 'another Lord [*Senhor*] of some lands they call *Cauralle* [perhaps from *Korale*, a territorial unit]; he, too, became a Christian.'[54] Friar João de Vila do Conde mentions the 'Princes [*Princepes*] of *Benachim* with their principal men [*seus primcipaes*]', equally in this area.[55] All three episodes allow us precious glimpses into the workings of tributary overlordship and layered kingship or lordship on the eastern fringes of the Lankan system, replicating locally, in a region that we have very little historical evidence for, the political and diplomatic logics of the symbolic centre of *cakravartiship*. There is much reason to believe that these polities were generally active diplomatically, each entertaining their own networks to counterbalance the hegemony of Kandy. In 1547, Barreto was however fixated enough on the highland capital to ignore all he saw. In this sense, Kandy's radiance was considerable, and the little kings subjected to it were indeed left empty-handed.

When Barreto finally arrived in Kandy, Jayavīra was in a relatively positive conjunction as a new alliance with Bhuvanekabāhu had begun to take shape. The reception was sobering. The Portuguese leader had to wait for over a week to see the ruler. And when he asked Jayavīra to make his baptism public, the king declared that he had no intention of doing so before the Portuguese 'gave him the *Reyno* of Madune [i.e. Sītāvaka], and this whole island up to Jaffna'. Clearly, Jayavīra was upping his game. The recurrent theme of Lankan unification was presented to the Portuguese as irradiating from the central highlands to engulf parts of the southwest controlled by Māyādunnē, and all the north towards the strait. Jayavīra styled himself as much more than the ruler of an isolated realm in the mountains: his was a stance as expansive and imperial as that of any other ruler in the lowlands. As Barreto observed the situation, he began to understand the wider implications of Kandy's quest for overlordship, its geographic logics, and how he himself was already caught up in it. Discovering his own Lankan self in the looking glass, he

[52] Simão de Coimbra to John III, Goa, 25 December 1546, *Ceylon*, pp. 431–3.
[53] On the voyage see António Moniz Barreto to João de Castro, Kayalpatnam, 22 April 1547, *Ceylon*, pp. 459–62. The itinerary is not entirely clear.
[54] António Moniz Barreto to João de Castro, Colombo, 11 October 1547, *Ceylon*, pp. 463–4.
[55] João de Vila do Conde to João de Castro, Colombo, 11 October 1547, *Ceylon*, p. 474.

began to realize that 'all these *régulos* ['little kings' of *Vylaçem, Cauralle* etc.] were becoming [Christians] because they are neighbours of Kandy and fear that if they remain pagans [*gentyos*] and the king of Kandy [becomes] a Christian, I might destroy them and take their lands and give them to the Christians of Kandy'.[56]

As the days went by in Kandy, the Portuguese began to feel trapped, surrounded as they were by 'very high uninhabited mountain ranges where we could all get lost [and] starve to death'. Finally, the men decided to burn their belongings and attempt an escape to Colombo.[57] The mountain pass at Balane, connecting Kandy with the southwestern lowlands, proved difficult to cross as Jayavīra wished to keep the Portuguese in his kingdom. Barreto panicked. Feeling that he was caught between the lines 'in the middle of the jungle and thirty leagues from the sea', he began to wander around pillaging villages. He did so in a rural area that no Portuguese had ever crossed before as far as we know, around the temple of Gadaladeniya.[58] These headless wanderings are remarkably different from what we used to imagine European 'explorations' in Asia to be. Finally, the party forced its way through into lands controlled by Māyādunnē, where they were well received.[59] In contrast, when they passed through areas controlled by Kōṭṭe between Negumbo and Colombo, things were worse again. About three months after his triumphant disembarking at Batticaloa, Barreto arrived in Colombo 'exhausted and devastated'.[60]

A series of twists and turns now led to an improbable Portuguese alliance with the traditional arch-enemy Māyādunnē. Barreto, confused and disillusioned with both Kandy and Kōṭṭe, went up the Kelani River in a boat to meet the king of Sītāvaka halfway between the capitals.[61] The Portuguese leader oscillated between despair and a slightly hysterical euphoria at the prospect of picking his allies. He was by now clearly overwhelmed by it all—a feeling quite easily shared by the modern reader. Māyādunnē hoped to secure Portuguese support for the conquest of Kōṭṭe; Bhuvanekabāhu, eager to salvage his relationship with John III, wished to defend his kingdom and secure the succession of Dharmapāla;[62] and Jayavīra, distressed by the prospect of being left out of the deal, soon sent apologies along with some artillery that the party had left behind, a gift of 10,000 *pardaus* for the

---

[56] Barreto to Castro, Colombo, 11 October 1547, *Ceylon*, p. 465.

[57] Barreto to Castro, Colombo, 11 October 1547, *Ceylon*, p. 467. See however the slightly different version in Gaspar Correia, *Lendas da Índia*, edited by M. Lopes de Almeida (Porto: Lello & Irmão, 1975), vol. IV, pp. 674–8.

[58] Barreto to Castro, Colombo, 11 October 1547, *Ceylon*, p. 468. Cf. Fernão de Queiroz, *Conquista Temporal e Espiritual de Ceilão* (Colombo: Government Press, 1916), pp. 215 and 217.

[59] The most detailed narrative is in Diogo do Couto, *Da Asia* (Lisbon: Livraria de São Carlos, 1973–1975), vol. VI, book iv, chapter 7, pp. 333–6.

[60] Barreto to Castro, Colombo, 11 October 1547, *Ceylon*, p. 469. The dates can only be inferred, but it seems that Barreto was in Batticaloa in May 1547 and arrived at Colombo in August.

[61] Māyādunnē to Castro [between Kōṭṭe and Sītāvaka], 26 October 1547, *Ceylon*, p. 478. Schurhammer suggests that the meeting may have taken place at Gurubewila. Perniola mentions Hanwella, another name for the same place. *The Catholic Church*, vol. I, p. 231.

[62] According to Queiroz, *Conquista*, pp. 215–16, Bhuvanekabāhu was absent for a pilgrimage to the great shrine of Trincomalee and came back hurriedly when he heard about the Portuguese marching through the lands of Māyādunnē. No other information about such distant voyages by the king of Kōṭṭe is extant.

soldiers, and an epistle to the Franciscans urging them to return to Kandy to accomplish their mission.[63]

A letter sent by Māyādunnē to Goa around this time illustrates well how the old ideal of attracting Portuguese forces to Lanka by building up a relationship of vassalage remained alive, and how it kept fuelling projects of military intervention, concocted by the Lankan elite to attract Portuguese resources to the Native Ground:

> I [Māyādunnē] have for many years desired the peace and friendship of the King of Portugal, and to be his vassal [...] For this reason I offer myself with my people to go and take [for him] the kingdom [of Kandy], if [the viceroy] grants it to me in the name of the king of Portugal for a son of mine [possibly the future king Rājasiṃha]. And for this [I ask] to be assisted with 200 well-armed Portuguese men, and I shall pay the expenses of the armada and the salary of the Portuguese as soon as they arrive. And one half of the treasure of Kandy shall be for the king of Portugal. And [I ask you to] order the captain not to leave me before the war is completed.[64]

The letter was remarkably clear with regard to the spatial configuration of powers. Māyādunnē mentions his ambition in principle to control the 'ten sea ports that are in this island' whilst also asking specifically, perhaps in order not to be too blunt about his desire to replace Bhuvanekabāhu, to be granted the port of Chilaw, where he hoped to conduct his trade with the Portuguese Crown—that is, to set up a new *feitoria*. There, about halfway between Colombo and Jaffna, Māyādunnē would pay his own tribute to John III. Amidst the initiatives of Kandy and Kōṭṭe, Māyādunnē's ambitions were equally intact, and indeed vast, covering a long belt of lands stretching from the far South all the way to the *korale* of Pitigal in the North.

The Portuguese stood at a crossroads, but had no clear idea of where to go. As soon as Bhuvanekabāhu heard about Māyādunnē's diplomatic offensive, he offered money to make sure Barreto did *not* take the Sītāvakan ambassador to Goa.[65] Māyādunnē's ambassador did make it to Goa in November 1547,[66] prompting Bhuvanekabāhu to send his own envoy after him.[67] Whilst no documents exist about the dealings of the two rival ambassadors in Goa, the chorus of militant voices surrounding the events, again reacting to complexity with one-dimensional answers, is well documented. Together, Juan de Albuquerque, friar João de Vila do Conde, and Francis Xavier all claimed for more blood to be shed in the name of Christ. The bishop urged the viceroy to keep his promise of making war.[68] The friar insisted how 'God is powerful, and He can resuscitate in the petrified hearts of these people the [souls of the] sons of Abraham; and because they place such obstacles in the way of the Holy Spirit, I believe this will not be possible without employing force'.[69] The new apostle of the Indies, in his turn, did not hesitate to

[63] Couto, *Da Asia*, vol. VI, book iv, chapter 7, p. 337.
[64] Māyādunnē to João de Castro [between Kōṭṭe and Sītāvaka], 26 October 1547, *Ceylon*, p. 477.
[65] João de Vila do Conde to João de Castro, Cochin, 27 November 1547, *Ceylon*, pp. 492–3.
[66] Cf. Register of the gifts sent by Māyādunnē to Dom João de Castro, Goa, 27 November 1547, *Ceylon*, p. 498.
[67] Rui Gonçalves de Caminha to João de Castro [Cochin], 9 January 1548, *Ceylon*, p. 500.
[68] Juan de Albuquerque to João de Castro, Cochin, 26 November 1547, *Ceylon*, p. 483.
[69] João de Vila do Conde to João de Castro, Colombo, 11 October 1547, *Ceylon*, p. 473.

go on proclaiming to the world that 'the island of Ceylão will be all Christian within a year, and [along with it] many kings of the Malabar [Coast], and around Cape Comorim and in many other parts' with due military support.[70]

What none of these grand strategists wished to acknowledge was the extreme vulnerability of Portuguese expeditionary forces in the island, and how they were most likely to continue being tossed around between various, fully operational foci of Lankan royal power, even if they were to be given some sort of officially sanctioned, religiously legitimated mandate in Goa or Lisbon.

## A STEP TOWARDS THE ABYSS: THE FIRST PORTUGUESE DISASTER, 1548–1550

The swelling of belligerent voices was interrupted unexpectedly when João de Castro died on 6 June 1548, being replaced by the elderly Garcia de Sá (gv. 1548–9). Sá reacted as Castro once had upon arriving at Goa: rather than sending troops, he sent letters in an attempt to understand the situation.[71] Although he was an uncle of Martim Afonso de Sousa and had close ties with Francis Xavier,[72] and even though people in Goa kept talking about the need to take revenge for the massacre of Mannār in 1544,[73] Sá refused to invade Jaffna.[74] He may have been reluctant due to continuing Turkish pressures in the North.[75] Possibly as well, the orders arriving from Portugal were slightly less encouraging than in previous years. Whilst Francis Xavier continued to agitate against Bhuvanekabāhu, the cause did not have the full support of the Portuguese crown.[76]

This may be the reason why there is hardly anything left in the official documentation from 1548–9 regarding Kandy and Sītāvaka: John III may have ceased considering these kingdoms as serious alternatives to Kōṭṭe. As a matter of fact, the relationship between Bhuvanekabāhu and the Portuguese royal family appears at its best again during these years. Queen Catherine was sending her personal goldsmith to the island to coordinate work on prestige objects, and Bhuvanekabāhu assisted them personally in the recruitment of local craftsmen.[77] As a major creditor of John III and a well-seasoned vassal, he seems to have regained some space for manoeuvring. Contrarily to Māyādunnē or Jayavīra, he had in his favour a well-working network of contacts connecting Kōṭṭe directly with Lisbon.[78] Long-distance

---

[70] Francis Xavier to John III, Cochin, 20 January 1548, *Ceylon*, pp. 505–6.

[71] Bhuvanekabāhu VII to John III, Kōṭṭe, 7 December 1548, *Ceylon*, p. 520.

[72] On Sá, see Schurhammer in *Ceylon*, p. 520.

[73] Rui Gonçalves de Caminha to John III, Goa, 30 December 1548, *Ceylon*, p. 526.

[74] António do Casal to John III, Cochin, 12 January 1549, *Ceylon*, pp. 527–8.

[75] On Garcia de Sá and the financial crisis, Correia, *Lendas*, vol. IV, pp. 661–3.

[76] Xavier to John III, Cochin, 26 January 1549, *Ceylon*, pp. 532–4.

[77] Bhuvanekabāhu VII to Catherine, Kōṭṭe, 11 December 1549, *Ceylon*, pp. 538–9.

[78] We thus see him writing with relative familiarity, in 1548 and 1549 (*Ceylon*, pp. 520–5 and 538–46), to John III, his wife, his brother, and the Count of Castanheira, the chief financial overseer of the kingdom (*vedor da fazenda*) since 1530 and one of the men who had solemnly received Śrī Rāmarakṣa in Lisbon in 1542. Cf. Queiroz, *Conquista*, p. 185.

diplomacy at the highest level trumped the initiatives launched by other Lankan rulers. For a moment, everything seemed to be falling back into place. Far from desperate, Bhuvanekabāhu VII struck a forthcoming, energetic tone. He stressed how he would 'kiss the hands of Your Highness' if John III agreed to forbid any Portuguese subjects from trading in any other ports than Colombo.[79] In the previous year already, he had briskly ordered Portuguese traders not to go to Sītāvaka[80] and mobilized the *feitor* António Pessoa to support this position.[81] Pessoa also argued that fomenting war in the lowlands could make it more difficult to obtain cinnamon for the Crown.[82] The moment was one of relative *détente*. Even friar António do Casal, the Franciscan custodian in Asia, expressed hope for a peaceful development: having only a few churches along the coast of southwestern Ceylon was not a bad start, he argued, and with patience and diplomacy more would come.[83] Faithful to his firmly established convictions, Bhuvanekabāhu VII maintained at the same time in a letter to John III how he had only two priorities in life: 'your friendship, and my God'.[84]

When, in mid 1549, Māyādunnē laid yet another siege on Kōṭṭe,[85] Bhuvanekabāhu asked for help from Goa and, in exchange for an increased tribute, obtained it. The new governor Jorge Cabral (gv. 1549–50) sent a relief armada in January 1550.[86] As so many times before, Māyādunnē lifted the siege. It soon came to a showdown further inland, and Māyādunnē was forced to accept the overlordship of Kōṭṭe.[87] Interestingly, however, the Portuguese captain Jorge de Castro also had orders from Goa to proceed to the highlands to assist the disgruntled prince Karaliyaddē Baṇḍāra—certainly not something that was in the interest of Bhuvanekabāhu.[88] In April 1550, Jorge de Castro walked into a trap.[89] The Portuguese were soon surrounded in the mountains and unable to retreat.[90] The first major military disaster of a European power in Ceylon cost the life of around

[79] Bhuvanekabāhu VII to John III, Kōṭṭe, 11 December 1548, *Ceylon*, p. 525.

[80] Cristóvão Rebelo and other inhabitants of Ceylon to João de Castro, Colombo, 27 November 1547, *Ceylon*, p. 496.

[81] 'Livro que trata das cousas da Índia e do Japão', edited by Adelino de Almeida Calado, *Boletim da Biblioteca da Universidade de Coimbra*, 24 (1960), p. 38. On the evolution of the trade monopolies see Luís Filipe Thomaz, *A questão da pimenta em meados do século XVI. Um debate político do governo de D. João de Castro* (Lisbon: CEPCEP, 1998), pp. 76–88.

[82] 'Livro que trata das cousas da Índia e do Japão', p. 37.

[83] António do Casal to John III, Cochin, 21 January 1549, *Ceylon*, p. 529. On the churches, see friar João Noé to John III, Cochin, 28 January 1552, *Ceylon*, p. 608. On the ports and their status, see C. R. De Silva, 'The First Portuguese Revenue Register of the Kingdom of Kotte – 1599', *The Ceylon Journal of Historical and Social Studies*, New Series, 5, 1–2 (1975), pp. 71–153.

[84] Bhuvanekabāhu VII to John III, Kōṭṭe, 7 December 1548, *Ceylon*, p. 521.

[85] Śrī Rāmarakṣa to Queen Catherine, Cochin, 28 January 1551, *Ceylon*, pp. 559–68. Couto, *Da Asia*, vol. VI, book viii, chapters 3–4, pp. 150–6 and VI, viii, 6–7, pp. 165–79.

[86] Couto, *Da Asia*, vol. VI, book viii, chapter 3, pp. 150–2.

[87] Couto, *Da Asia*, vol. VI, book viii, chapter 6, pp. 169–75. Śrī Rāmarakṣa to Queen Catherine, Cochin, 28 January 1551, *Ceylon*, p. 560.

[88] Couto, *Da Asia*, vol. VI, book viii, chapter 4, pp. 154–5.

[89] According to Śrī Rāmarakṣa, Bhuvanekabāhu tried to convince the Portuguese not to go to Kandy. *Ceylon*, p. 563. Cf. De Silva, 'The Rise and Fall of the Kingdom of Sitawaka (1521–1593)', *The Ceylon Journal of Historical and Social Studies*, 7, 1 (1977), p. 20.

[90] Couto, *Da Asia*, vol. VI, book viii, chapter 7, p. 177.

200 Portuguese men.[91] Despite the ensuing pause in activities, Bhuvanekabāhu VII had no reason to jubilate. Soon rumours circulated—not without some plausibility— that the disaster had been orchestrated by him. The king of Kōṭṭe was now facing not only the fragmented political landscape that had traditionally opposed centrifugal forces in the island. It is not even the intertwinement of the Lankan galactic system with wider regional politics, as in the 1530s, that must have worried him most. The problem for him was a fragmented landscape along with a situation where virtually *all* the rulers in the island were capable of forging alliances with the disoriented Portuguese, and appealing to their fast-evolving imperial imagination to make them come to the island.

## DREAMS, BUT NO STRATEGY: SRI LANKA AS A NEW ELDORADO (1550–1551)

After Castro's defeat, no-one in Ceylon expected any high-ranking Portuguese officer to visit the island anytime soon. But on 17 October 1550 a freshly appointed viceroy from Lisbon, Afonso de Noronha, came through Colombo surprisingly, on his way to Goa. Noronha did not carry new orders regarding the island,[92] and indeed John III was asking for more information to be gathered before decisions could be made in Lisbon.[93] But the disaster of Kandy was fresh in people's minds.[94] Many in Colombo accused Bhuvanekabāhu of having orchestrated it.[95] The Franciscans were upset about the demolition of a clandestine church in the south. Perhaps most importantly, Diogo de Noronha, a nephew of the new viceroy, began lobbying again for an alliance with Māyādunnē.[96] The viceroy grew ambiguous. In his letters to John III and Catherine, written in January 1551, he did not raise his voice openly against Bhuvanekabāhu. But he recommended giving both Bhuvanekabāhu and Māyādunnē a chance.[97]

Behind the scenes, Noronha was already pulling other strings. He believed that Māyādunnē might indeed have more to offer than Bhuvanekabāhu, even though the latter had just sent another loan of 10,000 *pardaus* to Cochin through his veteran ambassador, Śrī Rāmarakṣa.[98] The viceroy thought that the *Estado* should

---

[91] *Ceylon*, pp. 178 and 564. Couto, *Da Asia*, vol. VI, book viii, chapter 7, p. 179.

[92] The royal orders are summarized in Francisco de Andrade, *Crónica de D. João III*, edited by M. Lopes de Almeida (Porto: Lello, 1976), 4a parte, cap. 73, p. 1075.

[93] Andrade, *Crónica*, p. 1076. The same cautious stance shines through the orders given in 1552. John III to Afonso de Noronha, Almeirim, 20 March 1552, reported in Queiroz, *Conquista*, p. 235.

[94] Afonso de Noronha to John III, Cochin, 16 January 1551, *Ceylon*, pp. 550–1. Cf. Śrī Rāmarakṣa to Catherine, Cochin, 28 January 1551, *Ceylon*, p. 565.

[95] Afonso de Noronha to John III, Cochin, 16 January 1551, *Ceylon*, p. 550.

[96] Śrī Rāmarakṣa to Catherine, Cochin, 28 January 1551, *Ceylon*, pp. 564–5. This poorly documented individual came to India in 1545 and arrived in Ceylon in 1550 with Jorge de Castro. He is not identical with Diogo de Noronha, the son of Álvaro de Noronha (*Ceylon*, p. 564, note 2).

[97] Afonso de Noronha to John III, Cochin, 16 January 1551, *Ceylon*, p. 553.

[98] Śrī Rāmarakṣa to Catherine, Cochin, 28 January 1551, *Ceylon*, p. 559. According to a passage in the same letter, pp. 566–7, the envoy was not received with much warmth.

keep an open mind, and that Lisbon should not worry excessively about the supply of ivory objects so dear to the queen.[99] A part of Noronha's strategy on the ground was to stretch the Sinhalese ruler's patience, for example by asking him for a further, impossibly large loan. Immediately after Bhuvanekabāhu refused, Noronha received an ambassador from Sītāvaka on his ship. Predictably enough, Māyādunnē asked to 'be a vassal' ('*ser vasalo*') of John III and supported his claim by displaying a banner that João de Castro had sent him in 1547. Noronha staged a pompous reception and confirmed Māyādunnē as a vassal.[100] But why?

The question of how to control land and in particular the production of spices, but also foodstuff, was a matter of some debate during these years. In one of his letters, the viceroy developed a vision of the island in which the old Lankan *topos* of salubrity and fertility still played its role, but now under a new, decidedly Portuguese aegis: Ceylon appears as being 'very fertile' and yielding rich harvests, and these resources should be put in the service of the empire.[101] Conversions could be made, Muslims expelled,[102] and a new foothold gained to which the Portuguese could retreat from India in case of necessity.[103] Noronha also proposed to build a new fort at Colombo, as a basis for further meddling in local politics, increasing tributes, and even extracting land revenues. The project encompassed Kandy, where Jayavīra was to be 'taken out' and 'the kingdom [...] conquered' with the help of Māyādunnē. John III was there promised a Christian kingdom yielding as richly as a 'mine of precious stones'.[104]

Historians have asked themselves in vain what orders precisely Noronha may have given upon leaving the island. According to the viceroy himself, in a letter written over a year later in January 1552, he ordered the *alcaide-mor* Gaspar de Azevedo to avoid new conflicts between Bhuvanekabāhu and Māyādunnē.[105] But in fact, leaving Colombo and Kōṭṭe without assistance at the end of the sailing season, in January 1551, amounted to encouraging Māyādunnē to attack. Hostilities erupted soon indeed, and rumours began to spread that Māyādunnē had managed to hire someone close enough to Bhuvanekabāhu to get the monarch killed. Bhuvanekabāhu moved to Kelaniya with his personal guard of eighty Portuguese soldiers but there, on a veranda of the royal palace, he was assassinated. The exact circumstances remain obscure.[106] But it is certainly significant that not much was done to clarify the matter and that, incidentally or not, the viceroy had left detailed

---

[99] Noronha to John III, Cochin, 16 January 1551, p. 556. Diogo Vaz came back with over 1000 rubies, 500 emeralds, a large rock crystal, and numerous objects made of gold. Sebastião Ferreira to Catherine, Cochin, 24 January 1551, *Ceylon*, p. 558.

[100] Noronha to John III, Cochin, 16 January 1551, pp. 551–3.

[101] Noronha to John III, Cochin, 16 January 1551, p. 554.

[102] Baltasar Gago to the Jesuits in Portugal, Cochin, 20 January 1552, *Ceylon*, pp. 575–6.

[103] Simão de Coimbra to John III, 25 December 1546, *Ceylon*, p. 425; Correia, *Lendas*, vol. III, p. 819; Couto, *O Soldado Prático*, p. 195.

[104] Noronha to John III, Cochin, 16 January 1551, *Ceylon*, p. 555.

[105] Afonso de Noronha to John III, Cochin, 27 January 1552, *Ceylon*, p. 582.

[106] Couto describes the assassination in *Da Asia*, vol. VI, book ix, chapter 16, p. 339. Cf. Noronha to John III, Cochin, 27 January 1552, *Ceylon*, pp. 584–5 and De Silva, 'The rise and fall of the kingdom of Sitawaka', pp. 21–2.

instructions about how to proceed if Bhuvanekabāhu happened to die.[107] Years later, a Portuguese soldier confessed to having killed the Sinhalese monarch unwittingly when aiming at a pigeon—but this soldier had been a servant of the viceroy.[108] And, as one chronicler put it, 'it would be difficult to persuade anyone that human eyes could mistake a man for a pigeon'.[109]

With Bhuvanekabāhu VII dead, his closest followers in Kōṭṭe proclaimed the appointed heir Dharmapāla as the new king. Dharmapāla's father, Vīdiyē Baṇḍāra, was to serve as regent. The royal *alvará* passed by John III in 1543 to confirm this line of succession was presented to the Portuguese commander Gaspar de Azevedo along with a promise of increasing the annual cinnamon tribute.[110] But as soon as the news arrived in Goa, the viceroy decided to take a large fleet to the island. The campaign, launched in September 1551, was more than just a military relief mission. It involved a number of high-ranking personalities such as the bishop of Goa, the highest-ranking financial officer of the *Estado* (the *vedor da fazenda*), the Franciscan custodian for Asia, and a number of other Franciscans, Dominicans, and Jesuits.[111] But now that the plans forged over the years finally materialized, it also began to emerge how easily tensions could arise between the military and the missionary actors at play. As the *vedor* Simão Botelho put it, 'it seems that, because the aims [of the campaign] were treasures and Christianity, [two] things so different from each other, Our Lord did not wish for any of the two to be achieved'.[112]

Once on the ground, the viceroy admitted some embarrassment about the murder of Bhuvanekabāhu—it was too obviously to his own advantage. But he also made it clear that it was important to move on.[113] His aims included imposing law and order in Colombo, and getting a share of the royal treasure at Kōṭṭe. This grand theft was later described as a logical measure—indeed, a 'remedy'—at a time of acute financial pressures.[114] Noronha made sure that critical voices in the capital of the *Estado* were neutralized. In Ceylon, he further upped his game by telling Vīdiyē Baṇḍāra and Śrī Rāmarakṣa that Dharmapāla's succession to the throne could only be validated if the prince converted to the Catholic faith. The reaction was predictable on the one hand: the Kōṭṭe leaders considered a conversion of Dharmapāla to be risky. On the other hand, they did not rule out moving towards a royal conversion along with substantial tributary payments as long as their military needs were taken into account. The proposed solution was that the Portuguese should first 'pacify' the lowlands, reimpose Kōṭṭe's authority within the boundaries of 1521, subdue Sītāvaka, and leave a contingent of special troops. In exchange,

---

[107] Noronha to John III, Cochin, 27 January 1552, *Ceylon*, pp. 582–3. News of the death were not sent to Goa before mid May.

[108] Couto, *Da Asia*, vol. VI, book ix, chapter 16, p. 341.      [109] Queiroz, *Conquista*, p. 234.

[110] Noronha to John III, Cochin, 27 January 1552, *Ceylon*, pp. 585–6.

[111] On the bishop's presence in Colombo and Kōṭṭe, see Noronha to John III, Cochin, 27 January 1552, *Ceylon*, p. 588. On António Pessoa, p. 589. On the Jesuits and Dominicans, see friar João Noé to John III, Cochin, 28 January 1552, *Ceylon*, p. 608.

[112] Simão Botelho to John III, Cochin, 30 January 1552, *Ceylon*, pp, 612–13.

[113] Noronha to John III, Cochin, 27 January 1552, *Ceylon*, pp. 584–5.

[114] Afonso de Noronha to Queen Catherine, Cochin, 27 January 1552, *Ceylon*, p. 605.

the Kōṭṭe leaders offered to then hand over the royal treasure. This was the Matrioshka Principle in action again—though now, for the first time at the top of the Kōṭṭe hierarchy, with a Catholic twist. Noronha agreed to consider the deal before he marched to Kōṭṭe to meet the new vassal king.[115]

It was soon clear for all to see that the prospect of pillage trumped almost anything else among Noronha's priorities. Two ecclesiastic leaders were sent to 'receive the treasure' of Bhuvanekabāhu VII at Kōṭṭe and 'weigh, count and measure [it] in public'. However, the materials, valued around 40,000–50,000 *pardaus*, did not meet the viceroy's expectations, and attempts made during the following days to locate further valuables remained unsuccessful. Eventually Vīdiyē Baṇḍāra proposed to pay 200,000 *pardaus* to finance a campaign against Sītāvaka: 100,000 immediately, and another 100,000 after the viceroy's return from Sītāvaka. The second payment was to be complemented with more materials, to be taken from the Kōṭṭe Temple of the Buddha's Tooth. It is difficult not to feel reminded of comparable discussions around royal treasures in Mexico and especially Peru. Noronha swiftly broke his promises and proceeded straight to Kōṭṭe to 'receive' the contents of the Temple of the Buddha's Tooth, adjacent to the royal palace. What ensued was the officially sanctioned looting, over two days, of one of the central institutions of Buddhist kingship in Sri Lanka—indeed, one of the holiest places in all Asia.[116] The list of what was taken, compiled meticulously by the royal financial overseer, bears witness to an act of desecration comparable to the worst doings of Spanish conquistadors in the New World—except, of course, that we shall see yet another four decades go by before conquest as such began. It is disturbing to note that neither the event as such, nor the sources documenting it, have received much attention at all.

The acts of violence thus perpetrated were immediately followed by events revealing a more complex balance of powers than, say, those conditioning the actions of Cortés and Pizarro. Many leading nobles abandoned Kōṭṭe, and Noronha felt forced to devolve part of the treasure. When the regent Vīdiyē Baṇḍāra put down his foot, Noronha retreated to Colombo. It was decided that the promised expedition to Sītāvaka had to be carried out. Noronha marched to Sītāvaka and defeated Māyādunnē. Yet the Kōṭṭe leadership now saw an opportunity to retract from the deal in their own turn.[117] False information was given repeatedly regarding the whereabouts of the royal treasure, leading to increasingly grotesque Portuguese attempts to locate it. Noronha's immature tactics failed in the face of the Lankan elite's political resourcefulness. By the end of 1551, the viceroy was sufficiently demoralized to sail off to the Malabar Coast. Perhaps this is the sort of thing that would have awaited the Spanish in Mexico and Peru, had the forces holding their empires together not been weakened so much in the immediate run-up to the key

---

[115] Noronha to John III, Cochin, 27 January 1552, *Ceylon*, pp. 586–90.

[116] Noronha to John III, Cochin, 27 January 1552, *Ceylon*, pp. 590–3. The inventory is published in Sousa Viterbo, *O thesouro do rei de Ceylão* (Lisbon: Typographia da Academia Real das Sciencias, 1904). An English translation is currently under preparation.

[117] Noronha to John III, Cochin, 27 January 1552, *Ceylon*, pp. 593–8. Cf. Couto, *Da Asia*, vol. VI, book ix, chapter 17, p. 350.

encounters between Cortés and Pizarro on the one hand, and the local monarchs on the other.

Before leaving, the Portuguese viceroy decided to set up a new garrison of 300 men in Colombo. Its mandate was to keep the lowlands 'at peace', 'accomplish the destruction of Māyādunnē', and work towards locating the treasure of Kōṭṭe.[118] Further negotiations were held with the Kōṭṭe leaders. Soon the Portuguese garrison received from Kōṭṭe a sum of money sufficient to cover six months of salaries.[119] The arrangement may not have looked fundamentally different from what had been in place repeatedly since 1518. Tribute was paid and money lent in exchange for a garrison at Colombo that could assist Kōṭṭe against Māyādunnē. But by now the Portuguese presence in the island had become substantially more disruptive than before. It was much more fragile than the Spanish presence in Mexico and Peru, but also much more aggressive than it had been just five years earlier in Sri Lanka. The Portuguese juggled with multiple allies in the island. A viceroy had looted the Temple of the Buddha's Tooth. And the *Estado* was being led by a group of men ideologically and materially driven, in principle at least, to take further action without respecting the policy guidelines of John III. Global and regional forces, albeit not yet sanctioned by the monarch whose global imperial mandate they drew legitimacy from, were beginning to disrupt with novel brutality the mechanisms of local politics.

---

[118] Noronha to John III, Cochin, 27 January 1552, *Ceylon*, pp. 597–9. Cf. Couto, *Da Asia*, vol. VI, book ix, chapter 18, p. 352.

[119] Noronha to John III, Cochin, 27 January 1552, *Ceylon*, p. 601.

# 6

## *Translatio Imperii* in the Tropics
### Colombo, the Spectre of Cortés in Asia, and the Unification of Iberian Empires

How did the 'Native Ground' become a ground for conquest? One cannot set out to conquer something that is not in one's imagination as a conquerable entity. The key to understanding the transition from low- to high-cost intervention, and the gradual shaping of the Portuguese idea of conquering and colonizing Sri Lanka, is to be found in the second half of the sixteenth century. The 1550s to 1570s, however, are poorly documented, forcing us to move forward at a faster pace than up to now. The present chapter highlights how Kōṭṭe was pushed into a defensive position by its Lankan enemies after 1550, how a *mestiço* colony was formed in Colombo precisely by those military pressures, and how the realities of war produced a legal document that finally paved the way, between the new Luso-Lankan capital and Lisbon, for the policy renewal of the final decades of the century. We are approaching the moment of conquest, but are still not quite there yet.

### OF REBELS AND CONQUERORS: THE LOCAL CONTINGENCIES OF EMPIRE BUILDING

In 1552, the Jesuit Manuel de Morais complained about the lack of religious orthodoxy among the Portuguese living in Colombo:

> [Portuguese] men were publicly living in a sinful state with Pagan and Christian [women]; they were eating meat in public on Fridays and Saturdays, both at the tables of the captains and in the private homes; they made bread on Sundays and holidays like on any other day, and [also on Sundays] they worked as carpenters and blacksmiths like anyone else. Most people did not go to confession, there were more unmarried than married women, and more women than men; most of the latter were convicted criminals, and many were rebels, and in alliance with the Pagans, and all this was so common and normal, that it was not considered to be sinful, nor strange in any way.[1]

By 'rebels', of course, the author meant people who refused to recognize the authority of the Portuguese Crown at all times. Between Goa on the one hand and the informal colonies of the Bay of Bengal on the other, Colombo began to emerge as

---

[1] Manuel de Morais to the Company in Coimbra, Colombo, 28 November 1552, in Georg Schurhammer and Ernst August Voretzsch, *Ceylon zur Zeit des Königs Bhuvaneka Bahu und Franz Xavers 1539–1552* (Leipzig: Verlag der Asia Major, 1928) (henceforth cited as '*Ceylon*'), p. 625.

an original frontier formation in its own right. It was both a city of the empire and something else. It hosted crown officials and a sizeable garrison responding to orders from Goa. When Afonso de Noronha, the viceroy anxious to find the treasure of the deceased king of Kōṭṭe, moved back to India in 1551, he left a garrison of 400 men.[2] Work began on a fortification to protect only the western half of what is today central Colombo, that is, the area delimited by the bay, the lagoon, and the rivulet running between the two. No map survives of this structure, but we can imagine it by looking at later vistas (Figure 6.1) and imagining only half the city of Colombo—the western part bordering on the ocean, where the Franciscans and some private traders had settled in the previous decade—defended by walls.[3] Had it survived, this defensive structure would have created a division between a 'Portuguese' town of sorts and the old port town of Kolambā. But this soon turned out to be an ephemeral solution.

Behind the official façade, older power structures and cultural habits persisted. The Portuguese military presence in Colombo and Kōṭṭe may have been formalized in 1551 but, as during the previous period, the Portuguese rarely took the lead militarily, rather participating, and often reluctantly so, in campaigns they had little to do with in the first place. Very quickly, the situation got out of hand. With the viceroy gone, the Kōṭṭe leadership convinced the Portuguese captain, João Henriques, not only to quit the treasure hunt, but also to support a new dynastic project. The house of Kōṭṭe was now to be united with that of the Seven Korales, an inland area extending north of the old capital, where Māyādunnē had exerted influence in the past.[4] When the Portuguese captain died in May 1552, and his successor Diogo de Melo Coutinho opposed the plan,[5] the queen regent (Vīdiyē Baṇḍāra's wife, the daughter of Bhuvanekabāhu and mother of Dharmapāla), abandoned Kōṭṭe with a large retinue. She set up quarters at Rayigama, south of Colombo, where once the third kingdom of the lowlands had had its capital. By the time Duarte de Eça, the next captain, arrived from India later that year, the situation was too complicated for words.[6]

A peculiar episode may give us an idea of how antagonisms in this period worked along complex lines of fracture, and how the Portuguese acted mostly in response to unexpected circumstances, tactically, rather than following a solid strategy. Imprisoned in Colombo, the regent Vīdiyē Baṇḍāra promised to convert and escaped through a tunnel connecting his cell to the garden of the Franciscan convent around the end of 1552. Once he reached the Galle area in the south, he gathered people to attack 'all the churches and Christians that he could find'.

---

[2] Diogo do Couto, *Da Asia* (Lisbon: Livraria de São Carlos, 1973–5), vol. VI, book ix, chapter 18, pp. 352–3.

[3] Fernão de Queiroz, *Conquista Temporal e Espiritual de Ceilão* (Colombo: Government Press, 1916), p. 246.

[4] *Da Asia*, vol. VI, book ix, chapter 19, p. 365. Dharmapala was to marry a sister of the lord of the Seven Korales, who was a first cousin of Vīdiyē Baṇḍāra.

[5] *Da Asia*, vol. VI, book x, chapter 7, pp. 442–3. 'Deyagu de Mel' appears in the *Rājāvaliya*, p. 81.

[6] Couto, *Da Asia*, VI, book x, chapter 8, p. 451. Fernão de Queiroz describes a similar episode, but places it around late 1554. *Conquista Temporal e Espiritual de Ceilão* (Colombo: Government Press, 1916), pp. 249–51.

He eventually settled in Pālanda, not far to the south from Kōṭṭe, defying the authority of his own son, Dharmapāla.[7] Because Māyādunnē was a more concrete rival though, Vīdiyē soon negotiated again with Dharmapāla and the Portuguese captain, Duarte de Eça. The captain, in his turn, followed what was by now a tradition in its own right: he took money from Vīdiyē Baṇḍāra and then refused to dispatch the soldiers he had promised. Only after additional payments were made did he mobilize about twenty men, thirty less than promised. As Vīdiyē's campaign against Sītāvaka now unfolded, it was soon rumored that Eça was in fact seeking a deal with Māyādunnē. To complete the imbroglio, however, Vīdiyē Baṇḍāra came to an agreement with Māyādunnē against the Portuguese. Vīdiyē now planned to take as his second wife a widowed daughter of Māyādunnē. A daughter of this woman would, in turn, be married to a second son of Vīdiyē, that is, a half-brother of Dharmapāla.[8] Together, the dissident forces would launch a final assault on Kōṭṭe.

Bizarre as it may seem, this confusing arrangement, once again almost entirely beyond the imperial ambitions of Portugal, put Dharmapāla, a young man of 13 or 14 years, under considerable pressure. The years of 1552–4 saw an exponential growth of Vīdiyē Baṇḍāra's power in the southwest of Sri Lanka, along with a violent movement against freshly converted Christian communities.[9] It has indeed been argued convincingly that religious motives stood at the heart of the conflict, but it seems difficult to deny that dynastic politics and factional rivalries also played a key role.[10] Vīdiyē Baṇḍāra was carving out his own pocket of authority by enlisting anyone willing to support him. His ambitions appear to have been considerable, even though his is perhaps the least well documented case of an aspirant to higher kingship in sixteenth-century Sri Lanka. According to Queiroz, Vīdiyē Baṇḍāra wished to claim the title of 'great Emperor [*emperador grande*] of the whole island'.[11]

Faced with such a successful offensive, the Portuguese saw themselves forced into an alliance with Māyādunnē. In April 1555, a new captain arrived in Colombo.[12] This man, Afonso Pereira de Lacerda, was talked by Māyādunnē into launching a two-pronged attack on Vīdiyē Baṇḍāra so that he would be 'completely destroyed'.[13] A close reading of the agreement indicates that, once again, Māyādunnē was de facto doing the equivalent to paying tribute to the *Estado*, in the hope of harnessing Portuguese military resources for his project.[14] Indeed, he redeclared himself a vassal of the Portuguese crown on this occasion.[15] Captain Lacerda failed to spot

---

[7] Couto, *Da Asia*, vol. VI, book x, chapter 12, pp. 479–80. Cf. VI, ii, 4, p. 132, and Queiroz, *Conquista*, p. 252. Cf. *Rājāvaliya*, p. 81.

[8] *Da Asia*, vol. VI, book x, chapter 12, pp. 481–3.

[9] *Da Asia*, vol. VII, book ii, chapter 7, p. 132. Cf. Queiroz, *Conquista*, p. 252 for a similar episode.

[10] Cf. Strathern, *Kingship and Conversion*, pp. 170–1.    [11] Queiroz, *Conquista*, p. 255.

[12] Queiroz, *Conquista*, pp. 253–4. Cf. Couto, *Da Asia*, vol. VI, book x, chapter 12, p. 484 and vol. VII, book ii, chapter 4, p. 133.

[13] Couto, *Da Asia*, vol. VII, book ii, chapter 4, p. 133.

[14] C. R. De Silva, 'The rise and fall of the kingdom of Sitawaka', p. 25 has argued that it was the Portuguese who conceded, in exchange for Māyādunnē's assistance, lands that after 1521 had fallen to Kōṭṭe. Yet in practice 1555 saw the return to Portuguese control of a series of ports held by Māyādunnē. Couto, *Da Asia*, vol. VII, book ii, chapter 4, pp. 133–4. Queiroz, *Conquista*, p. 254.

[15] Queiroz, *Conquista*, p. 254.

the danger. He gathered 300 men to help Māyādunnē. When the rebellious Vīdiyē Baṇḍāra moved north to the Seven Korales,[16] killed the local ruler, and forced a number of lesser warlords into submission, the latter offered Lacerda a substantial sum of money for a Portuguese platoon. In Couto's words, the Portuguese soldiers 'were happy to go'—not to conquer a chunk of Ceylon, but 'because of the generous pay they were promised.'[17]

In the end, Vīdiyē Baṇḍāra was dislodged and eventually died in Jaffna in early 1556.[18] The death of this meteor-like figure allowed Māyādunnē to extend his influence through the Seven Korales again[19] and, around March or April 1556, lay siege on Kōṭṭe. The conflict dragged on until early 1557 without a decisive turn. To quote the chronicler Diogo do Couto, the entire year was spent in 'many confrontations [...] and because there was a great number of small [battles], and because I did not find notice of anything remarkable, I shall refrain from dwelling on them'.[20]

## CONVERTING THE KING OF KŌṬṬE: DHARMAPĀLA'S DEAL IN 1557

If the beginning of 1557 brought some tranquility,[21] then this is interesting because it coincides with the conversion of the young king Dharmapāla at Kōṭṭe.[22] The baptism of the last Buddhist monarch of Kōṭṭe can and has been interpreted as a significant defeat of the Lankan elite in the face of Portuguese temporal and spiritual imperialism, the first in a series of events that led the polity down the path of colonialization. This is, of course, not entirely wrong. Yet once again, the context shows very clearly that such an interpretation is excessively reductive. With Vīdiyē Baṇḍāra dead, Dharmapāla felt the full brunt of Māyādunnē's forces and was still not sure about the *Estado*'s support. Śrī Rāmarakṣa and Tammiṭa Sūriya Baṇḍāra, two outstanding figures of the kingdom of Kōṭṭe, had taken baptism in 1552 and 1555.[23] The king was the last figure that could cause a major diplomatic impact by doing the same.

By converting, Dharmapāla certainly betrayed the spirit of Bhuvanekabāhu's decade-long resistance to Franciscan pressures. The royal baptism as such took a heavy toll, prompting yet more leading families to break away and offer their obedience to Māyādunnē.[24] Cutting off the Buddhist *Sangha* from crown sponsorship at Kōṭṭe must, as Strathern has emphasized, have been perceived as a major

---

[16] Couto, *Da Asia*, vol. VII, book ii, chapter 4, pp. 135–6. Cf. Queiroz, *Conquista*, pp. 257–8.
[17] Couto, *Da Asia*, vol. VII, book iii, chapter 5, pp. 208–9. Cf. Queiroz, *Conquista*, pp. 256 and 260. The killed ruler was Edirimanna Sūriya Baṇḍāra. *Rājāvaliya*, p. 84.
[18] Couto, *Da Asia*, vol. VII, book iii, chapter 5, pp. 210–11. Cf. Queiroz, *Conquista*, pp. 260–1 and *Rājāvaliya*, p. 86.
[19] *Rājāvaliya*, p. 85.       [20] Couto, *Da Asia*, vol. VII, book iii, chapter 5, pp. 212–13.
[21] Queiroz, *Conquista*, p. 269.
[22] On the date see Vito Perniola, *The Catholic Church in Sri Lanka. The Portuguese Period. Original Documents translated into English* (Dehiwala: Tisara Prakasakayo, 1989–91), vol. I, p. 352.
[23] Cf. Perniola, *The Catholic Church*, vol. I, p. 350.       [24] Queiroz, *Conquista*, p. 271.

tear in the social-political fabric of the kingdom.[25] Dharmapāla transferred the goods of the Temple of the Tooth and the Kelaniya Maha Vihara, two grand institutions of Theravada Buddhism, to the Franciscan Order.[26] However, conversion per se, in the ample and accommodative sense of the word, was not unthinkable for rulers in Sri Lanka. Royal overtures to Shaivism did occur in the island during the same period.[27] Dharmapāla's move had a primarily political objective, and as such it proved relatively successful. By becoming a Catholic, Dharmapāla shook the moral grounds upon which some Portuguese were questioning the alliance with Kōṭṭe. After 1557, it became significantly more difficult for anyone in the *Estado* to argue in favour of a pact with Māyādunnē (or his upcoming successor, Rājasiṃha) than ever before. This was something Bhuvanekabāhu VII had not been able to achieve despite all his diplomatic skill. In this sense, then, Dharmapāla's conversion was a victory of sorts: it secured the survival of Kōṭṭe as a nominally independent kingdom for another four decades.

The upheaval that ensued in Kōṭṭe in June 1557 was as much an anti-Portuguese and anti-Catholic rebellion as a part of the internal power struggles that had traversed the Lankan southwest before. The violence reflects the social depth of the antagonism, more than the drama of anti-colonial politics. On 22 June 1557, Portuguese troops left Colombo for Kōṭṭe to assist Dharmapāla in crushing the uprising. Thirty Buddhist monks who had led the protests were executed.[28] With hindsight, one might say that this was European religious strife—and, even worse, the confessional politics of Tridentine Catholicism—making its entry into Sri Lanka. But for the moment, this was still in significant part a matter of renegotiating power within Kōṭṭe, between rival factions and indeed competing social groups. A number of leading families left Kōṭṭe, but this exodus also allowed for a renewal of the local elite. According to the *Rājāvaliya*, 'from this day, the principal men of Kōṭṭe [...] and also many people of a lowly caste, ignoring the modesty of their natural condition, married Portuguese people and became Christians'.[29] A single line in our sources serves as a powerful nod to better-known processes of upward mobility supported by imperial powers elsewhere. For some families, staying in Kōṭṭe and, sooner or later, converting to Catholicism, became part of a social ascent that had not been possible before. For others, such a stance was anathema—and their sentiment expressed some years later in the xenophobic verses of the Sītāvaka Hatana, a war poem from the 1580s that mentions 'half-castes' (*tuppahin*) as debased allies of the Portuguese.[30]

---

[25] Strathern, *Kingship and Conversion*, repeatedly emphasizes the importance of Buddhist patronage for Lankan kingship, and the difficulties that this posed to conversion.

[26] Original donation made in 1557, repeated in 1562, ratified in 1591, copied in Trindade, *Conquista Espiritual*, vol. III, pp. 48–9 and Queiroz, *Conquista*, pp. 264–5.

[27] Cf. Elizabeth Nissan and R. L. Stirrat, 'The generation of communal identities', in *Sri Lanka. History and the Roots of Conflict*, edited by Jonathan Spencer (London/New York: Routledge, 1990), pp. 19–44. Strathern, *Kingship and Conversion*, pp. 183–93 discusses the possible conversion of Rājasiṃha, king of Sītāvaka.

[28] Queiroz, *Conquista*, p. 271.

[29] *Rājāvaliya*, p. 80. There are numerous references to mixed marriages from this period onward in Queiroz, *Conquista*.

[30] See Strathern, *Kingship and Conversion*, p. 178.

Still in 1557, 300 soldiers were sent from Goa to Sri Lanka by the new governor Francisco Barreto (gv. 1555–8). The *Estado* was now doing what Bhuvanekabāhu VII had always hoped for, offering relief to Kōṭṭe and refusing to negotiate with its rivals. When Māyādunnē besieged Kōṭṭe again, the Portuguese remained faithful to the freshly converted vassal. The victory was celebrated with the first major Catholic procession in the history of Ceylon, now including as participants some of the highest-ranking personalities of Kōṭṭe.[31] After years of hesitations and diplomatic distractions, the *Estado* found itself bound up with the upcoming elite of a formerly Buddhist kingdom in transition to becoming a client state.

These are, then, the main novelties of the late 1550s: a Portuguese garrison more closely tied than ever to the interests of the royal house of Kōṭṭe; a renewed understanding that, to keep things afloat under such circumstances, Sītāvaka needed to be kept in check; and a growing assumption that the consolidation of Kōṭṭe's position would go hand in hand with further conversions—not on the grand stage of Lanka as a whole, but at least in this part of the island. The situation was paradoxical: whilst in earlier decades there had been opportunities for power building in the island and no political will to pursue them, now Portuguese troops stood close to a Sinhalese monarch with a nominal imperial project, but Kōṭṭe was reduced militarily to a shadow of its former self. It is a further irony that the Portuguese monarch who had crowned Dharmapāla in effigy did not live to see him as a Catholic on the throne. John III passed away in June 1557 before news of Dharmapāla's conversion arrived in Portugal. With the advent of the regency of Catherine of Habsburg, a capable leader but not one to rewrite the rules of imperial expansion in Asia, no space was left for rethinking crown policy in Ceylon.[32] Over the course of the following two and a half decades, Kōṭṭe remained an embattled polity. Its area of influence shrank until there was little more left than the city itself, barely connected with Colombo: a tiny enclave protected by Portuguese troops, and increasingly a social and political pressure cooker that was to come out of the conflict as a new, Luso-Lankan capital.

## A NERVE-CUTTING INTERLUDE: CONSTANTINO DE BRAGANÇA IN JAFFNA AND MANNĀR

We are getting close to a situation where Portuguese imperialism could effectively merge with Kōṭṭe-based 'cakravartism' and generate a new dynamic of conquest. But the realities on the ground remained too complex for such a merger to occur. As things ground to a halt in the Lankan southwest, the viceroy Constantino de Bragança (vr. 1558–61) decided in August 1560 to end his triennium in great

---

[31] Queiroz, *Conquista*, pp. 272–5.
[32] On Portugal's Asian policy during the regency see Maria do Rosário Themudo Barata, *As regências na menoridade de D. Sebastião. Elementos para uma história estrutural* (Lisbon: IN-CM, 1992), vol. II. Also see Luís Filipe Thomaz, 'A crise de 1565–1575 na história do Estado da Índia', *Mare Liberum*, 9 (1995), pp. 481–519.

glory, attacking not in the area of Kōṭṭe, but at Jaffna.[33] As the memory of the massacre of the Christians of Mannār in 1544 remained an open wound to many in the *Estado*, such an expedition was easy to justify. There were also implications for Kōṭṭe, since it was abundantly clear that the war with Sītāvaka had never been an isolated conflict. Māyādunnē received supplies from his allies on the Indian mainland. To intervene somewhere along the channel that connected Sītāvaka with Muslim polities in Kerala and with the Nāyaks of Thanjavur meant, as Bragança put it, 'to cut through a nerve'.[34] This was thought to be not only more cost-effective than sending hundreds of soldiers into the forests and paddy fields of the southwest, but also strategically more promising.

The crucial aspect to emphasize in this is that the invasion of Jaffna, in October 1560, still reflected the old thalassocratic impulses of the *Estado*. To be sure, the plan involved actions on the land. Bragança aimed for the removal of king Caṅkili (r. 1519–61).[35] He also wished to relocate to Jaffna the Portuguese colony of São Tomé de Meliapor, along with the Indian Christians of the Fishery Coast.[36] According to Queiroz, the viceroy even nominated a number of future administrative officials and made arrangements for lands to be registered and, one assumes, repossessed.[37] He may have hoped that by removing the Meliapor Portuguese from the Coromandel Coast, the *Estado* would not have to make costly concessions to Vijayanagara to ensure their security there.[38] This was in line with a proposal made in 1542 by Francis Xavier and Martim Afonso de Sousa for the island of Mannār, but it also went a step further.[39] For the first time, one senses that a Portuguese viceroy was playing with the idea of taking an entire kingdom, redistributing its lands and replacing its elite. But before we jump to conclusions about Constantino de Bragança's visions of a firmly controlled Catholic Sri Lanka, it is also important to underline that the project was more about establishing control over a maritime space with the help of some territorial occupation (a very small polity) than, inversely, a quest for extended territorial rule with naval backing. In fact, the more one attempts to understand Bragança's plans for Ceylon, the less it is clear how much of a plan there was at all. As we shall see soon, the viceroy's personal stance regarding the Lankan southwest may well have been to leave things very much as they were.

[33] The expedition is documented in a viceregal letter to Catherine, Cochin, 20 January 1561. See António dos Santos Pereira, 'A Índia a preto e branco: uma carta oportuna, escrita em Cochim, por D. Constantino de Bragança, à rainha Dona Catarina', *Anais de História de Além-Mar*, 4 (2003), pp. 449–84. Also see Couto, *Da Asia*, vol VIII, book ix, chapters 1–4, pp. 300–34 and Queiroz, *Conquista*, pp. 282–304.

[34] Bragança to Catherine, Cochin, 20 January 1561, in Pereira, 'A Índia a preto e branco', p. 458.

[35] Cf. De Silva and Pathmanathan, 'The Kingdom of Jaffna up to 1620', in *University of Peradeniya History of Sri Lanka*, vol. II, edited by K. M. de Silva (Peradeniya: University of Peradeniya, 1995), pp. 106–7.

[36] Bragança to Catherine, Cochin, 20 January 1561, in Pereira, 'A Índia a preto e branco', p. 458.

[37] Queiroz, *Conquista*, p. 297.

[38] On this problem, see Bragança to Catherine, Cochin, 20 January 1561, in Pereira, 'A Índia a preto e branco', p. 463.

[39] Xavier to Loyola, Tuticorin, 28 October 1542, *Epistolae S. Francisci Xaverii*, vol. I, pp. 150–1.

Even while he raided Jaffna, Bragança showed a remarkable willingness to negotiate with Māyādunnē. He may have felt that the war in the southwest could not be won. Seeing no breakthrough around Kōṭṭe, and not being interested at all in strengthening the crown's position there, the viceroy wrote to Lisbon: 'no war in India is more expensive [than this one] [...] 800 or 1000 men would hardly make a difference there, nor can [it] be properly finished if not with all the power of [the Portuguese garrisons in] India'.[40] The key phrase here is 'all the power of India' (*'todo o poder da Índia'*), identical with the wording of the letter of Lourenço Caracão written forty years earlier, and preluding similar formulas repeated over the decades to come.[41] Yet the argumentative logic is here, crucially, inverted. It is precisely because all the power of the *Estado* would be needed that the project is deemed impractical and undesirable. We shall see soon why Bragança should have been of such an opinion.

## CORTÉS IN THE EAST INDIES? EARLY SIGNS OF A SPANISH CONNECTION

While Constantino de Bragança, the highest-ranking Portuguese nobleman to have served in India in the sixteenth century, showed a renewed reluctance to intervene on the Sri Lankan land, the possibility of taking the island was still being discussed in Goa. The old topos of an enthused, militarily capable, and belligerently minded lower nobility standing up to a more hesitant, morally corrupt leadership interested in trade was alive. This is well illustrated in a treatise written in Goa between 1563 and 1573, Diogo do Couto's *Soldado Prático*.[42] Perhaps this text was even written in reaction to Bragança's decisions concerning Jaffna and Kōṭṭe, although the author was in principle well connected with the viceroy. The *Soldado Prático* praises the virtues of 'practical soldiers' with no vested interests in Asia other than serving their king. Regarding Ceylon, Couto argued that a large armada should be dispatched from Goa with a strong political and military mandate to break the status quo.

Couto suggested that the successful conquest of the island would be down to two factors: first, the mobilization of at least 2000–3000 men, along with 100,000 *cruzados* to pay for food, ammunition and additional mercenaries. That this was difficult to obtain was evident: Couto himself remarks that 'if even the king of Spain would find it difficult [to conquer Ceylon], how much more [difficult will it be for the king of] Portugal?' But the problem could be resolved, so the chronicler argued in a subsequent passage, by investing more time than had been the case so far. Taking the island with its 'jungles, high mountains and rivers' was challenging

---

[40] Bragança to Catherine, Cochin, 20 January 1561, in Pereira, 'A Índia a preto e branco', p. 477. Also see Couto, *Da Asia*, vol. VIII, book ix, chapter 5, p. 340.

[41] Cristóvão Lourenço Caracão to Manuel I, Cochin, 13 February 1522, in Geneviève Bouchon, 'Les rois de Kotte au début du XVIe siècle', in *Mare Luso-Indicum*, 1 (1971), p. 167.

[42] Diogo do Couto, *O Primeiro Soldado Prático*, edited by António Coimbra Martins (Lisbon: CNCDP, 2001), pp. 476–86. On the date of the text, p. 19.

but, Couto believed, an energetic viceroy might be able, 'in two years, without danger or loss of men' to become

> absolute lord of Ceylon, cut the head of Māyādunnē and [all] those wishing to take the name of kings, and obtain a large kingdom, a land of great advantage for the preservation of the *Estado*, for His Highness.[43]

For the first time, we see a project for a major military action emerging from a context other than that of men directly involved with the Lankan elite. And this was a project of conquest in the sense of transforming and taking over, not just of intervening. Diogo do Couto shared social and cultural values with the petty nobles we have already seen in action in the island, but in terms of imperial imagination his was a wider, global horizon, and one largely detached from local, Lankan narratives. For the first time, we witness a truly exogenous projection of Iberian ideas of conquest onto the island. Couto proposed to cut heads not as a means of extending suzerainty, but of working towards Portuguese sovereignty in the island. His text is the first document to argue for a systematic elimination of Lankan rulers to allow the Portuguese to become 'absolute lords' of the island. These were the preconditions for turning Ceylon into a proper colony.

It is striking that this project emerged in Goa in connection with the earliest Portuguese references to Spanish conquests, not only in the New World but also, fittingly for the late 1560s, in the Philippines. News of the deeds of Cortés in the early 1520s, Pizarro in the 1540s, and Legazpi in the 1560s circulated across the Portuguese world. The letters of Cortés were printed in numerous Castilian editions that would naturally have made it across the border at a time when bilingualism was still common in Portugal. But if these had an impact—and we know nothing about the history of their reception—then it also deserves emphasizing that it would have been very different in distinct parts of Portuguese society. To cautious imperialists like John III, or outright commercialists like the Gamas, it would be clear that any emulation of the New World conquests was out of question, except perhaps in Morocco, where symbolically the pursuit of Holy War remained important.[44] To militarily more expansive men like Couto and other practical soldiers, *conquista* in the hard-hitting sense of the word made perfect sense in South Asia as well as elsewhere.

This was a matter of resonance as much as, if not more than, Spanish influence. Ideas of conquest had been present among the Portuguese in Asia from very early on. Before news from Mexico could even have reached them in Asia, two men jailed by the Chinese authorities served up a spectacular plan for the conquest of the Middle Kingdom in the so-called 'Letters of Guangzhou'.[45] Conquest in the

---

[43] Couto, *O Primeiro Soldado Prático*, pp. 478 and 480.

[44] See Maria de Lourdes Rosa, 'Velhos, novos e mutáveis sagrados... um olhar antropológico sobre formas 'religiosas' de percepção e interpretação da conquista africana (1415–1521)', *Lusitania Sacra*, 2ª série, 18 (2006), pp. 13–85.

[45] The letters have been dated to 1524–6 or, alternatively, 1534–6, but the key aspect is that the authors were out of touch with the *Estado* from 1522. Cf. Biedermann, 'Imperial Reflections: China, Rome and the Logics of Global History in the *Ásia* of João de Barros', in *Empires on the Move/Empires en marche*, edited by François Lachaud and Dejanirah Couto (Paris: EFEO, 2017), pp. 23–47. The

sense of taking full and direct possession by means of an armed invasion had also been put into practice in Goa and Malacca, in 1510 and 1511, reproducing a model that went back to the very beginnings of Portuguese expansion, in Ceuta, in 1415. Whilst conquest was generally less dominant in the Portuguese crown's strategy in the East than other forms of negotiated settlement in forts and *feitorias*, it was not entirely absent from it. Generating military opportunities for nobles had, along with commercial prospects, been one of the drivers of Portuguese expansion from its very beginnings. With it came a predisposition, especially among those unable to make a livelihood from trade, for thinking about frontier warfare in ideologically charged, often anti-Islamic ways. To such an audience—subaltern but aspirational, often degraded by the squalid conditions of being a soldier in Asia, but 'honoured' and willing to invoke a hierarchy of values where warfare trumped trade—it made much sense to establish mental connections with what was going on in the Spanish empire. To make the connection even more plausible, many of the protagonists of conquest in America had also been members of the lower and middle nobility.

A second development of these years was Catholic radicalization on the ground. Religious zeal began to transpire not only from letters expounding Utopian projects, but also from the actual violence unfolding in Sri Lanka. The most spectacular instance of Catholic zeal ruthlessly put into action was the theft of the Lankan Tooth Relic, which Constantino de Bragança found in 1560 to have ended up in Jaffna after the turmoil of the 1550s. The viceroy had the relic taken to Goa and, there, publicly destroyed.[46] The religious aspect of this act is evident, but there is an equally important political dimension to it, as the relic was a key signifier of royal authority in Lanka.[47] A savage attack against pilgrims at the Temple of Alutgama in 1576 is another, even starker example of how religious strife was coming into the picture on the ground. The development was far from linear though, and not all religiously meaningful violence was necessarily religion-driven. The destruction of the Maha Vihara in Kelaniya, in 1574, for example, was a complex affair. It dealt a major blow to Buddhism in the lowlands, but that had not been its main purpose. Much of the town of Kelaniya was razed for strategic reasons in the fight against Sītāvaka, and indeed the campaign as such was not led by the Portuguese.[48] In other words, the event was extremely brutal, but not simply on grounds of an import of European confessional violence to Asia.

Nor was Constantino de Bragança with his attack on Jaffna and his aggressive religious performances paving the way for the conquest of Ceylon. As we will see,

---

letters are published in *Enformação das cousas da China. Textos do século XVI*, edited by Raffaella d'Intino (Lisbon: IN-CM, 1989), pp. 7–53 and *Cartas dos cativos de Cantão (1524?)*, edited by Rui Manuel Loureiro (Lisbon: Instituto Cultural de Macau, 1992).

[46] The story is explored, and partly questioned, in John Strong, '"The Devil was in that Little Bone": The Portuguese Capture and Destruction of the Buddha's Tooth-Relic, Goa, 1561', *Past and Present*, 206, Supplement 5, 1 (2010), pp. 184–98.

[47] See Strathern, *Kingship and Conversion*, p. 170, on how the relic may have served the political project of Vīdiyē Baṇḍāra explored above.

[48] Both events in Queiroz, *Conquista*, p. 344.

a conquest such as that proposed by Diogo do Couto was quite exactly what he wished to avoid. He may have had some ideas about setting up a Catholic colony in the straits and allow it to be run directly by Portuguese officials. But this was within a very limited frame and against the backdrop of firmly established cautions. Whilst Bragança needed to avoid coming across as a pure commercialist because of his very high social status, behind the religious façade he was a man disinclined to conquest. The gulf between the militarist discourses of opportunity-hungry petty nobles, on the one hand, and the more complex, at times tension-ridden, but overall cautious approach in the highest strata of the imperial elite, on the other, was still in place when it came to Sri Lanka, regardless of the religious zeal that appeared to connect them.

## KŌṬṬE, COLOMBO AND THE MAKING
## OF A NEW IMPERIAL CAPITAL

The plan formulated by Diogo do Couto in Goa was as out of tune with the intentions of Constantino de Bragança, as with the situation of the Portuguese in Kōṭṭe. Not only were there no conquests in sight, but the area controlled by Kōṭṭe and Colombo continued to shrink even further.[49] By 1565, the situation was militarily untenable, and Dharmapāla faced a difficult decision: to defend Kōṭṭe at the risk of letting the city with its imperial paraphernalia fall into the enemy's hands, or move his court to Colombo. In an atmosphere of hardening warfare, the old Lankan capital was abandoned, its court and remaining population transferred to the nearby port city, and the fortifications there enlarged drastically to secure the new royal seat. The entire area that is today known as old Colombo—including the so-called Fort District (a more recent name) and the Pettah—were fortified.[50] Colombo thus underwent a profound transformation towards becoming a fully fledged capital city (Figure 6.1). The new defences transformed old *Kolambā* into a vast fortress housing the Portuguese garrison, but also the court of Kōṭṭe and all the Lusitanian and Lankan institutions that came along with this. From being a port city with primarily commercial purposes, Colombo grew into a conurbation combining commercial, religious, military and, crucially, political functions. This was clearly a new imperial (and sub-imperial) capital in the making. One that could house the potential *cakravarti* of Kōṭṭe *and* serve as a focus of action for the local Portuguese elite in collaboration with the *Estado*.[51]

After the transfer of the royal household, the Portuguese town citizens (*casados*) of Colombo soon emphasized how the city had inherited the pedigree of 'the royal

---

[49] Queiroz, *Conquista*, pp. 319–20. Cf. De Silva, 'The rise and fall of the kingdom of Sitawaka', p. 29.

[50] Queiroz, *Conquista*, p. 341. Couto, *Da Asia*, vol. VI, book ix, chapter 18, pp. 352–3. Cf. S. G. Perera, *The City of Colombo 1505–1656* (Colombo: Ceylon Historical Association, 1926), pp. 13–14. For a detailed study see Biedermann, 'Colombo versus Cannanore: Contrasting Structures of Two Early Colonial Port Cities in South Asia', *Journal of the Economic and Social History of the Orient*, 53, 2 (2009), pp. 413–59, revised in *The Portuguese in Sri Lanka and South India. Studies in the History of Empire, Diplomacy and Trade, 1500–1650* (Wiesbaden: Harrassowitz, 2014), pp. 103–48.

[51] Cf. A. F. Burghardt, 'A hypothesis about Gateway Cities', *Annals of the Association of American Geographers*, 61, 2 (1971), pp. 269–85.

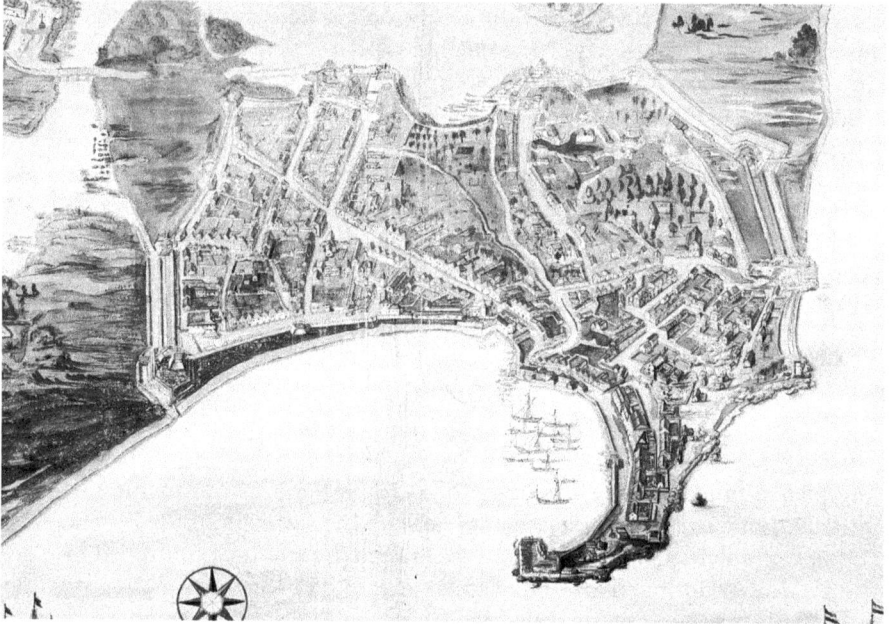

**Figure 6.1** Colombo as a capital with fortifications begun in 1565. Detail from a Dutch view drawn after 1656. Atlas Johannes Vingboons, Nationaal Archief, The Hague, Inv.-nr. VELH_619.115. South on top. Image in the public domain.

city of Kōṭṭe, metropolis and head of kingdom'.[52] Whilst in 1565 Colombo was still, in the terms of Lusitanian law, a town (*vila*)[53], by 1580 it was officially recognized as a city (*cidade*). The new *caput regni* came to host a magistrate (*juíz ordinário*), a *tabelião público* (notary public), and an *ouvidor* (crown judge).[54] Behind these formal changes indicating a rapprochement with the symbolic order of the *Estado*, however, the most fascinating aspect is the consolidation of the new elite that had started emerging in the 1550s, accommodating Portuguese and Mestizo traders, converted Kōṭṭe families with increasing ties to the Portuguese, and Buddhist and Hindu families still resisting conversion, but seeing more advantages in coming to Colombo than moving elsewhere.

The last three decades of the sixteenth century were a period of considerable ethnic and religious dynamism in Colombo. Many of the most prestigious inhabitants, including Christians speaking Portuguese, served Dharmapāla, not the Lusitanian crown. They remained members of his entourage and received money

[52] Record of Dharmapala's donation of Ceylon to the Portuguese crown, Colombo, 12 August 1580, *As Gavetas da Torre do Tombo* (Lisbon: CEHU, 1960–77), vol. III, p. 608, my translation. Also available in Perniola, *The Catholic Church*, vol. I, pp. 87–91.

[53] Dharmapala to Sebastian, Colombo, 10 January 1566, Arquivo Nacional Torre to Tombo, *Corpo Cronológico*, 1-107-100.

[54] Donation, Colombo, 12 August 1580, *Gavetas*, vol. III, pp. 608–10. List of the expenses of the *Estado*, 1581, in Matos, *O Estado da Índia*, p. 178.

and land grants from him.[55] With the growth of the garrison, conflicts increasingly arose between *casados* and *soldados*, not between 'Portuguese' and 'Lankans'. The Franciscan convent stood next to Dharmapāla's new residence, continuing an old tradition of physical proximity between palace and temple.[56] Many inhabitants of the city avoided conversion until well into the seventeenth century.[57] In theory, there was a legal divide in the Portuguese empire between Christians and non-Christians since 1562—when Catholics of foreign birth were granted the status of Portuguese subjects in Goa—but in practice, the religious and ethnic boundaries remained porous, conversions a complex affair involving adaptations in both directions. Full state or ecclesiastic control remained a distant reality.[58] The 1570s certainly saw the beginnings of a Catholicization and Iberianization of Colombo, but what really seems most significant is the increasing intertwinement of the various political realities at the intersection of the *Estado* and the old kingdom of Kōṭṭe.

If any doubts remained about the self-confidence of the *casado* community, the city came to boast a municipal council (*câmara*), the standard governing institution of all cities in the Portuguese world, by 1583. This was an institution for which, interestingly, there does not seem to have been an equivalent in the Lankan tradition.[59] However, even here we are far from seeing the outright transplanting of a foreign institution into the Lankan body politic. The municipal council represented the married residents of Portuguese origin, usually with wives and often parents of local or mixed background. The attachment of many members of this community to the kings of Kōṭṭe contributed to their self-esteem. Whilst they were building, as Queiroz later put it, a new Rome in Sri Lanka, they were also continuing an old and prestigious Lankan tradition.[60] Their growth at the intersection of the Kōṭṭe-based *cakravarti* project, European imperial ideas, and globalized Portuguese municipalism, reveals the striking confidence of a community creating new institutions in the vicinity of, and not in opposition to, an Asian king. It was in this context that the *casados* began to collect symbolic capital and build their own memory archive, structured around the military defence of Portuguese institutions *and* the Lankan monarchy during the challenges of the 1560s and 1570s: those are the stories populating numerous chapters of Fernão de Queiroz's *Conquista*, taken directly from narratives compiled by earlier writers in Colombo.[61] There could hardly be a better example of the intertwinement of city and empire—one city entertaining links with two imperial traditions. All this unfolded while Colombo barely dominated more than a few square miles of land.

[55] See among others: Phillip II to Matias de Albuquerque, Lisbon, 22 February 1591, British Library, *Additional Manuscripts*, 20,861, fol. 135. António Giralte to Phillip II, Goa, December 6, 1589, Archivo General de Simancas, *Secretarías Provinciales: Portugal*, Codex 1551, fols. 608–611v.

[56] *Gavetas*, vol. III, p. 52. Trindade, *Conquista*, vol. III, pp. 48–9. Queiroz, *Conquista*, pp. 264–5.

[57] Cf. Abeyasinghe, *Portuguese Rule*, p. 78.

[58] On this and the ensuing 'cultural conversions' in Goa, see Ângela Barreto Xavier, *A invenção de Goa: poder imperial e conversões culturais nos séculos XVI e XVII* (Lisbon: ICS, 2008).

[59] See C. R. Boxer, *Portuguese Society in the Tropics. The Municipal Councils of Goa, Macao, Bahia, and Luanda, 1510–1800* (Madison/Milwaukee, WI: University of Wisconsin Press, 1965).

[60] Queiroz, *Conquista*, p. 341.

[61] Alan Strathern, 'Re-reading Queirós: some neglected aspects of the *Conquista*', *Sri Lanka Journal of the Humanities*, 26, 1–2 (2000), pp. 1–28.

## TRANSLATIO IMPERII, THE LANKAN WAY:
## THE DONATION OF KŌṬṬE (1580)

In 1574, when the *Estado* once again hesitated, for reasons unclear, to commit resources to the defence of Colombo, Dom João Dharmapāla wrote to pope Gregory XIII (1572–85).[62] The Lankan ruler was firmly committed to the local imperial tradition of Kōṭṭe, but also willing to use his access to a global network of communications to pursue it. Predictably, he argued that the governor should come from Goa with 2000 or 3000 men (a figure identical with that mentioned in Couto's *Soldado Pratico*, perhaps indicating that this was a broadly circulating topos by now). Reference was made to religion, but essentially Dharmapāla expressed his wish to 'conquer' Māyādunnē and 'win over this very large island'. He had already made it clear that he regarded Colombo as his possession, rather than the *Estado's*.[63] And whilst a superficial glance at the situation in the 1560s and 1570s shows that the number of military campaigns in which the Portuguese participated was considerable, a closer reading shows that Dharmapāla's military leaders were still the ones taking the initiative. The Portuguese garrison assisted them, but not one of the numerous assaults launched between 1565 and 1576 to relieve Colombo from Sītāvakan pressure was led by them. It is not surprising that very little information about these campaigns, best described in the *Conquista* of Queiroz, has survived in the official record.[64]

The fact that Dharmapāla remained militarily and diplomatically active has been ignored by historians because the assumption has been that he was merely a puppet in the hands of the Portuguese. Even in the most reliable study on this period, we can read that the Portuguese relentlessly 'spurned any suggestion of a truce [with Sītāvaka]', and that in 1574, after the death of Dharmapāla's first queen, they thus 'obtained for him a Kandyan princess'.[65] In reality, Dharmapāla was still engaging vigorously in the same diplomatic game that Bhuvanekabāhu VII had played before. If the Kandyan princess chosen by Dharmapāla was nominally a Catholic—we know her by her Christian name, Dona Margarida—this should by no means suggest that in marrying her the king followed Portuguese orders. In fact, the same

---

[62] Dharmapala to Gregory XIII, Colombo, 26 January 1574, *Bullarium Patronatus Portugalliae Regum in Ecclesis Africae, Asiae Atque Oceaniae*, edited by Levy Maria Jordão (Lisbon: Typographia Nacional, 1868–1879), vol. II, pp. 219–20. In 1568, the general orders issued in Lisbon on 27 February to the future viceroy Luís de Ataíde did not even mention Ceylon. *Archivo Portuguez-Oriental*, edited by Joaquim Heliodoro da Cunha Rivara, reprint (New Delhi: Asian Educational Service, 1992), fasc. 3, pp. 1–26. Note how 1568, the year of the handover from the cardinal regent Henry to king Sebastian, also saw the end of the old secretariat of Indian matters, once controlled by Pedro de Alcáçova Carneiro under John III. The new *Secretaria de Estado da Índia* under Duarte Dias de Meneses showed no interest in reinforcing central control over Lankan matters. Cf. Francisco Paulo Mendes da Luz, *O Conselho da Índia. Contributo ao Estudo da História da Administração e do Comércio do Ultramar Português nos Princípios do Século XVII* (Lisbon: Agência Geral do Ultramar, 1952), pp. 69–73.

[63] Dharmapala to Sebastian, Colombo, 10 January 1566, Arquivo Nacional Torre do Tombo, *Corpo Cronológico*, 1-107-100.

[64] I explored these campaigns extensively in 'A aprendizagem de Ceilão' (PhD dissertation, École Pratique des Hautes Études/Universidade Nova de Lisboa, 2006).

[65] De Silva, 'The rise and fall of the kingdom of Sitawaka', p. 31.

princess had been courted in vain by Rājasiṃha, the son of king Māyādunnē.[66] Dharmapāla needed to build alliances across the island like any other king of Kōṭṭe before. Bearing in mind the efforts of Kandy in the 1540s to establish alliances with Kōṭṭe, Dharmapāla's marriage was probably heavily indebted to the diplomatic vigour of Karaliyaddē, the new highland king, about whom we shall hear more soon.[67] Some years earlier, around 1565, Dharmapāla had even presided over a symbolically laden diplomatic exchange with Pegu (Myanmar), replicating earlier Buddhist links originating in a Pāli cosmopolis, without interference from the *Estado*.[68] Neither Lisbon nor Goa had a plan for Ceylon, but Kandy, Colombo, and Sītāvaka all had plans for the island and, within it, the Portuguese. Incidentally, it has also been overlooked that soon after Dharmapāla became a widower again, around 1585, he kept pushing for yet another marriage, and indeed two letters from 1589 show that his efforts were crowned by success.[69]

In May 1578, the king of Sītāvaka, Māyādunnē, finally handed over the throne to his son Rājasiṃha. Sītāvakan troops besieged Colombo with renewed vigour for a full 22 months, from 1579 to 1581.[70] As the siege went into its final phase and Dharmapāla struggled to rally, again, additional support from Goa, he resorted to a final stratagem. On 12 August 1580, the middle-aged king signed a testamentary donation of his kingdom to the Portuguese crown. If he was to die without an heir— which he still hoped he would not—then the royal title and all that came with it would go to the king of Portugal. This extraordinary document became a cornerstone of Portuguese policy in the island some years later. Well into the nineteenth century, it would fuel Portuguese claims that Ceylon was legally a Lusitanian possession.[71] Here again, a significant aspect has been ignored though by historians on both sides of the postcolonial divide. The donation, like everything that Bhuvanekabāhu VII and Dharmapāla had negotiated with the Portuguese before, remained firmly grounded in Lankan assumptions of inter-imperial mutuality. The document as such may have been drafted by someone familiar with Iberian law—possibly one

[66] The marriage is dated 1573 in 'De como os Reys de Portugal são legitimos herdeiros dos Reinos de Ceylão, principalmente do Reino de Candea', Goa, 8 April 1643, in *Collecção de Tratados e Concertos de Pazes que o Estado da India fez*, edited by Júlio Biker (Lisbon: Imprensa Nacional, 1881–87), vol. I, pp. 225–8.

[67] Cf. Abeyasinghe, 'The kingdom of Kandy', pp. 144–5 and *Rājāvaliya*, p. 82.

[68] Couto, *Da Ásia*, vol. VIII, chapters 12–13. Cf. Tilman Frasch, 'A Pāli cosmopolis? Sri Lanka and the Theravāda Buddhist Ecumene, c. 500–1500', in *Sri Lanka at the Crossroads of History*, edited by Zoltán Biedermann and Alan Strathern (London: UCL Press, 2017), pp. 66–76.

[69] Phillip II to viceroy, Lisbon, 21 January 1588, *Archivo Portuguez-Oriental*, fasc. 3, p. 119. The queen, Dona Isabel, appears in Dharmapala to Phillip II, Colombo, 29 November 1589, Archivo General de Simancas, *Secretarías Provinciales: Portugal*, Codex 1551, fol. 796 and in Dom Antão (son of the *mudaliyār* Dom Teodósio and brother of Dona Isabel) to Phillip II, Colombo, 29 November 1589, Archivo General de Simancas, *Secretarías Provinciales: Portugal*, Codex 1551, fol. 799.

[70] Queiroz, *Conquista*, pp. 349–54.

[71] Cf. António de Vasconcelos Saldanha, 'O problema jurídico-político da incorporação de Ceilão na coroa de Portugal. As doações dos Reinos de Kotte, Kandy e Jaffna (1580–1633)', *Revista de Cultura*, 13/14, Ano V, vol. 1 (1991), pp. 233–57. Cf. by the same author, *Iustum Imperium. Dos tratados como fundamento do império dos portugueses no Oriente. Estudo de história do direito internacional e do direito português* (Lisbon/Macao: Fundação Oriente/Instituto Português do Oriente, 1997), pp. 501–17. Jorge Flores, 'Recuperar Ceilão em meados do século XIX: atribulações de um diplomata português em Londres', *Oriente*, 3 (2002), pp. 21–30.

of the Franciscans at Colombo—but above all, it served to prevent Rājasiṃha from getting hold of the Kōṭṭe throne. Dharmapāla would either retain it with Portuguese support or, once he died, the throne would go to the king of Portugal, who would then have to battle to protect the community, and indeed the polity, attached to it. Secondly, the document is again very explicit about the role of Portuguese military assistance not only to Dharmapāla, but also to Kōṭṭe as a more abstract repository of Lankan imperial authority. The dismembered realm claimed by Kōṭṭe was to be rebuilt with Portuguese arms, precisely because it would eventually be inherited by the Portuguese monarch.[72]

Some interesting tensions do appear in the text as well. Whilst Dharmapāla insisted that his status as a vassal was equal, if not higher, than that of the viceroys at Goa, he also admitted, for the first time, that the war 'for the restoration of his kingdoms' ('*seus reynos*') was to be financed by the *Estado*. To be more precise, he demanded it. This inversion of the cash flow, on which there is no indication elsewhere in the record of the 1570s, but which probably has its roots in the abandonment of Kōṭṭe in 1565, may be crucial for an understanding of the further developments. It indicates a tilting of the symbolic balance of powers and the gradual submission of Dharmapāla, who was now placing himself under the financial umbrella of the Portuguese crown.[73] The transfer of financial responsibilities also meant, as we shall see, that within a few years the accounts of the Portuguese crown at Colombo were to slide deep into the red. So much so that a new policy for Ceylon had to be devised—but this was not, of course, anticipated in 1580. As imagined at the time, the kingdom of Kōṭṭe would, once it went to the Portuguese crown, carry on its local imperial mission in the island as a part of the global empire of the Portuguese. The transition initiated in 1580 may have opened the doors to conquest, but it also shows how Lankan statehood, earlier linked to a markedly South Asian concept of sacred kingship, had a potential for carrying on under the aegis of Catholic Universalism.[74]

Crucially, Dharmapāla handed over two things, not just one, to his distant heirs: first, the right to take possession of his devastated lands generally known as the kingdom (*reino*) of Kōṭṭe. This was a relatively small area contained by a loose set of borders going back to the time before the 1521 partition, thus including what we have been treating as the kingdoms of Kōṭṭe, Sītāvaka, and Rayigama. Second, the donation also included Kōṭṭe's imperial mandate, the mandate to submit all the other kingdoms of the island to Kōṭṭe's suzerainty. This was a fully fledged *translatio imperii* to a foreign power that had not until then been willing to take

---

[72] Donation, Colombo, 12 August 1580, *Gavetas*, vol. III, 607–11.

[73] The grant is not mentioned in the donation, but there is a change in the Portuguese royal budget for Colombo between 1574 and 1581, when Dharmapala appears as being in receipt, 'for his sustenance', of 300,000 *réis* per year. Matos, *O Estado da Índia*, p. 178. The captain of Colombo received 400,000 *réis*. At the same time, the 1581 budget does mention a cinnamon tribute coming to the Portuguese coffers, but from Māyādunnē. This may be a copist's mistake (since Māyādunnē was then much talked about as 'king of Ceylon'), or the king of Sītāvaka may indeed have continued to send cinnamon.

[74] For a view that differs from mine on this point, see Strathern, *Kingship and Conversion*.

part whole-heartedly in Lankan warfare, but would now be obliged to do so. Whoever was to inherit the realm, Dharmapāla made sure to spell out,

> shall legitimately wage war on the land and on the sea until they become entirely lords [*senhores*] of all the said kingdoms [*reinos*] along their ancient demarcations, and over-lords, as the kings of Kōṭṭe formerly were, to the other kings of this island, which is and has always been due to them.[75]

The latter part of the original Portuguese sentence is particularly difficult to translate into English. The Portuguese version reads very much like an elaborate formula rendering the fact that it was a part of Kōṭṭe's exclusive historical heritage to lay claim to overlordship over the rest of the island. The prospect was rather radical: the Lankan nesting empire might one day become an integral part of the Portuguese monarchy, rather than an empire nesting inside it. Any possibility of the larger empire cutting the smaller out of its own body was thus, in that future scenario, done away with. The Matrioshka Principle, if not entirely suppressed (Dharmapāla remained king of Kōṭṭe until his death in 1597), was transformed into a new imperial hybrid that neither the Portuguese nor the Lankan crowns had originally intended to create. But this was only one part of the equation.

## TRANSLATIO IMPERII, THE HABSBURG WAY

The 1580 donation is a decisive document for the histories of Sri Lanka *and* Eurasia more widely. Produced at the intersection between Lankan and Portuguese imperial discourses, it ended up putting Kōṭṭe at the mercy of global processes well beyond Dharmapāla's control. By a fatidic coincidence, Portugal itself ceased to be an independent kingdom almost exactly at the time when the contract was signed. King Sebastian (r.1568–78) of the Avis dynasty had died in Morocco in 1578, leaving the country in disarray. His successor, an elderly cleric, was incapable of ruling or producing an heir. Over the course of the years 1580–1, the Portuguese crown passed into the hands of Phillip II of Spain (r.1556–98). Phillip, it was said, 'conquered, inherited and bought' Portugal in a process involving invasion, negotiations with the Portuguese parliaments (*cortes*), and subornment on a large scale, including a considerable increase in privileges granted to the high nobility.[76] Although the two halves of the Catholic Monarchy remained formally separate,

---

[75] 'Poderam lisetamente fazer guerra por terra e por maar ate de todo estarem senhores de todos os ditos reynnos per suas antigoas demarquasóis e senhorios que tem como tiveram os reis da Cota sobre os outros reis desta ilha que lhes he e foi sempre devida.' *Gavetas*, vol. III, p. 609.

[76] Mafalda Soares da Cunha, 'A questão jurídica na crise dinástica', in *História de Portugal*, edited by José Mattoso (Lisbon: Círculo de Leitores, 1993–4), vol. III, pp. 552–9. Joaquim Romero de Magalhães, 'Filipe II (I de Portugal)', ibid., pp. 563–6. Whereas the Portuguese and Spanish historiography of the past twenty years has emphasized the negotiated dimension of the transition, Rafael Valladares has recently reclaimed some ground for the acknowledgement of conquest as a key factor. Each element, he argues, had its preponderance at a specific moment of the transition. *La conquista de Lisboa. Violencia militar y comunidad política en Portugal, 1578–1583* (Madrid: Marcial Pons, 2008).

things soon started to change in the *Estado*, and Ceylon is in many ways an example of these transformations.

Once the donation of Kōṭṭe reached Phillip II in Lisbon (the monarch remained there from 1581 to 1583), it was examined by a council of jurists (*letrados*). It was found to be valid and worthy of being archived in the repository of state papers, the *Torre do Tombo*. Whilst Portuguese expansion had clearly had its own obsession with laws, legalism—yet another Universalist fiction grounded in the Roman past and projected across the globe through Iberia—was immensely powerful in the Castilian imperial imagination. It helped achieve, for Kōṭṭe, what 'cakravartism' and Catholic Universalism had set in motion, but not quite accomplished: the full, legally binding integration of Sri Lanka into the Iberian imperial body. A connection that had worked in a variety of ways involving complex acts of translation, but had always remained reliant on negotiations to sustain, could now be made into something permanent, written in stone as Roman law had been.

The legalistic fiction was powerful also because it could be articulated with performative acts of imperial affirmation on the ground. As Phillip's jurists had it, 'the said document came in a convenient form', but

> in order to strengthen this inheritance, it should be demanded of the king of Ceylon that, his relatives being against him [and] at war [with him], he should disinherit them explicitly. This shall by law be right and sufficient to deprive them of the succession to the kingdom [...].

Additionally, the 'people of Ceylon' were expected to elect Phillip II 'as king of that kingdom, based on the said document and donation of the King of Ceylon'. The legitimacy deriving from such an election, the jurists declared to dissipate any doubts, would extend to Phillip's successors.[77] After the fictions of global political, commercial, and religious hegemony entertained for decades by the Portuguese crown, the fiction of global law now helped the Iberian elite to think about Sri Lanka as a conquerable whole, as it had been presented to them by Dharmapāla. This was, then, a key translation of the Lankan ideal of unity into the idiom of Iberian imperialism. The power of legal rhetoric achieved at the Habsburg court what decades of a less formalized epistolography and diplomacy had not been able to bring about in the palaces of Lisbon and Goa. Enticed by the utterly readable legality of the donation, Phillip II, a man for whom inheriting kingdoms was no novelty, bit the bait that John III had avoided for so long. With the throne of Kōṭṭe, he inherited the *cakravarti* mandate without even noticing it. It is quite remarkable how the new Spanish-Portuguese imperial administration managed such a problematic *translatio* in a well-lubricated process of bureaucratic incorporation.

Equally remarkable is how the juridical details analyzed by the imperial administrators with their global outlook were digested locally, in the new imperial city that had grown around Dharmapāla, his *casados*, and the Portuguese garrison. What the authorities wished to see was a public performance of imperial rituals,

---

77 Phillip II to Duarte de Meneses, Lisbon, 10 March 1584, British Library, *Additional Manuscripts*, 20,861, fols. 2v–3.

finally staged in Colombo in 1583. While Catholic nobles swore their oath on the Bible, others affirmed their allegiance with 'their bracelets and pagodas'—which are likely to have included some Lankan regalia.[78] On the same day, a public acclamation was staged. The Kōṭṭe elite recognized the donation of Dharmapāla in the name of the Lankan people, swearing that they would, after his death, accept the King of Portugal 'as their own natural king' ('*como a seu proprio rey natural*'). Phillip, the Spanish monarch with Austrian, Burgundian, and Portuguese ancestry, was to function in the island as if he had been born there.[79] The Kōṭṭe nobles were here addressing the issue of identity on two fronts: that of a Habsburg monarch whose father Charles had struggled when he arrived as a foreigner in Castile; and that of Lankan kingship, where foreigners were welcome to rule but, as anywhere else, needed to be accepted by the local elite. The latter was soon to become a challenge, but in an altogether unexpected way.

[78] Donation with ratification by Dom João to Phillip II, Colombo, 4 November 1583, *Gavetas*, vol. III, p. 50.
[79] Acceptance of the donation of Ceylon by Dom João to Phillip II, Colombo, 4 November 1583, *Gavetas*, vol. III, pp. 615–18.

# 7

# From Allies to Invaders
## Sri Lanka at the Crossroads of Global Iberian Imperialism

Few historians have a clear idea of how the Iberian union of crowns played out in the Portuguese 'half' of the world. We know that, whilst the two main constituents of the new global empire remained juridically separate, united only by a common monarch, some changes did begin to occur. Perhaps the most widely recognized aspect is the growth, after 1581, of Brazil, rendering the old dividing line created at Tordesillas in 1494 obsolete. But what happened in the rest of the Portuguese sphere, in Africa and Asia, is much less clear. If historians mention the matter at all, the most common reference is to a gradual shift from maritime to terrestrial expansion, often vaguely, or even just implicitly, attributed to some sort of Spanish influence on the Portuguese realm. So, what *exactly* can we say about how the *Estado* began to change under Habsburg rule, and what may the Sri Lankan case add to the picture?

The story is substantially more complex than has been assumed. The testamentary donation of Kōṭṭe in 1580 forfeited Dharmapāla's realm, as I argued in the previous chapter, in a last bid to halt the expansion of Sītāvaka. It was, needless to say, a Lankan affair in the first place, and there can be little doubt that Dharmapāla himself still hoped to produce an heir who would have made the contract irrelevant. His aim was certainly not to encourage an invasion of Ceylon by forces he could not control. If the *Estado* had to be begged even for small contingents of soldiers, who would expect it to embark on a larger mission anyway? However, once the donation made it to Lisbon, now occupied by Spanish forces, the stage was set juridically, on the Iberian side, for a prospective integration of Kōṭṭe, and indeed Lanka as a whole, into the Catholic Monarchy. In this sense, it is very tempting indeed to draw a direct line from the events of 1580–81 to the formal beginning of the conquest. After all, the chain of causation would seem to be straightforward: Kōṭṭe fell into the hands of Portugal, Portugal fell into the hands of Spain, and with Kōṭṭe thus at the mercy of Phillip II it was doomed to become yet another case of direct, hard-hitting *conquista*. After Mexico, Peru, the Low Countries and the Philippines, it was Sri Lanka's turn to feel the full brunt of Habsburg power.

In all fairness, some historians have attempted to formulate more subtle interpretations. It has been argued that the changes in various parts of the Portuguese empire were fiscal before becoming military in nature, with the *Estado* shifting its focus to include more terrestrial revenues than before. The most recent attempt at taking stock of this change, owed to Sanjay Subrahmanyam, is rightly cautious. It shows, on the one hand, that signs of a 'terrestrial turn' of the *Estado* go back to the 1570s, well before the Union of Crowns; on the other, whilst the reader is still left with a vague impression of some sort of Castilian-inspired inflection, it also allows room for doubts about whether the tendency to improve the empire's agrarian fiscal base during the late sixteenth century amounts to a Castilian-led strategic turn.[1] Rather than moving towards a conclusion at this point of our narrative, then, we need to take 1580—or rather 1581, when Phillip officially became king in Portugal—as a moment that made the buildup to conquest possible, but not inevitable. It is through a complex concatenation of decisions and communicational acts at the local, regional, and global level that the conquest of Ceylon got under way, but only about a decade and a half *after* the Union of Crowns was declared.

## ATTEMPTING THE CONQUEST OF KANDY: RĀJASIṂHA I, NOT PHILLIP II

The main military campaign launched in Sri Lanka after the donation of 1580 was an initiative not of Goa, Lisbon or Madrid, but of Sītāvaka with its new king Rājasiṃha I (r. 1578–93). Having had to abort the siege of Colombo, which caused Dharmapāla to sign his donation of the Lankan throne to the Portuguese crown, this ambitious, freshly crowned man turned inland. A single decisive battle at the mountain pass of Balane in 1582 allowed him to enter Kandy, replace Karaliyaddē on the throne, and subject key areas of the highlands to his overlordship.[2] Within a few weeks, he extended his authority further than anyone else had since the mid fifteenth century, uniting much of the southwestern lowlands and central highlands under a single imperial umbrella. This said, the 'conquest' remained an extremely fragile reality.[3] To stabilize his rule in the mountainous interior, Rājasiṃha was compelled into fighting a series of smaller campaigns. In fact, a reading of the events in line with everything we have learned so far must acknowledge the fact that Rājasiṃha had again been lured to Kandy by a powerful local aristocrat, Vīrasundera Baṇḍāra, who used the Sītāvakan forces to overthrow his own king, but did certainly not wish to be a vassal of the invader indefinitely.[4]

---

[1] Sanjay Subrahmanyam, 'Holding the World in Balance: The Connected Histories of the Iberian Empires, 1500–1640', *American Historical Review*, 112, 5 (2007), pp. 1379–81. Cf. Sanjay Subrahmanyam and Luís Filipe Thomaz, 'Evolution of Empire: The Portuguese in the Indian Ocean during the Sixteenth Century', in *The Economy of Merchant Empires*, edited by James D. Tracy (Cambridge: Cambridge University Press, 1991), pp. 298–331. Also see the cautious position taken by Luís Filipe Thomaz in 'A crise de 1565–1575 na história do Estado da Índia', *Mare Liberum*, 9 (1995), pp. 494–508, which underlines that there was no coherent strategy, not even in the wake of the fall of Vijayanagar in 1565. Cf. Matos, *O Estado da India*.

[2] Fernão de Queiroz, *Conquista Temporal e Espiritual de Ceilão* (Colombo: Government Press, 1916), p. 356. Cf. Chandra Richard De Silva, 'The Rise and Fall of the Kingdom of Sitawaka (1521–1593)', *The Ceylon Journal of Historical and Social Studies*, 7, 1 (1977), pp. 34–5.

[3] Cf. *Rājāvaliya*, p. 89.

[4] On Vīrasundera Baṇḍāra and his son Konnappu Baṇḍāra, see Abeyasinghe, *Portuguese rule*, p. 13.

Once their detested king was gone, the rebels turned against Rājasiṃha. Pacifying and governing such a socially, not just topographically difficult terrain soon proved to be beyond Rājasiṃha's means.[5]

Much like the Portuguese, Rājasiṃha underestimated the centrifugal elements in the Kandyan realm. He also miscalculated the power of diplomacy and the ability of his enemies to reach out to South India. The deposed Karaliyaddē escaped. Before he died en route to Jaffna, his nephew Yamasiṃha Baṇḍāra was acclaimed as the rightful heir to the throne of Kandy, and wedded to the deposed king's young daughter Kusumāsana Devi. The new throne pretender set off through Jaffna to Goa, where he was received by the new viceroy, Duarte de Meneses (vr.1584–8). In the capital of the *Estado*, Karaliyaddē took baptism and, as a signal of the new era of global imperialism, chose a name that left little doubt about his ambitions: Dom Filipe.[6]

Around the same time, in 1585, Rājasiṃha was attacked at the Kandyan court. Vīrasundera Baṇḍāra, solidly established as a local lord in Peradenyia, at a short distance from the capital, now openly competed with him for the throne. When Rājasiṃha finally managed to eliminate Vīrasundera Baṇḍāra,[7] the latter's son Konappu Baṇḍāra did what other Kandyan leaders found to be most advisable at the time: he too fled, and chose to take refuge with the Portuguese. Konappu travelled through Colombo to Goa, was baptized, and given yet another ominous name: Dom João de Áustria, after the son of Phillip II and hero of the battle of Lepanto. In Goa, this determined young man became part of the entourage of Dom Filipe Yamasiṃha, and together they began to forge new plans.[8]

Clearly, the tentacular Lankan royal family continued to function as a formidable generator of political projects, and the space of South Indian exile—again best documented for Goa, but certainly including other hotspots—as the perfect powerhouse to boost their chances. Dom Filipe Yamasiṃha, nephew and heir to the deposed king Karaliyaddē of Kandy, began to lobby Phillip II to allow him to enter the highland kingdom with Portuguese troops. The terms used in the letters were in many ways similar to those of earlier times.[9] There was talk about the Catholic Monarch 'having him placed in that kingdom with troops and a fleet', and of course mass conversions were to be expected. The prince included a request to be allowed to travel to Europe to present his project. He was ready to take risks and go global not just in writing, but also in person.[10]

---

[5] Cf. Abeyasinghe, 'The kindgom of Kandy', pp. 142–5.

[6] Queiroz, *Conquista*, p. 356. The *Rājāvaliya*, p. 82 mentions a similar episode sometime between 1565 and 1582.

[7] This seems to be the episode narrated in the *Rājāvaliya*, p. 90, where Vīrasundera is said to have been tricked into falling into a pit.

[8] De Silva, 'The rise and fall of the kingdom of Sitawaka', pp. 34–5. On their story, see Biedermann, 'Cosmopolitan Converts. The Politics of Lankan Exile in the Portuguese Empire', in *Sri Lanka at the Crossroads of History*, edited by Zoltán Biedermann and Alan Strathern (London: UCL Press, 2017), pp. 141–60.

[9] Dom João is in fact mentioned explicitly as the relevant precedent: Phillip II [signed Miguel de Moura] to Duarte de Meneses, Lisbon, 6 February 1589, *Archivo Portuguez-Oriental*, edited by Joaquim Heliodoro da Cunha Rivara, reprint (New Delhi: Asian Educational Service, 1992), fasc. 3, p. 187.

[10] The original request is lost, but indirect evidence suggests that it was first made at the beginning of 1586 or even the end of 1585. Phillip II [signed Miguel de Moura] to Duarte de Meneses, Lisbon, 28 January 1588, *Archivo Portuguez-Oriental*, fasc. 3, p. 126.

## DEFENDING THE STATUS QUO: THE
## GAMA-BRAGANÇA LOBBY AT WORK

The royal response drafted in Lisbon in January 1587 was, however, remarkably evasive. The matter was referred back to Goa, and here the viceroy was equally hesitant.[11] Such had been the dominant attitude of the crown authorities during the entire decade. In 1581, a *regimento* issued by viceroy Francisco Mascarenhas (vr.1581–4) to the captain of Colombo João Correia de Brito (1581–8) had suggested to strengthen the local garrison by allowing convicts to be taken there for military service, but the emphasis was still on regulating (rather liberally) the cinnamon trade.[12] In 1585, a royal letter reminded Goa, in a tone reminiscent of the cautious style of John III, of the importance of treating Dharmapāla well. There was not a word about Kandy.[13] When news reached Lisbon of the attempted poisoning of Rājasiṃha, the response remained focused on the defence of Colombo and Mannār and the now emerging problem of spiralling expenses. In January 1587, the crown revealed disappointment over how more negotiations were not held with Rājasiṃha to save military resources.[14] Six years after the Habsburg takeover, there was still no strategy for Sri Lanka other than keeping down the costs. A cautious central administration kept shuffling inconclusive letters back and forth while on the ground the relevant actors struggled to rebuild military might.

The earliest inflection to this hyper-cautious stance appears in a letter from Lisbon dated March 1587. This missive is of key importance because it documents a new kind of connection being forged. A certain António Araújo de Carvalho had come from India to Lisbon in the previous year and was about to leave again. He had succeeded in presenting a project for Ceylon to someone at the Portuguese court and pointed out ways in which war might be waged upon Rājasiṃha, not just to keep him in check, but in order to prepare the terrain 'so that that island may be conquered'. Crucially as well, someone in Lisbon found the plan interesting enough to issue orders to Goa for a discussion to be held about it with other 'men of experience'. A transcript was sent, along with recommendations to also look into a second proposal made by Carvalho regarding the building of a fort at Galle, which might serve as a hub on the way from the Arabian Sea to Southeast Asia.[15]

Whilst there is no sign that the viceroy took these ideas on board, the project seems to have met with some interest in Iberia because it combined a rhetoric of

[11] Phillip II to Duarte de Meneses, Lisbon, 28 January 1587, British Library, *Additional Manuscripts*, 20,861, fol. 102v.
[12] Francisco Mascarenhas, *Regimento* for João Correia de Brito, [Goa], [end of 1581], British Library, *Additional Manuscripts*, 28,433, fols. 63–5v.
[13] Phillip II [signed Miguel de Moura] to Duarte de Meneses, Lisbon, 11 February 1585, *Archivo Portuguez-Oriental*, fasc. 3, p. 42. Note that the request for a trading privilege was later refused. Phillip II [signed Miguel de Moura] to Duarte de Meneses, Lisbon, 10 January 1587, *Archivo Portuguez-Oriental*, fasc. 3, p. 75.
[14] Phillip II [signed Miguel de Moura] to Duarte de Meneses, Lisbon, 10 January 1587, *Archivo Portuguez-Oriental*, fasc. 3, pp. 72–3.
[15] Phillip II [signed Miguel de Moura] to Dom Duarte de Meneses, Lisbon, 21 March 1587, *Archivo Portuguez-Oriental*, fasc. 3, p. 108.

conquest with a larger plan to articulate the two basins of the Indian Ocean. These were years of grand strategic planning in the Monarchy, with a view to creating a state of global hegemony, after all. It was not only the plan to invade England that occupied parts of the Spanish-Portuguese military apparatus in 1587, but also an offensive against another key enemy of the Catholic faith. Precisely at the end of March 1587, orders were issued to invade Aceh with a large armada carrying 4000 men, at the substantial cost of 300,000 *cruzados*. This major project, seen as a strategic move against the perceived Islamic axis extending from the Balkans to the Moluccas, only came to a halt due to military emergencies in Malindi, Johor, and Ceylon.[16] Between northwestern Europe and Southeast Asia, Ceylon appears to have emerged as a new focus of strategic planning in 1587. The actions discussed may still have been predominantly maritime, but in a royal letter from February 1588, which is unfortunately mostly illegible, there is talk about 'Raju, and the conquest of Ceylon'.[17]

In Goa, to be sure, viceroy Meneses resisted any intervention until his death in May 1588.[18] He declared to be sceptical about the plan of conquest proposed by Araújo de Carvalho, and ditched it.[19] True, he expressed worries about the second siege that Rājasiṃha laid on Colombo in June 1587.[20] In a letter written to the monarch in April 1588, he underlined how he supported a rescue armada with 800 men carrying permission to 'fight on the land'.[21] But much of the campaign was really down to naval manoeuvres. The Portuguese destroyed a group of ships heading for the Red Sea, and whilst they also attacked two temples,[22] there is no sign of a concerted terrestrial strategy. In fact, the viceroy soon saw his cautions confirmed by another royal letter, issued in Lisbon in February 1589, which, whilst passingly mentioning the importance of doing something to lift the siege of Colombo,[23] did not even allude to the idea of conquest recommended the previous year. One could be forgiven for beginning to suspect that not all royal letters were being written by the same hand.

[16] Phillip II to Duarte de Meneses, Lisbon, 30 March 1587, Arquivo National da Torre do Tombo, *Corpo Cronológico*, 1-112-19. Cf. Paulo Jorge Sousa Pinto, *Portugueses e Malaios. Malaca e os Sultanatos de Johor e Achém, 1575–1619* (Lisbon: Sociedade Histórica da Independência de Portugal, 1997), p. 92.

[17] Phillip II to Duarte de Meneses, Lisbon, 5 February 1588, *Archivo Portuguez-Oriental*, fasc. 3, p. 127.

[18] Duarte de Meneses to Phillip II, Goa, 15 April 1588, Archivo General de Simancas, *Secretarías Provinciales: Portugal*, Codex 1551, fols. 295–302v. Cf. Diogo do Couto, *Da Asia* (Lisbon: Livraria de São Carlos, 1973–1975), vol. X, x, 19. Note that starting at this point the valuable narrative of Couto is interrupted due to the loss of the eleventh *Década*, which would have covered the years 1588–96. For an attempt at reconstructing the lost events, see Donald Ferguson, *The History of Ceylon, from the Earliest Times to 1600 A.D.* (Colombo: Royal Asiatic Society, 1909), pp. 388–409.

[19] Duarte de Meneses to Phillip II, Goa, 23 November 1587, Archivo General de Simancas, *Secretarías Provinciales: Portugal*, Codex 1551, fol. 77v.

[20] Duarte de Meneses to Phillip II, Goa, 11 December 1587, Archivo General de Simancas, *Secretarías Provinciales: Portugal*, Codex 1551, fol. 60.

[21] Duarte de Meneses to Phillip II, Goa, 15 April 1588, Archivo General de Simancas, *Secretarías Provinciales: Portugal*, Codex 1551, fol. 297v.

[22] Duarte de Meneses to Phillip II, Goa, 15 April 1588, Archivo General de Simancas, *Secretarías Provinciales: Portugal*, Codex 1551, fols. 297v–298.

[23] Phillip II [signed Miguel de Moura] to Duarte de Meneses, Lisbon, 2 February 1589, *Archivo Portuguez-Oriental*, fasc. 3, p. 175.

An impression emerges that a powerful lobby may have been blocking policy changes specifically with regard to Ceylon. The blockade functioned both in Lisbon and in Asia, supporting a group of interests which is rarely directly mentioned in the sources, but shows strong signs of having revolved around trading arrangements established on the semi-periphery of the *Estado* earlier in the century, connecting Cochin with Colombo and involving vast transactions of cinnamon and other Sri Lankan goods.[24] On the surface of it, it was primarily the Gama family (the counts of Vidigueira) who, as descendants of Vasco da Gama, derived substantial revenues from the trading of cinnamon. They had little interest in seeing the status quo—including well-established trading practices that flourished in a moderately unstable, opaque environment such as that perpetuated by the petty wars of the 1560s to early 1590s—challenged. It is certainly no coincidence that Duarte de Meneses, the staunchest opponent to any changes of policy around Ceylon in the late 1580s, married his daughter to Francisco da Gama, a man later confronted by the authorities for standing in the way of the crown's interests.[25]

But behind the Gamas one discerns the contours of a far more powerful family. Despite the scarcity of direct evidence, there are strong signs that it may have been the Dukes of Bragança who had the greatest interest in maintaining Ceylon in limbo. The Braganças—including Duchess Catherine (1540–1614), a grand-daughter of Manuel I and, as such, a cousin of Phillip II and serious contender for the throne in 1580—enjoyed a princely cinnamon trading allowance.[26] They were the most powerful family in Portugal and, in the transition of 1580–1, the one that Phillip's agents had had to placate with the most substantial concessions.[27] They were the patrons of the Gamas and had, regarding Asia, a long history of opposing royal policy. Whilst the idea of two 'parties' fighting each other in Lisbon along the lines proposed by Luís Filipe Thomaz for the early 1500s may not do full justice to the complexity of the situation, it is still possible to see a commercialist, centrifugal logic at work in the resistance to a more centralistically, militarily minded approach, for which momentum was now slowly building up between the periphery and some people in the metropolis.

[24] Cf. Sanjay Subrahmanyam, 'Making India Gama: The Project of Dom Aires da Gama (1519) and Its Meaning', *Mare Liberum*, 16 (1998), pp. 43–7 and the accusations later made by Nicolau Petro, *feitor* of Cochin, to Phillip II, Cochin, 14 January 1587, Archivo General de Simancas, *Secretarías Provinciales: Portugal*, Codex 1551, fol. 212–212v.

[25] On the wider logics at work see James C. Boyajian, *Portuguese Trade under the Habsburgs 1580–1640* (Baltimore, MD/London: Johns Hopkins University Press, 1992), pp. 43–5 and Mafalda Soares da Cunha, 'A Casa de Bragança e a Expansão, séculos XV-XVII', in *A Alta Nobreza e a Fundação do Estado da Índia*, edited by João Paulo Oliveira e Costa and Vítor Luís Gaspar Rodrigues (Lisbon: CHAM/ IICT, 2004), pp. 303–19. The evidence for Sri Lanka is patchy, but a later document reveals that the Count of Vidigueira purchased cinnamon from at least 1580 to 1593 through his private agent Nicolau Pinto. Phillip III to viceroy João Coutinho, Lisbon, 31 December 1617, *Documentos Remettidos da India ou Livros das Monções*, edited by Raymundo Antonio Bulhão Pato and António da Silva Rego (Lisbon: Academia Real das Sciencias/Imprensa Nacional, 1880–1982), vol. IV, pp. 239–40.

[26] A royal letter from 1588 mentions how Catherine maintained the right to purchase 100 quintals of cinnamon per year in Ceylon and bring it to Portugal. Phillip II to Duarte de Meneses, Lisbon, 16 March 1588, *Archivo Portuguez-Oriental*, fasc. 3, p. 151.

[27] On the negotiations and the House of Braganza, see Joaquim Veríssimo Serrão, *História de Portugal*, 2nd edition, vol. IV (Lisbon: Verbo, 1990), pp. 14–19 and 304–8.

Controlling Portuguese networks active in the 'shadow empire' was a thorny issue for the new Habsburg administration, not only because it involved challenging the interests of powerful families, but also because the Spanish-Portuguese monarchy was still under consolidation. Rumours circulated that the *Estado* might declare itself independent under the leadership of Dom António, the Portuguese throne contender ousted by Phillip II in 1581, with a new headquarters precisely in Ceylon. António had attempted to govern as a king in the Azores in 1582, his dogged insular resistance remaining fresh in everyone's mind. The prospect of awakening comparable ghosts in the East must have left many a councillor to the monarch cautious, especially considering that António obtained asylum in England, where oceanic explorations were gaining momentum.[28] For a few years, the defenders of the status quo benefitted precisely from the Catholic Monarchy's global exposure. Although changes were under way, the hands of the reformers remained tied.

## OVERCOMING THE IMPASSE (1): SIGNS OF IMPERIAL REFORM, 1587–8

Seen under such a light, the flurry of letters concerning Ceylon that reached Lisbon (and Madrid, as we shall see) between 1588 and 1590 must have come as a shock. Whilst the proposals varied widely in scope, the very fact that they are all bound together in a single volume of Portuguese state papers in the Spanish state archive at Simancas is telling. Clearly, someone high up in the hierarchy was developing an interest in the matter. In fact, one of the earliest letters in the bundle combines precisely a critique of the trading practices of the Gamas with a military approach to Lankan politics. Written in Cochin in January 1587 by the king's *feitor* Nicolau Petro Cochino, this letter takes a strong stance on defending royal against private interests established in the region.[29] According to the author, the Gamas were using middlemen illegally to send large cargoes (up to 1000 *quintals*) of cinnamon to Lisbon every year, evading taxes and hurting the Crown's own trade interests. This state of affairs, Petro added, was supported by corrupt officers in the island.[30]

---

[28] Cf. 'Configurações do Império', in *História da Expansão Portuguesa*, edited by Francisco Bethencourt and Kirti Chaudhuri (Lisbon: Círculo de Leitores, 1998), vol. II, pp. 276–83. An interesting reference to how the Portuguese in Asia pinned their hopes on Dom António whilst the Spanish authorities attempted to spread news of his death is in the account of Thomas Cavendish in Richard Hakluyt, *Voyages and Discoveries. The Principal Navigations, Voyages, Traffiques and Discoveries of the English Nation*, edited, abridged and introduced by Jack Beeching (London: Penguin, 1972), p. 293.

[29] Nicolau Petro Cochino to Phillip II, Cochin, 14 January 1587, Archivo General de Simancas, *Secretarías Provinciales: Portugal*, Codex 1551, fol. 212–212v.

[30] Nicolau Petro Cochino to Phillip II, Cochin, 14 January 1587, Archivo General de Simancas, *Secretarías Provinciales: Portugal*, Codex 1551, fol. 205 (due to binding). Note how, at the same time, there were rumours that Petro himself was in touch with Rājasiṃha, negotiating in cinnamon on behalf of the king of Cochin. If this is true, then the letter quoted above would need to be read essentially as a counter-offensive to discredit critics. Cf. Phillip II to Duarte de Meneses [signed Miguel de Moura], Lisbon, 6 February 1589, *Archivo Portuguez-Oriental*, fasc. 3, pp. 175–6.

Whilst such accusations may have seemed commonplace and not necessarily trustworthy, one aspect stands out which was to have consequences: the plan to regulate trade and rationalize the Estado was bound up with the idea of conquest. Against the current, costly state of affairs, Nicolau Petro affirmed that the crown stood to benefit if 'the entire island' was 'taken' at last (the verb is '*tomar*'). For this to happen, war needed to be waged 'truly', that is, with appropriate conviction, as others had proposed in Goa before. Whatever the resonances of the *feitor*'s arguments with the official logics of Spanish empire building, it seems important to emphasize though how this was still a project generated in South Asia, in dialogue with power networks operating at a different, slightly lower level than the global polity. Petro's project, whilst serving up centralist topoi, also included intriguing details such as a mention of the *rāja* of Cochin, who was offering 5000–6000 Nāyar musketeers in support of the expedition.[31] A considerable corpus of diplomatic activity involving various parties in Sri Lanka and South India is probably buried beneath the silence of our sources.

Another letter preserved at Simancas, written in Colombo in December 1587 by an otherwise obscure individual called Nuno Álvares de Atouguia, confirms the aggressive trend set by Nicolau Petro, though with nuances.[32] The name of the author might seem to indicate an affiliation with the house of Bragança, the town of Atouguia being one of their many possessions in Portugal. The contents of the letter, however, are very much in opposition to it. Atouguia had arrived in Colombo in mid 1587 from Quilon, leading a fleet of six vessels.[33] In his view, 'to conquer this island would not be an arduous task for the *Estado*, but rather a very simple one'. It could be carried out with less than 3000 men, and once the *Estado* was 'in possession' of the island, or at least Rājasiṃha had been fragilized, the Portuguese could occupy key ports. Garrisons with less than 200 men each could control Galle in the South, Chilaw in the West, and Batticaloa in the East. Interestingly, though, the proposal then turns seawards rather than inland, as if the author sensed that this might still be more acceptable in Lisbon than a plan of terrestrial conquest. Mention is made of the vast potential of the cinnamon trade in connection with other parts of the Indian Ocean such as Persia, Arabia, Aceh, Malacca, and China. The author wished to emphasize the importance of dominating the sea to subdue ('*sojugar*' and '*senhorear*') the lords of the land.

Atouguia's proposal is at its most interesting where it introduces a third argument for military action—again, one that could only unfold with such persuasiveness at the intersection of Lankan and Iberian political discourses. Taking military action, the author affirmed, was not just about boosting the Habsburg coffers. It was rather, essentially, a matter of 'just and divine right'—a barely veiled allusion not so much to Catholic Universalism, but to the Ibero-Lankan juridical fiction created

[31] Nicolau Petro Cochino to Phillip II, Cochin, 14 January 1587, Archivo General de Simancas, *Secretarías Provinciales: Portugal*, Codex 1551, fol. 205.

[32] Nuno Álvares de Atouguia to Phillip II, Colombo, 20 December 1587, Archivo General de Simancas, *Secretarías Provinciales: Portugal*, Codex 1551, fols. 109–109v.

[33] Duarte de Meneses to Phillip II, Goa, 23 November 1587, Archivo General de Simancas, *Secretarías Provinciales: Portugal*, Codex 1551, fol. 75.

by the donation of 1580. Clearly, this had by now become yet another topos talked about by nobles with ambitions of military leadership. As an heir to the throne of Kōṭṭe, Phillip II had an 'obligation' to destroy Rājasiṃha, Atouguia claimed. It seems quite significant that a man purporting to be part of the household of the Portuguese king connected these various aspects into a single line of thought: the need to fight private trading interests, the need to set up forts around the island and use them to channel the power of maritime hegemony towards the control of lands, the importance of destroying Rājasiṃha as a potential all-Lankan overlord, the right and indeed obligation of Phillip II to do this as a beneficiary of the testament of Dharmapāla and as a patron of Catholicism, and the possibility of achieving all this with 3000 men.[34]

Complementing this epistolary wave, others wrote about the advantages of dealing a blow to Rājasiṃha in connection with the matter of growing expenses at Colombo. By the time Nicolau Petro was writing again in 1588,[35] he was joined in his efforts by Dom Mateus, the bishop of Cochin.[36] João Gomes da Silva, the captain of Hormuz, urged the metropolitan authorities to go ahead with the conquest of Ceylon in two letters of his own. He invoked, again, the '*soldados practicos* of those parts', men with experience in Lankan matters who, according to Silva, recognized the fragility of Rājasiṃha's demoralized army. Silva thought that an offensive should be launched before the king produced an heir. He also asked for a new fortification to be built, possibly at Galle, alluding to an earlier letter which, unfortunately, is lost.[37] That the captain of Hormuz was taking a position on matters pertaining to Sri Lanka is intriguing. But the Persian Gulf port had become a major thoroughfare for the (largely illicit) cinnamon trade connecting Colombo and Cochin with the Middle East, so Silva may well have been positioning himself against the dominant trading network mentioned above, sensing a potential reward from the crown.[38]

One of the constant references in this flurry of letters is to the costliness of defending Colombo and the need for new, more rational fortifications. Preoccupations in this field may have been among the first to arise after the Union of Crowns, though, again, not necessarily in Iberia. Whilst explicit orders from Lisbon appear in 1589, a letter written in Goa in 1587 by Manuel de Sousa

---

[34] Atouguia to Phillip II, Colombo, 20 December 1587, Archivo General de Simancas, *Secretarías Provinciales: Portugal*, Codex 1551, fols. 109–109v.

[35] Nicolau Petro Cochino to Phillip II, Cochin, 14 January 1587, Archivo General de Simancas, *Secretarías Provinciales: Portugal*, Codex 1551, fols. 205–205v.

[36] Mateus, bishop of Cochin, to Phillip II, Cochin, 16 January 1588, Archivo General de Simancas, *Secretarías Provinciales: Portugal*, Codex 1551, fols. 312–312v.

[37] João Gomes da Silva, captain of Hormuz, to Phillip II, Hormuz, 4 July 1588 and 11 July 1588, Archivo General de Simancas, *Secretarías Provinciales: Portugal*, Codex 1551, fols. 551–551v and fols. 293–294v.

[38] A later document also refers how Francisco da Gama infringed upon the crown's cinnamon trade at Hormuz. Biblioteca Nacional de Portugal, *Reservados*, Codex 1976, fols. 149–52. Gama was incidentally said to be issuing licenses for cinnamon to be taken not only to Hormuz, but also Diu and even Jiddah. Biblioteca Nacional do Rio de Janeiro, *Rendas da Índia*, Codex 2, 2, 10, fols. 241–247v and 'Livro das merces geraes do dito Conde', Biblioteca Nacional de Portugal, *Reservados*, Codex 1987, fol. 112v. I thank Susana Miranda for drawing my attention to these documents.

Coutinho before he became head of the *Estado* mentions that he had written about redrawing the fortifications of Colombo to three successive governors already— which would take us back to the governorship of Fernão Teles de Meneses in 1581.[39] The matter was widely acknowledged as being one that required attention.[40] That this came to be perceived in Iberia as a major issue in connection specifically with private trade emerges from a royal missive written in March 1589. This document offers, in dramatic contrast with the more evasive royal letters produced in February of the same year, the most ambitious and elaborate strategic plan drafted in Lisbon during the 1580s. The missive opens with a remarkably energetic request for the viceroy to react to a set of notes that, in the understanding of the author of the orders, had not been properly addressed in Goa—quite probably the above-mentioned proposal by António de Araújo de Carvalho, from 1586. While vast sums of crown money were being spent on the local garrison and even on such aspects of local life as feeding the cinnamon peelers, the royal *feitoria* hardly received any cinnamon any more.[41] The bitterest complaints in the royal missive of March 1589 regarded not Rājasiṃha, but the Portuguese private traders.

The orders were for Colombo to adapt, and radically so. What the central authorities proposed in 1589 was a solution that would later be adopted by the Dutch VOC, after 1656, precisely to cut costs at its new Lankan headquarters.[42] The full integration of the city into the official empire was to go along with a profound reformulation of its urban space.[43] The idea was to cut through the fabric of the city with a new wall, separating a heavily fortified, officially Portuguese area west of the old rivulet from the rest of the conurbation. Half of the city, including the municipal council, various churches and numerous noble households pertaining to the mixed Luso-Lankan elite formed during the previous decades would have been simply left outside. That the *casados* never even considered obeying these orders is hardly surprising: they must have seen them as absurd. But the plan set the tone for a new type of discourse emanating from Iberia: more centralistic, more rationalistic, and less tolerant of local idiosyncrasies.

Before we proceed, it is worth pointing out that drawing excessively rigid lines between the various parties involved in the discussion in the late 1580s may not do justice to the complexity of the situation. It is a legitimate and useful exercise to

[39] Manuel de Sousa Coutinho to Phillip II, Goa, 14 December 1587, Archivo General de Simancas, *Secretarías Provinciales: Portugal*, Codex 1551, fol. 176.

[40] Manuel de Sousa Coutinho to Phillip II, Panaji, 10 December 1588, Archivo General de Simancas, *Secretarías Provinciales: Portugal*, Codex 1551, fols. 251–251v.

[41] Phillip II to Duarte de Meneses, *Archivo Portuguez-Oriental*, fasc. 3, pp. 217–18. A later list shows that the cinnamon price was particularly high in 1585–9 (40 to 50 *xerafins* the *quintal*), and then dropped back in 1590 to the 1584 level, around 10 *xerafins*. Viceroy to crown *procurador* Pedro Alves Pereira, Goa, 10 December 1618, *Documentos Remettidos da India ou Livros das Monções*, vol. IV, p. 242.

[42] On the VOC measures taken after 1656 see Remco Raben, 'Trade and urbanization. Portuguese and Dutch urban attitudes in Ceylon. Colombo: mirror of the colonial mind', *Mare Liberum*, 13 (1997), pp. 95–120.

[43] Phillip II to Dom Duarte de Meneses, Lisbon, 7 March 1589, *Archivo Portuguez-Oriental*, fasc. 3, p. 217. The same order was given again in a royal letter from Lisbon, 2 March 1590, Arquivo Histórico Ultramarino, Codex 281, fols. 73v–74.

identify tensions between two analytical extremes—centralists versus free traders—
but reality was usually more complicated. Simão de Brito de Castro, the captain of
Colombo, had gone to Madrid in 1584 and agreed to use one third of his own
cinnamon allowance to support the crown's efforts in improving the existing fortifications.[44] But whilst this allowed the crown to save some money and Castro to
style himself as a loyal subject, the latter's actions also meant in practice the
consolidation of a physical structure that would require ever more money for its
defence. Being in Colombo and experiencing these twists and intertwinements
certainly resulted in a healthily nuanced appreciation—but also some understandable despair. In a letter written in November 1589, the captain requested financial
support for the building of a proper royal residence in Colombo, in what was
evidently a move inspired by Dom João Dharmapāla. He recommended supporting a rebellion in Kandy to destabilize Sītāvaka, reviving an old Kōṭṭe
project. He complained bitterly about his frictions with the financial supervisor
dispatched by the governor, accusing Goa of undermining his authority by negotiating with Rājasiṃha and facilitating the illicit cinnamon trade. It is little wonder
that, as he prepared the ground for his own exit, Castro requested a lifelong
captaincy in a 'calmer' place. Cochin, he believed, would do, or even Sofala in
East Africa.[45]

How is it, then, that things moved forward at all? Whilst the citizenry of
Colombo simply ignored any orders to reconfigure the fortifications, the crown—
and we shall attempt soon to clarify what exactly that word may be taken to
mean—showed no signs of relenting. In 1589, despite the very recent trauma of
the Great Armada affecting both Spain and Portugal, the central administration
presented a remarkably elaborate plan for the renewal of Lusitanian naval
hegemony in the Sea of Ceylon. The plan was to create a permanent fleet capable
of blocking the ports of the island instead of sending annual reinforcements.
Again, the enemy to be tamed was not just Rājasiṃha. To deal with the rampant
corruption in and around Colombo, orders were that the armada should remain
independent from the jurisdiction of the captain of the fort.[46] The gesture was
reminiscent of mid century proposals discussed under John III, where the Sri Lanka
Portuguese were to be subjected to the authority of a captain who, annually, would
go from India to visit the island in the company of a judge. In those days, cinnamon
had still been abundant in the royal warehouses, so the crown ended up not pursuing the matter. By now the corruption of the system had reached breaking point
as the crown itself was deep in the red.[47]

[44] Simão de Brito de Castro to Phillip II, Ceylon, 20[?] December 1588, Archivo General de
Simancas, *Secretarías Provinciales: Portugal*, Codex 1551, fol. 269.
[45] Simão de Brito de Castro to Phillip II, Colombo, 24 November 1589, Archivo General de
Simancas, *Secretarías Provinciales: Portugal*, Codex 1551, fols. 798–798v.
[46] Phillip II to Duarte de Meneses, Lisbon, 7 March 1589, *Archivo Portuguez-Oriental*, fasc. 3, p. 216.
[47] On 'corruption' and how to conceptualize it in the Portuguese context in Asia, see Nandini
Chaturvedula, 'Imperial excess: Corruption and decadence in Portuguese India (1660–1706)'
(PhD dissertation, Columbia University, 2010).

## OVERCOMING THE IMPASSE (2): PRODUCTIVE COMMUNICATIONAL GAPS

But how could the impasse caused by the existence of at least two widely disparate Portuguese visions for Sri Lanka in the 1580s be overcome? Part of the answer is to be found not so much in a gradual build-up of central power, eventually triggering action on the ground, but on a deeply convoluted and often flawed process of intra-imperial communications. The late 1580s became a key moment in Luso-Lankan history essentially on grounds of an uneven effectiveness of communications between Asia and Europe, along with the disarticulation between (often contra-dictory) central orders, uncoordinated peripheral projects and policies, and changes of fortune in Sri Lanka itself. As communicational voids appeared here and there, the space for game-changing agency also increased.

There are many signs that communication along the traditional Cape route suf-fered severe disruptions precisely during these years. News about the death of the viceroy Duarte de Meneses in April 1588 took over a year to reach Lisbon. A letter written by the governor Manuel de Sousa Coutinho in November 1590 would not have reached Portugal at all, had a copy not been sent through the Middle East, along the murky channels connecting Goa with the Mediterranean through Hormuz and Cairo.[48] It does not appear mentioned before the dispatch of a reply letter dated September 1592.[49] In March 1593, Lisbon complained about not receiving, during the previous year, the much-awaited letters of viceroy Matias de Albuquerque (vr.1591–7).[50] And, from a royal missive dated March 1594, it tran-spires that a letter sent from Colombo in November 1592 had just arrived.[51] Such delays added to the already substantial difficulty in articulating central decision making with military actions on the ground. It thus became increasingly plausible for men with a sense of opportunity to jump into the gaps, short-circuit the network, and take initiative.

One of the decisive moments allowing for a transition at the level of imperial policy in 1588–9 involved a temporary geographical shift in the *Estado*'s Lankan policy from Colombo to Mannār, and an attempt at using Mannār as a spring-board to Kandy. Whether this was anyone's conscious decision or a half-hearted concession to the prolonged diplomatic petitioning of Dom Filipe Yāmasiṃha, a particularly persistent candidate to the Kandyan throne, is not clear. After the

---

[48] Duarte de Meneses to Phillip II, Goa, 23 November 1587, Archivo General de Simancas, *Secretarías Provinciales: Portugal*, Codex 1551, fol. 70. On the landroute see Anthony Disney, 'The gulf route from India to Portugal in the sixteenth and seventeenth centuries: couriers, traders and image-makers', in *A carreira da Índia e as rotas dos estreitos: actas do VIII Seminário Internacional de História Indo-Portuguesa*, edited by Luís Filipe Thomaz and Artur Teodoro de Matos (Lisbon: CEPCEP/CHAM/IICT, 1996), pp. 530–9.

[49] Phillip II to Simão de Brito de Castro, s.l., 6 September 1592, Arquivo Histórico Ultramarino, Codex 281, fol. 209.

[50] Phillip II to Dom João Dharmapala, [Lisbon], 9 March 1593, Arquivo Histórico Ultramarino, Codex 281, fol. 234.

[51] Phillip II to Dom João Dharmapala, Lisbon, 5 March 1594, Arquivo Histórico Ultramarino, Codex 281, fol. 274.

death of Duarte de Meneses, the new viceroy Manuel de Sousa Coutinho (gv. 1588–91), a man who had spent years in the island, agreed to dispatch Dom Filipe with some troops and a letter of recommendation to Mannār around December 1588.[52] The prince set up quarters in the fort of Mannār with a pension and some other means of sustenance granted by Coutinho.[53] As the Portuguese enclave of Mannār came to host this little court, the island's inhabitants began to claim more attention from the Portuguese crown.[54] True, Coutinho doubted the reliability of Yāmasiṃha,[55] but the prince was far from relying on the governor alone. One of his strongest supporters was the bishop of Cochin, who had been a close ally (and *procurador*) of Dharmapāla since the 1560s.[56] In fact, the king of Kōṭṭe himself supported the idea of Yāmasiṃha being helped by the *Estado* in his venture to overthrow Rājasiṃha and take the Kandy throne. This is where our story of the intertwinement of Portuguese and Sri Lankan ideas of conquest comes full circle— or almost.

In a letter from 1589, Dom João Dharmapāla, still the potential *cakravarti* of the island, explained to Phillip II how Dom Filipe Yāmasiṃha had a place in the wider scheme of things, designated above as the Matrioshka Principle.[57] He emphasized that, whoever might come to sit on the throne of Kandy, would also necessarily have to acknowledge the overlordship of Kōṭṭe. Dharmapāla still styled himself as the sole legitimate vassal of the Portuguese crown in Sri Lanka, so that any other lordships added to the sphere of influence of Phillip II would come into the picture *through* their links of submission to Kōṭṭe. What Dharmapāla hoped Phillip II would support was the extension—or rather restoration—of the suzerainty of Kōṭṭe by means of 'new tributes and various vassalages' ('*nouos tributos e vassalagens deferentes*').[58] As we shall soon see, this is where a major

---

[52] Queiroz, *Conquista*, p. 356. Dom Filipe may have gone in September–December 1588. This would explain the sudden enthusiasm of the captain of Mannār at a time when the captain of Colombo was not yet aware of things. Simão de Brito de Castro to Cardinal Archduke Albert, Colombo, 7 December 1588, Arquivo Nacional Torre do Tombo, *Corpo Cronológico*, 1-112-51. A royal letter written in Lisbon in February 1589 reveals the extent to which the authorities were unaware of the prince's expedition to Ceylon. Phillip II to Dom Duarte de Meneses, Lisbon, 6 February 1589, *Archivo Portuguez-Oriental*, fasc. 3, p. 187.

[53] Phillip II to Matias de Albuquerque, Lisbon, [beginning 1591], *Archivo Portuguez-Oriental*, fasc. 3, pp. 254–5.

[54] Phillip II to Duarte de Meneses, Lisbon, 7 February 1586, *Archivo Portuguez-Oriental*, fasc. 3, pp. 61–2; Phillip II [signed Miguel de Moura] to Dom Duarte de Meneses, Lisbon, 6 February 1589, *Archivo Portuguez-Oriental*, fasc. 3, p. 202.

[55] Coutinho defended the idea of sending an expedition in one letter, only to boast about his resistance to the plan in another. Letter to Phillip II, Pangim (Goa), 4 December 1589, Archivo General de Simancas, *Secretarías Provinciales: Portugal*, Codex 1551, fols. 768–790 and Phillip II [signed Miguel de Moura] to Matias de Albuquerque, Lisbon, [c.1591], *Archivo Portuguez-Oriental*, fasc. 3, pp. 254–5.

[56] Phillip II to Matias de Albuquerque, Lisbon, [c.1591], *Archivo Portuguez-Oriental*, fasc. 3, pp. 254–5. On the bishop, André de Santa Maria, see Trindade, *Conquista Espiritual*, vol. I, pp. 222–5 and vol. III, p. 45.

[57] Dom João Dharmapala to Phillip II, Colombo, 29 November 1589, Archivo General de Simancas, *Secretarías Provinciales: Portugal*, Codex 1551, fols. 796–796v.

[58] Dom João Dharmapala to Phillip II, Colombo, 29 November 1589, Archivo General de Simancas, *Secretarías Provinciales: Portugal*, Codex 1551, fol. 796.

misunderstanding began to arise between two increasingly different imperial traditions: the Lankan and the Spanish. But in 1589, the Sinhalese king was not alone in seeing a Kandy project supported by the Portuguese crown as a potential boost to the symbolic prevalence of Kōṭṭe.[59]

Others came out in 1588 to support Dom Filipe Yamasiṃha from a slightly different angle. The captain of Mannār, João de Melo, laid out the advantages of conquering and evangelizing Kandy. He embraced the cause in the hope of gaining military protagonism, arguing that a major expedition to Kandy would not only weaken Rājasiṃha, but also open up new perspectives of conquest in other places such as Aceh. Melo must have had a keen interest in the projects of the Monarchy at the time. But again, this was not just a Portuguese noble drawing attention to himself; it was a Portuguese noble drawing attention to himself *and* appropriating the ideas of a Lankan throne pretender in connection with the assumed wider interests of the Monarchy. One of the key arguments was, again, that the Kandyan prince would soon, as a Catholic, gain the support of a majority of the highland population.[60]

Crucially though, the mobilization of Goan resources and their deployment through Mannār into the heart of Sri Lanka ended up being once more ignited *outside* of the correspondence we have at our disposal. Dom Filipe Yamasiṃha was still bracing himself for another year of waiting in Mannār, when the political situation in Kandy reached breaking point. Towards the end of 1589, a *mudaliyār* known as Dom Francisco Visugo rebelled against Rājasiṃha. He governed Kandy for about six months, before sending word to Mannār to offer the throne to Dom Filipe. One chronicler states that the latter's legitimacy as a successor to Karaliyaddē was key.[61] Certainly calculations to obtain Portuguese military support played an equally important role. The process as such—a relatively obscure individual taking the throne in Kandy, only to pass it on to a legitimate candidate enjoying foreign support—was not unheard of in Sri Lanka.

This is not to say that things were going according to a well-rehearsed script. The Kandyans remained as divided as ever, and Dom Filipe ended up leaving Mannār rather hastily, at an unfavourable moment of the southwestern monsoon, between June and August 1590.[62] After eight years of lobbying in exile, the prince of Kandy ended up being dispatched with a rather meagre retinue of thirty Portuguese soldiers and 200 *lascarins*.[63] But for a brief moment his decision seemed to pay off. Soon he was acclaimed at Wahakotte (today a large Catholic pilgrimage site) north of Kandy, and again in a large public gathering at Gannoruwa, closer to the capital.[64]

---

[59] In this he was supported again by the Franciscans. Guardian to Phillip II, Colombo, 29 November 1589, Archivo General de Simancas, *Secretarías Provinciales: Portugal*, Codex 1551, fols. 794–794v.

[60] João de Melo to Phillip II, Mannār, 28 December 1588, Archivo General de Simancas, *Secretarías Provinciales: Portugal*, Codex 1551, fols. 539–539v.

[61] Trindade, *Conquista Espiritual*, vol. III, p. 70.

[62] Trindade, *Conquista Espiritual*, vol. III, p. 71.

[63] *Conquista*, p. 356 and Trindade, *Conquista Espiritual*, vol. III, p. 71.

[64] Queiroz, *Conquista*, p. 361. Cf. Trindade, *Conquista Espiritual*, vol. III, p. 71.

Sometime later that year, Dom Filipe finally saw the arrival of 300 to 400 Portuguese soldiers. They helped him consolidate his authority in the highlands and lead a successful offensive against Sītāvaka.[65] In addition to all this, the captain of Colombo, Simão de Brito de Castro, led a series of naval raids against ports controlled by Rājasiṃha, from Chilaw in the North to Dondra in the South.[66] For a moment, it looked as if the idea of placing a Sinhalese Catholic ruler on the throne of Kandy and building up maritime power to consolidate inland processes might work.

Then, however, sometime during the first half of 1591, Dom Filipe died in Kandy, quite possibly of poisoning.[67] The Kandyan elite remained as restless as it had ever been. Dom João Konappu Baṇḍāra seized the throne, apostatized, and cut off the supply routes of the Portuguese troops still present in the kingdom.[68] He had kept close to Dom Filipe Yamasiṃha for some time, but taking into consideration his family history, it is rather surprising that no-one saw the risks of such a cooperation. Konappu was the son of Vīrasundera Baṇḍāra, the very man who had helped assassinate king Karaliyaddē, the father-in-law of Yamasiṃha, in 1582. These two young men, temporarily united by a quest for Portuguese support, remained the figureheads of two rival Kandyan factions.

Once on the throne, Konappu Baṇḍāra became Vimaladharmasūriya I. The chronicler Queiroz commented a century later how 'this was the beginning of the new family that still reigns in Ceylon, holding the crown in the mountains of Candea at the cost of many Portuguese lives'.[69] It was also where a new strand of *cakravartism* took its roots, in powerful defiance of the hegemonic discourse of Kōṭṭe—creating a new focus of 'genuine' Lankan overlordship, constitutive of national identity until today. The Portuguese presence in Kandy became unsustainable, showing just how hollow the entire project had been. Others had failed in taking control of Kandy before, including Parākramabāhu VI and Rājasiṃha himself. Kandy was a difficult conquest not just in terms of its physical topography, but most importantly in terms of its persistently complex social landscape and slippery constellations of powers. How Vimaladharmasūriya learned to gain a grip on this realm—by embracing what was already an embryonic anti-Christian and anti-Portuguese discourse of Sinhalaness—is a different story that has been told elsewhere.[70] The Portuguese, so much is clear, failed once again to establish a foothold in the mountainous interior of Ceylon.

---

[65] A royal letter dated 1592 mentions receipt, by means of the land route, of a letter by the governor Manuel de Sousa Coutinho, written in Goa on 6 November 1590, which contained the news that Rājasiṃha was 'almost' defeated—suggesting that the battle of Ganetenna may have happened before, perhaps in mid October. Phillip II to Simão de Brito de Castro, [Lisbon], 6 September 1592, Arquivo Histórico Ultramarino, Codex 281, fol. 209.

[66] Queiroz, *Conquista*, pp. 360–1.

[67] According to Queiroz, *Conquista*, pp. 361, 364, and 366, Dom Filipe died a few days after his victory, but the Portuguese troops only returned to Mannār in October 1591.

[68] Queiroz, *Conquista*, pp. 361–2.

[69] *Conquista*, p. 362. Note how the *Rājāvaliya*, p. 92 does not mention Dom Filipe Yamasiṃha, presenting Konnappu as the man who, after spending some years in Goa, seized the Kandyan throne.

[70] Strathern, *Kingship and Conversion*, pp. 214–21.

# THE ADVENT OF THE CAPTAINCY-GENERAL OF THE CONQUEST OF CEYLON, 1591–1594

Then, in 1591, a revolt in the Seven Korales opened up some space for a northward extension of Dharmapāla's authority. The kingdom of Kōṭṭe, now based in Colombo, could start pulsating again. In 1592, a successful campaign involving Portuguese troops reinforced the impression that Rājasiṃha was retreating. Finally, in 1593, Rājasiṃha died and Sītāvaka imploded.[71] It was in this year that, according to Queiroz, the arrival in Colombo of a new captain, Pedro Homem Pereira, prompted the beginning of the 'good fortunes of Ceylon'.[72] In reality, the campaign attributed to Pereira was almost entirely organized by Dharmapāla's own military, involving the *casados* of Colombo, well before the new Portuguese captain arrived. As for orders from Portugal or Spain to attack, there were none. The royal missives that arrived in Goa in 1593, written in September 1592, were still responding to news sent from Asia in November 1590.[73]

A second military campaign, launched from Colombo in September 1593, was largely down to the initiative of a Lankan commander known as Manamperuma Mohoṭṭāla.[74] This man, who had originally come from South India to serve Rājasiṃha, had ambitious plans to control the southwestern lowlands. Again, the Portuguese hurried after him rather than leading the way. A crucial reinforcement of 200 men led by Julião de Noronha left Goa on 20 February 1594, five months after the campaign began.[75] When Manamperuma Mohoṭṭāla established himself as Jayavīra, the new king of Sītāvaka, he relied on Portuguese troops as auxiliaries only.

What is it then that made the wars of 1593–4 so important? According to the chronicler Queiroz, it was this specific season of war-making that alerted the Portuguese to the possibilities of conquest in the island—most notably when they say how easily Jayavīra took Sītāvaka and pacified vast stretches of the southwest. According to Queiroz, 'the Portuguese opened their eyes and saw how the best part of Ceylon was conquered and subjected with so little power'. In addition to this, they now felt that 'the right to [claim] those lands was conserved in a king [Dharmapāla] with no hope of succession'.[76] In other words, Ceylon was soon to belong to the Portuguese crown, and the opportunity created by the death of

---

[71] Silva, 'The rise and fall of Sitawaka', p. 40.   [72] Queiroz, *Conquista*, p. 381.
[73] Phillip II to Simão de Brito, [unsigned copy] s. l., 6 September 1592, Arquivo Histórico Ultramarino, Codex 281, fol. 209.
[74] Phillip II to Matias de Albuquerque, Lisbon, 18 February 1595, Arquivo Histórico Ultramarino, Codex 281, fol. 302–302v. Also see Strathern, *Kingship and Conversion*, p. 207.
[75] 'Vida e Acções De Mathias de Albuquerque, cappitao e visRey Do Estado da Inda [...] Tresladado No anno de 1749', Biblioteca Nacional de Portugal, Codex 482, fol. 62v. An almost identical version is in Biblioteca Pública de Évora, CXV/1-13. The first is published, with notes referring to the second, by Antonella Vignati in 'Vida e acções de Mathias de Albuquerque Capitão e Viso-Rei da Índia', *Mare Liberum*, 15 (1998), pp. 139–245 and 17 (1999), pp. 267–360. As noted by Abeyasinghe, the *Vida* follows closely the *Lembrança dos Galeões [...] que mandey com provimentos e socorros às fortalezas de Maluco, Malaca, Manar, Ceilão [...]*, s.l., [c. 1597], BL, *Additional Manuscripts*, 28,432, fols. 124–131. Abeyasinghe, 'Portuguese Documents on the Last Days of the Sitawaka Kingdom 1593–1594', *Journal of the Royal Asiatic Society of Sri Lanka*, New Series, XXIV (1978-9), pp. 86–91.
[76] Queiroz, *Conquista*, p. 387.

Rājasiṃha was hard not to seize. The irony is that Jayavīra still acted according to the old logic of layered overlordship: acknowledging the superiority of Kōṭṭe and subjecting, in his own turn, the lesser warlords around him. The 'ease' with which he 'conquered' was due precisely to the logics of tributary overlordship that now came increasingly under pressure from some Iberian decision-makers advocating for full conquest.

At the end of 1594, a second armada left Goa under the command of a man whose name would be remembered: Pero Lopes de Sousa. For the first time, something genuinely new was happening. Not only did Sousa travel with a sizeable retinue of 600 soldiers. He also carried a new kind of mandate, sailing to the island as the first 'captain general of the conquest of Ceylon'. To be sure, he was in practice still jumping on a moving train rather than launching a campaign of his own. Sousa arrived just in time to take part in a new mission that was being set up by Jayavīra to attack Kandy. This was a re-enactment of the expedition of Dom Filipe Yamasiṃha, now involving the defunct prince's sister, Dona Catarina. She was, after all, the daughter of Karaliyaddē, the king deposed by Rājasiṃha some years earlier.[77] But, nevertheless, Sousa carried a formal title of conquest, and this does suggest that a new kind of conquest project was about to be grafted onto the existing culture of Luso-Lankan warfare.

Sousa and Jayavīra entered Kandy triumphantly in July 1594. But who was to sit on the throne? Sousa took a novel approach: he suggested marrying off Dona Catarina to a nobleman born in Portugal who would become 'King of Kandy, tributary to the [king] of Portugal'. This was a halfway solution between traditional vassalage on the one hand, and the elimination of Lankan ruler figures, on the other. Again, Queiroz saw this as a key moment that prompted many Lankans to cease seeing the Portuguese as allies of the king of Kōṭṭe. From now on, the chronicler argues, they began to perceive them as foreign intruders—not quite conquerors, but self-governing competitors for local thrones.[78] Soon Sousa and Jayavīra clashed. When Sousa murdered Jayavīra, the forces of resistance were unleashed. The 'disaster of Danture', as it came to be known, saw the death of Pero Lopes de Sousa and a majority of his men. Vimaladharmasūriya, the ousted king, reappeared in Kandy, captured princess Catarina, and married her. This gave him all the legitimacy he needed. Militarily and symbolically, 1594 marked a radical strengthening of Kandy as an independent kingdom. This, in turn, soon made it possible to pitch Portuguese military projects against a single, stable polity in the high mountains of Lanka. Suddenly, clear contrasts appear in a picture previously dominated by multiple tones of grey.

In Goa, the viceroy Matias de Albuquerque decided to press ahead. A second, hastily appointed, captain-general, Jerónimo de Azevedo, was sent to Colombo, where he arrived around Christmas 1594. A week later, Azevedo was marching inland with 700 Portuguese soldiers and 2000 *lascarins* to 'pacify' the old lands of Kōṭṭe. Even though Lankan leaders and troops were still essential to this campaign, agency was

---

[77] Queiroz, *Conquista*, pp. 389–90.        [78] Queiroz, *Conquista*, p. 392.

finally in the hands of the invaders. By September 1595, Azevedo was writing to Lisbon about his successes in the 'conquest of Ceylon'. The news was over-optimistic, and setbacks swiftly followed.[79] But the tone was given for the years to come. By 1596, Phillip II was of the opinion that the conquest of Ceylon needed to be 'finished'. But before we come to that fatidic formal decision, which was made in Madrid, we do need to pause one last time to ask what exactly had triggered such radical transformations—and where.

## INFLUENCE OR CONFLUENCE? SPANISH AND PORTUGUESE FORCES IN TRANSITION

It is naturally tempting to see a direct causal relation between the Iberian Union of Crowns and the strategic inflection towards territorial conquest in Ceylon after 1590. Once the *Estado* was nominally a part of the Catholic Monarchy, the argument goes, it was only natural for 'Spanish' strategies from the New World to be taken to Asia.

But once we examine the institutional changes that took place after 1581—that is, *where, how,* and *by whom* decisions may have been made that changed imperial policy—the complexities involved are substantial. First, virtually all the letters sent to Asia with royal orders after 1581 were still written in Lisbon. That royal missives were not usually authored by the monarch himself is evident, not only because Phillip II left the Portuguese capital in 1583, but mainly because a large majority was signed by Miguel de Moura, the chief Portuguese minister left in charge of running state affairs.[80] Many carry notes about the need to have such letters seen by the king, or at least someone close. They often identify the nominal author as 'King' (or at times 'Cardinal', for the Archduke Cardinal Albert, who officially governed Portugal from 1583 to 1593), and the actual signatory as 'Miguel de Moura'. Letters then name the addressee (e.g. 'To the viceroy'), and finally add the formula 'For Your Majesty to see' ('*Rey/ Miguel de Moura/ Pera ho VisoRey. Pera Vossa Magestade ver*'). In other words, decisions were apparently made by Moura on behalf of the monarch. But in practice, Moura was known to have delegated the running of the bulk of Asian affairs to Diogo Velho, the Secretary of State of India, Guinea and Brazil, in November 1584. Velho remained in office until the creation of the Portuguese Council of the Indies (*Conselho da Índia*) in August 1604. Attached to the office run by Velho was the *Secretaria das Mercês*, which dealt with requests for grants and privileges, a key tool of imperial policy.

Some decisions did also go through Madrid (and at times Valladolid), where papers sent from Lisbon led to a blockage of the *Consejo de Portugal*, eventually triggering the reform of this organ in 1602.[81] The most senior Portuguese figure at

---

[79] Queiroz, *Conquista*, p. 407.

[80] On Miguel de Moura, see Francisco Loureiro, 'Miguel de Moura (1538–1599): Secretário de Estado e Governador de Portugal' (PhD dissertation, Lourenço Marques, 1974).

[81] Francisco Paulo Mendes da Luz, *O Conselho da Índia. Contributo ao Estudo da História da Administração e do Comércio do Ultramar Português nos Princípios do Século XVII* (Lisbon: Agência Geral do Ultramar, 1952), pp. 74–8.

the *Consejo* was Cristóvão de Moura, the man who had taken Phillip II through the *Cortes* of Tomar against the opposition of the Braganças. That the Cardinal Archduke Albert, regent of Portugal, was not a central figure for Asian matters is an impression further supported by a rare autobiographical narrative from someone whom we have met already: Simão de Brito de Castro, the captain of Colombo, who before being nominated in Portugal had gone to see the Archduke in Lisbon, but then travelled to Madrid to 'kiss His Majesty's hand'. Only because Phillip was away in Aragon did Castro return to Lisbon. Here, the Cardinal went through his papers, but the decisive documents came later, by official post from Madrid, suggesting that they did go through the hands of Cristóvão de Moura or someone else at the *Consejo de Portugal*, possibly in consultation with the king.[82] Understanding such itineraries in detail is often complicated by the fact that a number of additional people sometimes signed as '*Rey*'.[83] In fact, when one reads the royal missives sent from Lisbon in the late 1580s, the ones signed off in March are often more aggressive than the ones from January—suggesting perhaps that they reflect the mood in Madrid, from where reactions to news from Asia would take longer to materialize. A wider examination of the decision-making processes between the two parts of the Monarchy is still outstanding, and will certainly throw more light on the mechanisms of power building at play.

An important administrative innovation was the creation, in 1591, of a council deciding on financial matters. Phillip II extinguished a series of old Portuguese directorates known as *vedorias* and replaced them by a new council, the *Conselho da Fazenda*. This was a consultative and executive organ with vast, ground-breaking political competences in the Portuguese empire. The council became, in the words of its main historian, 'the sole competent authority immediately beneath the king in any matters pertaining to the royal treasury, be it in the kingdom of Portugal or its colonial possessions'. It made decisions on any matter involving money, that is, practically everything from appointments of officials to decisions over war and peace.[84] Though this view is now partly under revision, there is no doubt that the new council threatened to break the status quo. It could be made to function as a tool for wider political reform.[85] Reformatory processes were under way, it must swiftly be added, in Portugal *and* in Castile. The venerable *Consejo de Indias* lost its competency to manage New World revenues around the same time.

---

[82] Simão de Brito de Castro to the Cardinal Archduke Albert, Colombo, 7 December 1588, Arquivo Nacional Torre do Tombo, *Corpo Cronológico*, 1-112-51.

[83] Pedro Álvares Pereira to Cristóvão de Moura, Valladolid, 14 February 1600, in Luz, *O Conselho da Índia*, p. 78.

[84] Luz, *O Conselho da Índia*, pp. 81–9. The new *Conselho da Fazenda* consisted of four counsellors (two being *letrados* versed in law), and four scribes. Each counsellor would be in charge of one of the following areas: a) Portugal; b) India, Guinea, Brazil, São Tomé, Cape Verde; c) Military Orders, Azores, Madeira; and d) Conquests in Africa, Tribunal of Accounts.

[85] José Manuel Subtil, 'A administração central da Coroa', in *História de Portugal*, edited by José Mattoso, vol. III, pp. 78–90. On the position of the *Conselho de Portugal* see José Antonio Escudero, 'La creación del Consejo de Portugal', offprint from *Boletim da Faculdade de Direito de Coimbra*, special issue (Coimbra: Imprensa da Universidade, 1983).

Another change, so far overlooked by historians, occurred at the level of social practice, rather than institutional reform. At least two of the governors of India appointed during this period of transition, and one captain of Colombo, travelled, before embarking to India, to Madrid. Simão de Brito de Castro, whom we have encountered already as a captain and active letter-writer in Colombo, reminded the monarch of how he had visited Madrid in 1584 to try to see him at the Pardo palace, after having travelled all the way from India to Lisbon to request compensation for 32 years of service in the East.[86] From the memoirs of the viceroy Matias de Albuquerque, we learn of a trip to Castile during the winter of 1589–90, just before Albuquerque's departure to Goa, in what was to become one of the most militarily aggressive triennia of the century.[87] This trip coincided with the avalanche of letters that came from Asia between 1587 and 1589, proposing the conquest of Ceylon. Some years later, Francisco da Gama, a young man who had accepted the job of governing India rather reluctantly, was summoned to Madrid. It was there, as we shall see, that he received the order to conquer the island.[88]

Again, however, it is crucial not to read such changes automatically as signalling a growth of 'Castilian influence' over, or even interference with, 'Portuguese affairs'. There is a distinct—and, as we shall see, highly plausible—possibility of interpreting them as manifestations of reformist impulses, set against a background of factional strife, rather than squabbles between two 'nations'. But could it not be argued that in the upper strata of Spanish society the full conquest of a territory the size of Sri Lanka—much smaller than Peru, and far bigger than Goa—may simply have seemed a more feasible and desirable solution than in Lisbon? The cultural contrast between the Portuguese understanding of *conquista* in Asia as a right to impose tribute—a *ius ad rem*—in opposition with the Spanish practice of conquest in core areas of the New World (and since in 1565 in the Philippines)—establishing a *ius in re*—could not be starker after all. Indeed, this perceived contrast of political cultures was often conjured by subjects of both crowns at the time, from jurists in the Peninsula to *soldados práticos* serving in the East.[89]

But here again, caution is required. The comparative history of territorialization in the two Iberian empires remains largely to be written. True, many Portuguese may have appreciated the deeds of Cortés and Pizarro, but one would have to add to the picture a longstanding admiration, on the Spanish side, for the maritime capabilities of the Portuguese.[90] The importance of maintaining a vigorous navy to project power anywhere was undisputable. Even the exequies of Charles V were

---

[86] Simão de Brito de Castro to Phillip II, Ceylon, 20[?] December 1588, Archivo General de Simancas, *Secretarías Provinciales: Portugal,* Codex 1551, fol. 269.

[87] *Vida e Acções De Mathias de Albuquerque,* fol. 49v/p. 78.

[88] Phillip II to Francisco da Gama [signed Miguel de Moura], Lisbon, 30 January 1597, *Archivo Portuguez-Oriental,* fasc. 3, pp. 665–7.

[89] See below, chapter 8, and Diogo do Couto, *O Primeiro Soldado Prático, introdução, ensaio de leitura, glossário e índice onomástico,* edited by António Coimbra Martins (Lisbon: CNCDP, 2001), pp. 476–86. Cf. Antonio M. Molina, *Historia de Filipinas* (Madrid: Instituto de Cooperación Iberoamericana, 1984), vol. I.

[90] Rafael Valladares, *Castilla y Portugal en Asia (1580–1680). Declive imperial y adaptación* (Leuven: Leuven University Press, 2001).

charged with maritime symbolism. At Brussels, in 1558, an enormous 'ship of state' was built in front of the Cathedral, its deck decorated with the banners of the many territories of Charles' empire on both sides of the ocean.[91] Notably as well, there had been impulses in Portugal to support various territorial projects in America, Africa, and Asia during the 1570s, partly in reaction to the discovery of the silver mines of Potosí in 1545, which leaves us with a very indirect kind of Spanish 'influence'.[92] It is important not to assume, even at the level of what historians once called *mentalités*, that the Union of Crowns brought about a clean territorial 'turn' in the Portuguese imperial imagination. With regard to Sri Lanka, the royal policy of the late 1580s—as opposed to the mid 1590s—was still largely about saving money and establishing crown control rather than conquering lands. There was often, indeed, a strong focus on maritime power, which is best seen in connection with Castilian aspirations to emulate Portuguese naval hegemony.[93] Even the Portuguese system of vassalage and the idea that revenue could be generated through tributary arrangements had its declared adepts in Castile during the reign of Phillip III.[94] In other words, none of the traditional 'explanatory' notions attached to the perceived Castilian-provoked inflection of Portuguese imperial policy is entirely satisfactory. We need to look elsewhere.

## THE LOCAL AND THE REGIONAL: IMAGINING CONQUEST IN GOA, COLOMBO, AND MALACCA

If developments in the Iberian Peninsula explain only part of the change of policy we are attempting to understand, then it is logical that we travel back to Asia for further evidence. The Catholic Monarchy was a multi-centric realm, and Goa in particular serves as a reminder of the complexities involved. Between Lisbon and Madrid on the one hand, and Colombo on the other, the capital of the *Estado* was both centre and periphery. In 1594, Goa played a key role in articulating the Lankan military events led by Jayavīra with decisions to make war in the name of the empire, while orders from Iberia were still missing. The fact that communication was often difficult between Iberia and South Asia and that the 1590s saw further disruptions to the flow of letters adds plausibility to the thesis of Goan sub-imperialism. For example, the news that with the death of Rājasiṃha in early

---

[91] Jonathan Brown and John H. Elliott, *A Palace for a King: The Buen Retiro and the Court of Philip IV* (New Haven, CT: Yale University Press, 1980), p. 152.

[92] Anthony Disney, *A History of Portugal and the Portuguese Empire* (Cambridge: Cambridge University Press, 2009), vol. II, pp. 165–8.

[93] Cf. Fernando Bouza Álvarez, 'Portugal en la política internacional de Felipe II: *por el suelo el mundo en pedazos*', in *A União Ibérica e o Mundo Atlântico*, edited by Maria da Graça Ventura (Lisbon: Colibri, 1997), pp. 29–46 and 'Portugal en la Monarquía Hispánica (1580–1640). Felipe II, las Cortes de Tomar y la Génesis del Portugal Católico' (PhD dissertation, Universidad Complutense de Madrid, 1997), pp. 65–95. As Luís Filipe Thomaz underlines, the naval capabilities of the *Estado* were also a matter of preoccupation in the *Soldado Prático* of Diogo do Couto. 'A crise de 1565–1575 na história do Estado da Índia', *Mare Liberum*, 9 (1995), p. 488.

[94] See for example Pedro Ordóñez de Cevallos, *Viage del Mundo* (Madrid, 1616), quoted in Bouza Álvarez, 'Portugal en la Monarquía Hispánica', p. 69.

1593 an extraordinary opportunity had arisen for a major campaign ('the gates stood open for this conquest', as the viceroy put it) only arrived in Iberia sometime in 1594, and any royal orders reacting to it could never have arrived in Asia before late 1595.[95]

So, what exactly happened in Goa? After the dispatch of Julião de Noronha to Colombo in February 1594, which had stood largely in the tradition of the usual maritime '*socorros*', Pero Lopes de Sousa was nominated 'captain general of the conquest of Ceylon' in March or April. This appointment was pushed through with unusual vigour by a single high-ranking officer of the *Estado*: the viceroy himself. It appears that, alerted about the death of Rājasiṃha, Matias de Albuquerque convoked a first meeting, where a majority of counsellors was still in favour of concentrating on military threats to Chaul, near Mumbai, rather than investing resources in Ceylon. Soon, however, the viceroy single-handedly overruled that decision and put together an armada for Pero Lopes de Sousa. He took full personal responsibility for any consequences, a highly uncommon gesture for a decision of inscrutable magnitude.[96]

Inspired by Sousa, Albuquerque imposed a strategy at the level of the *Estado* for which there were no royal orders. He did this against a majority of sceptics among his own counsellors, hoping—correctly, as it turned out—for a sympathetic reception of the news once they arrived in Lisbon and Madrid.[97] But what prompted him to take the gamble? A socio-cultural factor may have played a role. Matias de Albuquerque was a great-grandson of Lopo de Albuquerque, cousin of Afonso, conqueror of Goa.[98] This connection may seem remote by current standards, but it played an important role in the viceroy's symbolic economy as a military leader. The first part of Matias de Albuquerque's *Vida* ends with a complete transcription of the text engraved on Afonso's tomb.[99] When Pero Lopes de Sousa appeared in Goa, Albuquerque decided to act quite like his ancestor Afonso in the 1510s, interpreting an absence of explicit royal orders as a mandate to create military facts in Asia—and, by doing so, deal a heavy blow to his greatest enemy, the free-trading lobby. If Afonso had created the great chain of possessions that became the backbone of the early *Estado* (Hormuz, Goa, Malacca), Matias was to inaugurate the amplification of the *Estado* under the Habsburg crown.

What was it though about Sousa in particular that prompted the viceroy to see such an opportunity and take such a risk? It seems that Sousa himself created the impression that he was the right man in the right place at the right time. Before his arrival in Goa, Sousa had been captain of Malacca for several years. He had also,

[95] Albuquerque, *Vida*, fol. 62v/p. 94. The earliest Iberian reaction to Rājasiṃha's demise dates from February 1595. Arquivo Histórico Ultramarino, Codex 281, fols. 323v-324 and 328v.
[96] Francisco Rodrigues da Silveira, *Reformação da Milícia e Governo do Estado da Índia Oriental*, edited by Benjamin N. Teensma (Lisbon: Fundação Oriente, 1996), p. 66.
[97] This is what transpires from the royal reaction to the nomination of Pero Lopes de Sousa. Phillip II to Matias de Albuquerque, Lisbon, 26 February 1595, *Archivo Portuguez-Oriental*, fasc. 3, pp. 503–4.
[98] Anselmo Braamcamp Freire, 'Genealogia dos Albuquerques', in *Brasões da Sala de Sintra*, reprint of the second edition (Lisbon: IN-CM, 1996), vol. II, pp. 216–17.
[99] Albuquerque, *Vida*, fol. 68/p. 100.

on his way back to Goa at the end of his term, sometime in early 1594, briefly stopped over at Colombo.[100] This regional itinerary is crucial because it suggests that Sousa was exposed to a whole range of ideas of conquest. The Lankan element in this exposure is now abundantly familiar to us. At Colombo, Sousa spoke with Pedro Homem Pereira, the acting captain, who mentioned the opportunity that had arisen from the death of Rājasiṃha, naturally much talked about in the Lankan southwest in direct reference to the logics of Lankan galactic politics.[101] The talk was, in and around Colombo, about relaunching the suzerainty-driven empire of Kōṭṭe. In this sense, Sousa was yet another receptacle for Lankan ideas.

But why was Sousa so receptive to such talk, to the point of not only promising Pereira to lobby the viceroy for a massive intervention, but also, on his way to Goa, deciding that this was his own opportunity of becoming a proper *conquistador*? Crucially, Sousa had been exposed during his time in Malacca to another, very specific environment of military exaltation where numerous plans of territorial conquest were forged. The bishop of Malacca, Dom João Ribeiro Gaio (1581–1601), was a vigorous advocate of invading Aceh and other parts of Southeast Asia. Malacca was teeming with projects that dwarfed even the boldest ideas formulated by Diogo do Couto in Goa. Such plans thrived there in part due to the connection with the nearby Spanish colony of Manila, where plans of conquest mushroomed in the aftermath of the sweeping military expansion across the Pacific. Between the main Portuguese port of the Malay World and the new Spanish capital of the Philippines, itself the product of a sub-imperialist initiative launched from the west coast of Mexico in 1565, a number of grandiose plans were discussed during the 1580s to conquer Burma, Cambodia, Chiampa, Siam and even China.[102] Some of them were fully territorial in scope, at times expressing a desire for sweeping conquests as they had unfolded on the other side of the ocean. The understanding was that through such initiatives the Catholic Monarchy as a whole might realize its full potential in Asia.

That this was not just a series of Utopian ramblings in two distant outposts of the empire ought to be underlined. The Philippines had been invaded in 1565, and the new colony consolidated over the following years, with relative ease.[103]

---

[100] Queiroz, *Conquista*, p. 385. Note how this reference may help clarify the duration of Sousa's captaincy at Malacca. Cf. Pinto, *Portugueses e Malaios*, p. 229.

[101] As explained above in chapter 2. Cf. Stanley J. Tambiah, 'The Galactic Polity in Southeast Asia', *Culture, Thought, and Social Action. An Anthropological Perspective* (Cambridge, MA: Harvard University Press, 1985).

[102] Charles Ralph Boxer, 'Portuguese and Spanish Projects for the Conquest of Southeast Asia, 1580-1600', *Journal of Asian History*, 3 (1969), pp. 118–36. Among the most important texts written in Malacca are the *Roteiro das cousas do Achém*, by Ribeiro Gaio, from 1584, published as *O Roteiro das Cousas do Achem de D. João Ribeiro Gaio*, edited by Jorge dos Santos Alves and Pierre-Yves Manguin (Lisbon: CNCDP, 1997); a *Relación [...] de las cosas de Patani* and a *Relaçion y derrotero del Reyno de Çian*, also by Ribeiro Gaio (now in the Boxer Collection at the Lilly Library), and the *Historia dos cercos [...] de Malaca* of Jorge de Lemos, printed in Lisbon in 1585. Other projects were written up by Luís Pérez Dasmariñas and friar Diego Aduarte (Boxer Collection) and by Father Alonso Sánchez. See Boxer, *The Christian Century in Japan 1549–1650* (Los Angeles, CA/Cambridge: University of California Press/Cambridge University Press, 1951), pp. 257–9.

[103] Romain Bertrand, *Le long remords the la conquete. Manille-Mexico-Madrid: l'affaire Diego de Ávila (1577–1580)* (Paris: Seuil, 2011).

The proposal for the conquest of Aceh, much talked about in the region especially the 1580s, was eventually approved by Phillip II in 1591 and only called off after a truce was signed locally in 1592.[104] Ideas to invade China and other parts of Asia were discussed officially at a high level, and whilst the lunacy of it all may be manifest to us, it was not to most actors at the time. Through Manila, Macao, and Malacca, it seemed to make sense to reach further into Asia, continuing the Pacific expansion until it would vigorously link up with the Atlantic-Indian Ocean axis of the Portuguese—which was, at the same time, also expected to serve as the backbone to a series of new territorial conquests in Angola, Mozambique, and other parts.[105] Pero Lopes de Sousa had every reason to be euphoric when he heard in Sri Lanka about the possibility of launching an invasion following the death of Rājasiṃha. At that precise moment, the local notion that Kōṭṭe should fill the political void and reinstate its own *cakravarti* project met another, not just globally connected, but globally mushrooming idea of *conquista* as a possibility of extending the Iberian Monarchy. This was, then, a local imperial project finally linked up with the global ambitions of Habsburg subjects with a keen sense of opportunity.

What we have under our lens is an extraordinary conjugation of factors at a very precise moment in time. First, the death of Rājasiṃha and the inexistence of a strong successor allowed the warlord Jayavīra, originally from South India, to seize Sītāvaka on grounds of established Lankan power-building practices—and the Colombo elite, *including* the captain of the Portuguese forces, to dream of a restoration of Kōṭṭe's old, suzerainty-based, empire; second, a captain arrived from Malacca after an intensive exposure to plans of direct conquest generated at the Pacific intersection of the Portuguese and the Spanish empires, ultimately connecting Colombo with Mexico through Malacca and Manila—thus allowing the local plan to resonate with bigger ideas of conquest in Goa and in Madrid; third, a viceroy taking inspiration from his anti-commercialist ancestor Afonso de Aluquerque, the original maker of the *Estado*'s own military backbone running through Hormuz and Goa to Malacca, to mount an expeditionary force opposed by a majority of counsellors, thus breaking the status quo; and finally, a lack of clear royal orders, which allowed for flexible interpretations of the crown's best interest anywhere in a universe where royal letters could take years to reach their destination. At the confluence of these factors, conquest could finally begin to happen.

But given that all this resulted, in 1594, in the greatest military disaster the Portuguese had ever suffered in Sri Lanka, why did things not immediately come to a halt? How is it that the defeat at Danture in October 1594 did not prompt the *Estado* to retract immediately and go back to the old tactics? To answer this question, we need to stay in South Asia for yet another moment, only then to head back to Portugal—and finally to Spain.

[104] Cf. Pinto, *Portugueses e Malaios*, pp. 90–2.
[105] On Angola and Mozambique, see Disney, *History of Portugal and the Portuguese Empire*, vol. II, pp. 70–5 and 165–6.

## REFORMING THE EMPIRE THROUGH
## THE CONQUEST OF CEYLON

After the death of Pero Lopes de Sousa at Danture, a new captain-general was appointed in Goa by Albuquerque. Jerónimo de Azevedo had served as a commander of the Malabar fleet for a decade and a half and soon became associated in the imperial memory with the existence of orders to conquer Ceylon issued 'by the King of Spain'.[106] In reality, his ad hoc nomination still had nothing to do with letters from Madrid or Lisbon, where news of the defeat of Sousa were not received before 1596. Only towards the end of 1595, after almost a year spent in the island, did Azevedo begin to act on grounds of explicit royal orders, though these were still not addressed to him. A set of letters left Lisbon in February 1595 which, based on information generated in Sri Lanka in late 1593 and thus including, for the first time, news of Rājasiṃha's death, signalled a new approach. Their contents converged with (rather than generating) what the viceroy in Goa had de facto begun to implement on the ground in April 1594. Sousa's and Albuquerque's gamble was starting to pay off, albeit benefitting a new captain, Azevedo.[107]

In the first of the 1595 letters, the viceroy was told to 'strive by all possible means to win over that island and, especially, to disrupt the designs of Dom João Modelliar [king Vimaladharmasūriya] who has rebelled in the kingdom of Camdia'.[108] Whoever wrote the orders also believed, almost certainly on grounds of advice received from South Asia, that it was important not to miss the 'opportunity' that Rājasiṃha's death offered 'for the conquest of the entire island of *Ceillam*'. The project, it was added, could now be put into practice 'with less expenses and effort' than at any other time, certainly a key aspect given the discourse of austerity of earlier years.[109] When news arrived in Iberia about the disastrous campaign of Pero Lopes de Sousa, they caused consternation only for a brief moment. In fact, sometime around the end of 1595 a set of letters issued in Goa in February that year arrived by way of the Middle East, neutralizing any negative effect that the news might have had. The new letters reported the successes of Jerónimo de Azevedo and emphasized how there was now hope 'not only to regain what has been lost, but also to gain what is desired'.[110]

---

[106] 'Descendencia dos Imperadores e Reys da ilha de Ceylão', anonymous, undated document, in *Collecção de Tratados e Concertos de Pazes que o Estado da India fez com os Reis e Senhores com que teve relações nas partes da Asia e Africa Oriental*, edited by Júlio Biker (Lisbon: Imprensa Nacional, 1881–7), vol. I, p. 223.

[107] Couto, *Da Asia*, XII, i, 1, pp. 1–2.

[108] Phillip II to Matias de Albuquerque, Lisbon, 18 February 1595, Arquivo Histórico Ultramarino, Codex 281, fol. 298. A copy is at the British Library, *Additional Manuscripts*, 20,861, fols. 148-53v.

[109] Phillip II to Matias de Albuquerque, Lisbon, 18 February 1595, Arquivo Histórico Ultramarino, Codex 281, fols. 298v-299 and 302.

[110] Phillip II to Dom Francisco da Gama, Lisbon, 1 March 1596, *Archivo Portuguez-Oriental*, fasc. 3, pp. 595–6, with copies in Arquivo Histórico Ultramarino, Codex 281, fols. 370v-371 and Biblioteca Nacional de Portugal, Codex 1815, fol. 379-379v. Another letter went in reply to Pedro Homem Pereira, who had written from Colombo on 12 December 1594 after the Danture disaster. Phillip I to Pedro Homem Pereira, Lisbon, 1 March 1596, Arquivo Histórico Ultramarino, Codex

Thus the centre of the empire began, in 1595–6, to issue explicit orders for the conquest of a distant Indian Ocean island where, for almost a century, the Portuguese crown had been happy to hold its imperial umbrella over a rather murky status quo. Once the decision was reached in Iberia, long-held and long-ignored arguments in favour of conquest were brought to the fore. Among these, an important one was the idea that, were the Portuguese possessions in India ever to be lost (a fear boosted by the implosion, not long before, of the South Indian empire of Vijayanagara and the resulting instability in the region), they might be regained from a base in Ceylon. The donation of Dharmapāla was invoked as a source of a legal obligation for the crown to proceed.[111] Although the donation as such would only generate a transfer of power after the death of the Sinhalese monarch—which did not occur until 1597—it was already perceived as a document that left the imperial overlord no other option than to press ahead through conquest.

Crucially as well, orders were issued not only in writing. As we have seen already, future governors like Francisco da Gama could be summoned by the highest officers of the Monarchy to hear orders personally. The young man chosen, during the winter of 1595–6, to replace Matias de Albuquerque as the head of the *Estado*, was a leading figure of precisely the group of interest that centralist forces were now putting under attack. That the conquest of Ceylon should have been imposed upon a descendant of Vasco da Gama holding vast commercial interests in the East is not just ironic, it is key to our understanding of the story. Originally, Fernando de Noronha, Count of Linhares, had been chosen to lead the *Estado*, but he had backed out on grounds of ill health.[112] Phillip II asked the governors of Portugal to make a new appointment, leading to a decision in July 1595. The choice of Gama was made public towards the end of August, and considered inappropriate by many.[113] Over the following months, up to his departure to Goa in April 1596, Francisco da Gama assisted the governors in their meetings, but received little sympathy.[114] Clearly, the ground was being prepared for a major power struggle to unfold, albeit not necessarily following a grand strategic plan. For reform, too, there had to be a moment of opportunity.

Gama was against the conquest of Ceylon for obvious reasons. If the *Estado* was to move in with a full mandate of conquest and set up a model colony in coordination with the centralist forces of the Monarchy, many well-established commercial interests in the region, including his own, would be at risk. It was because everyone knew about this that Gama ended up humiliated in Madrid. He may or may not have faced Phillip II in person, but he did receive the orders of the king through Miguel de Moura—Moura being a man who certainly did what

---

281, fol. 387. The tone of approval extends to a letter written to Julião de Noronha, Lisbon, 28 February 1596, Arquivo Histórico Ultramarino, Codex 281, fol. 387v.

[111] Phillip II to Francisco da Gama, *Archivo Portuguez-Oriental*, fasc. 3, p. 596.

[112] On this issue, see João da Silva, Count of Portalegre, to Phillip II, November 1594, Biblioteca Nacional de España, Manuscritos, Codex 981, fols. 121v-123.

[113] João da Silva to Cristóvão de Moura, August 1595, Biblioteca Nacional de España, Manuscritos, Codex 981, fol. 25v-27v.

[114] Couto, *Da Asia*, XII, i, 1, p. 2.

he could to impose authority on Gama in Lisbon, but ended up adding the weight of a meeting in Madrid to achieve his goal.[115] The meeting was followed up by letters that could not have been clearer in their harshly authoritarian, even threatening tone. These were letters signed in the name of the monarch by Miguel de Moura, and they may well not even have gone through the *Consejo de Portugal*.[116] But they left no doubt about who was in charge.

It was made clear to Gama that, whilst he was widely known not to be in favour of the conquest of Ceylon, his only way of maintaining the crown's trust would be to do everything he could to achieve it. No 'interpretations' of the orders, no delays, nor any other of the means traditionally used by governors to deflect centralist orders would be tolerated. The severity of the letter in which Gama was reminded of his duties in 1596 lays bare the mechanisms of power that finally began to matter, over a decade and a half after the Union was created. Its final sentence stated: 'I order you to go ahead with the said conquest of Ceylon, in case it should not be finished already.'[117] This was Madrid—the complex Madrid of the late 1500s, populated by Portuguese courtiers engaging in a reform of their own imperial sphere—finally making its move to break the status quo in Asia. The orders are so bleakly explicit about the absence of any margin for negotiation that one could be forgiven for feeling that the main attack launched by the crown was not against any rival ruler in Lanka, but its own defiant subjects:

> In this matter, you shall do the possible and the impossible, remembering precisely what I have ordered you to do, as I practically forced you not to express your judgment and opinion on the matter, and I shall only consider your actions to be in my service if you follow my instructions.[118]

What has been seen as a case of Castilian influence or even interference is much more appropriately interpreted as a long-desired change of policy nurtured by many in Portugal and South Asia that, to take effect, was staged in Madrid instead of just crawling through the traditional channels of the Portuguese imperial administration. At stake was the breaking up of an age-old constellation of interests that had allowed a series of well-connected families to draw vast profits from a largely illegal trade, ironically subsidized by the crown through an increasingly onerous military support for fleets and forts. When Francisco da Gama was summoned to Madrid, he was not there primarily as a *Portuguese* noble, but as a member of a network that had resisted royal control in South India and Sri Lanka for too long. A faction that had always had its enemies in Goa, Lisbon and other places, but had worked efficiently enough to maintain its privileges over many decades, was now being challenged.

---

[115] Miguel de Moura is mentioned as the interlocutor of Gama in a later letter: King to Francisco da Gama [signed Miguel de Moura], Lisbon, 10 December 1598, *Archivo Portuguez-Oriental*, fasc. 3, pp. 932–4. Phillip II died at the Escorial on 13 September 1598.

[116] Cf. Phillip II to the Municipal Council of Goa, Aranjuez, 8 March 1596, Arquivo Histórico Ultramarino, Codex 281, fol. 382v.

[117] Phillip II to Gama, Madrid, 1 March 1596, *Archivo Portuguez-Oriental*, fasc. 3, p. 596.

[118] Phillip II to Francisco da Gama [signed Miguel de Moura], Lisbon, 30 January 1597, *Archivo Portuguez-Oriental*, fasc. 3, pp. 665–7.

In sum, what began in the mid 1590s was an attempted centralization and rationalization of Luso-Lankan matters that, given the historical opportunity created by the Union of Crowns, gained momentum via Madrid. As irrational and 'Spanish' as the decision to conquer Ceylon may seem to us, it made perfect sense to Portuguese administrators and counsellors who believed in a fundamental renewal and reconfiguration of the power relations and decision-making channels in their empire.[119] For this, they obviously had the support of the monarch. But it was not Phillip who devised the project or pushed it ahead.

Once in Asia, Gama did of course attempt to evade his responsibilities. In 1597, he tried to halt the military offensive under way by replacing Jerónimo de Azevedo with a more moderate leader—André Furtado de Mendonça—heading only a relatively weak contingent capable of prolonging the war in Ceylon, but not resolving it. The reaction of the crown, however, was unambiguous: Azevedo was to stay in charge. In the same letter, Gama was also told to concede the habit of the Order of Christ to one of the chief military leaders of Kōṭṭe, Dom Fernando Samarakone, underlining how Phillip II wished to be in tune with all loyal subjects, as long as they were fully invested in the conquest.[120] To add to Gama's misery, even the ancient missionary monopoly of the Franciscans in the island was now under attack. Azevedo himself was personally connected with the Jesuits, who soon entered Ceylon along with Dominicans and Augustinians. He was a brother of Inácio de Azevedo, the Jesuit provincial of Brazil. The end of Franciscan hegemony was sealed by the next governor, Aires de Saldanha, a willing follower of crown policy in this regard.[121]

It is important, of course, to clarify what exactly 'centralization' could mean in this particular context. The word itself is rightly deemed problematic by many historians of the Catholic Monarchy. Its usefulness in explaining, for example, territorial expansion in Brazil under the Union of Crowns has been questioned very vigorously after decades of uncritical usage.[122] Anyone familiar with the workings of Spanish imperialism in the New World will be aware of the limited effectiveness of crown policies on the ground. The 'polycentric' empire, as some historians now call it, was an utterly complex affair.[123] But we are here talking about centralization at very different levels. What was de facto at stake in Sri Lanka in 1596–7 was not the creation of a highly efficient, centralized administration,

---

[119] Anthony Disney has spoken of a 'late resurgent expansionism' with roots in the 1570s. *A History of Portugal and the Portuguese Empire*, vol. II, p. 165.

[120] Phillip III to Francisco da Gama [signed Miguel de Moura], Lisbon, 10 December 1598, *Archivo Portuguez-Oriental*, fasc. 3, pp. 932–4.

[121] On Saldanha's support for the Jesuits see Phillip III to viceroy, Madrid, 29 February 1608, *Documentos Remetidos*, vol. I, p. 197. Cf. Queiroz, *Conquista*, p. 468. On the politics of Franciscan writing about Lankan space, see Biedermann, 'The Temporal Politics of Spiritual Conquest: History, Geography and the Logics of Franciscan Orientalism in the Work of Friar Paulo da Trindade', in *Culture and History Digital Journal*, 5, 2 (2016).

[122] Guida Marques, 'L'invention du Brésil entre deux monarchies. L'Amérique portugaise et l'Union ibérique (1580-1640): un état de question', *Anais de História de Além-Mar*, 6 (2005), pp. 109–37.

[123] Cf. Pedro Cardim, Tamar Herzog, José Javier Ruiz Ibáñez and Gaetano Sabatini, *Polycentric Monarchies. How did Early Modern Spain and Portugal Achieve and Maintain a Global Hegemony?* (Eastbourne: Sussex Academic Press, 2012).

capable of reaching from Madrid into the remote Sri Lankan countryside—or at least, not yet. The orders given to Gama were centralistic in the very basic sense of attempting to break, in the name of the Monarchy, a status quo that had maintained a solid centrifugal grip on Portuguese imperial practices for a long time. Nothing more than that, but also nothing less.

Crucially as well, the centralist impulses were still, in the mid 1590s, only one part of the equation. Colombo as a receptacle of Lankan imperialism at the intersection with an *Estado* under reformist pressure still *produced* empire rather than just *reproducing* it. It functioned as a part of a global body politic not just in the sense proposed by Charles Boxer, who saw Iberian institutions replicating across the globe the organizational models of the imperial centre. Nor are we fully in the realm of Thomaz's more abstract network model, which concedes vast centrifugal powers to each node, but still sees the varying fortunes of two courtly factions rooted in Portuguese society as a driving force of the system. Along with these realities, what we see emerge from the Sri Lankan case is a multi-centric, network-like empire, extending far beyond the narrow boundaries of the crown's official possessions into realms with their own imperial traditions. In this empire, a city such as Colombo could function not only as a resonating body for signals emitted by a distant imperial centre in Europe, but more decisively as a place where various imperial traditions could meet and a new imperial reality in its own right emerge.

We are in the presence of the vertiginously global *and* local logics of early modern empire building at the same time, mediated by the regional movement of people and ideas. We have witnessed how the death of a king in a remote Lankan village became connected with the anxieties of a gout-ridden universal monarch sitting in the Escorial, through a series of communicational and political acts (and failures) staged in Colombo, Goa, Malacca, Manila, and Lisbon. The great paradox is that the ultimate imperial connectivity allowing for the intertwinement of the destinies of two such distant figures as Rājasiṃha I and Phillip II—in many ways the culmination of nine decades of history—also signalled the approaching end of it all. The imperial centre could now envisage a direct course of action at last, and ambition to level the old intricacies of Luso-Lankan empire building through the imposition of a fully fledged project of conquest. Inter-imperial diplomacy gave way to intra-imperial power building, connection to conquest. To explore this crucial shift whilst still maintaining a sense of the complexities at work is the proposition of the final chapter of this book.

# 8

# Anatomy of a Divergence
## Habsburg Sovereignty and the End
## of the Lankan Island Empire

Whilst the central question posed by Kenneth Pomeranz in *The Great Divergence*—'why did sustained industrial growth begin in Northwest Europe, despite surprising similarities between advanced areas of Europe and East Asia?'—is clearly key to an understanding of the global twentieth century, historians of the early modern period may prefer to ask questions pertaining to the realm of the political and cultural.[1] Ours has been: why did people from southwestern Europe begin to conquer an Asian country—and dream up other conquests in the continent—after decades of *comparatively* constructive interactions? What could possibly have generated such a breakdown when the process leading up to it was grounded precisely in the perception that political practices and values could be shared? How could conquest begin to happen just as a local Mestizo elite was attaining critical mass? To frame the Sri Lankan-Iberian imperial encounter in connection with a wider horizon of conquests in the early modern world may seem disproportionate, but there are reasons to push the argument in such a direction at this point. Not only because our case *is* broadly connected with imperial processes elsewhere, but also because, even if we were to attempt a reading of the Sri Lankan-Portuguese encounter as an entirely isolated affair, it would resonate with other encounters across the continents.

The complexity of the process with its ample ramifications and numerous twists certainly suggests that we are dealing with more than just a linear transition from one imperial regime, built around 'diplomacy' and 'commerce', to another, characterized by 'conquest'. We have seen imperial ideas structure arrangements that historians in the past perceived as essentially trade-driven, and conquest in the hard-hitting sense emerge from projects of financial and commercial rationalization. We have observed how closely matters maritime and terrestrial could be intertwined. And it has also become evident that describing the actors in our play as strictly 'indigenous' or 'exogenous' makes limited sense. In this final chapter, I suggest taking a hard look at some of the analytical binaries that still haunt early modern

---

[1] Kenneth Pomeranz, *The Great Divergence. China, Europe, and the Making of the Modern World Economy* (Princeton, NJ: Princeton University Press, 2000). Note the retraction offered by Pomeranz himself, whose original title would have been *A Great Divergence*. 'Writing about divergences in global history: some implications for scale, methods, aims, and categories', in *Writing the History of the Global. Challenges for the 21st century*, edited by Maxine Berg (Oxford: Oxford University Press, 2013), p. 117.

global history. But rather than simply doing away with them, I shall attempt to identify the places where they might still be relevant.

Two aspects in our story point to something that the Latin Americanist Walter Mignolo has, irritatingly but not without his own strong reasons, called the 'Darker Side of the Renaissance'.[2] The first is that, even during the heyday of Portuguese-Sri Lankan diplomacy, the power of letters written on paper and palm leaves circulating between Kōṭṭe and Lisbon was not evenly spread. The semantic bridges connecting the two parties were always under some strain, and the disadvantages accrued on the Lankan side in the long term. Bhuvanekabāhu VII may have felt optimistic about interacting with John III, but he struggled to obtain what he most needed in order to survive as a Lankan monarch in Sri Lanka—and thus also felt increasingly misunderstood.

The second aspect, which we have seen emerge as the inter-imperial dialogue began to break down at the end of the sixteenth century, is connected to the first, but of a qualitatively different nature. It was not just a matter of increasing tension but, as I shall argue, of impending, radical incompatibility and collapse. As the Lankan side held on to a person-centred notion of power—in one of his last letters to Phillip II, Dharmapāla still insisted on describing himself as the sole conduit of Iberian imperial power into Sri Lanka, and still requested soldiers to be placed under his direct authority[3]—the Iberian side went over to thinking about its power in relation to territory directly. For the new imperial administration, power in Sri Lanka was to find its principal expression through the unchallenged command by Phillip II over land, not people; or rather, to put it more accurately, over people *on grounds of* an undivided dominion of the land, rather than labouring for the control of a fragmented political space through the vassalage of local leaders. This is a major point of difference, and yet we are still well advised not to rush to conclusions about a historical contrast that, if isolated all too neatly, may take us dangerously close again to crude ideas about 'pre-modern' and 'modern' types of imperial authority and power, or about 'European' versus 'Asian' political cultures. Rather than delving straight into the incompatibilities that made a smooth integration of Sri Lanka into the Catholic Monarchy impossible, I suggest that we stay for one more moment with the commonalities that, to some actors at the time, still seemed to make it possible. This shall allow us to sharpen our understanding of the contrasts at stake, and to clarify where they will be most significant on the new map of early modern (dis)connections.

## COMPATIBILITIES AND INCOMPATIBILITIES

The empire into which Sri Lanka was to be incorporated on grounds of the 1580 donation was a composite monarchy: a vast, geographically discontinuous and

---

[2] Walter D. Mignolo, *The Darker Side of the Renaissance. Literacy, Territoriality & Colonization*, 2nd edition with a new afterword by the author (Ann Arbor, MI: University of Michigan Press, 2003).

[3] Dharmapala to Phillip II, Colombo, 10 December 1594, *Archivo Portuguez-Oriental*, fasc. 3, p. 736.

administratively heterogenous body of juridically distinct territories.[4] The union of these territories was formally conceived of as being among equals—*aeque princi- paliter*—entailing a sustained treatment of each unit as a distinct entity with its own political lore. In other words, the monarchy of Charles V and Phillip II favoured the incorporation of polities without necessarily imposing radical changes to their internal political structures.[5] Even between Kōṭṭe and the Spanish empire, the scope for accommodation was thus wider than one might expect. This was not just a matter of political geography, but of commensurable aspects in the way people conceived of royal authority in the various parts of the Monarchy. Contractual readings of kingship were comparably strong in early modern Spain and South Asia, and they did resonate powerfully across the complex political and spatial order of the Habsburg realm. This complexity had, in part, to do with the fact that the Iberian system in the sixteenth century was in its very core built on a combin- ation of two different political traditions. Charles V was as much *imperator* or *unus princeps* in the sense proposed by Roman Law, as *rex regum* or *princeps principum* in the Ecclesiastic corporatist school of thought—the latter of which had, import- antly, experienced its own developments in medieval Iberia, and allowed strong centrifugal forces to thrive.[6] There was scope for the cultivation of more *or* less intrusive forms of imperial power.

Over the course of the Medieval period, the crown of Castile had come to include a multitude of distinct territories, ranging from Asturias to Granada, which only adapted to each other slowly, if at all. The union of 1479 between Isabel of Castile and Ferdinand of Aragon stood precisely in that tradition of glueing together separate realms without changing their internal structures. Aragon itself had aggregated Valencia, Majorca, Catalonia, and Naples during the late medieval period, but each of these territories was run separately throughout the 1500s. In fact, viceroyalty as an institution, taken to the New World by Castile and to Asia by Portugal, was originally tested by Aragon in Italy. There remained much space for local autonomy and local political institutions and lore in such a complex imperial body, to which the monarchs bowed due to the physical distance and numerous legal arrangements. Hence the powers of local parliaments (*cortes*) such as those of Navarre and Portugal, whilst both territories had their own political councils (*consejos*) in Madrid.[7] Even at the height of their power, Charles V and Phillip II had to negotiate constantly with such bodies.

This should in principle have been good news for the kingdom of Kōṭṭe and its elite as it merged into the Monarchy. But of course there was one major unfavourable

---

[4] See above all John H. Elliott, 'A Europe of Composite Monarchies', *Past & Present*, 137 (1992), pp. 48–71.

[5] Manuel Fernández Álvarez and Ana Díaz Medina, *Los Austrias Mayores y la culminación del Imperio (1516–1598)*, vol. VIII of *Historia de España*, edited by Ángel Montenegro Duque (Madrid: Gredos, 1987), p. 180.

[6] Franz Bosbach, *Monarchia Universalis. Ein politischer Leitbegriff der frühen Neuzeit* (Göttingen: Vandenhoek & Ruprecht, 1988), pp. 38–9.

[7] On the polysinodal or multi-council system, see Francisco Tomás y Valiente, 'El sistema polisino- dial: el todo y las partes', in *Historia de España Menéndez Pidal*, edited by José María Jover Zamora, vol. 25, *La España de Felipe IV*, 3rd edition (Madrid: Espasa Calpe, 1982), pp. 124–50.

condition that had to be imported, too, once Dharmapāla would die and his donation take effect: each of the kingdoms forming the larger imperial body had to recognize the same monarch as its king. Phillip II was a sovereign simultaneously in each of his *reinos*, and Iberian political theory had it that the logically ensuing absence of the monarch from most of his realms was a lesser issue than its reverse. 'Whilst there cannot be a King without a Kingdom', it was said, 'there can well be a Kingdom without a King.'[8] A king could be absent from his realm and still rule alone over it. When news arrived in Madrid, in 1598, that Dom João Dharmapāla had passed away the previous year, the first and foremost reaction of the king—by then Phillip III—was to affirm that the viceroy in India should treat the realm as 'mine *in solidum* [...] as are all the others of my Crown'.[9] This was the juridical ground rock upon which the incorporation would be performed.[10] Whether the latter would then be fully achieved and materialized through military conquest was, in terms of political discourse, almost a secondary aspect. Portugal, for example, had been added to the Monarchy by combining strategies of inheritance, purchase, and conquest.[11] The legitimacy of it all was grounded in the first of the three aspects: the absence of a local ruler.

This was a considerable issue for the Kōṭṭe elite: for a kingdom to become part of the Monarchy, its throne needed to be genuinely vacant and at the disposal of Phillip II. Only then could a new contract be made between the local community and its 'chosen' monarch. After the death of Dom João Dharmapāla, a ceremony of disinheritance had to be staged not only to ensure the loyalty of the new political subjects, but also to deny legitimacy to any other throne candidates. On the new map of empire, there was no space left for vassal kings. The transition implied a drastic departure from the indirect, suzerainty-driven imperialism of the Portuguese dynasty of Avis and its complex dialogues with segmentary and galactic polities. The Portuguese monarchs had been lords in Asia without 'possessing' kingdoms, to take a word used by the chronicler Queiroz.[12] Phillip II, in contrast, was not a king of kings, but assumedly and exclusively a king of kingdoms. In his absence, local matters needed to be dealt with by an official of the empire, for example a captain-general—and not a member of the Lankan royal family.[13] This was something neither John III nor the Lankan elite had ever envisaged as a solution. When some Portuguese soldiers spontaneously suggested placing a Portuguese noble on the throne of Kandy in 1594, they met with vehement opposition from their Lankan allies. The creation of the office of captain-general with its vast array of powers in

---

[8] Fernando Bouza Álvarez, *Portugal no Tempo dos Filipes. Política, Cultura, Representações (1580–1668)* (Lisbon: Cosmos, 2000), p. 24 and 114.

[9] Phillip III to Gama [signed Miguel de Moura], Lisbon, 21 November 1598, Historical Archives of Goa, *Monções*, Codex 2, fols. 419–420, also in *Archivo Portuguez-Oriental*, fasc. 3, p. 918.

[10] Cf. Saldanha, *Iustum Imperium*, p. 515.

[11] See Rafael Valladares, *La conquista de Lisboa. Violencia militar y comunidad política en Portugal, 1578–1583* (Madrid: Marcial Pons, 2008).

[12] Fernão de Queiroz, *Conquista Temporal e Espiritual de Ceilão* (Colombo: Government Press, 1916), p. 431.

[13] See Saldanha, *Iustum Imperium*, pp. 333–41.

the same year, three years before Dom João Dharmapāla passed away, was received with great outrage, and had to be dropped.[14]

Was this then the decisive point completing the rupture between Habsburg-Portuguese rule and Lankan politics? Perhaps it was, in the sense that the 'absent king' doctrine proved profoundly incompatible with a political culture in which kingdoms stood and fell with the kings sitting at their centre. In Sri Lanka, a kingdom could hardly survive without a king. In fact, kingdoms as such existed in practice as a function of the authority of kings. All this being said, however, as we look deeper into the realities of the transition to Iberian rule, the answer is still less straightforward than expected. The handover after Dharmapāla's death in May 1597 was, by any standards, remarkably smooth. A gathering of the principal nobles who had remained attached to Dharmapāla was organized in Colombo, the main participants being nominated by a larger assembly and then taken to swear an oath accepting Phillip II as the 'universal heir' (*universal herdeiro*) of the Sinhalese monarch. They agreed to 'keep faith and loyalty, obey and be vassals to him and to his successors [. . .] or to his viceroys, governors or captains'. Then people went into the streets publicly to acclaim the new, absent king.[15] In fact, it may well be that this went down so easily because the local elite felt the system could be bent in their own favour at thousands of miles from Lisbon and Madrid. Soon a second ceremony of succession was staged in the royal palace at Malwāna, a few hours' march away from Colombo. According to Queiroz, '*cortes*', a parliament-style gathering like those of Iberia, namely the ones held in Tomar in 1580–1 to acclaim Phillip as king of Portugal, were held. Before the Lankan aristocrats voted to accept the new status quo, they were promised 'in the name of His Majesty' that the 'Naturals of Ceylon' could keep their own laws.[16]

Although the gathering is only documented indirectly, there are compelling reasons to believe that it took place and played a key role in the transition to Iberian rule.[17] The Colombo acclamation alone would simply have left too many fundamental issues unresolved. The donation of 1580 made no mention of the Sinhalese ruler's non-Christian subjects, non-Christian courts and administrative offices, or the way revenues would be collected after the Sinhalese ruler's death. The main negotiations must have taken place within an assembly comparable to the *cortes* which, in Portugal, had so very recently paved the way for the Habsburg takeover. We do know that the years after the Lankan *translatio* were marked by a considerable increase in the local nobility's rights and privileges, much like had been the

---

[14] Queiroz, *Conquista*, pp. 388–92. Dharmapala to Phillip II, 10 December 1594, *Archivo Portuguez-Oriental*, fasc. 3, 736.

[15] Diogo do Couto, *Da Asia* (Lisbon: Livraria de São Carlos, 1973–5), vol. XII, i, 6, pp. 45–6. Queiroz, *Conquista*, p. 430.

[16] Queiroz, *Conquista*, p. 834. Cf. João Ribeiro, *Fatalidade Histórica*, pp. 20–3.

[17] Cf. Tikiri Abeyasinghe, 'The Myth of the Malvana Convention', *Ceylon Journal of Historical and Social Studies* 7, 1 (1964), pp. 67–72, against which I argue in 'The "Malwana Convention" and the Lankan Transition to Colonial Rule', in *The Portuguese in Sri Lanka and South India. Studies in the History of Diplomacy, Empire and Trade* (Wiesbaden: Harrassowitz, 2014), pp. 87–102.

case in Portugal in 1581 after the negotiations leading to Phillip's acclamation.[18] To make the transition acceptable, the contract between the monarch and his new political subjects had to include substantial concessions. And perhaps the main concession of the empire had to do with the throne that, after all, was not left *as* vacant as Lisbon and Madrid may have imagined.

Jerónimo de Azevedo, the charismatic captain-general of the conquest of Ceylon from 1597 to 1612, kept a second official residence at Malwāna, less than twenty kilometres from Colombo. There, a palace was maintained to serve as a political hub for the Lankan polity. A symbolically crucial aspect of Dharmapāla's late Mestizo Colombo—its role as a political and ritual centre of Lankan empire-building—was thus detached from the city again and taken inland. Azevedo found a place to hold the traditional annual *däkum mangalle* ceremonies, during which the local nobility renewed their allegiance to their king as they had done at Kōṭṭe before.[19] The *däkum* was, as we have seen at the beginning of this study, a key component of the Lankan system connecting each *rāja* with his subjects in the villages through the inter-mediary level of local leaders. To put it bluntly, Azevedo was made to serve like a king in the Lankan tradition: a warrant, on grounds of his power to attract and maintain loyalties, of the order of the realm. Although fundamental elements of Buddhist kingship were abandoned—in fact, the Sinhalese king's patronage of the *Sangha* had been dropped four decades earlier when Dharmapāla converted—the performance of Azevedo during these *däkum* gatherings retained forms that made it possible for the Kōṭṭe elite to accept and digest the new arrangement. However debased of religious legitimacy all this may have seemed from a Buddhist point of view, Azevedo's *däkum* ceremonies succeeded in maintaining the political ties between the crown and its subjects, and those were the fundamental ties upon which the unity of the polity still rested, whichever the supernatural apparatus invoked.[20] If men from South India could become kings in Sri Lanka, then a com-mander like Azevedo, too, stood a chance of being made to work as a royal figure. This was not—or at least not entirely—an instance of, as Geertz put it, 'systematic misunderstanding' reducing 'traditional form to social farce'.[21] What may seem like a farce, an arrangement apparently too strange to carry authentic political clout, did in fact work for some time.

Why, then, is it that things soured so intensely in the early 1600s, plunging Sri Lanka into six decades of devastating warfare? Whilst the period between 1550 and 1590 had been conflict laden already, and Lankan history in the longer run does not strike one as particularly peaceful either, warfare in seventeenth-century Sri Lanka took on a novel intensity. Year after year, thousands of men, women and

---

[18] Cf. Abeyasinghe, *Portuguese Rule*, pp. 82–3 and 110–11, and Serrão, *História de Portugal*, vol. III, pp. 16–19 and 21–3.

[19] Cf. Abeyasinghe, *Portuguese Rule*, pp. 76–7 and 91.

[20] Cf. K. W. Goonewardena, 'Kingship in XVIIth Century Sri Lanka: Some Concepts, ceremonies and other practices', *Sri Lanka Journal of the Humanities*, 3 (1977), pp. 10 and 23. Strathern, *Kingship and Conversion*, pp. 210–11 and 247–9, disagrees with me on the capability of the Portuguese to slip into such a position as local kings.

[21] Clifford Geertz, *The Interpretation of Cultures: selected essays* (New York: Basic Books, 1973), p. 9.

children lost their lives to the senseless brutality of conquest warfare. To be sure, much of the story of the seventeenth-century wars in Sri Lanka calls to be revisited, too, and may well reveal a much more complex picture than that painted by historians in the past.[22] Probably some of the logics at play in the seventeenth century were in practice not entirely different from those of the previous period. After initial attempts at conquering and beheading the Kandyan polity, one might be forgiven for feeling that the campaigns of the 1610s to 1640s slid back into a mode where, on the ground (as opposed to the letters ordering such campaigns) the periodical measurement of forces prevailed over definitive military solutions. Comparisons with some of the more protracted conquests of the Spanish in America may be of use here, for example with the already mentioned case of Yucatán, or others such as New Galicia in the North of Mexico or the protracted campaigns in southern Chile.[23] Conquest was, after the initial shockwave, a slow affair in many parts of the world, and systematic comparisons along that front are something the present volume cannot deliver. A definitive comparative answer to what went wrong (or indeed, from a Kandyan perspective, what went right) after 1600 will be down to future research.

But the story as we have seen it unfold during the sixteenth century does suggest that two closely intertwined aspects may have characterized the rupture at the level of high political power and discourse around 1600. First, there was the way in which Habsburg-Portuguese sovereignty was imposed in the southwestern territories pertaining directly to Kōṭṭe—that is, roughly the lands originally considered to be those of the 'kingdom' partitioned in 1521. It has been noted, quite crucially, that the multiplicity of political and institutional practices in the European kingdoms of the Spanish Habsburgs—that is, their toleration of local political institutions—was never quite matched by an equal acceptance of diversity outside of Europe. There, conquest was more commonly accompanied by the 'notional implantation and reproduction of imported institutions',[24] and of course the massive enterprise of converting populations to a new religion. In other words, the extra-European possessions of the composite monarchy were generally subjected to deeper institutional and cultural changes than, say, Iberian kingdoms such as Navarre or even Majorca. Despite what seems to have been an initial promise to maintain much of the internal political and social status quo, the early seventeenth century also brought an increasing Iberianization of Sri Lanka's southwest, as the Portuguese

---

[22] For example, the radicalization of the colonial wars resulted in increased diplomatic activities to harness the power of third parties—England in the case of Portugal, the VOC and other South Indian powers in the case of Kandy. In this sense, Sri Lanka with its long tradition of vassalage and alliance-building across the sea proved, in the long run, more resilient than the imperial formations of Central and South America which, when faced with a penetration of the logics of conquest into deeper levels of culture and society found no comparable means to react. In other words, the tradition that had made Sri Lanka so open to Portuguese intervention during the sixteenth century may *also* have helped Kandy resist conquest in the seventeenth and eighteenth centuries.

[23] See especially Ida Altman, *The War for Mexico's West. Indians and Spaniards in New Galicia, 1524–1550* (Albuquerque, NM: University of New Mexico Press, 2010).

[24] Sanjay Subrahmanyam, 'A Tale of Three Empires. Mughals, Ottomans, and Habsburgs in a Comparative Context', *Common Knowledge*, 12, 1 (2006), pp. 75–6.

proceeded to take possession of the lands, draft the first revenue register (finished in 1599), transform the institutions of Kōṭṭe, and extend the activities of missionary orders.

After 1597, the treatment of the members of the Sinhalese royal family changed radically for the worse. Princes and princesses of royal blood were now perceived as a threat, not an asset, and the authorities did whatever they could to neutralize them. Some were assassinated, others were sent into exile to Goa, and still others ended up in Portugal and Spain, where they legally renounced their claims in exchange for royal grants.[25] In the island, offices and positions formerly held by Lankans were Lusitanized: whereas in 1597 only one higher office in the kingdom of Kōṭṭe—tellingly, a military position—had been held by a Portuguese man (married to a Sinhalese woman of royal lineage), by 1615, shortly after Phillip III (r.1598–1621) ordered a systematic cleansing of this sphere of power in 1608, a single Sinhala *mudaliyār* was left in charge in the entire kingdom.[26] An analogous process would begin in Portugal in the 1620s as the Count-Duke of Olivares attempted to undermine the legal integrity of Portugal as a separate realm (his perception was that the elites of the various kingdoms composing the Monarchy needed to be woven together more closely to foster unity), but in Sri Lanka the effects of the policy were incomparably more dramatic. Pressure increased on non-Catholics to convert. Missionary activities intensified as Jesuits, Augustinians, and Dominicans moved in to compete with the Franciscans for Lankan souls and sliced up the Lankan southwest to create their own territories of spiritual conquest. Although much remains to be said about the missions, they certainly generated an increase in religiously motivated hostility—or at least they led to religious interpretations of ongoing conflicts, making them even worse than they already were.[27]

The ambition became increasingly to take possession of lands and create the material infrastructure of a settler colony—not necessarily always in the sense that thousands of new colonists would arrive every year as they did in the Americas (Portugal remained hopelessly overstretched demographically to populate a global empire), but in the sense that local *casado* families with a Portuguese connection, and increasingly also newcomers from other parts of the empire, could settle in Colombo and reach out from there to gain control over village lands previously owned by Lankans.[28] New maps were drawn, villages and lands listed to be taxed

---

[25] For example, the donation of Kandy by Dom Filipe (Yamasiṃha Baṇḍāra) to the Portuguese crown, made in Mannār in 1590, was said to have no legal effect before Filipe's son Dom João personally renounced his heritage on a trip to Madrid in 1609. Queiroz, *Conquista*, 576–8. Cf. Biedermann, 'Cosmopolitan Converts. The Politics of Lankan Exile in the Portuguese Empire', in *Sri Lanka at the Crossroads of History*, edited by Zoltán Biedermann and Alan Strathern (London: UCL Press, 2017), pp. 141–60.

[26] Abeyasinghe, *Portuguese Rule*, p. 78.

[27] On the missionary history of this period, which deserves further exploration, see the chapters in Abeyasinghe, *Portuguese Rule*, pp. 192–223 and De Silva, *The Portuguese*, pp. 236–46.

[28] For a more radical plan to bring in women from Portugal so that 'our nation would not discredit itself by degenerating here, by mixing with [...] the vilest and lowest people', and thus create an Island colony capable of replacing Goa as the centre of the *Estado*, see Francisco Rodrigues da Silveira, *Reformação da Milícia e Governo do Estado da Índia Oriental*, edited by Benjamin N. Teensma (Lisbon: Fundação Oriente, 1996), pp. 219–22.

and, when possible, transferred to new owners. Fiscality and geographical knowledge making went hand in hand. The ghost of the *Relaciones Geográficas*, the system of geographical inventorization applied in New Spain from the 1570s onwards, began to haunt the paddy fields and cinnamon woods of Sri Lanka.[29] These were, in essence, the first steps towards a complex process of territorial appropriation and colonization. Although never completed, they gradually undermined the powers of the elite that had initially made the transition possible.

All this happened at the level of the kingdom of Kōṭṭe in the first place, but it unfolded its most tragically disruptive potential when it came to the imposition of power *beyond* the limits of the old kingdom—that is, across the island as a whole. When Phillip II agreed to become the successor of Dharmapāla, he misunderstood (or chose to misunderstand, or a little of both) a single, but overwhelmingly important aspect of his duty as king of Kōṭṭe. What he was expected to do across the island was not to impose his sovereignty in other kingdoms, but his suzerainty over other kings. His mission beyond the heartlands of the kingdom of Kōṭṭe— and an obligation it was, according to the donation of 1580—was not to recon- quer the entire island in the narrow sense of the word, to impose direct control. The 'conquest' he was *expected* to put into practice was the one that Kōṭṭe and the Portuguese had ambitioned for a long time before, following the old traditions of Lankan imperialism. Phillip's duty was not to expand the military, administrative, fiscal, and juridical reach of Kōṭṭe into increasingly distant areas, but to see to it that the rulers of those distant places accepted to pay him tribute.[30] Apparently, Dom João Dharmapāla even alerted the Portuguese, shortly before he died, that Kandy and Jaffna were *not* to be subjected to the new monarch's rule directly, quite possibly a sign that he sensed he had not made himself clear enough about this point—but to no avail.[31] The political *translatio* originated a radical mis-transla- tion of the Lankan imperial project by the Habsburg administration.

One might wonder how two Iberian courts teeming with experienced generals, lawyers, literati and other scholars, several paper-crunching royal councils, and one of the greatest monarchs on earth could possibly have made such a mistake. And yet, they did. One might also wonder how Dom João Dharmapala thought that Phillip might adopt a political praxis so manifestly distinct from everything he did. Dharmapala's mistake was probably still rooted in an overestimation of the power of local political tradition. Phillip's, on the other hand, must be seen as resulting from an overestimation of the global applicability of his own political praxis. Partly, perhaps, this was due to the conjunctural illusion that a much-awaited opportun- ity for an extensive military takeover had come with the death of Rājasiṃha I,

---

[29] See Abeyasinghe, *Portuguese Rule*. On the *relaciones* and their associated mapping practices, see José Miguel Morales Folguera, *La construcción de la utopía. El proyecto de Felipe II (1556–1598) para Hispanoamérica* (Madrid/Málaga: Editorial Biblioteca Nueva/Universidad de Málaga, 2001), and Barbara Mundy, *The Mapping of New Spain. Indigenous Cartography and the Maps of the Relaciones Geográficas* (Chicago, IL/London: University of Chicago Press, 1996).

[30] Cf. Sheldon Pollock, *The Language of the Gods in the World of Men: Sanskrit, Culture, and Power in Premodern India* (Berkeley/Los Angeles: University of California Press, 2009), pp. 274–7.

[31] Ribeiro, *Fatalidade Histórica*, p. 20.

King of Sītāvaka, in 1593. The fact that Rājasiṃha, for some time the most powerful ruler in the island, left no successor certainly played a role in creating a notion that there was a power vacuum, and that the rules of the game might be changed. Partly as well, it may have been down to an ambition of reforming the empire as we have seen in the previous chapter: consciously to disrupt an older political tradition for the sake of breaking the status quo. Fundamentally, though, the misunderstanding was down to an underestimation of political and cultural difference between Iberia and Lanka, particularly in connection with the way royal power was conceived of. Nobody in Madrid seems to have felt the need genuinely to reflect about why the Portuguese crown's relation with Kōṭṭe had been what it was for almost a century, and how exactly it had worked. In the Catholic Monarchy, there may have been much space for difference in legal and political lore, but not for a questioning of the fundamental logic of having a single monarch rule and tax all his territories directly, extensively, and intensively. Whilst it is naturally important not to picture Habsburg Spain as a precociously modern state in 1600—in fact, relations between central and local authorities remained very complex throughout the seventeenth century—it certainly does bear relevance that the Spanish Habsburgs managed to control large parts of the judicial system across Castile during this period and thus developed a sense of how to reach into distant corners of the realm.[32]

As the Spanish empire incorporated the Portuguese, the contrasts between the American and the Asian empires created during the 1500s produced a pressure that, perhaps inevitably, elicited a semantic tension and then a shift around the word *conquista*. As an Augustinian friar based in the Philippines put it, it became increasingly frivolous to 'speak of a [Portuguese] Conquest of India [...] as if therein anything were conquered'.[33] Language, one is compelled to argue here at a somewhat different level than before—for this is a matter not just of vocabulary and grammar, but of semantic hegemony—was a matter of prime importance in the consolidation of empire. A little later, another sceptic of the Portuguese system, Anthony Shirley, would write with noticeable exasperation: 'Portugal is opposed to the rule of Castile [...] and in the same way as it is different in language, it differs as much as it can in fashion, and all customs: it is an ancient foe and an unreliable vassal, never firmly to be trusted.'[34] In fact, Shirley would come to believe that it was precisely in Ceylon, the largest territorial conquest of the Spanish Habsburgs in the *Estado*, that the Monarchy should impose itself and gain a lasting foothold from which to launch the wider conquest of Asia. There, Spain could prove that *conquista* meant conquest in the Spanish, not the Portuguese sense of the word.

Like many others, Shirley did not hesitate to map the contrast onto a perceived terrain of rival 'national' cultures. It was then, as it has remained ever since for many historians, the easiest way to go. Ceylon—and it is remarkable how Shirley

[32] See Victor Pérez-Díaz, 'State and public sphere in Spain during the Ancien Régime', *Daedalus*, 127, 3 (1998), pp. 251–79.

[33] Fray Rodrigo de Aganduru Móriz, 'Historia general de las Islas Occidentales a la Asia adyacentes', quoted in Valladares, *Castilla y Portugal en Asia (1580–1680). Declive imperial y adaptación* (Leuven: Leuven University Press, 2001), pp. 6–7.

[34] Anthony Shirley, *Peso Político de todo el Mundo del Conde D. Antonio Xerley*, edited by Carmelo Viñas Mey (Madrid: Instituto Balmes de Sociología, 1961), p. 3.

here echoes unconsciously the old topos of Lanka as a blessed land, while attempting to connect the island with the myth of Eldorado—'is very large, and has an
excellent air and climate, and is most fertile [...] it is a forest of cinnamon, has
great mines of gold and, so it is thought, also of silver'. It 'reverberates [...] above
all the nations of Africa facing the Indic Sea, as well as those of Asia and Arabia
Felix all the way to China, in brief, it is the only place that may [reasonably] be
chosen and desired to be had in the middle of it', that is, of the Orient—instead of
Goa, of course, where Diogo do Couto had spun quite precisely the same thoughts
half a century earlier, inspired by the deeds of Castilians in the New World. And
Shirley could not go full circle without concluding that 'infallibly, five thousand
Spaniards would finish this conquest'.[35] Needless to say, behind the binary opposing Portuguese to Spanish capabilities there was a much larger opposition luring,
which had to do with the global imperial prospects of Europe as opposed to those
of the other continents.

Advising Phillip IV on how to proceed in this regard, Shirley insisted that, 'had
the conquest of this island fallen into the remit of the Spanish nation, which does
not restrict is ambitions to profit, but to domination [*señorio*]', then the empire
would have a proper, substantial and coherent body ('*un cuerpo substanzial y entero*')
in those parts. It is hard not to see how it is precisely our own point of departure
in this study—the notion that polities can be fairly unsubstantial and still function
as empires—that came under fierce attack in the 1600s. This was one kind of
empire, one kind of *imperial idea*, supplanting the other. It was the Ancien Régime
readying itself to crush the remainders of the Renaissance with its global reverber-
ations and experimentations. 'Following the reason of state' Shirley added, 'it cannot
be sufficient in any manner to have only an ambition of power, without it being
accompanied and sustained by true power and force'.[36] Projecting authority across
the globe through symbolic acts of overlordship was one thing; imposing power
effectively and permanently was another, and this was now to be the true manifest-
ation of the imperial idea. The quest for extended sovereignty was on in the tropics.

That this may have been construed as a matter of Luso-Castilian antagonism
and contrasting national cultures at the time should not make us forget that, at the
heart of the conflict, there were transnationally significant ideas about how royal
power ought to function in an imperial system. Are we here in the realm of an
emerging political modernity? Perhaps, but we are also today in a position to handle
the notion of the early modern without clinging to its Eurocentric heritage. As the
Goan chronicler Diogo do Couto criticized the Portuguese kings in particular for
not aspiring to true military and administrative dominion, Spain was not his only
point of comparison. He also invoked vividly the example of the Ottoman sultans,
who he believed made an effort to match their rhetorical aspirations to universal
lordship (as '*Senhores do Mundo*') with deeds of conquest aimed at effectively placing
lands 'under their power', to the utter humiliation of the Portuguese.[37] The crux of
the matter was not for a 'western' model to be imposed in the 'East', but for the

---

[35] Shirley, *Peso Politico*, p. 77.    [36] Shirley, *Peso Politico*, pp. 76–7.
[37] Luís Filipe Thomaz, 'A crise de 1565–1575 na história do Estado da Índia', *Mare Liberum*, 9
(1995), p. 488, n. 73.

crown—any crown—to take control: to move beyond the realm of diplomatically sanctioned hegemony into proper, full conquest.

## FROM SISYPHUS TO LEVIATHAN: RE-MAPPING THE CONQUEST AROUND 1600

A glance at two maps produced during the period scrutinized in this book helps to illustrate the transition and make some final points about the territorialization of the word 'conquest'—and now, finally, we can also think about embracing the term 'territorialization' in its most specific sense, pointing to the making of the Ancien Régime state as a spatial form participating in the homogeneity of early modern cartographic space.

Our first map, to be sure, illustrates quite exactly the opposite (see Figure 8.1).[38] Sometime during the third quarter of the sixteenth century, a map of Sri Lanka had been drawn in Goa by a certain Fernão Vaz Dourado, a Luso-Indian *mestiço*

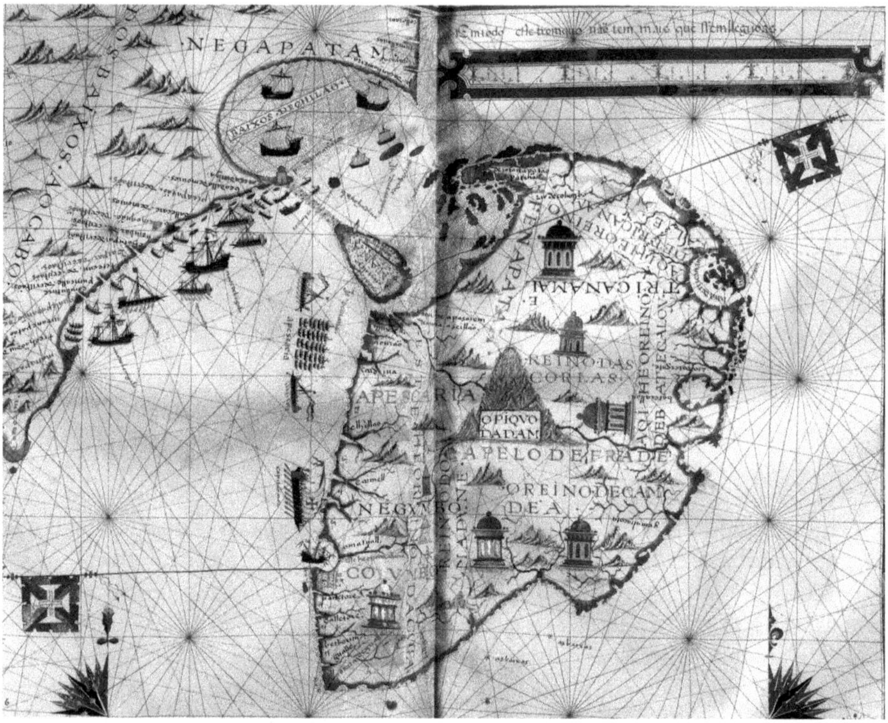

**Figure 8.1** Sri Lanka as a galactic polity on a map in the Atlas of Fernão Vaz Dourado, Goa, 1568. Biblioteca de los Duques de Alba, Madrid.

[38] Michael Biggs, 'Putting the State on the Map: Cartography, Territory, and European State Formation', *Comparative Studies in Society and History*, 41, 2 (1999), pp. 374–405.

with links to the viceroy Dom Luís de Ataíde (vr.1568–71). This map, finished in 1568, was the first of its kind since the myth of Taprobane had evaporated six decades earlier.[39] Not a single map of the island as a whole, at a scale comparable to this, had been produced during all those years. The freshly drawn picture signals, at first sight, the growing spatial awareness of the Portuguese with regard to Ceylon after decades of representing the island as little more than a blip on larger maritime charts. It does include parts of South India and thus begs questions about how maritime and terrestrial matters were thought about in connection with each other. But it also takes us straight into the years when Portuguese men began to criss-cross the island as such, carrying letters for Lankan rulers, leading troops to support one or the other pretender to a local throne, and dreaming up military projects at the intersection between the Lankan polity and the reluctant Portuguese crown.

Most significantly, the map of Fernão Vaz Dourado engages with the political (one might say the 'regal'), not the physical landscape of Sri Lanka. It does so by structuring the island space around a set of political central places: royal capitals acting as the nodes of a network or constellation, pulsating like stars in a galaxy. Kōṭṭe, Sītāvaka, and Kandy are there, as one would expect; but also others, such as the Four Korales and the kingdoms of Jaffna, Batticaloa, and Trincomalee, knowledge about which appeared in Goa along with the diplomatic fragmentation of the mid to late 1540s. Each political centre has been marked with an icon resembling a little temple topped by a crown, but none is surrounded by a fixed border. Dourado has thus rendered cartographically what was perhaps the most disconcerting characteristic of the Sri Lankan space: the absence of the very notion of territory. Borderlines were absent from the Lankan political landscape in the sixteenth century. There had of course been 'boundary books' and land grants with considerable topographical information in Medieval Sri Lanka, but much of what those texts dealt with was at the level of agricultural lands around villages.[40] Kingdoms as a whole were only described very occasionally, and by the sixteenth century any clear limits that may have existed earlier were blurred by decades of political turmoil.[41] To be sure, we need to be wary not to label this system as inherently 'pre-modern'. I shall come back to this point.[42] But the fact of the matter is that not a single document of the sixteenth century mentions the crossing of a border in the island. Whenever emissaries, adventurers, missionaries, and troops marched through Lanka, they crossed from one polity into the other in remote, often uninhabited areas. Somewhere—or rather nowhere—in the middle of a forest,

---

[39] For a deeper exploration see Biedermann 'Imagining Space before Conquest: Two Contrasting Maps of Sri Lanka, 1568–1606' in *The Portuguese in Sri Lanka and South India. Studies in the History of Diplomacy, Empire and Trade* (Wiesbaden: Harrassowitz, 2014), pp. 73–86.

[40] Cf. H. A. P. Abhayawardana, *Boundary Books of Mediaeval Sri Lanka* (Colombo: Academy of Sri Lankan Culture, 1999). See for example a case of an area at Mannār leased out to a Tamil individual for the collection of revenues in 1545, in Simon Casie Chitty, 'A Royal Grant Engraved on a Copper Plate', *Journal of the Ceylon Branch of the Royal Asiatic Society*, 1, 3 (1848), pp. 109–10.

[41] Cf. Strathern, 'Sri Lanka in the long Early Modern Period: Its Place in a Comparative Theory of Second Millenium Eurasian History', *Modern Asian Studies* 43, 4 (2009), especially pp. 828–30 and 855–60.

[42] See already Lucien Febvre, 'Limites et Frontières', in *Annales E.S.C.* (April–June 1947), pp. 201–7.

an uncultivated stretch of land or a mountain range, the sphere of influence of one lord would end, and that of another begin. Wandering across the island, individuals would enter and leave the realms of particular lords like meteors flying through the solar system, their trajectories inflected by the gravitation of successive planets, but often travelling through vast swathes of empty, unpopulated space. And the gravitational force of each ruler fluctuated with high frequency: even in the absence of any concrete military activity in a given area, its political whereabouts could change.

When António Moniz Barreto and Māyādunnē agreed to meet in 1547, the former went up the Kelani four leagues in a boat, and the latter came down four leagues. There was no border line to meet at. Somewhere, they talked, and then parted again.[43] To 'enter' a kingdom in sixteenth-century Lanka was not in itself a meaningful act. The difficulty lay not in crossing borders, but in getting to the political centres. In fact, Śrī Rāmarakṣa explained this to Queen Catherine in a letter about Sītāvaka. It was not on the border, he argued, but 'further inside' ('*mais dentro*') of the lands of Māyādunnē that the latter's forces were.[44] In military terms, there were generally no lines of defence *around* a realm, but, in case of war, *along* the roads or rivers leading from one centre to the other: for example, fort after fort along the Kelani river, in a constellation that may have extended its roots as far back as the classical period.[45] When Moniz Barreto arrived in Kandy, he entered the realm without passing any particular line, only to be received by the king in close vicinity to the capital itself. In fact, the rite of passage was then extended through time, as if to compensate for a lack of structure in space: Barreto was left to wait for eight days before he was allowed into the presence of the king again. In the meantime, he was visited by a number of Kandyan nobles, allowing him to come closer to the realm's centre socially, when topographically he was already there.[46]

The Dourado map is, in fact, a remarkable example of how the non-territorial quality of the Lankan galactic polity could be put on the paper without creating an illusion of territoriality. It is, in this sense, far superior to most maps circulating in history books today. The map could even have been used to illustrate precisely the intricacies and inscrutabilities of Lankan power building, where polities took their names from capital cities, or even from their rulers, in increasing contrast with Europe at the same time. Travelling across the map with a finger whilst consulting about the possibilities of dispatching troops from Goa, one would inevitably be reminded how, even if one *rāja* in the system was to be brought under nominal control, most probably other, unexpected and disconcerting alliances would pop up between the remaining nodes—as indeed they did, most spectacularly during the 1540s to 1560s. Conquering the island depicted by Fernão Vaz Dourado would come close to the travails of Sisyphus: not because it would be a realm difficult to invade, but because it would be almost impossible to hold on to.

---

[43] Māyādunnē to João de Castro, Ceylon, 26 October 1547, in Georg Schurhammer and Ernst August Voretzsch, *Ceylon zur Zeit des Königs Bhuvaneka Bahu und Franz Xavers 1539–1552* (Leipzig: Verlag der Asia Major, 1928) (henceforth cited as '*Ceylon*'), p. 478.

[44] Śrī Rāmarakṣa to Catherine, Cochin, 28 January 1551, *Ceylon*, p. 564.

[45] See Wilhelm Geiger, *Culture of Ceylon in Medieval Times*, edited by Heinz Bechert (Wiesbaden: Harrassowitz, 1960), p. 162.

[46] António Moniz Barreto to João de Castro, Colombo, 11 October 1547, *Ceylon*, p. 465.

The growing contrast here with sixteenth-century Portugal is remarkable. Building fortifications along the border with Spain following a logic of 'lines' (*linhas* of castles built alongside the border) had been a preoccupation of Portuguese rulers in the medieval period already. When Manuel I commissioned the artist Duarte de Armas to draw vistas of his frontier castles in the early 1500s, many of them appeared facing another, similarly linear structure just across the border, on the Spanish side.[47] This material structure, in itself already unparalleled in Sri Lanka, then began to gain an added political and symbolic significance in the sixteenth century. When Manuel I married for the first time, shortly after becoming king in 1495, he spontaneously marched into Castile with his retinue to fetch his future wife. By the time of his third marriage, in 1518, the situation was different. To cross the border now involved veritable rites of passage. The Portuguese reception committee waited on the Portuguese bank of the border river, following the strict Burgundian-inspired protocol that had begun to pervade Spanish court culture. When the princess arrived, the Portuguese Count of Vila Nova walked across the bridge to kiss her hand, as she stood between the Duke of Alba and the Bishop of Cordoba. He then took her across the bridge into Portugal, where she was received by the Duke of Bragança, and eventually handed over to the king. This was a rite of passage staged in space, not time.[48]

The construction of a border imbued with deep political meaning went hand in hand with the project of mapping the realm. Recent research has shown that, for Portugal, this began in the early years of the reign of John III, or even possibly under Manuel I, precisely after his marriage to Isabel, well before it materialized in the first printed map in 1561.[49] John III ruled not only without the threat of ever being challenged as king (something we have identified above as a possible obstacle to a full appreciation of Bhuvanekabāhu's situation in the 1530s and 1540s), but also of seeing the Portuguese borders dented by his neighbour and brother-in-law Charles V. The reign was one of relative consolidation, of mapping the metropolitan realm, of referring back to Constantine's Rome with confidence and investing in the fiction of a stable *Pax Lusitana*. Such developments, which had no parallel in Sri Lanka at the time, took Portugal down a diverging path. The growing gap, it must be emphasized again, did not sever communications. A *relative* proximity of political cultures allowed for a certain degree of translatability, and of course, the distant *Estado* remained a territorially much more blurry affair than the metropolis anyway. But under the surface the tension was mounting.

[47] The illustrations of the *Livro de Duarte d'Armas* are published in *Portugaliae Monumenta Cartographica*, edited by Armando Cortesão and Avelino Teixeira da Mota (Lisbon: PMC, 1960), vol. I, plates 28–33.

[48] Damião de Góis, *Crónica do Felicíssimo Rei Dom Manuel*, part III, chap. 23 and 24, both quoted in J. Romero de Magalhães, 'O enquadramento do espaço nacional', in *História de Portugal*, edited by José Mattoso (Lisbon: Círculo de Leitores, 1993–4), p. 24.

[49] On the map of Álvares Seco, printed in Rome in 1561, see Romero de Magalhães, 'As descrições geográficas de Portugal: 1500–1650', *Revista de História Económica e Social*, 5 (1980), p. 42. A recent study by Suzanne Daveau places the earliest sign of a map of Portugal in 1525. *Um mapa corográfico de Portugal (c. 1525). Reconstituição a partir do Códice de Hamburgo* (Lisbon: Centro de Estudos Geográficos, 2010).

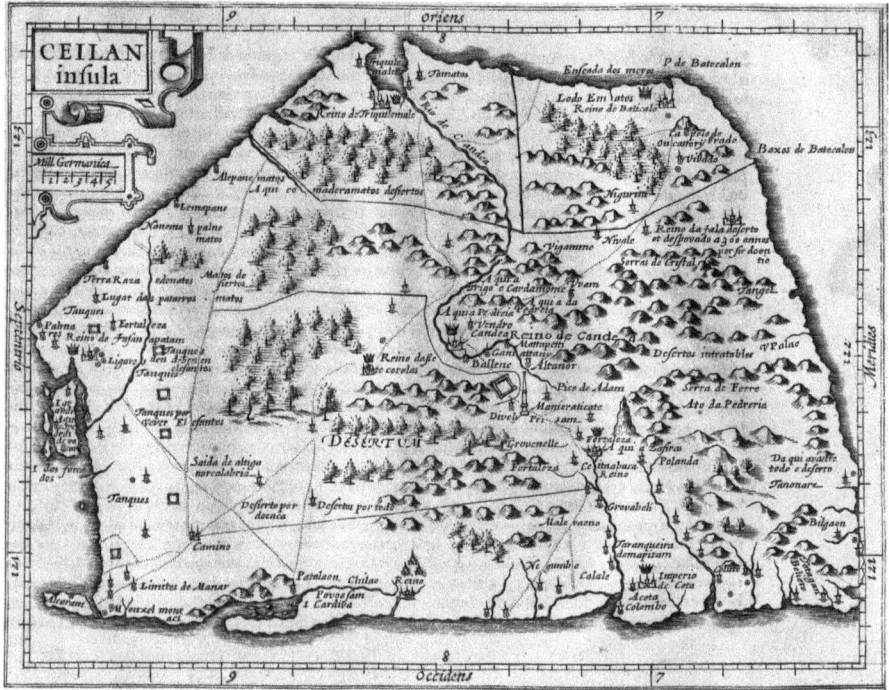

Figure 8.2  *Ceilan Insula* as a conquerable territory. Map from the Mercator Atlas edited by Jodocus Hondius, Antwerp, 1606, based on a lost map by Cipriano Sánchez. David Rumsey Collection, Stanford. Image in Creative Commons.

The distinctively non-territorial quality of the Dourado map just discussed, and the way it was being challenged in the minds of an increasing number of people, becomes particularly evident if we compare it with a later map that has come down to us through a print made in Antwerp, repeatedly from 1606, by Jodocus Hondius, for an edition of the famous Mercator Atlas (see Figure 8.2). Antwerp was the foremost centre of printing and mapmaking in the Spanish Low Countries. Much of what was produced there found its way into the libraries of the king, his various governors, and noble families across the Monarchy. The map carries the title *Insula Ceilan quae incolis Tenarisin dicitur* and, according to the information given in a cartouche in the lower right-hand corner, it was based on an earlier image originally drafted by a certain Cipriano Sánchez Villavicencio.[50]

In comparison with the Dourado map made in Goa, the Sánchez-Hondius map made in Antwerp downplays the importance of the many different political centres and kingdoms of Sri Lanka. In fact, they are barely visible as one throws a first glance at the print. Instead, the map creates an image that conveys a great deal of order, unhindered visibility, and manageability. The interior of the island is, despite

---

[50] On Sánchez, whose other extant maps are technically and visually very unlike the one depicting Ceylon, see *Portugaliae Monumenta Cartographica*, vol. III, pp. 111–13.

a relatively large number of mountains, represented as an essentially homogenous and almost uniformly accessible space where the imaginary traveller can easily plan journeys from any particular point to any other. Naturally, some places are still marked by captions as the centres of kingdoms, and they, like any toponym, bear the potential of disrupting the homogenous continuity of cartographic space by 'punctuating' it, as the map theoretician Christian Jacob puts it.[51] But in comparison with the Dourado map, the central places where Sri Lankan politics unfolded happened most dramatically have been tamed, the space surrounding them smoothed and evened out. Lanka's multiple political centres have been subjected to the graphic conventions developed in the Low Countries to represent 'towns' anywhere in the empire, anywhere in the world.

The might of Sri Lanka's pulsating political centres has been subdued by the homogenous, quantifiable, manageable space of early modern, neo-Ptolemaic geography.[52] Nothing in the picture bends the (undrawn, but powerfully present) lines of latitude and longitude emanating from the frame of the map, covering Sri Lanka with the same grid that was now being applied everywhere else across the globe. As so often in maps, it is precisely this invocation of a given, abstract quality of geographical space that carries the most powerful political message. Thanks to its graphical clarity, its grounding in mathematically calculable space and its reliance on conventional signs and icons taken from Europe across the continents, the Sánchez-Hondius map neutralizes the complexities of the Lankan political landscape and naturalizes the upcoming imperial order reaching across the globe.

From here, it was only one little step to imagining the island as a surface onto which a new territorial reality could be built—not intertwined with the help of endless negotiations, but directly imposed, because in essence this was already a territory in potency. As the cartographic historian David Woodward put it well before Walter Mignolo expounded such ideas for New Spain, the cartographic rationalization of space during the Renaissance carried the seeds of a world 'over which systematic dominance was possible'. Euclidean space was not only global in itself, it also created globality, providing a 'powerful framework for political expansion and control', a most plausible surface for the projection of new ideas of sovereignty anywhere on the planet.[53] An image such as the Hondius map could only serve as an encouragement to anyone thinking about the possibilities of conquest in the increasingly dominant sense of the word. This is not to state that the map and the science underlying it necessarily inspired the conquest, but that the map participates in a significant shift in the way overseas space was perceived and understood by the elites of the Catholic Monarchy. The making, printing, and distributing of this map coincides in time with some of the most brutal campaigns of the Portuguese in Sri Lanka.

[51] Christian Jacob, *The Sovereign Map. Theoretical Approaches in Cartography through History* (Chicago: University of Chicago Press, 2006), p. 203.
[52] David Woodward, 'Cartography and the Renaissance: Continuity and Change', in *The History of Cartography*, vol. III, *Cartography in the European Renaissance*, edited by David Woodward (Chicago, IL/London: University of Chicago Press, 2007), pp. 3–24.
[53] David Woodward, 'Maps and the rationalization of space', in *Circa 1492. Art in the Age of Exploration*, edited by J. A. Levenson (New Haven, CT: Yale University Press, 1991), p. 87.

Misled by an excess of self-confidence and a failure to understand the Lankan imperial model, the decision-makers of the 1590s and early 1600s felt capable of dealing with Ceylon simply by going for its conquest: *conquista* in the percussive, hard-edged, deeply transformative sense of taking full and permanent possession of territory by military means.[54] This kind of conquest was something the empire had dealt with successfully before. If Tenochtitlán and Cuzco, or indeed Brabant and the Philippines, had been 'pacified' by the global Leviathan, how could Ceylon—more neatly prepared for conquest on the map than any of those earlier victims—not be subdued? It was only too logical that, once the door stood open to conquest thanks to a legally binding donation and the death of a key enemy, the empire would effectively proceed to take possession of what it now, on grounds of its transformative reading of the testament of Dharmapāla, believed to be its own. The new Universalism of the Catholic Monarchs could still make claims on grounds of the older Universalism of the Kōṭṭe *cakravartis*, but between these two ideologies, a fundamental gap had by now formed—and it is into the resulting abyss that the dialogue collapsed.

## APOCALYPSE THEN AND NOW: THE REINVENTION OF 'CEYLON'

This abyss is of the greatest significance—not primarily in the sense of a static onto-logical contrast between two 'cultures', but of a dynamic, contingent disjunction, the roots of which we may uncover by proceeding comparatively, but the workings of which we can only understand through a critical connected history of successive combinations of dialogue and monologue. In marked contrast with the first nine decades of Luso-Lankan relations, shaped by the interactions of two suzerainty-driven imperialisms, the Portuguese presence in Ceylon between 1597 and 1658 can be read as a series of frustrated attempts, at least as far as the centrally formulated strategies are concerned, at conquering and consolidating territories so they could be ruled by a single king. The *cakravarti* mandate, derived from classical Indic uni-versalism and reshaped over the centuries to adapt to Lankan political plurality and diversity, was transformed by the Catholic Monarchy into yet another *conquista*—not in the supple, heterogeneous sense handled earlier by the Portuguese dynasty of Avis, but in the sense used by the reformers of the empire, now under the aegis of Habsburg Spain. Emphasis shifted from winning over people (members of the local elites) to ruling directly and imposing power over lands; from controlling centres to creating territory; from extracting royal tribute to introducing laws, making justice and levying taxes; and from exploring the circulation of goods to controlling their production.

---

[54] A number of subtly divergent meanings of the word *conquista* can still be found in Rafael Bluteau, *Vocabulario Portuguez e Latino*, vol. II (Coimbra: No Collegio das Artes da Companhia de Jesu, 1712), p. 471.

The madness of it all is most dramatically evident when it comes to the island as a whole. What the *Estado* decided to conquer was an imagined kingdom that had never existed before. It was now called the '*conquista de Ceilão*' or simply '*Ceilão*', but the Asian root of the toponym should not fool us into ignoring its radical novelty and conceptual incompatibility with Lankan political culture. This was the old idea of Lanka (an Island Empire *protected* on the outside by a global king of kings) metamorphosed into a new idea of *Ceilão* (an Island Kingdom *aggregated* and *incorporated* into a global empire). It was to be a unified territorial realm ruled by a single (Iberian) sovereign, inhabited by followers of a single, state-sanctioned (Christian) confession, and circumscribed by a clearly defined, visually and emotionally compelling (territorial) border. Regarding the latter, the coastline of the island was readily at hand. Sri Lankans themselves had, to be sure, long cultivated the ideal of the symbolic unity of the island, an ideal made plausible in many cultures by the notion of insularity itself.[55] Islands in general are prone to serve in such a manner as apparently self-evident repositories of human collectives. Strathern and Roberts have indeed argued compellingly that the island offered a shell for surprisingly old, medieval manifestations of Lankan identity, anchoring society in a vision of locatedness that acted as a counterweight to cultural and political exposure to the wider world.[56] However, it is also clear now that this idealized single outer border had been largely compliant with a vast array of internal divisions which it could not, and did not even wish to, erase. The Lankan shore had never been a territorial border in the modern sense of the word. That is precisely why it had been so easy for the Portuguese to cross it in the first place.

At the dawn of the seventeenth century, the island as a whole was reinvented, its natural borderline re-coded by the Habsburg administration to serve a new imperial project geared towards the progressive integration and assimilation of *Ceilão* as a territory. The island's diverse polities and communities were ignored, levelled into the flat surface of the paper map. Lanka as a sacred shell, as a blessed, sensuously beautiful insular space calling for a generously tolerational imperial umbrella, as had been the case in the earlier political and poetic imagination, was replaced by a novel idea of Lanka as a receptacle for full and unshared sovereignty—a territory, I am tempted to venture, out of which an island colony might grow, and one day in the distant future a nation state. However much the British may have done to flesh out this notion and put it into practice through various strategies of 'islanding' after 1800, it is in the years around 1600 that we ought to seek the roots of the process.[57]

Of course much remains to be said about the following two centuries, and none of what was imposed by the Portuguese compares to the fully fledged sovereignty

---

[55] See Steven Collins, *Nirvana and Other Buddhist Felicities. Utopias of the Pāli Imaginaire* (Cambridge: Cambridge Uiversity Press, 1998).

[56] Alan Strathern, *Kingship and Conversion* and Michael Roberts, *Sinhala Consciousness in the Kandyan Period 1590s to 1815* (Colombo: Vijitha Yapa Publications, 2003).

[57] Cf. Sujit Sivasundaram, *Islanded: Britain, Sri Lanka, and the Bounds of an Indian Ocean Colony* (Chicago, IL: University of Chicago Press, 2013). Tariq Jazeel, 'Reading the geography of Sri Lankan island-ness: colonial repetitions, postcolonial possibilities', *Contemporary South Asia*, 17, 4 (2009), pp. 399–414.

of nineteenth-century textbooks on the modern state—but in relation to what had been the dominant praxis of previous decades, the change was fundamental. The radicalization of the Portuguese empire's policy after 1590 had a deeper impact in Sri Lanka than the first encounter of 1506, the desecration of the Temple of Kōṭṭe in 1551, or King Dharmapāla's baptism in 1557. The most dramatic of all translations and transformations in our story is the one that, as historians far too inclined to believe in modern maps, we may have expected to be the least of all problems, or simply overlooked: it was the appropriation and radical reinvention of the island itself.

# Conclusion

## (Dis)connected Histories and the Beginnings
of European Conquest in Asia

The question asked at the beginning of this book—*why conquer?*—implied a specific approach to the word 'conquest', but also to the word 'why' as something signalling potentially complex, unstraightforward, reversible forms of causality. This approach is not necessarily the one most commonly taken by global historians. In a recent, forcefully argued attempt at answering the question *Why did Europe Conquer the World?*, Philip T. Hoffman has ventured that, thanks to a very idiosyncratic kind of infighting among European monarchs, military specialists in this continent perfected their techniques and technology to a point where they had a significant advantage over fighting forces in other continents.[1] Similar theories involving geographical, biological, and other factors explaining European successes abound. Yet we still need to ask ourselves: why would anyone in Europe *wish* to conquer another part of the world? One cannot set out to take possession of a place (an island, a continent) without first imagining that place as something that a) can and b) should be taken possession of. Military history matters a great deal, of course, but we are still compelled to dig into the deeper layers of history and seek out cultural explanations for the global projection of European power. There can be no global history of empire without a global history of the imperial imagination. And there can be no global history of the imperial imagination without a critical approach to global connections.

## TERRITORIALIZATION IN GLOBAL EARLY MODERNITY

Revisiting a small, but extraordinarily rich corner of the Eurasian colonial archive has allowed us to take the pulse of a century of suzerainty-driven imperial interactions, crushed in the end by the overwhelming weight of a new, sovereignty-driven idea of imperial conquest—*conquista* in a hard-hitting sense deemed by late sixteenth-century reformers of the Portuguese empire to offer a solution to problems inherited from the past. Conquest was to replace diplomacy as a tool of power building in Sri Lanka under its new Habsburg monarchs. But how can this shift be

[1] Philip T. Hoffman, *Why Did Europe Conquer the World?* (Princeton, NJ: Princeton University Press, 2017).

made to generate meaning on a broader scale? I have insisted on the non-territorial and often unstable quality of the Portuguese empire, of South Asian polities, and of the constellations of power that sprang up at the intersection of the two during the sixteenth century. The intention has been to de-territorialize them in a specific sense: not to affirm that they possessed no extension in terrestrial space—the initial question was precisely what encouraged the Portuguese to move into the land in spite of their reticence to do so—but to argue that those political formations operated on grounds of relationships between royal authority and terrestrial space differing from the paradigm that became dominant in Europe in the seventeenth century. A relationship, that is, contrasting with the increasing material and symbolic investments of early modern European rulers in the making of consolidated territories defined by unambiguous territorial borders.

There is a long tradition of scholarship suggesting that people have—as Owen Lattimore once put it—generally tended to belong to groups before identifying with territories.[2] It is largely on such grounds that Benedict Anderson asserted that 'in the older imagining, where states were defined by centres, borders were porous and indistinct, and sovereignties faded imperceptibly into one another'. This, Anderson thought, was in contrast with 'the modern conception' where 'state sovereignty is fully, flatly, and evenly operative over each square centimetre of a legally demarcated territory'.[3] The idea that Europe was at the heart of the transformation has been further consolidated by projects such as that of Daniel Nordman on the making of borders in early modern and modern France.[4] By the turn of the millennium, Yi-Fu Tuan felt encouraged to theorize, in the language of anthropologists but with a distinct emphasis on Europe, that late medieval societies in this continent began to evolve from a system where rulers mediated a vertically organized cosmos towards a system where people lived in a horizontally organized world.[5]

Two brief caveats, followed by a broader qualification, shall help us move towards a conclusion. First, we ought to remain cautious about mapping differences in political culture linearly onto our own, problematic, map of continents.[6] As with other changes in the early modern period, namely in military and diplomatic praxis, territorialization may have to be brought into connection with processes other than European state formation and expansion. Islamization appears to have put pressure on Indic societies structured around vertical symbolic centres in insular

---

[2] See Owen Lattimore, *Inner Asian Frontier of China* (New York: American Geographical Society, 1940) and 'Origins of the Great Wall of China: A Frontier Concept in Theory and Practice', in *Studies in Frontier History. Collected Papers, 1928–1958* (London: Oxford University Press, 1962), pp. 97–118.

[3] Benedict Anderson, *Imagined Communities. Reflections on the Origin and Spread of Nationalism*, revised edition (London/New York: Verso, 1991), p. 19.

[4] Daniel Nordman, *Frontières de France. De l'espace au territoire, XVIe-XIXe siècle* (Paris: Gallimard, 1998). Before this author, see John A. Armstrong, *Nations before Nationalism* (Chapel Hill, NC: University of North Carolina Press, 1982), pp. 65–90. Cf. also Charles Tilly, *The Formation of National States in Western Europe* (Princeton, NJ: Princeton University Press, 1972).

[5] Foreword to Kenneth Robert Olwig, *Landscape, Nature and the Body Politic. From Britain's Renaissance to America's New World* (Madison, WI: University of Wisconsin Press, 2002), pp. xix–xv.

[6] Martin W. Lewis and Kären Wigen, *The Myth of Continents. A Critique of Metageography* (Berkeley/Los Angeles: University of California Press, 1997).

Southeast Asia, for example, long before the arrival of Europeans.[7] Whether this can be taken to suggest historiographical opportunities along the Islamicate, and not only the Iberian, frontiers of Asia with regard to territoriality, is something I must leave to others to discuss. Second, whilst the territorial shift originated a profound crisis in Lankan history, this does not mean that Lankan societies could not digest it to some extent at least. We know that in the highland kingdom of Kandy, the invigorated institutions of Buddhist kingship gained legitimacy from the early 1600s as a focus of indigenist opposition to lowland power. Once the global empire with which Kōṭṭe had been bound up on the littoral appeared as a genuinely foreign invading force, Kandy may have started adopting a more rigid territorial border along which to defend itself against Portuguese assaults. The revision of this realm's history has only just begun.[8]

Territorialization theory is fortunately nuanced enough to offer us some wriggling space. Historians of early modern Europe have been able to contend that territory-building (or 'horizontality') was not entirely incompatible with some ruler-centric power structures (or 'verticality').[9] Rather than focusing on the appearance and swift imposition of territoriality as a hegemonic modernizing force, it may be most rewarding to observe the slowness of its emergence and the way it remained entangled with unevenly evolving notions of societal space, royal authority and law.[10] Nordman himself has admitted that the transition from a state of affairs where the centre structured the realm to one where the boundary performed that function was *long*.[11] Early modern Europe, even as the Westphalian system was coming into bloom, still turns out to have been full of ambiguous 'places of imperfectly superimposed and unequally territorialized sovereignties and rights'.[12] The methodological hazard lies not primarily in the identification of distinct ideal-typical modes of power building, but in the notion that a linear shift from one to the other occurred abruptly, irreversibly, and essentially in Western Europe, to then cause a straightforward impact around the globe.[13]

One might imagine a more malleable framework then, into which early modern polities could be inserted analytically and yet allowed to remain mobile as they interact with each other historically. This could take the shape of a coordinate system,

[7] Denys Lombard, *Le Carrefour javanais. Essai d'histoire globale* (Paris: Éditions de l'École des Hautes Études en Sciences Sociales, 1990), vol. II, Les réseaux asiatiques, chapter 3.
[8] Cf. Strathern, *Kingship and Conversion*, pp. 214–19 and Gananath Obeyesekere, 'Between the Portuguese and the Nāyakas: the many faces of the Kandyan Kingdom, 1591– 1765', in *Sri Lanka at the Crossroads of History*, edited by Zoltán Biedermann and Alan Strathern (London: UCL Press, 2017), pp. 161–77.
[9] 'La typologie de l'état moderne, le droit, l'espace', in *L'État moderne: le droit, l'espace et les formes de l'état*, edited by Noel Coulet and Jean-Philippe Genet (Paris: Éditions du CNRS, 1990), pp. 7–14.
[10] Cf. Lauren Benton, *A Search for Sovereignty. Law and Geography in European Empires, 1400–1900* (Cambridge: Cambridge University Press, 2009), pp. 279–81.
[11] Nordman, *Frontières de France*, pp. 514–24.
[12] Bernard Lepetit speaks of a 'logique de « marches », lieux de souverainetés et de droits imparfaitement superposés et inégalement territorialisés', in his preface to Peter Sahlins, *Frontières et identités nationales. La France et l'Espagne dans les Pyrénées depuis le XVIIe siècle* (Paris: Belin, 1996), p. 3.
[13] See for example the twelfth–thirteenth century processes described in Nora Berend, 'Défense de la chrétienté et naissance d'une identité. Hongrie, Pologne et péninsule ibérique au Moyen Âge', *Annales HSS*, 58, 5 (2003), p. 1023.

one axis of which might measure size, while the other would evaluate power-building strategies, suspended between two ideal-types: suzerainty-driven imperialism at one extremity, and sovereignty-driven imperialism at the other. To describe the cases examined in this book, we would start by locating Portugal and Sri Lanka with regard to the second axis and conclude that they were close enough to each other on the canvas, around 1500, to start a dialogue. They were probably part of a larger cluster comprising other suzerainty-driven polities across the globe, a possibility that should encourage us to invest more in the study of early global diplomacy. They certainly also appreciated this proximity and understood that 'connections' could be established here on grounds of a perceived commensurability of political idioms. Whilst the connections were unquestionably fraught by misunderstandings and disjunctions, they nevertheless functioned well enough for the platform itself to remain meaningful, allowing both sides to emit and absorb impulses, and change each other's development, in an inter-imperial dialogue. As Lankan ideas of imperial unification hit the Portuguese imagination, the resulting plans of intervention carried territorial elements, but only to a limited extent. Interestingly as well, the perceived commensurability of imperial power-building strategies proved potent enough to defuse problems arising from a difference in size. The principle of nesting empires—the Matrioshka Principle—offered a relatively effective vision of imperial formations cohabitating despite operating on different scales: the smaller, Lankan polity with its complicated ambitions in the island could—or so it was hoped—thrive inside the larger, Portuguese imperial project, as in a bubble. 'Large' here means not that the Portuguese possessed many lands, but that they could reach across oceans, impose themselves militarily almost anywhere on the Asian seas and, with a loosely formulated mandate of conquest in the older sense of the word, begin to imagine possible instances of power building on the land.

As we have seen, tensions arose early on. Not only was the dialogue between John III and Bhuvanekabāhu VII always fraught but, more importantly, in some less visible corners of Portuguese imperial society the Lankan ideas of *cakravarti*-led unification reacted with more radical expansionist impulses to produce proposals of military and religious intervention and even conquest in a more hard-hitting sense. The signals sent out by the Lankan elite were read and digested by some Portuguese as an encouragement to build a more muscular empire: one that, having global reach, could also penetrate the polity locally, on the ground, possess it, and transform it. Over the decades, such thoughts coalesced into a political discourse of conquest that, whilst failing to become policy, began to put pressure on the platform upon which the Houses of Kōṭṭe and Avis communicated. Towards the later sixteenth century, the now dominant imperial reformists of Habsburg Portugal and Spain entered the game. Theirs was an empire larger than any other. Theirs was also an impulse to move away vigorously from the old, suzerainty-centred imperial cluster that had produced such exchanges as those of John III and Bhuvanekabāhu VII. The reformists heard the decades-old calls of discontented nobles and missionaries for military occupation and mass conversion, and read them as a recipe for the furthering of royal administrative and fiscal power. They asked why such ideas had not been taken on board by policymakers. They began to imagine a

Portuguese imperial body rejuvenated through the conquest and consolidation of a new and exhilarating tool of the political imagination: taxable, manageable, colonizable territories. In the 1590s the lively, albeit ever strained, Luso-Lankan dialogue finally broke down. The vectorial forces pulling the two parties apart were too substantial for the connection to survive.

## IMAGINING THE GLOBAL AND THE LOCAL

Importantly, this may also be the point where the proposal of a coordinate system reaches its limits. It is visually suggestive, but does not do justice, for example, to the complex heritage of Lankan imperial politics present even in the darkest orders of conquest issued by Phillip II. To appreciate this baggage, we need to resort to something else than a diagram. Perhaps the case studied in the book is indeed most widely relevant not at the level of the territorial shift as such, but of what this shift, and especially the way it was prepared over nearly a century, can tell us about the much-invoked yet still poorly understood early modern interface between the local and the global. The imperial triangle that we have observed is a site of local narratives that went global, and global narratives that went local. It is at this point that the question asked at the very beginning of this book may arise again: *where* exactly do connections—and, logically, disconnections—sit on the map? Can we put them on a map at all? How shall we talk about them without falling into outdated schemes opposing the Asian to the European, the medieval to the modern, or the (immobile) local to the (dynamic) global? And is there a possibility that *through* their histories we can understand both the making and the unmaking of that vast 'Afro-Eurasian continuum' that historians sometimes invoke?[14]

We could, here, attempt to retain a narrative that emphasizes connection, intertwinement, and even hybridity. For much of the sixteenth century, the story we have seen unfold was one of imperial projects encountering each other and growing, together, into something new. We might imagine Portuguese imperialism as, for example, one of those Ivies growing abundantly in Central European cemeteries. Naturally, they start from somewhere, but as they grow, they also begin to reach into the ground, here and there, through new adventitious roots, until at some point it becomes very difficult to see where they were born in the first place. Sri Lanka offered not just a particularly fertile local ground for such an adventitious root to grow out of the global plant into the island soil; it actively encouraged the larger empire to come to the island. Rather than reaching randomly into this or that piece of local ground, the global imperial plant that we customarily call 'Portuguese' was attracted to a specific site in South Asia thanks to an army of disgruntled princes and translators, go-betweens and adventurers, missionaries and other letter-writers inspired by the old imperial project of Kōṭṭe. Two insights result

---

[14] Jos Gommans, 'Continuity and change in the Indian Ocean basin', in *The Cambridge World History*, vol. 6, The Construction of a Global World, 1400–1800 CE, edited by Jerry H. Bentley, Sanjay Subrahmanyam and Merry E. Wiesner-Hanks (Cambridge: Cambridge University Press, 2015), p. 182.

from this. First, as we observe the larger empire extend across the globe and implanting itself in various places, we realize how important the local ground was for it to succeed. The Lankan case suggests that the global empire could not have gone on growing without a fertile local environment. In fact, the categories are further complicated by the fact that, when necessary, the local imperial project was able to reach out diplomatically (albeit relying on the transportation and communicational channels of the *Estado*) over large distances to where it felt it needed to grab the attention of its global counterpart: be that in Cochin, or Goa, or Lisbon. It could then be argued that, after decades of such reaching out, intertwining and cross-fertilizing, the very categories of local and global become blurred. This is exactly what the donation of 1580 suggests, where a Lankan monarch went to the point of entrusting a global monarch with his local imperial project as if a seamless takeover was indeed possible. Second, whilst we may here struggle to find an appropriate botanical simile, the intertwinement of global and local imperial project was so intense that the two parts of the new 'plant' were, by the 1580s, virtually inseparable in terms of what we would call their DNA. After a certain amount of exposure to local politics, an empire such as the Portuguese cannot be explained solely on grounds of its European heritage any more—a realization that calls to be linked up with Stern's reading of the early history of the EIC.[15] Whilst we still know, at one level, that the 'Portuguese empire' had its original root in Iberia, we are also compelled to ask, as Frances Yates might have if she had been offered this larger picture, to what extent that still mattered in Sri Lanka after decades of such profound interaction and hybridization.

In this sense, then, even the shock of the 1590s could be subjected to a relatively optimistic interpretation. As the reformers of the global empire cut through the (in their eyes) abhorrent, hybrid political body they wished to transform, they may have ended up grafting their own imperial policy onto a vigorous hybrid stem with deep South Asian roots. This could be a suggestive image to retain, then: a *graft* placed upon a *hybrid stem*, even in the darkest of moments.[16] However, this generates intriguing questions again about the global and the local—and these may take us down a much more sinister path than the one described so far. Clearly, the reformed, sovereignty-centred imperial project embraced by Portuguese administrators and military leaders under the Habsburgs, grafted onto the older Luso-Lankan stem, saw itself as more decidedly global and independent from the local than the empire of the House of Avis had ever been. It did so precisely because it felt that the empire was strong enough to impose itself locally without having to take into account the idiosyncrasies of the existing political system.

At the end of the day, we need to ask a disheartening question. Here, the role played by the local may *not* give rise to any kind of optimistic, locally inflected reading of the global. What if, in the turmoil of the 1590s, the only local 'contribution' that really mattered was an entirely passive presence of the local on the new global map? Was it perhaps in the vision of a defenceless, flat, conquerable island, as shown in

---

[15] Cf. Philip J. Stern, *The Company-State. Corporate Sovereignty and the Early Modern Foundations of the British Empire in India* (New York: Oxford University Press, 2011).

[16] The grafting metaphor appears, carrying a slightly different, but overall comparable, meaning in Luís Filipe F. R. Thomaz, *De Ceuta a Timor*, 2nd ed. (Lisbon: Difel, 1994).

atlases produced by printers in Europe, that the Iberian advocates of conquest saw the figure of full territorial sovereignty emerge with the greatest clarity? The conquest of Ceylon appeared to the imperial reformers of the late 1500s and early 1600s as an eminently feasible enterprise—as it would, later, to the Dutch and to the English, and this may have to do with the way the new global gaze fell on a very specific version of the local. It is 'empty spaces' after all—those flat, apparently tame surfaces appearing on maps such as that distributed by Jodocus Hondius—that invite colonial inscription most powerfully. Perhaps the phantasm of full sovereignty gained plausibility, in the eyes of Iberian imperial reformers, precisely in the more distant and apparently tame, defenceless, 'local' corners of the world—possibly even before it coagulated into a coherent system in Europe, where the checks on royal power were much more immediately apparent to any observer. Generally speaking, Phillip II and Phillip III did not care too much about the details of the grafting process described above, as long as the results were favourable: the Spanish Habsburg monarchs cared about furthering Iberian, Catholic supremacy in Europe and, with renewed vigour in the face of English and Dutch interloping, around the world. In this sense, then, their empire was a potent, all-encompassing, crushing combination of Leviathan and Behemoth, an empire of the sea and of the land operating globally, taking possession of places locally wherever the opportunity appeared, and (still) capable of believing that it might thus come to dominate the world.[17]

If we now zoom in again on the local theatre of imperial incorporation of the 1590s, we may feel that the most appropriate image is not necessarily that of a 'thread' connecting two distant polities being 'wrested' and 'torn' as one polity moved away from the other. At the core of the story, something else occurred. It was precisely when the Catholic Monarchy of Phillip II incorporated the Kōṭṭe kingdom of Dharmapāla, that the dialogue collapsed. 'Collapse' is, in fact, a striking metaphor for the institutional transformation in the Lankan lowlands, in that it suggests not just a breakdown of communications, but also the folding and burying of one party's ideas into and under those of the other. The global empire crushed the local empire precisely as it made its decisive move to inhabit it, to have Phillip II sit, as an absentee monarch represented by a *Portuguese* captain-general, on the throne of Kōṭṭe. Sovereignty in the emerging sense of the word proved much too large a pair of feet for the imperial shoes of Kōṭṭe to fit.

When a polity such as Kōṭṭe is transformed from vassal state into crown possession, a strange, scrambled monologue replaces the dialogue. Between the diplomatic letters of Bhuvanekabāhu VII and, say, a land register drawn up for the Habsburg administration in the seventeenth century, political space has been flattened, the polyphony of voices muted. Even though we may still distinguish many interesting signs of Lankan agency in the conquered territories, as historians do in the conquered territories of Spanish America, the complex habitat of interacting imperial themes appears in the process of being reduced to host a single, all-encompassing imperial body that sees itself as carrying the same weight globally and in every single place it inhabits. The Native Ground is being obliterated, compressed into that very different surface where subjugation is expected to be implemented in a way that was not conceivable

---

[17] Cf. David Armitage, 'The Elephant and the Whale: Empires of Land and Sea,' *Journal for Maritime Research*, 9, 1 (2007), pp. 23–36.

before: the Colonial Ground. The points of contact where the local had connected with the global, and vice versa, are gone, diluted, obliterated by a surface allowing for only one kind of empire: the kind that sees itself as a global polity uninflected by the local (and *then* all the 'negotiations' cherished by colonial historians may get under way).

## DISSONANCES IN THE POLYPHONY
## OF EARLY MODERN EURASIA

Two conclusions are possible, and indeed necessary, as we reach the end of our journey. The first will barely require spelling out to the reader who has followed the storyline from beginning to end, as it has been ubiquitous throughout this book: once we question the binaries of old imperial history and embrace the possibilities of global connected history, the origins of conquest and the making of colonial Ceylon become astonishingly complex, locally and globally interconnected affairs. The official inauguration of a policy of conquest in Sri Lanka in the mid 1590s may look similar to other instances of Iberian empire building in the New World and the Philippines, but what in Central Mexico had been condensed into months of negotiations and confrontation in 1519–21, took almost a century in our case to unfold. It involved a prolonged flow of people, letters, objects, and ideas between such distant places as Colombo, Goa, Manila, Lisbon, Madrid, and Rome. It involved, above all, a steady Lankan input of ideas, enticements, and requests, originating an increasing flow of Portuguese resources to an island that was not a Lusitanian crown possession.

This conclusion is very much in line with the notion, now quite comfortably established, of a 'polyphonic' early modern world.[18] It encourages us to keep looking for comparable cases of imperial cooperation and transimperial flows of ideas, information, and power. 'Islanding' for example, as described by Sujit Sivasundaram for early nineteenth-century Sri Lanka, may have had other sources than the British imperial imagination. The Iberian tradition has come into the picture very forcefully,[19] but the more we can also acknowledge the Asian input that went into Iberian projects in the first place, the better. To understand the early modern and how it fed into the modern, we still need to work towards detaching ourselves from the cartographies and chronologies that structured the world of previous generations of historians. We must acknowledge that western scholars have been allowed to be masters of the map and the narrative for far too long. Really, ever since Matteo Ricci declared about his interlocutors in Asia, rather than about himself, that 'it is a marvel how little they know'.[20]

[18] Sanjay Subrahmanyam, 'Introduction', in *The Cambridge World History*, vol. 6, The Construction of a Global World, 1400–1800 CE, edited by Jerry H. Bentley, Sanjay Subrahmanyam and Merry E. Wiesner-Hanks (Cambridge: Cambridge University Press, 2015), p. 7.

[19] The Spanish contribution to French absolutism has been studied, but nothing comparable exists for the British case. See Jean-Frédéric Schaub, *La France espagnole. Les racines hispaniques de l'absolutisme français* (Paris: Seuil, 2003).

[20] Quoted in Mary Laven, '"From His Holiness to the King of China". Gifts, Diplomacy and Jesuit Evangelization', in *Global Gifts. The Material Culture of Diplomacy in Early Modern Eurasia*, edited by

There is also a much darker inference to be spelt out, however, and it can be made to derive precisely from the assertion just cited. It may seem particularly compelling when we go back into the local, post-colonial theatre of Sri Lanka today, but it is of equal relevance to the global reader. Hindsight suggested from the onset that the connected histories of the three ruling houses under scrutiny—the houses of Kōṭṭe, Avis, and Habsburg—would end in calamity. After all, whilst European ships frequented Asian shores, we know that the opposite was never the case. And whilst this can be read optimistically as a sign of European trade gravitating to the economic powerhouses of Asia, it also means quite plainly that some polities had more reach and, alas, more impact than others. The Luso-Lankan divergence examined in this study may seem niche, a story of minute significance in the face of other, more balanced imperial exchanges on the Eurasian mainland, involving more stable polities such as the Mughal or the Savafid empires. Yet if we listen carefully, an unpleasant note is audible amid the great polyphony of early modern Eurasia. Once it has found its way into our ears, it becomes difficult to ignore it.

Can we even speak of 'connections' without sounding frivolous when it comes to the origins of three and a half centuries of conquest and colonization? Only under certain conditions. First, we ought to make sure that we do not insulate the old ecumene (as a realm of 'connections') from the Americas (as a realm of 'conquests'). Otherwise, how will we ever be able to compare the contemporaneous processes leading up to of British colonization *and* Latin American decolonization by the early 1800s?[21] Second, and following from the first point, connectivity as such needs to be as thoroughly politicized in our narratives as anything else pertaining to the history of empires, including conquest. Most disturbingly perhaps, the case of Sri Lanka reminds us of how communication can work for some time but also deteriorate until a dialogue falls apart. Commensurability and translatability may increase or decrease over time. Commensurable political cultures can be a fertile breeding grounds for ideas of imperial conquest. Connections can *breed* conquest, and global historians need to continue exploring this dilemma along with the general 'fragility of global connections and the dynamics of disruption'—or they will be accused of painting an uncritical picture of globalization.[22] A tension has emerged between the way the more connective aspects of our narrative of the Luso-Lankan encounter have unfolded, on the one hand, and what the experience of modernity—early, high, and late—means in the collective memories of South Asians, and indeed the Global South, today. All the intricacies and human subtleties of the sixteenth-century communicative process apart, we still end up confronted with a

Zoltán Biedermann, Anne Gerritsen and Giorgio Riello (New York: Cambridge University Press, 2018), p. 226. Cf. Walter D. Mignolo, 'The movable center: geographical discourses and territoriality during the expansion of the Spanish empire', in *Coded Encounters: Writing, Gender and Ethnicity in Colonial Latin America*, edited by Francisco Cevallos-Candau et al. (Amherst, MA: University of Massachussetts Press, 1994), pp. 15–45; reissued in Mignolo, *The Darker Side of the Renaissance*, pp. 219–58.

[21] Cf. Ronald Robinson, 'Non-European foundations of European imperialism: sketch for a theory of collaboration', Studies in the Theory of Imperialism, edited by Roger Owen and Bob Sutcliffe (London: Longman, 1972), pp. 117–42.

[22] Richard Drayton and David Motadel, 'Discussion: the futures of global history', *Journal of Global History*, 13, 1 (2018), pp. 1–21 highlights the important critical efforts of global historians.

European-based empire—the paper-obsessed, unforgivingly universalistic and transformative, heavily armed empire of Phillip II—setting out to crush the rest. It is impossible not to see here a precursor to the most brutal, least accommodating policies of the British Raj—the ones that spread once imperial policy was in the hands of men aspiring to dominion with or without the consent of local elites. What we are looking at is a global force attempting to replace the local, assuming from the onset that it could simply cannibalize it in order to succeed.

However encouraged we may feel by the complex combinations of thought and action that, over the course of the sixteenth century, allowed two distant cultures to exchange ideas and formulate commensurable, even mutually compatible projects; however much we may be tempted to see, for a moment, the forces of interpersonal politics, representation and diplomatic performance as culturally more fertile than the severe logics of the nascent bureaucratic state; Sri Lanka, at the end of the day, was hit by the invading armies of an empire unwilling to compromise. All this ends up taking us back, almost full circle, into close proximity to where, in our attempt at revisiting a case of early European-Asian interaction and breaking down historiographical atavisms, we hoped for a moment that we might manage not to be: with the blunt realities of territorial conquest, confessionalization, and bureaucratization, created by a European-based political elite willing to take on other, more flexible forms of imperial interaction and crush them. It ought to be clear enough that this book, whilst opening up a window on a wonderfully idiosyncratic century that complicates narratives, was never intended as an escape from the horrors of colonial history. In their own remarkable manner, the 1500s did pave the way for the realities of colonialism, and however much the origins of conquest may be a cross-cultural, simultaneously local and global affair, the armed conflicts, the colonial massacres, the rapes, the destruction of heritage and wealth, occurred in Sri Lanka, not in Iberia.

It is also there that a bloodstained crisis persists today, despite the apparent quiet since the end of the civil war in 2012, around the imagined territorial unity of the island. Poignantly enough, Spain, the Netherlands, and the United Kingdom have all become polities where, whilst full fragmentation is still resisted, substantial powers are shared between central and other authorities. The same cannot be said of Sri Lanka, where the indivisibility of the island territory, brought to the realm around 1600 from Goa, Malacca, and Madrid, possibly absorbed and reworked by Kandy as a centre of Lankan state building, and certainly reinforced (or possibly reintroduced, we simply do not know yet) by the British, has become the most deeply entrenched of all political notions. Sri Lanka today sees itself not as an Island Empire, but as an Island Nation. The profound and persistent impossibility of complexifying sovereignty experienced by the Lankan state may well be the ultimate sign that the legacy of colonialism—and not just British colonialism— remains disturbingly alive in the post-colonial nation.

*

History keeps producing connections and disconnections, convergences and divergences. Historiography pulsates in similar ways. Whenever a paradigm comes along, voraciously consuming our attention for a decade or two, the next paradigm is already around a corner, readying itself for a chase. There are signs that a backlash to global history might be in the making, either as an act of genuine soul-searching in the face of the current global crisis, or as a rather cynical response to what is sometimes perceived as the excessive optimism and cosmopolitanism of global historians.[23] It would be perfect if we could pause for a moment, free to grasp the global sixteenth century with all its contradictions, and allowed not to resolve them. Perhaps we could indeed describe this methodological state of grace as conducive to a '(dis)connected history' or a 'critical connected history' of global early modernity.

Islands tell us all that we need about the challenge we face.[24] They tend to be open to the world *and* capable of cordoning themselves off, connected and disconnected, ready to converge with and diverge from the rest of the planet as they are exposed to, but not defenceless in the face of, moving people, things and ideas. No society, no single person ever lives in full isolation, and yet each and every human being has the ability to activate boundaries as well as breaking them down. To understand past societies, to understand ourselves, it seems unreasonable not to embrace the full set of contradictions built into our archipelagic condition. It is also more helpful than ever to remind ourselves of the deceptively prosaic warning heard in the mother of all novels, written when Spain and Portugal dreamed of ruling the world, by the little man who dreamed of ruling an isle: 'look, Sancho, from just one side you can't see all of whatever you may be looking at'.[25]

[23] See Introduction and Chapter 1.
[24] I have taken much inspiration throughout this book from Alan Strathern, *Kingship and Conversion*. This final paragraph owes even more to our conversations about *Sri Lanka at the Crossroads of History* (London: UCL Press, 2017), and especially the portentous summary offered therein by Strathern on 'The digestion of the foreign in Lankan history, c. 500–1818', pp. 216–38.
[25] Miguel de Cervantes, *Don Quixote*, translated by Edith Grossman (New York: Harper Collins, 2003), second part, chapter 41, p. 726.

# Glossary and List of Rulers

*Ārachchi*: military leader

*Cakravarti*: literally, 'Turner of the Wheel', emperor

*Câmara municipal*: municipal council

*Casados*: official residents, married subjects of the Portuguese crown

*Däkum*: tributary ceremony

*Estado*: *Estado da Índia*, includes all Portuguese crown possessions east of the Cape

*Feitor*: chief officer in charge of a *feitoria*

*Feitoria*: official crown trading post

*Governador*: governor of the *Estado*; some were also *vice-reis*

*Lascarins*: Asian soldiers fighting for the Portuguese

*Língua*: interpreter

*Ouvidor*: crown official with juridical functions

*Mahārājan*: great king

*Mudaliyār*: high-ranking leader

*Purohita*: alter ego of the Lankan monarch

*Rāja*: ruler, King

*Vedor*: royally appointed overseer

*Vice-rei*: viceroy of the *Estado*; every viceroy was also *governador*, but not vice-versa

## KINGS OF PORTUGAL

John II (1481–95)

Manuel I (1495–1521)

John III (1521–57)

Regencies of Catherine and Henry (1557–68)

Sebastian (1568–78)

Henry (1578–80) Anthony (publicly acclaimed, 1580–82)

Phillip II of Spain (1581–98)

Phillip III of Spain (1598–1621)

## KINGS OF KŌṬṬE

Parākramabāhu VI (c.1411–67)

Jayavīra Parākramabāhu (1466–9)

Bhuvanekabāhu VI (1469–77)

Paṇḍita Parākramabāhu VII (1477)

Vīra Parākramabāhu VIII (1477–89)

Dharma Parākramabāhu IX (1489–1513)

Vijayabāhu VI (1513–21)

Bhuvanekabāhu VII (1521–51)

Vīdiyē Baṇḍāra (regent 1551)

Dharmapāla (1551–97), known as Dom João from 1557

## KINGS OF SĪTĀVAKA

Māyādunnē (1521–78/81)

Rājasiṃha I (1578/81–93)

Rājasūriya (1593–4) Jayavīra (1594)

## KINGS OF UDARAṬA/KANDY

Sēnāsammata Vikramabāhu (1469–1511)

Jayavīra or Vijayavīra Baṇḍāra (1511–52)

Karaliyaddē Baṇḍāra (1552–82)

Rājasiṃha I (1582–9)

Dom Francisco Vesugo (regent, c.1589–90)

Yamasiṃha, baptised as Dom Filipe (1590–2)

Vimaladharmasūriya I, formerly Konappu Baṇḍāra (1592–1604)

Senarat (1604–35)

Rājasiṃha II (1635–87)

## KINGS OF JAFFNA

Singai Pararājasekaran (1478–1519)

Caṇkili Segarājasekaran (1519–61)

Puvirāja Paṇḍāram Pararājasekaran (1561–5 and 1582–91)

Periyapillai (1565–82)

Ethirimanna ciṅkam Pararājasekaran (1591–1616)

Caṇkili Kumaran II (1616–20)

## GOVERNORS AND VICEROYS AT GOA

Francisco de Almeida (vr 1505–9)

Afonso de Albuquerque (1509–15)

Lopo Soares de Albergaria (1515–18)

Diogo Lopes de Sequeira (1518–22)

Duarte de Meneses (1522–4)

Vasco da Gama (vr 1524)

Henrique de Meneses (1524–6)

Lopo Vaz de Sampaio (1526–9)

Nuno da Cunha (1529–38)

Garcia de Noronha (vr 1538–40)

Estêvão da Gama (1540–2)

Martim Afonso de Sousa (1542–5)

João de Castro (vr 1545–8)

Garcia de Sá (1548–9)

Jorge Cabral (1549–50)

Afonso de Noronha (vr 1550–4)

Pedro Mascarenhas (vr 1554–5)

Francisco Barreto (1555–8)

Constantino de Bragança (vr 1558–61)

Francisco Coutinho (vr 1561–4)

João de Mendonça Furtado (1564)

Antão de Noronha (vr 1564–8)

Luís de Ataíde (vr 1568–71)

António de Noronha (1571–3)

António Moniz Barreto (1573–6)

Diogo de Meneses (1576–8)

Luís de Ataíde (vr 1578–80)

Fernão Teles de Meneses (1581)

Francisco Mascarenhas (vr 1581–4)

Duarte de Meneses (vr 1584–8)

Manuel de Sousa Coutinho (1588–91)

Matias de Albuquerque (vr 1591–7)

Francisco da Gama (vr 1597–1600)

Aires de Saldanha (vr 1600–5)

Martim Afonso de Castro (vr 1605–7)

Aleixo de Meneses (1607–9)

# Bibliography

## ARCHIVAL MATERIALS

**Lisbon:**
- Arquivo Histórico Ultramarino: *Caixas da Índia*; *Códices*
- Arquivo Nacional da Torre do Tombo: *Cartas dos Vice-Reis*; *Chancelaria de D. João III*; *Corpo Cronólogico*; *Gavetas*; *São Lourenço*; *Monções*
- Biblioteca Nacional de Lisboa: *Reservados*

**London:**
- British Library: *Additional Manuscripts*; *Egerton*

**Goa:**
- Historical Archives of Goa: *Monções*

**Madrid:**
- Biblioteca Nacional de España: *Manuscritos*

**Rio de Janeiro:**
- Biblioteca Nacional: *Rendas da India; Reservados*

**Simancas:**
- Archivo General de Simancas: *Secretarías Provinciales—Portugal*

## PUBLISHED PRIMARY MATERIALS

*Alakesvara Yuddhaya,* edited by A. V. Suravira (Colombo: Ratan Book Publishers, 1965).

Albuquerque, Afonso de, *Cartas de Afonso de Albuquerque, seguidas de documentos que as elucidam,* edited by Raimundo António de Bulhão Pato, 7 vols. (Lisbon: Academia Real das Ciências, 1884–1935).

Albuquerque, Brás de, *Comentários de Afonso de Albuquerque, 5a edição, conforme à 2a edição, de 1576,* edited by Joaquim Veríssimo Serrão (Lisbon: IN-CM, 1973).

Albuquerque, Luís de and José Pereira da Costa, 'Cartas de "serviços" da Índia (1500–1530)', in *Mare Liberum,* 1 (1990), pp. 309–96.

Andrade, Francisco de, *Crónica de D. João III,* edited by M. Lopes de Almeida (Porto: Lello & Irmão, 1976).

Anonymous, 'Livro que trata das cousas da Índia e do Japão', editado por Adelino de Almeida Calado, in *Boletim da Biblioteca da Universidade de Coimbra,* 24 (1960), pp. 1–138.

*Archivo Portuguez-Oriental,* edited by Joaquim Heliodoro da Cunha Rivara, reprint, 6 fascicles in 10 parts (New Delhi: Asian Educational Service, 1992).

*Atlas du Vicomte de Santarém. Edition fac-similée des cartes définitives,* edited by Martim de Albuquerque (Lisbon: Administração do Porto de Lisboa/CNCDP, 1989).

Barbosa, Duarte, *O Livro de Duarte Barbosa, edição crítica e anotada,* edited by Maria Augusta da Veiga e Sousa, 2 vols. (Lisbon: MCT/IICT/CNCDP, 1996–2000).

Barros, João de, *Ásia de João de Barros. Dos feitos que os Portugueses fizeram no descobrimento e conquista dos mares e terras do Oriente,* edited by António Baião and Luís F. Lindley Sintra, reprint, 4 vols. (Lisbon: IN-CM, 1988–2001).

Biker, Júlio Firmino Júdice, *Collecção de Tratados e Concertos de Pazes que o Estado da India fez com os Reis e Senhores com que teve relações nas partes da Asia e Africa Oriental: desde o princípio da conquista até ao século 18*, 14 vols (Lisbon: Imprensa Nacional, 1881–7).

Bluteau, Rafael, *Vocabulario Portuguez e Latino*, 10 vols. (Coimbra: No Collegio das Artes da Companhia de Jesu, 1712–28).

Bracciolini, Poggio, *De l'Inde. Les voyages en Asie de Nicolò de' Conti. De varietate fortunae. Livre IV*, edited and translated by Michèle Guéret-Laferté (Turnhout: Brepols, 2004).

Brásio, António, 'Uma carta inédita de Valentim Fernandes', *Boletim da Biblioteca da Universidade de Coimbra*, 24 (1960), pp. 338–58.

*Bullarium Patronatus Portugalliae Regum in Ecclesis Africae, Asiae Atque Oceaniae*, edited by Levy Maria Jordão, Viscount of Paiva Manso, 3 vols. (Lisbon: Typographia Nacional, 1868–79).

Castanheda, Fernão Lopes de, *História do Descobrimento e Conquista da Índia pelos Portugueses*, edited by M. Lopes de Almeida, 2 vols. (Porto: Lello & Irmão, 1979).

Castro, João de, *Obras completas de D. João de Castro*, edited by Armando Cortesão and Luís de Albuquerque, 4 vols. (Coimbra: Imprensa da Universidade de Coimbra, 1968–81).

Castro, João de, *Cartas de D. João de Castro a D. João III*, edited by Luís de Albuquerque (Lisbon: Alfa, 1989).

Chitty, Simon Casie, 'A Royal Grant Engraved on a Copper Plate', *Journal of the Ceylon Branch of the Royal Asiatic Society*, 1, 3 (1848), pp. 109–10.

Correia, Gaspar, *Lendas da Índia*, edited by M. Lopes de Almeida, 4 vols. (Porto: Lello & Irmão, 1975).

Cortés, Hernán, *Cartas de Relación*, edited by Mario Hernández Sánchez-Barba (Madrid: Dastin, 2000).

Cortesão, Armando and Avelino Teixeira da Mota, *Portugaliae Monumenta Cartographica*, 5 vols. (Lisbon: PMC, 1960).

Couto, Diogo do, *Da Asia de Diogo do Couto Dos Feitos, que os Portuguezes fizeram na Conquista, e Descubrimento das Terras, e Mares do Oriente*, 15 vols. (Lisbon: Livraria de São Carlos, 1973–5).

Couto, Diogo do, *O Soldado Prático. Texto restituído, prefácio e notas*, edited by M. Rodrigues Lapa, 3rd edition (Lisbon: Sá da Costa, 1980).

Couto, Diogo do, *O Primeiro Soldado Prático*, edited by António Coimbra Martins (Lisbon: CNCDP, 2001).

*Cūlavamsa, being the more recent part of the Mahavamsa*, transl. into German by W. Geiger and from the German into English by C. R. Rickmers, 2 vols. (London: n. p., 1929).

D'Intino, Raffaella, ed., *Enformação das cousas da China. Textos do século XVI* (Lisbon: IN-CM, 1989).

*Documenta Indica*, edited by Joseph Wicki (Rome: Monumenta Historica Societatis Iesu, 1948–).

*Documentação Ultramarina Portuguesa*, edited by António da Silva Rego, 5 vols. (Lisbon: CEHU, 1960–7).

*Documentos Remettidos da India ou Livros das Monções*, edited by Raymundo Antonio Bulhão Pato and António da Silva Rego, 10 vols. (Lisbon: Academia Real das Sciencias/ Imprensa Nacional, 1880–1982).

*Documentos sobre os Portugueses em Moçambique e na África Central, 1497–1840/Documents on the Portuguese in Mozambique and Central Asia, 1497–1840*, 9 vols. (Lisbon: CEHU/ National Archives of Rhodesia), 1962–89.

*Epigraphia Zeylanica: being lithic and other inscriptions of Ceylon*, 8 vols. (London/Colombo: Henry Frowde/Sri Lanka Archaeological Survey, 1912–2001).

Ferguson, Donald, *The History of Ceylon, from the Earliest Times to 1600 A.D., related by João de Barros and Diogo de Couto* (Colombo: Royal Asiatic Society, 1909).

*Gavetas (As) da Torre do Tombo*, 12 vols. (Lisbon: CEHU, 1960–77).

Góis, Damião de, *Crónica do felicíssimo rei D. Manuel, edição nova conforme à de 1566*, 4 vols. (Coimbra: Universidade de Coimbra, 1949–55).

Gonzaga, Francisco, *De origine Seraphicae Ordinis Franciscanae ejusque progressibus de Regularis observantiae institutione* (Rome: Ex Typographia Dominici Basae, 1587).

Loureiro, Rui Manuel, *Cartas dos cativos de Cantão (1524?)* (Lisbon: Instituto Cultural de Macau, 1992).

*Māha Hatana (The Great War)*, edited by Albert De Silva (Colombo: Vidyasagara Printers, 1896).

*Mahāvamsa or the Great Chronicle of Ceylon*, translated into English by Wilhelm Geiger (London: Oxford University Press for the Pali Text Society, 1912).

Mercator, Gerardus and Jodocus Hondius, *Gerardi Mercatoris Atlas sive Cosmographicae Meditationes de Fabrica Mundi* (Amsterdam: In aedibus Iudoci Hondij, 1606).

Paranavitana, Karunasena Dias and Rajpal Kumar de Silva, *Maps and Plans of Dutch Ceylon. A representative collection of cartography from the Dutch period* (Colombo: The Central Cultural Fund/Sri Lanka—Netherlands Association, 2002).

Pereira, António dos Santos, 'A Índia a preto e branco: uma carta oportuna, escrita em Cochim, por D. Constantino de Bragança, à rainha Dona Catarina', *Anais de História de Além-Mar*, 4 (2003), pp. 449–84.

Perniola, Vito, *The Catholic Church in Sri Lanka. The Portuguese Period. Original Documents translated into English*, 3 vols. (Dehiwala: Tisara Prakasakayo, 1989–91).

Pieris, Paulus E. and M. A. Hedwig Fitzler, *Ceylon and Portugal*, Part I, Kings and Christians 1539–52 (Leipzig: Asia Major, 1927).

Pinto, Fernão Mendes, *The Travels of Mendes Pinto*, edited and translated by Rebecca Catz (London/Chicago, IL: University of Chicago Press, 1989).

Pires, Tomé, *A Suma Oriental de Tomé Pires e o Livro de Francisco Rodrigues*, edited by Armando Cortesão (Coimbra: Imprensa da Universidade, 1978).

Polo, Marco, *O livro de Marco Paulo—O livro de Nicolao Veneto*, edited by Francisco Maria Esteves Pereira (Lisbon: Biblioteca Nacional de Lisboa, 1922).

Polo, Marco, *Milione. Le divisament dou monde. Il Milione nelle redazioni toscana e franco-italiana*, edited by Gabriella Ronchi (Milan: Mondadori, 1982).

Queiroz, Fernão de, *Conquista Temporal e Espiritual de Ceilão* (Colombo: Government Press, 1916).

Queiroz, Fernão de, *The Temporal and Spiritual Conquest of Ceylon*, transl. Father S. G. Perera (Colombo: A. C. Richards Government Printer, 1930).

Radulet, Carmen M. and Luís Filipe F. R. Thomaz, *Viagens portuguesas à Índia (1497–1513). Fontes italianas para a sua história* (Lisbon: CNCDP, 2002).

*Rājasīnha Hatana (Rājasīnha's War)*, edited by H. M. Somaratna (Kandy, 1968).

*Rājāvaliya (The) or a Historical Narrative of the Sinhalese Kings from Vijaya to Vimala Dharmasuriya II*, edited by B. Gunasekara, reprint (New Delhi: Asian Educational Service, 1995).

Ribeiro, João de, *Fatalidade Histórica da Ilha de Ceilão*, edited by Luís de Albuquerque (Lisbon: Alfa, 1989).

Schurhammer, Georg and Ernst August Voretzsch, *Ceylon zur Zeit des Königs Bhuvaneka Bahu und Franz Xavers 1539–1552. Quellen zur Geschichte der Portugiesen, sowie der Franziskaner- und Jesuitenmission auf Ceylon, im Urtext herausgegeben und erklärt*, 2 vols. (Leipzig: Verlag der Asia Major, 1928).

Shirley, Anthony, *Peso Politico de todo el Mundo del Conde D. Antonio Xerley*, edited by Carmelo Viñas Mey (Madrid: Instituto Balmes de Sociología, 1961).

Silveira, Francisco Rodrigues da, *Reformação da Milícia e Governo do Estado da Índia Oriental*, edited by Benjamin N. Teensma, Luís Filipe Barreto and George Davison Winius (Lisbon: Fundação Oriente, 1996).

*Sītāvaka Hatana (The Sītāvaka War)*, edited by Rohini Paranavitana (Colombo: Ministry of Cultural Affairs, 1999).

Trindade, Frei Paulo da, *Conquista Espiritual do Oriente*, edited by Félix Lopes, 3 vols. (Lisbon: CEHU, 1962–7).

Vartema, Lodovico, 'Itinerario di Lodovico Barthema', in Giovanni Battista Ramusio, *Navigazione e Viaggi*, edited by Marica Milanesi (Turin: Giulio Einaudi, 1978), vol. I, pp. 755–893.

Vignati, Antonella, ed., 'Vida e Acções de Matias de Albuquerque Capitão e Viso-Rei da Índia', in *Mare Liberum*, 15 (June 1998), pp. 139–245 and 17 (June 1999) pp. 237–360.

Viterbo, Sousa, *O thesouro do rei de Ceylão* (Lisbon: Typographia da Academia Real das Sciencias, 1904).

Xavier, Francis, *Monumenta Xaveriana, ex autographis vel ex antiquioribus exemplis collecta*, 2 vols. (Madrid: Typis Augustini Aurial, 1899–1912).

Xavier, Francis, *Epistolae S. Francisci Xaverii aliaque eius scripta, nova editio ex integro refecta*, edited by Georg Schurhammer and Joseph Wicki, 2 vols. (Rome: Monumenta Historica Societatis Iesu, 1944–5).

Zainuddin Makhdoom, *História dos Portugueses no Malabar por Zinadím. Manuscrito árabe do século XVI traduzido e anotado*, edited by David Lopes, 2nd ed. (Lisbon: Antígona, 1998).

SECONDARY LITERATURE

Abeyasinghe, Tikiri, 'The Myth of the Malvana Convention', *Ceylon Journal of Historical and Social Studies* 7, 1 (1964), pp. 67–72.

Abeyasinghe, Tikiri, *Portuguese Rule in Ceylon 1594–1612* (Colombo: Lake House, 1966).

Abeyasinghe, Tikiri, 'The Politics of Survival: Aspects of Kandyan External Relations in the Mid-Sixteenth Century', *Journal of the Royal Asiatic Society of Sri Lanka*, New Series, XVII (1973), pp. 11–21.

Abeyasinghe, Tikiri, 'Portuguese Documents on the Last Days of the Sitawaka Kingdom 1593–1594', *Journal of the Royal Asiatic Society of Sri Lanka*, New Series, 24 (1978–9), pp. 86–91.

Abeyasinghe, Tikiri, 'The kingdom of Kandy: foundations and foreign relations to 1638', in *University of Peradeniya History of Sri* Lanka, edited by K. M. De Silva (Peradeniya: University of Peradeniya, 1995), vol. II, pp. 139–61.

Abhayawardana, H. A. P., *Boundary Books of Mediaeval Sri Lanka* (Colombo: Academy of Sri Lankan Culture, 1999).

Adelman, Jeremy, 'What is global History now?', *Aeon* (2017), https://aeon.co/essays/is-global-history-still-possible-or-has-it-had-its-moment (last accessed 20 September 2017).

Adelman, Jeremy and Stephen Aron, 'From Borderlands to Borders: Empires, Nation-States, and the Peoples in Between in North American History', *American Historical Review*, 104 (1999), pp. 814–41.

AHR Conversation 'On Transnational History', *American Historical Review*, 111, 5 (2006), pp. 1441–64.

Albuquerque, Luís de, *O Tratado de Tordesilhas e as dificuldades técnicas da sua aplicação rigorosa* (Coimbra: Universidade de Coimbra, 1973).

Alcock, Susan et al., eds., *Empires. Perspectives from Archaeology and History* (Cambridge: Cambridge University Press, 2001).

Alexandrowicz, Charles Henry, *An Introduction to the History of the Law of Nations (16th, 17th and 18th Centuries)* (Oxford: Clarendon Press, 1967).

Almeida, Onésimo T., 'Experiência a madre das cousas—experience, the mother of things —on the "revolution of experience" in 16th-century Portuguese maritime discoveries and its foundational role in the emergence of the scientific worldview', in *Portuguese Humanism and the Republic of Letters*, edited by M. Berbara and K. Enenkel (Leiden: Brill, 2011), pp. 381–400.

Altman, Ida, *The War for Mexico's West. Indians and Spaniards in New Galicia, 1524–1550* (Albuquerque, NM: University of New Mexico Press, 2010).

Alves, Ana Maria, *Iconologia do poder real no período manuelino. À procura de uma linguagem perdida* (Lisbon: IN-CM, 1985).

Alves, Ana Maria, *As Entradas Régias Portuguesas. Uma Visão de Conjunto* (Lisbon: Livros Horizonte, 1986).

Anderson, Benedict, *Imagined Communities. Reflections on the Origin and Spread of Nationalism*, revised edition (London/New York: Verso, 1991).

André, Jacques and Jean Filliozat, *L'Inde vue de Rome. Textes latins de l'Antiquité relatifs à l'Inde* (Paris: Belles Lettres, 1986).

Antoninus, A. J. B., *The Martyrs of Mannar. Second enlarged edition* (Colombo: St Joseph Press, 1945).

Antunes, Luís Frederico, 'Algumas considerações sobre os prazos de Baçaim e Damão', *Anais de História de Além-Mar*, 3 (2002), pp. 231–57.

Arasaratnam, Sinnappah, *Maritime India in the Seventeenth Century* (Oxford: Oxford University Press, 1994).

Armitage, David, *The Ideological Origins of the British Empire* (Cambridge: Cambridge University Press, 2000).

Armitage, David, 'The Elephant and the Whale: Empires of Land and Sea,' *Journal for Maritime Research*, 9, 1 (2007), pp. 23–36.

Armstrong, John A., *Nations before Nationalism* (Chapel Hill, NC: University of North Carolina Press, 1982).

Asch, Ronald and Dagmar Freist, eds., *Staatsbildung als kultureller Prozess. Strukturwandel und Legitimation von Herrschaft in der Frühen Neuzeit* (Cologne: Böhlau, 2005).

Assayag, Jackie, 'La caste entre histoire et anthropologie. Le "grand jeu" interprétatif', *Annales HSS*, 58, 4 (2003), pp. 815–30.

Aubin, Jean, 'L'apprentissage de l'Inde. Cochin, 1503–1504', *Moyen-Orient et Océan Indien, XVIe-XIXe siècles*, 4 (1987), pp. 1–96.

Bailey, Gauvin Alexander, *The Andean Hybrid Baroque: Converging Cultures in the Churches of Colonial Peru* (Notre Dame, IN: University of Notre Dame Press, 2010).

Barata, António Francisco, 'Regimento da Gente da Ordenança e das vinte lanças da Guarda', *Archivo Histórico Portuguez*, I (1903), pp. 80–8.

Barata, Maria do Rosário Themudo, *As regências na menoridade de D. Sebastião. Elementos para uma história estrutural*, 2 vols. (Lisbon: IN-CM, 1992).

Barreto, Luís Filipe, *Descobrimentos e Renascimento. Formas de ser e pensar nos séculos XV e XVI* (Lisbon: IN-CM, 1983).

Baud, Michel and Willem Van Schendel, 'Toward a Comparative History of Borderlands', *Journal of World History*, 8, 2 (1997), pp. 211–42.

Bayly, Christopher A., *Indian Society and the Making of the British Empire* (Cambridge: Cambridge University Press, 1988).

Bechert, Heinz, 'Mother Right and Succession to the Throne in Malabar and Ceylon', in *The Ceylon Journal of Historical and Social Studies*, 6 (1962), pp. 25–40.

Bell, Coral, *The End of the Vasco da Gama Era. The Next Landscape in World Politics* (Sydney: Lowy Institute for International Policy, 2007).

Bennett, Tony and Patrick Joyce, 'Material powers: Introduction', in *Material Powers: Cultural Studies, History and the Material Turn*, edited by Tony Bennett and Patrick Joyce (London/New York: Routledge, 2010), pp. 1–22.

Benton, Lauren, *A Search for Sovereignty. Law and Geography in European Empires, 1400–1900* (Cambridge: Cambridge University Press, 2009).

Berend, Nora, 'Défense de la chrétienté et naissance d'une identité. Hongrie, Pologne et péninsule ibérique au Moyen Âge', *Annales HSS*, 58, 5 (2003), pp. 1009–27.

Berger, Mark T., 'From Commerce to Conquest: The Dynamics of British Mercantile Imperialism in Eighteenth-Century Bengal, and the Foundation of the British Indian Empire', *Bulletin of Concerned Asian Scholars*, 22, 1 (1990), pp. 44–62.

Berkemer, Georg, *Little Kingdoms in Kalinga. Ideologie, Legitimation und Politik regionaler Eliten* (Stuttgart: Franz Steiner, 1993).

Berkemer, Georg, and Margret Frenz, 'Little Kingdoms or Princely States? Trajectories towards a (theoretical) conception', *Indian Historical Review*, 32, 2 (2005), pp. 104–21.

Berkwitz, Stephen C., *Buddhist Poetry and Colonialism: Alagiyavanna and the Portuguese in Sri Lanka* (Oxford: Oxford University Press, 2013).

Bertrand, Romain, *L'histoire à parts égales. Récits d'une rencontre, Orient-Occident (XVIe–XVIIe siècle)* (Paris: Seuil, 2011).

Bertrand, Romain, *Le long remords the la conquête. Manille-Mexico-Madrid: l'affaire Diego de Ávila (1577–1580)* (Paris: Seuil, 2011).

Bethencourt, Francisco, 'A Inquisição', in *Portugal: Mitos Revisitados*, edited by Yvette K. Centeno et al. (Lisbon: Edições Salamandra, 1993), pp. 99–138.

Bethencourt, Francisco, *História das Inquisições. Portugal, Espanha e Itália* (Lisbon: Temas e Debates, 1996).

Bethencourt, Francisco, 'Political configuations and local powers', in *Portuguese Oceanic Expansion, 1400–1800*, edited by Francisco Bethencourt and Diogo Ramada Curto (Cambridge: Cambridge University Press, 2007), pp. 197–254.

Bethencourt, Francisco and Kirti Chaudhuri, eds., *História da Expansão Portuguesa*, 5 vols. (Lisbon: Círculo de Leitores, 1998).

Betts, Raymond F., *Europe Overseas: Phases of Imperialism* (New York: Basic Books, 1968).

Biedermann, Zoltán, 'A última carta de Francisco de Albuquerque (Cochim, 31 de Dezembro de 1503)', *Anais de História de Além-Mar*, 3 (2002), pp. 123–53.

Biedermann, Zoltán, 'De regresso ao Quarto Império', in *D. João III e o Império. Actas do Congresso Internacional*, edited by Roberto Carneiro and Artur Teodoro de Matos (Lisbon: CHAM/CEPCEP, 2004), pp. 103–20.

Biedermann, Zoltán, 'Colombo versus Cannanore: Contrasting Structures of Two Early Colonial Port Cities in South Asia', *Journal of the Economic and Social History of the Orient*, 53, 2 (2009), pp. 413–59.

Biedermann, Zoltán, 'The Matrioshka Principle and How it was Overcome: Portuguese and Habsburg Attitudes toward Imperial Authority in Sri Lanka and the Responses of the Rulers of Kotte (1506–1656)', *Journal of Early Modern History*, 13, 4 (2009), pp. 265–310.

Biedermann, Zoltán, 'El espacio sujeto al tiempo en la cronística franciscana: una relectura de la "Conquista Espiritual do Oriente" de Fr. Paulo da Trindade', *Cuadernos de Historia Moderna*, Anejo XIII (2014), pp. 221–42.

Biedermann, Zoltán, *The Portuguese in Sri Lanka and South India. Studies in the History of Empire, Diplomacy and Trade, 1500–1650* (Wiesbaden: Harrassowitz, 2014).

Biedermann, Zoltán, 'The Temporal Politics of Spiritual Conquest: History, Geography and the Logics of Franciscan Orientalism in the Work of Friar Paulo da Trindade', in *Culture and History Digital Journal*, 5, 2 (2016), online publication.

Biedermann, Zoltán, 'Cosmopolitan Converts. The Politics of Lankan Exile in the Portuguese Empire', in *Sri Lanka at the Crossroads of History*, edited by Zoltán Biedermann and Alan Strathern (London: UCL Press, 2017), pp. 141–60.

Biedermann, Zoltán, 'Imperial Reflections: China, Rome and the Logics of Global History in the *Décadas da Ásia* of João de Barros', in *Empires on the Move/Empires en marche*, edited by François Lachaud and Dejanirah Couto (Paris: EFEO, 2017), pp. 23–47.

Biedermann, Zoltán, 'Diplomatic Ivories: Sri Lankan Caskets and the European-Asian Diplomatic Exchange, 1500–1600', in *Global Gifts. The Material Culture of Diplomacy in Early Modern Eurasia*, edited by Zoltán Biedermann, Anne Gerritsen and Giorgio Riello (New York: Cambridge University Press, 2018), pp. 88–118.

Biggs, Michael, 'Putting the State on the Map: Cartography, Territory, and European State Formation', *Comparative Studies in Society and History*, 41, 2 (1999), pp. 374–405.

Bosbach, Franz, *Monarchia Universalis. Ein politischer Leitbegriff der frühen Neuzeit* (Göttingen: Vandenhoek & Ruprecht, 1988).

Bouchon, Geneviève, 'Les rois de Kotte au début du XVIe siècle', in *Mare Luso-Indicum*, 1 (1971), pp. 65–96 and 163–8.

Bouchon, Geneviève, *Mamale de Cananor. Un adversaire de l'Inde portugaise (1507–1528)* (Genève/Paris: Librairie Droz, 1975).

Bouchon, Geneviève, 'A propos de l'inscription de Colombo (1501). Quelques observations sur le premier voyage de João da Nova dans l'Océan Indien', *Revista da Universidade de Coimbra*, 28 (1980), pp. 233–70.

Bouza Álvarez, Fernando, 'Portugal en la Monarquía Hispánica (1580–1640). Felipe II, las Cortes de Tomar y la Génesis del Portugal Católico' (PhD dissertation, Universidad Complutense de Madrid, 1997).

Bouza Álvarez, Fernando, 'Portugal en la política internacional de Felipe II: *por el suelo el mundo en pedazos*', in *A União Ibérica e o Mundo Atlântico*, edited by Maria da Graça Ventura (Lisbon: Colibri, 1997), pp. 29–46.

Bouza Álvarez, Fernando, *Portugal no Tempo dos Filipes. Política, Cultura, Representações (1580–1668)* (Lisbon: Cosmos, 2000).

Boxer, Charles, *Portuguese Conquest and Commerce in Southern Asia, 1500–1750* (London: Variorum Reprints, 1985).

Boxer, Charles Ralph, *The Christian Century in Japan 1549–1650* (Los Angeles, CA/ Cambridge: University of California Press/Cambridge University Press, 1951).

Boxer, Charles Ralph, *Portuguese Society in the Tropics. The Municipal Councils of Goa, Macao, Bahia, and Luanda, 1510–1800* (Madison/Milwaukee, WI: University of Wisconsin Press, 1965).

Boxer, Charles Ralph, 'Portuguese and Spanish Projects for the Conquest of Southeast Asia, 1580–1600', *Journal of Asian History*, 3 (1969), pp. 118–36.

Boyajian, James C., *Portuguese Trade under the Habsburgs 1580–1640* (Baltimore, MD/ London: Johns Hopkins University Press, 1992).

Bozeman, Adda B., *Politics and Culture in International History* (Princeton, NJ: Princeton University Press, 1960).

Brothers, Cammy, 'The Renaissance Reception of the Alhambra: The Letters of Andrea Navagero and the Palace of Charles V', *Muqarnas*, 11 (1994), pp. 79–102.

Brown, Jonathan and John H. Elliott, *A Palace for a King: The Buen Retiro and the Court of Philip IV* (New Haven, CT: Yale University Press, 1980).

Buescu, Maria Leonor Carvalhão, *O estudo das línguas exóticas no século XVI* (Lisbon: Instituto de Cultura e Língua Portuguesa, 1983).

Burghardt, A. F., 'A hypothesis about Gateway Cities', *Annals of the Association of American Geographers*, 61, 2 (1971), pp. 269–85.

Cañeque, Alejandro, *The King's Living Image: The Culture and Politics of Viceregal Power in Colonial Mexico* (New York: Routledge, 2004).

Cañizares-Esguerra, Jorge, *Puritan Conquistadors. Iberianizing the Atlantic, 1550–1700* (Stanford, CA: Stanford University Press, 2006).

Cañizares-Esguerra, Jorge, 'Entangled Histories: Borderland Historiographies in New Clothes?', *American Historical Review*, 112 (June 2007), pp. 787–99.

Cardim, Pedro, Tamar Herzog, José Javier Ruiz Ibáñez and Gaetano Sabatini, eds., *Polycentric Monarchies. How did Early Modern Spain and Portugal Achieve and Maintain a Global Hegemony?* (Eastbourne: Sussex Academic Press, 2012).

Cattaneo, Angelo, 'Venice, Florence, and Lisbon. Commercial routes and networks of knowledge, 1300–1550', in *Encompassing the Globe. Portugal and the World in the 16th and 17th centuries*, edited by Jay Levenson (Washington, DC: Freer and Sackler Galleries, 2007), vol. II, pp. 13–21.

Cattaneo, Angelo, *Fra Mauro's Mappamundi and Fifteenth-Century Venetian Culture* (Turnhout: Brepols, 2011).

Cervantes, Miguel de, *Don Quixote*, translated by Edith Grossman (New York: Harper Collins, 2003).

Chartier, Roger, 'Construção do Estado Moderno e formas culturais. Perspectivas e questões', in *A História Cultural entre Práticas e Representações*, edited by Roger Chartier (Lisbon: Difel, 1988), pp. 215–29.

Chitty, Simon Casie, 'A Royal Grant Engraved on a Copper Plate', *Journal of the Ceylon Branch of the Royal Asiatic Society*, 1, 3 (1848), pp. 109–10.

Clarence-Smith, William Gervase, Kenneth Pomeranz and Peer Vries, 'Editorial', *Journal of Global History*, 1, 1 (2006), pp. 1–2.

Clendinnen, Inga, *Ambivalent Conquest. Maya and Spaniard in Yucatan, 1517–1570* (Cambridge: Cambridge University Press, 1989).

Codrington, H. W., 'Medieval Mercenary Forces in Ceylon', *Ceylon Literary Register*, Third Series, III, 9 (1934), pp. 385–92.

Codrington, H. W., *Ancient Land Tenure and Revenue in Ceylon*, Colombo, 1938.

Cohn, Bernard S., 'Political Systems in Eighteenth Century India: the Benares Region', *Journal of the American Oriental Society*, 82, 3 (1962), pp. 312–20.

Collins, Steven, *Nirvana and Other Buddhist Felicities. Utopias of the Pāli Imaginaire* (Cambridge: Cambridge University Press, 1998).

Conrad, David C., *Empires of Medieval West Africa. Ghana, Mali and Songhay*, revised edition (New York: Chelsea House, 2010).

Costa, João Paulo Oliveira e, 'Do sonho manuelino ao realismo joanino. Novos documentos sobre as relações luso-chinesas na terceira década do século XVI', *Studia*, 50 (1991), pp. 121–56.

Costa, João Paulo Oliveira e, 'A nobreza e a expansão. Particularidades de um fenómeno complexo', in *A Nobreza e a Expansão. Estudos biográficos* (Cascais: Patrimonia Historica, 2000), pp. 13–51.

Costa, João Paulo Oliveira e, 'A diáspora missionária', in *História Religiosa de Portugal*, edited by Carlos Moreira Azevedo (Lisbon: Círculo de Leitores, 2000–2), vol. II, pp. 255–313.

Costa, João Paulo Oliveira e, 'O império português em meados do século XVI', *Anais de História da Além-Mar*, 3 (2002), pp. 87–121.

Costa, João Paulo Oliveira and Vítor Luís Gaspar Rodrigues, *Portugal y Oriente: El proyecto indiano del Rey Juan* (Madrid: Fundación Mapfre, 1992).

Couto, Dejanirah, 'Em torno da concessão da fortaleza de Baçaim (1529–46)', *Mare Liberum*, 9 (1995), pp. 117–32.

Couto, Dejanirah, 'Quelques observations sur les renégats portugais en Asie au XVIeme siècle', *Mare Liberum*, 16 (1998), pp. 57–85.

Cruz, Maria Augusta Lima, 'Exiles and renegades in early sixteenth-century Portuguese India', *The Indian Economic and Social History Review*, 23, 3 (July–Sept. 1986), pp. 249–62.

Cunha, Mafalda Soares da, 'A questão jurídica na crise dinástica', in *História de Portugal*, edited by José Mattoso (Lisbon: Círculo de Leitores, 1993–4), vol. III, pp. 552–9.

Cunha, Mafalda Soares da, 'A Casa de Bragança e a Expansão, séculos XV–XVII', in *A Alta Nobreza e a Fundação do Estado da Índia*, edited by João Paulo Oliveira e Costa and Vítor Luís Gaspar Rodrigues (Lisbon: CHAM/IICT, 2004), pp. 303–19.

Dalché, Patrick Gautier, *La Géographie de Ptolémée en Occident (IVe–XVIe siècle)* (Turnhout: Brepols, 2009).

Darby, Phillip, *The Three Faces of Imperialism: British and American Approaches to Asia and Africa, 1870–1970* (New Haven, CT: Yale University Press, 1987).

Darwin, John, *After Tamerlane. The Rise and Fall of Global Empires, 1400–2000* (London: Penguin, 2007).

Das, Rahul Peter, 'Little Kingdoms and Big Theories of History. Review of *Little Kingdoms in Kalinga: Ideologie, Legitimation und Politik regionaler Eliten* by Georg Berkemer', *Journal of the American Oriental Society*, 117, 1 (1997), pp. 127–34.

Daveau, Suzanne, *Um mapa corográfico de Portugal (c. 1525). Reconstituição a partir do Códice de Hamburgo* (Lisbon: Centro de Estudos Geográficos, 2010).

De Silva, Chandra Richard, *The Portuguese in Ceylon 1617–1638* (Colombo: H. W. Cave & Co., 1972).

De Silva, Chandra Richard, 'Trade in Ceylon Cinnamon in the Sixteenth Century', *The Ceylon Journal of Historical and Social Studies*, New Series, 3, 2 (1973), pp. 14–27.

De Silva, Chandra Richard, 'The First Portuguese Revenue Register of the Kingdom of Kotte–1599', *The Ceylon Journal of Historical and Social Studies*, New Series, 5, 1–2 (1975), pp. 71–153.

De Silva, Chandra Richard, 'The Rise and Fall of the Kingdom of Sitawaka (1521–1593)', *The Ceylon Journal of Historical and Social Studies*, 7, 1 (1977), pp. 1–43.

De Silva, Chandra Richard, 'Colonialism and Trade: The Cinnamon Contract of 1533 between Bhuvanekabahu, King of Kotte and António Pereira, Portuguese Factor in Sri Lanka', *University of Colombo Review*, 10 (1991), pp. 27–34.

De Silva, Chandra Richard, 'Beyond the Cape: The Portuguese encounter with the peoples of South Asia', in *Implicit Understandings. Observing, Reporting and Reflecting on the Encounters Between Europeans and Other Peoples in the Early Modern Era*, edited by Stuart Schwartz (Cambridge: Cambridge University Press, 1994), pp. 295–322.

De Silva, Chandra Richard, 'Sri Lanka in the Early Sixteenth Century: Political Conditions', in *University of Peradeniya History of Sri Lanka*, vol. II, edited by K. M. De Silva (Peradeniya: University of Peradeniya, 1995), vol. II, pp. 11–36.

De Silva, Chandra Richard, 'Islands and Beaches: Indigenous Relations with the Portuguese in Sri Lanka after Vasco da Gama', in *Vasco da Gama and the Linking of Europe and Asia*, edited by Anthony Disney and Emily Booth (New Delhi: Oxford University Press, 2000), pp. 280–94.

De Silva, Chandra Richard and S. Pathmanathan, 'The Kingdom of Jaffna up to 1620', in *University of Peradeniya History of Sri Lanka*, vol. II, edited by K. M. de Silva (Peradeniya: University of Peradeniya, 1995), pp. 105–21.

De Vries, Jan, 'Reflections on doing global history', in *Writing the History of the Global. Challenges for the 21st century*, edited by Maxine Berg (Oxford: Oxford University Press, 2013), pp. 32–47.

Dening, Greg, *Islands and Beaches: discourse on a silent land. Marquesas, 1774–1880* (Honolulu: University of Hawai'i Press, 1980).

Deswartes, Sylvie, *Les enluminures de la Leitura Nova 1504–1552. Etude sur la culture artistique au Portugal au temps de l'Humanisme* (Paris: Fondation Calouste Gulbenkian, 1977).

Dewaraja, Lorna, *The Kandyan Kingdom of Sri Lanka 1707–1782*, second revised edition (Colombo: Lake House, 1988).

Dias, João José Alves, *Gentes e espaços (em torno da população portuguesa na primeira metade do século XVI)* (Lisbon: JNICT, 1996).

Dias, João José Alves, Isabel Drumond Braga and Paulo Drumond Braga, 'A conjuntura', in *Nova História de Portugal*, edited by Joel Serrão and A. H. Oliveira Marques, vol. V (Lisbon: Presença, 1998), pp. 689–760.

Dias, José Sebastião da Silva, *A política cultural da época de D. João III* (Coimbra: Universidade de Coimbra, 1969).

Dias, Pedro, *À Maneira de Portugal. Uma tapeçaria inédita* (Porto: VOC Antiguidades, 2007).

Dirks, Nicholas, 'The Structure and Meaning of Political Relations in a South Indian Little Kingdom', *Contributions to Indian Sociology*, 13 (1979), pp. 169–206.

Dirks, Nicholas B., *The Hollow Crown. Ethnohistory of an Indian Kingdom* (Cambridge: Cambridge University Press, 1988).

Disney, Anthony, 'The gulf route from India to Portugal in the sixteenth and seventeenth centuries: couriers, traders and image-makers', in *A carreira da Índia e as rotas dos estreitos: actas do VIII Seminário Internacional de História Indo-Portuguesa*, edited by Luís Filipe Thomaz and Artur Teodoro de Matos (Lisbon: CEPCEP/CHAM/IICT, 1996), pp. 530–9.

Disney, Anthony, 'What was the Estado da Índia? Four Contrasting Images,' *Indica*, 38, 1–2 (2001), pp. 161–8.

Disney, Anthony, 'Portuguese Expansion, 1400–1800: Encounters, Negotiations, and Interactions', in *Portuguese Oceanic Expansion, 1400–1800*, edited by Francisco Bethencourt and Diogo Ramada Curto (Cambridge: Cambridge University Press, 2007), pp. 283–313.

Disney Anthony, *A History of Portugal and the Portuguese Empire*, 2 vols. (Cambridge: Cambridge University Press, 2009).

Doyle, Michael, *Empires* (Ithaca, NY: Cornell University Press, 1986).

Drayton, Richard and David Motadel, 'Discussion: the futures of global history', *Journal of Global History*, 13, 1 (2018), pp. 1–21.

DuVal, Kathleen, *The Native Ground. Indians and Colonists in the Heart of the Continent* (Philadelphia, PA: University of Pennsylvania Press, 2006).

Elbl, Ivana, 'Cross-Cultural Trade and Diplomacy: Portuguese Relations with West Africa, 1441–1521', *Journal of World History*, 3, 2 (1992), pp. 165–204.

Elliott, John H., 'A Europe of Composite Monarchies', in *Past and Present*, 137 (Nov. 1992), pp. 48–71.

Elliott, John H., *Empires of the Atlantic World. Britain and Spain in America, 1492–1830* (New Haven, CT: Yale University Press, 2006).

Emich, Birgit, 'Frühneuzeitliche Staatsbildung und politische Kultur. Für die Veralltäglichung eines Konzepts', *Zeitschrift für historische Forschung*, 35 (2005), pp. 191–205.

Escudero, José Antonio, 'La creación del Consejo de Portugal', offprint from *Boletim da Faculdade de Direito de Coimbra*, special issue (Coimbra: Imprensa da Universidade, 1983).

Falchetta, Pietro, *Fra Mauro's World Map, with a commentary and transcriptions of the inscriptions* (Turnhout: Brepols, 2006).

Febvre, Lucien, 'Limites et Frontières', in *Annales E.S.C.* 2, 2 (April–June 1947), pp. 201–7.

Febvre, Lucien, *Pour une histoire à part entière* (Paris: SEVPEN, 1962).

Ferguson, Donald, 'The Discovery of Ceylon by the Portuguese in 1506', *Journal of the Ceylon Branch of the Royal Asiatic Society*, XIX, 59 (1907), pp. 284–400.

Ferguson, Donald, *The History of Ceylon, from the Earliest Times to 1600 A.D.* (Colombo: Royal Asiatic Society, 1909).

Fernández-Albaladejo, Pablo, *Fragmentos de Monarquía* (Madrid: Alianza Editorial, 1992).

Fernández Álvarez, Manuel and Ana Díaz Medina, 'Los Austrias Mayores y la culminación del Imperio (1516–1598)', vol. VIII of *Historia de España*, edited by Ángel Montenegro Duque (Madrid: Gredos, 1987).

Fernández-Armesto, Felipe, 'Portuguese expansion in a global context', in *Portuguese Oceanic Expansion, 1450–1800*, edited by Francisco Bethencourt and Diogo Ramada Curto (Cambridge: Cambridge University Press, 2007), pp. 480–511.

Fletcher, Richard, 'The Early Middle Ages, 700–1250', in *Spain. A History*, edited by Raymond Carr (Oxford: Oxford University Press, 2000), pp. 63–89.

Flores, Jorge, 'A imagem do Oriente no Ocidente europeu: dos ecos da expansão mongol ao Portugal manuelino', *Revista da Biblioteca Nacional*, 2a série, 5, 2 (1990), pp. 21–40.

Flores, Jorge, '"Um homem que tem muito crédito naquelas partes": Miguel Ferreira, os "alevantados" do Coromandel e o Estado da Índia', *Mare Liberum*, 5 (1993), pp. 21–37.

Flores, Jorge, 'Portuguese entrepreneurs in the Sea of Ceylon (mid-sixteenth century)', in *Maritime Asia. Profit Maximization, Ethics and Trade Structure, c. 1300–1800*, edited by Karl Anton Sprengard and Roderich Ptak (Wiesbaden: Harrassowitz, 1994), pp. 125–50.

Flores, Jorge, *Os Portugueses e o Mar de Ceilão, 1498–1543. Trato, Diplomacia e Guerra* (Lisbon: Cosmos, 1998).

Flores, Jorge, 'A Ilha de Ceilão e o Império Asiático Português', *Oceanos*, 46 (2001), pp. 98–112.

Flores, Jorge, 'Recuperar Ceilão em meados do século XIX: atribulações de um diplomata português em Londres', *Oriente*, 3 (2002), pp. 21–30.

Flores, Jorge, '"They have discovered us". The Portuguese and the Trading World of the Indian Ocean', in *Encompassing the Globe. Portugal and the World in the 16th and 17th centuries*, edited by Jay Levenson (Washington, DC: Freer and Sackler Gallery, 2007), vol. II, pp. 185–93.

Flores, Jorge, 'The Iberian Empires, 1400–1800', in *The Cambridge World History*, vol. 6, The Construction of a Global World, 1400–1800 CE, edited by Jerry H. Bentley, Sanjay Subrahmanyam and Merry E. Wiesner-Hanks (Cambridge: Cambridge University Press, 2015), pp. 271–96.

Flores, Jorge and Maria Augusta Lima Cruz, 'A "Tale of two Cities", a "Veteran Soldier", or the struggle for endangered nobilities: The two *Jornadas de Huva* (1633, 1635) revisited', in *Re-exploring the Links. History and Constructed histories between Portugal and Sri Lanka*, edited by Jorge Flores (Wiesbaden: Harrassowitz, 2007), pp. 95–123.

Flynn, Dennis O. and Arturo Giráldez, 'Born Again: Globalization's sixteenth-century origins (Asian/Global versus European Dynamics)', *Pacific Economic Review*, 13, 3 (2008) pp. 359–87.

Fonseca, Luís Adão da and Maria Cristina da Cunha, eds., *O Tratado de Tordesilhas e a diplomacia luso-castelhana no século XV* (Lisbon: INAPA, 1991).

Frasch, Tilman, 'A Pāli cosmopolis? Sri Lanka and the Theravāda Buddhist Ecumene, c. 500–1500', in *Sri Lanka at the Crossroads of History*, edited by Zoltán Biedermann and Alan Strathern (London: UCL Press, 2017), pp. 66–76.

Freire, Anselmo Braamcamp, *Brasões da Sala de Sintra*, reprint of the second edition, 3 vols. (Lisbon: IN-CM, 1996).

Frenz, Margret, *Vom Herrscher zum Untertan. Spannungsverhältnis zwischen lokaler Herrschaftsstruktur und der Kolonialverwaltung zu Beginn der Britischen Herrschaft, 1790–1805* (Stuttgart: Franz Steiner, 2000).

Furber, Holden, 'Asia and the West as Partners before "Empire" and After', *Journal of Asian Studies*, 28, 4 (1969), pp. 711–21.

Furber, Holden, *Rival Empires of Trade in the Orient, 1600–1800* (Oxford/Minneapolis, MN: University of Minnesota Press, 1976).

Gaio, João Ribeiro, *O Roteiro das Cousas do Achem de D. João Ribeiro Gaio*, edited by Jorge dos Santos Alves and Pierre-Yves Manguin (Lisbon: CNCDP, 1997).

Gardiner, Patrick, *The Nature of Historical Explanation*, reprint (Oxford: Clarendon Press, 1980).

Geertz, Clifford, *The Interpretation of Cultures: selected essays* (New York: Basic Books, 1973).

Geertz, Clifford, *Negara: The Theatre State in Nineteenth-Century Bali* (Princeton, NJ: Princeton University Press, 1980).

Geiger, Wilhelm, 'Army and War in Mediaeval Ceylon', *Ceylon Historical Journal* 4 (1954–5), pp. 153–68.

Geiger, Wilhelm, *Culture of Ceylon in Medieval Times*, edited by Heinz Bechert (Wiesbaden: Harrassowitz, 1960).

Gellner, David N., *The Anthropology of Buddhism and Hinduism. Weberian Themes* (New Delhi: Oxford University Press, 2001).

Genet, Jean-Philippe, 'La typologie de l'état moderne, le droit, l'espace', in *L'État moderne: le droit, l'espace et les formes de l'état*, edited by Noel Coulet and Jean-Philippe Genet (Paris: Éditions du CNRS, 1990), pp. 7–14.

Ghobrial, John-Paul, *The Whispers of Cities. Information Flows in Istanbul, London, and Paris in the Age of William Trumbull* (Oxford: Oxford University Press, 2013).

Ghobrial, John-Paul, 'The Secret Life of Elias of Babylon and the Uses of Global Microhistory', *Past and Present*, 222, 1 (2014), pp. 51–93.

Gil, Juan, 'As Ilhas Imaginárias', *Oceanos*, 46 (Abril/Junho 2001), pp. 11–24.

Gillis, John R., *Islands of the Mind: How the Human Imagination Created the Atlantic World* (New York: Palgrave Macmillan, 2004).

Godinho, Vitorino Magalhães, 'A viragem mundial de 1517–1524 e o Império português', in *Ensaios* (Lisbon: Sá da Costa, 1978), vol. II, pp. 205–21.

Godinho, Vitorino Magalhães, *Os Descobrimentos e a Economia Mundial. 2a edição correcta e ampliada*, 4 vols. (Lisbon: Presença, 1981–3).

Gómez, Nicolas Wey, *Tropics of Empire: Why Columbus Sailed South to the Indies* (Cambridge, MT: MIT Press, 2008).

Gommans, Jos, 'Continuity and change in the Indian Ocean basin', in *The Cambridge World History*, vol. 6, The Construction of a Global World, 1400–1800 CE, edited by Jerry H. Bentley, Sanjay Subrahmanyam and Merry E. Wiesner-Hanks (Cambridge: Cambridge University Press, 2015), pp. 182–209.

Goonatilake, Susantha, *A 16th Century Clash of Civilizations. The Portuguese Presence in Sri Lanka* (Colombo: Vijitha Yapa, 2010).

Goonewardena, K. W., 'Kingship in XVIIth Century Sri Lanka: Some Concepts, ceremonies and other practices', *Sri Lanka Journal of the Humanities*, 3 (1977), pp. 1–32.

Grabar, Oleg, *The Formation of Islamic Art* (New Haven, CT: Yale University Press, 1973).

Grabar, Oleg, 'From Dome of Heaven to Pleasure Dome', *Journal of the Society of Architectural Historians*, 49, 1 (1990), pp. 15–21.

Grassotti, Hilda, 'Para la historia del botín y de las parias en León y Castilla', *Cuadernos de Historia de España*, 41–42 (1965), pp. 43–83.

Greenblatt, Stephen, *Marvelous Possessions. The Wonder of the New World* (Chicago, IL: University of Chicago Press, 1991).

Gruzinski, Serge, *The Mestizo Mind. The Intellectual Dynamics of Colonization and Globalization* (New York/London: Routledge, 2002).

Gruzinski, Serge, *Les quatre parties du monde. Histoire d'une mondialisation* (Paris: La Martinière, 2004).

Gschwend, Annemarie Jordan and Johannes Beltz, *Elfenbeine aus Ceylon: Luxusgüter für Katharina von Habsburg (1507–1578)* (Zurich: Museum Rietberg, 2010).

Guerreiro, Inácio and Luís de Albuquerque, 'A política de Portugal no Oriente e as suas flutuações', in *Portugal no Mundo*, edited by Luís de Albuquerque, reprint (Lisbon: Alfa, 1993), vol. II, pp. 460–3.

Guerreiro, Inácio and Vítor Luís Gaspar Rodrigues, 'O "grupo de Cochim" e a oposição a Afonso de Albuquerque', in *Studia*, 51 (1992), pp. 119–44.

Gunawardana, R. A. L. H., 'The People of the Lion. The Sinhala Identity and Ideology in History and Historiography', *Sri Lanka Journal of the Humanities*, V, 1–2 (1979), pp. 1–36.

Gupta, Akhil, 'Globalization and Difference: Cosmopolitanism before the Nation-State', *Transforming Cultures e-Journal*, 3, 2 (2008).

Guy, Jean-Sébastien, 'What is Global and What is Local? A Theoretical Discussion Around Globalization', *Parsons Journal for Information Mapping*, 1, 2 (2009), pp. 1–2.

Hakluyt, Richard, *Voyages and Discoveries. The Principal Navigations, Voyages, Traffiques and Discoveries of the English Nation*, edited, abridged and introduced by Jack Beeching (London: Penguin, 1972).

Hall, John R., 'Cultural Meaning and Cultural Structures in Historical Explanation', *History and Theory*, 39, 3 (2000), pp. 335–40.

Hämäläinen, Pekka, *The Comanche Empire* (New Haven, CT: Yale University Press, 2008).

Hämäläinen, Pekka and Samuel Truett, 'On Borderlands', *Journal of American History*, 98, 2 (2011), pp. 338–61.

Headley, John M., *Church, Empire and World. The Quest for Universal Order, 1520–1640* (Aldershot: Ahsgate Variorum, 1997).

Herrmann, Albert, 'Taprobane', in *Paulys Real-Encyclopädie der Classischen Altertumswissenschaft. Neue Bearbeitung begonnen von Georg Wissowa*, 2nd series, vol. IV (Stuttgart: Metzler, 1932), pp. 2260–72.

Hertel Ralf and Michael Kivak, eds., *Early Encounters between East Asia and Europe: Telling Failures* (Abingdon/New York: Routledge, 2017).

Hespanha, António Manuel, *As Vésperas do Leviathan. Instituições e poder político, Portugal— séc. XVII* (Coimbra: Livraria Almedina, 1994).

Hespanha, António Manuel and Catarina Madeira Santos, 'Os Poderes num Império Oceânico', in *História de Portugal*, edited by José Mattoso (Lisbon: Círculo de Leitores, 1993–1994), vol. 4, pp. 395–413.

*História da Arte Portuguesa*, vol. II, Do 'Modo' Gótico ao Maneirismo, edited by Paulo Pereira (Lisbon: Temas e Debates, 1995).

Hoffman, Philip T., *Why Did Europe Conquer the World?* (Princeton, NJ: Princeton University Press, 2017).

Holt, John C., *Buddha in the Crown. Avalokiteśvara in the Buddhist Traditions of Sri Lanka* (Oxford: Oxford University Press, 1991).

Holt, John C., *The Religious World of Kīrti Srī: Buddhism, Art and Politics in Late Medieval Sri Lanka* (Oxford: Oxford University Press, 1996).

Holt, John C., *The Buddhist Visnu: Religious Transformation, Politics and Culture* (New York: Columbia University Press, 2004).

Holt, John C., *The Sri Lanka Reader. History, Culture, Politics* (Durham, NC/London: Duke University Press, 2011).

Horn, James, *Adapting to a New World. English Society in the Seventeenth-Century Chesapeake* (Chapel Hill, NC/London: University of North Carolina Press, 1996).

Howland, Douglas, 'The Predicament of Ideas in Culture: Translation and Historiography', *History and Theory*, 42 (2003), pp. 45–60.

Jacob, Christian, *The Sovereign Map. Theoretical Approaches in Cartography through History* (Chicago, IL: University of Chicago Press, 2006).

Jaffer, Amin and Melanie Schwabe, 'A Group of Sixteenth-Century Ivory Caskets from Ceylon', *Apollo*, 445 (1999), pp. 3–14.

Jami, Catherine, 'Imperial Science Written in Manchu in Early Qing China: Does It Matter?', in *Looking at It from Asia: The Processes that Shaped the Sources of History of Science*, edited by F. Bretelle-Establet (Boston, MA: Springer, 2010), pp. 371–91.

Jazeel, Tariq, 'Reading the geography of Sri Lankan island-ness: colonial repetitions, postcolonial possibilities', *Contemporary South Asia*, 17, 4 (2009), pp. 399–414.

Johnson, Alan G., 'Opportunity structure, deviance', in *The Blackwell Dictionary of Sociology. A User's Guide to Sociological Language, Second Edition* (Oxford: Blackwell, 2000), pp. 214–15.

Kane, Anne, 'Reconstructing Culture in Historical Explanation: Narratives as Cultural Structure and Practice', *History and Theory*, 39, 3 (Oct. 2000), pp. 311–30.

Kaplan, Benjamin, *Cunegonde's Kidnapping: A Story of Religious Conflict in the Age of Enlightenment* (New Haven, CT/London: Yale University Press, 2014).

King, Blair L. and M. N. Pearson, *The Age of Partnership: Europeans in Asia before Dominion* (Honolulu: University Press of Hawai'i, 1979).

Koenigsberger, H. G., *Politicians and Virtuosi: Essays in Early Modern History* (London: Hambledon Press, 1986).

König, Daniel G., 'Übersetzungen und Wissenstransfer. Zu einem Aspekt der Beziehungen zwischen lateinisch-christlicher und arabisch-islamischer Welt', *Trivium*, 8 (2011), online publication.

Kubler, George, *A Arquitectura Portuguesa Chã. Entre as Especiarias e os Diamantes (1521–1706)*, 2nd ed. (Lisbon: Nova Vega, 2005).

Lach, Donald F., *Asia in the Making of Europe*, vol. I (Chicago, IL/London: University of Chicago Press, 1965).

Lamana, Gonzalo, *Domination without Dominance: Inca-Spanish Encounters in Early Colonial Peru* (Durham, NC: Duke University Press, 2008).

Lattimore, Owen, *Inner Asian Frontiers of China* (New York: American Geographical Society, 1940).

Lattimore, Owen, 'Origins of the Great Wall of China: A Frontier Concept in Theory and Practice', in *Studies in Frontier History. Collected Papers, 1928–1958* (London: Oxford University Press, 1962), pp. 97–118.

Laven, Mary, ' "From His Holiness to the King of China". Gifts, Diplomacy and Jesuit Evangelization', in *Global Gifts. The Material Culture of Diplomacy in Early Modern*

*Eurasia*, edited by Zoltán Biedermann, Anne Gerritsen and Giorgo Riello (New York: Cambridge University Press, 2018), pp. 217–34.

Leitner, Ulrich, 'Der imperiale Ordnungskomplex. Die theoretische Fiktion eines politischen Systems', in *Imperien und Reiche in der Weltgeschichte. Epochenübergreifende und globalhistorische Vergleiche*, edited by Michael Gehler and Robert Rollinger (Wiesbaden: Harrassowitz, 2014), vol. II, pp. 1415–52.

Lewis, Martin W. and Kären Wigen, *The Myth of Continents. A Critique of Metageography* (Berkeley/Los Angeles, CA: University of California Press, 1997).

Lombard, Denys, *Le Carrefour javanais. Essai d'histoire globale*, 3 vols. (Paris: Éditions de l'École des Hautes Études en Sciences Sociales, 1990).

Loureiro, Francisco, 'Miguel de Moura (1538–1599): Secretário de Estado e Governador de Portugal' (PhD dissertation, Lourenço Marques, 1974).

Luz, Francisco Paulo Mendes da, *O Conselho da Índia* (Lisbon: Agência Geral do Ultramar, 1952).

Luz, Francisco Paulo Mendes da, *O Conselho da Índia. Contributo ao Estudo da História da Administração e do Comércio do Ultramar Português nos Princípios do Século XVII* (Lisbon: Agência Geral do Ultramar, 1952).

McPherson, Kenneth, *The Indian Ocean: A History of the People and the Sea* (New Delhi: Oxford University Press, 1993).

Magalhães, Joaquim Romero de, 'As descrições geográficas de Portugal: 1500–1650', *Revista de História Económica e Social*, 5 (1980), pp. 15–56.

Magalhães, Joaquim Romero de, 'Filipe II (I de Portugal)', *História de Portugal*, edited by José Mattoso (Lisbon: Círculo de Leitores, 1993–1994), vol. III, pp. 563–6.

Maltez, José Adelino, 'O Estado e as Instituições', in *Nova História de Portugal*, edited by Joel Serrão and A. H. Oliveira Marques, vol. V (Lisbon: Presença, 1998), pp. 372–3.

Manukulasooriya, R., 'Transport in Sri Lanka in Ancient and Mediaeval Times', *Journal of the Royal Asiatic Society of Sri Lanka*, New Series, 24 (1978–9), pp. 49–85.

Marcocci, Giuseppe, *L'invenzione di un impero. Politica e cultura nel mondo portoghese (1450–1600)* (Rome: Carocci, 2010).

Marcocci, Giuseppe, 'Too Much to Rule. States and Empires across the Early Modern World', *Journal of Early Modern History*, 20, 6 (2016), pp. 511–25.

Marques, Guida, 'L'invention du Brésil entre deux monarchies. L'Amérique portugaise et l'Union ibérique (1580–1640): un état de question', *Anais de História de Além-Mar*, 6 (2005), pp. 109–37.

Matos, Artur Teodoro de, *O Estado da Índia nos anos de 1581–1588: Estrutura Administrativa e Económica. Alguns elementos para o seu estudo* (Ponta Delgada: Universidade dos Açores, 1982).

Matthew, Donald, *The Medieval European Community* (New York: St Martin's Press, 1977).

Mattingly, Garrett, *Renaissance Diplomacy* (Boston, MA/Cambridge: Houghton Mifflin/ Riverside Press, 1955).

Mattoso, José, *Identificação de um país. Ensaio sobre As Origens de Portugal, 1096–1325*, 2 vols. (Lisbon: Estampa, 1985).

Mattoso, José, ed., *História de Portugal*, 8 vols. (Lisbon: Círculo de Leitores, 1993–4).

Meegama, Sujatha Arundathi, 'The local and the global: the multiple visual worlds of ivory carvers in early modern Sri Lanka,' in *Sri Lanka at the Crossroads of History*, edited by Zoltán Biedermann and Alan Strathern (London: UCL Press, 2017), pp. 113–40.

Merrell, James H., *The Indians' New World. Catawbas and their Neighbors from European Contact through the Era of Removal* (Chapel Hill, NC: University of North Carolina Press, 1989).

Metcalf, Alida, *Go-betweens and the colonization of Brazil, 1500–1600* (Austin, TX: University of Texas Press, 2005).

Meyer, Éric, 'Comment caractériser les royaumes sri lankais anciens? Remarque critique sur les concepts de féodalisme et de société hydraulique', in *De la royauté à l'état, anthropologie et histoire du politique dans le monde indien*, edited by Jacques Pouchepadasse and Henri Stern (Paris: EHESS, 1991), pp. 207–16.

Mignolo, Walter D., 'The movable center: geographical discourses and territoriality during the expansion of the Spanish empire', in *Coded Encounters: Writing, Gender and Ethnicity in Colonial Latin America*, edited by Francisco Cevallos-Candau et al. (Amherst, MA: University of Massachussetts Press, 1994), pp. 15–45.

Mignolo, Walter D., *The Darker Side of the Renaissance. Literacy, Territoriality and Colonization*, 2nd edition with a new afterword by the author (Ann Arbor, MI: University of Michigan Press, 2003).

Mintz, Sidney, *Sweetness and Power: The Place of Sugar in Modern History* (New York: Viking Press, 1985).

Molina, Antonio M., *Historia de Filipinas*, 2 vols. (Madrid: Instituto de Cooperación Iberoamericana, 1984).

Morales Folguera, José Miguel, *La construcción de la utopía. El proyecto de Felipe II (1556–1598) para Hispanoamérica* (Madrid/Málaga: Editorial Biblioteca Nueva/ Universidad de Málaga, 2001).

Moreira, Rafael, 'A Arquitectura do Renascimento no Sul de Portugal. A encomenda régia entre o *Moderno* e o *Romano*' (PhD dissertation, Universidade Nova de Lisboa, 1991).

Moreira, Rafael, 'Cultura Material e Visual', in *História da Expansão Portuguesa*, edited by Francisco Bethencourt and Kirti Chaudhuri (Lisbon: Temas e Debates, 1998), vol. I, pp. 455–86.

Mota, Avelino Teixeira da, *Mar, Além-Mar. Estudos e ensaios de História e Geografia* (Lisbon: JIU, 1972).

Muchagato, Jorge, 'Os valores artísticos. A arquitectura', in *Nova História de Portugal*, vol. V, edited by João José Alves Dias (Lisbon: Presença, 1998), pp. 505–42.

Muldoon, James, *Empire and Order. The Concept of Empire, 800–1800* (London/New York: MacMillan/St Martin's, 1999).

Mumford, Jeremy Ravi, *Vertical Empire: The General Resettlement of Indians in the Colonial Andes* (Durham, NC: Duke University Press, 2012).

Mundy, Barbara, *The Mapping of New Spain. Indigenous Cartography and the Maps of the Relaciones Geográficas* (Chicago, IL/London: University of Chicago Press, 1996).

Murteira, André, 'A navegação portuguesa na Ásia e na rota do Cabo e o corso neerlandês, 1595–1625' (PhD dissertation, Universidade Nova de Lisboa, 2016).

Necipoğlu, Gülru, 'Suleyman the Magnificent and the Representation of Power in the Context of Ottoman-Hapsburg-Papal Rivalry', *Art Bulletin*, 71 (1989), pp. 401–27.

Newitt, Malyn, *A History of Portuguese Expansion, 1400–1668* (London/New York: Routledge, 2005).

Nirenberg, David, *Communities of Violence: Persecution of Minorities in the Middle Ages* (Princeton, NJ: Princeton University Press, 1996).

Nissan, Elizabeth and R. L. Stirrat, 'The generation of communal identities', in *Sri Lanka. History and the Roots of Conflict*, edited by Jonathan Spencer (London/New York: Routledge, 1990), pp. 19–44.

Nordman, Daniel, *Frontières de France. De l'espace au territoire, XVIe–XIXe siècle* (Paris: Gallimard, 1998).

Norkus, Zenonas, *An Unproclaimed Empire: The Grand Duchy of Lithuania from the view-point of Comparative Historical Sociology of Empires* (London/New York: Routledge, 2017).

Obeyesekere, Gananath, *Land Tenure in Village Ceylon* (Cambridge: Cambridge University Press, 1967).

Obeyesekere, Gananath, *The Cult of the Goddess Pattini* (Chicago, IL/London: University of Chicago Press, 1984).

Obeyesekere, Gananath, 'Between the Portuguese and the Nāyakas: the many faces of the Kandyan Kingdom, 1591–1765', in *Sri Lanka at the Crossroads of History*, edited by Zoltán Biedermann and Alan Strathern (London: UCL Press, 2017), pp. 161–77.

Olwig, Kenneth Robert, *Landscape, Nature and the Body Politic. From Britain's Renaissance to America's New World* (Madison, WI: University of Wisconsin Press, 2002), pp. xix–xv.

Osterhammel, Jürgen, 'Die Wiederkehr des Raumes. Geopolitik, Geohistorie und historische Geographie', *Neue Politische Literatur*, 43 (1998), pp. 374–97.

Pagden, Anthony, *Lords of All the World: Ideologies of Empire in Spain, Britain and France, c.1500–1800* (New Haven, CT/London: Yale University Press, 1995).

Pagden, Anthony, 'Fellow Citizens and Imperial Subjects. Conquest and sovereignty in Europe's overseas empires', *History and Theory*, 44, 4 (2005), pp. 28–46.

Paiva, José Pedro, 'Dioceses e organização eclesiástica', in *História Religiosa de Portugal*, (Lisbon: Círculo de Leitores, 2000–2002), vol. II, pp. 187–99.

Paiva, José Pedro, 'A Igreja e o Poder: Interpenetração da Igreja e do Estado', in *História Religiosa de Portugal*, edited by Carlos Moreira de Azevedo (Lisbon: Círculo de Leitores, 2000–2), vol. II, pp. 135–85.

Palomo, Federico, *A Contra-Reforma em Portugal, 1540–1700* (Lisbon: Livros Horizonte, 2006).

Panikkar, K. M., *Asia and Western Dominance. A Survey of the Vasco da Gama Epoch of Asian History, 1498–1945* (London: Alan & Unwin, 1953).

Paranavitana, Senarat, 'Aryan Settlement: the Sinhalese', in *University of Ceylon History of Ceylon*, edited by H. C. Ray, vol. I, part 1 (Colombo: Ceylon University Press, 1959), pp. 82–97.

Paranavitana, Senarat, 'Civilisation of the Period: Economic, Political and Social Conditions', in *University of Ceylon History of Ceylon*, edited by H. C. Ray, vol. 1, part 2 (Colombo: Ceylon University Press, 1960), pp. 713–44.

Paranavitana, Senarat, 'The Kotte Kingdom up to 1505', in *University of Ceylon History of Ceylon*, edited by H. C. Ray, vol. I, part 2 (Colombo: Ceylon University Press, 1960), pp. 663–83.

Parthasarathi, Prasannan, 'Comparison in global history', in *Writing the History of the Global. Challenges for the 21st century*, edited by Maxine Berg (Oxford: Oxford University Press, 2013), pp. 69–82.

Patton, Maryam, 'Global Microhistory: One or two things that I know about it', Blogpost on *JHIBLOG* (September 2015), https://jhiblog.org/2015/09/09/global-microhistory-one-or-two-things-that-i-know-about-it/ (last accessed 19 October 2017).

Pearson, M. N., *The Portuguese in India* (Cambridge: Cambridge University Press, 1987).

Pelúcia, Alexandra, *Martim Afonso de Sousa e a sua Linhagem. Trajectórias de uma Elite no Império de D. João III e de D. Sebastião* (Lisbon: CHAM, 2009).

Pereira, António dos Santos, 'A Índia a preto e branco: uma carta oportuna, escrita em Cochim, por D. Constantino de Bragança, à rainha Dona Catarina', *Anais de História de Além-Mar*, 4 (2003), pp. 449–84.

Perera, C. Gaston, *The Portuguese Missionary in 16th and 17th Century Ceylon: The Spiritual Conquest* (Colombo: Vijitha Yapa, 2009).

Perera, E. W., 'Alakeswara: His Life and Times', *Journal of the Ceylon Branch of the Royal Asiatic Society*, 18 (1904), pp. 281–312.

Perera, E. W., 'The Age of Sri Parākrama Bāhu VI', *Journal of the Ceylon Branch of the Royal Asiatic Society*, 22 (1910), pp. 6–45.

Perera, S. G., *The City of Colombo 1505–1656* (Colombo: Ceylon Historical Association, 1926), pp. 13–14.

Pérez-Díaz, Victor, 'State and public sphere in Spain during the Ancien Régime', *Daedalus*, 127, 3 (1998), pp. 251–79.

Pieris, Ralph, *Sinhalese Social Organization* (Colombo: Ceylon University Press, 1956).

Pinto, Augusto Cardoso, *A guarda del rei Dom João II: notas para a história das guardas reais portuguesas* (Lisbon: Centro Tipográfico Colonial, 1930).

Pinto, Paulo Jorge Sousa, *Portugueses e Malaios. Malaca e os Sultanatos de Johor e Achém, 1575–1619* (Lisbon: Sociedade Histórica da Independência de Portugal, 1997).

Pirani, Cenan, 'The Military Economy of Seventeenth-Century Sri Lanka. Rhetoric and Authority in a Time of Conquest' (PhD dissertation, UCLA, 2016).

Pollock, Sheldon, 'India in the Vernacular Millennium: Literary Culture and Polity, 1000–1500', *Daedalus*, 127, 3 (1998), pp. 41–74.

Pollock, Sheldon, *The Language of the Gods in the World of Men: Sanskrit, Culture, and Power in Premodern India* (Berkeley/Los Angeles, CA: University of California Press, 2009).

Pomeranz, Kenneth, *The Great Divergence. China, Europe, and the Making of the Modern World Economy* (Princeton, NJ: Princeton University Press, 2000).

Pomeranz, Kenneth, 'Writing about divergences in global history: some implications for scale, methods, aims, and categories', in *Writing the History of the Global. Challenges for the 21st century*, edited by Maxine Berg (Oxford: Oxford University Press, 2013), pp. 117–28.

Prange, Sebastian R., 'A Trade of No Dishonor: Piracy, Commerce, and Community in the Western Indian Ocean, Twelfth to Sixteenth Century', *American Historical Review*, 116, 5 (2011), pp. 1269–93.

Pratt, Marie-Louise, *Imperial Eyes. Travel Writing and Transculturation* (London/New York: Routledge, 1992).

Ptak, Roderich, 'China and Portugal at Sea. The Early Ming Trading System and the *Estado da Índia* Compared', *Revista de Cultura*, 13–14 (1991), pp. 21–38.

Queirós, Maria Helena, 'A Contra-Reforma em Portugal 1540–1700, Federico Palomo, Lisboa, Livros Horizonte, 2006, 130 p. Nota crítica à obra', in *Via Spiritus*, 16 (2009), pp. 175–86.

Raben, Remco, 'Trade and urbanization. Portuguese and Dutch urban attitudes in Ceylon. Colombo: mirror of the colonial mind', *Mare Liberum*, 13 (1997), pp. 95–120.

Raghavan, M. D., *The Karava of Ceylon. Society and Culture* (Colombo: K. V. G. De Silva & Sons, 1961).

Ramusack, Barbara N., *The Indian Princes and their States* (Cambridge: Cambridge University Press, 2004).

Rau, Virgínia, *Feitores e Feitorias. 'Instrumentos' do Comércio Internacional Português no Século XVI* (Lisbon: Brotéria, 1966).

Reid, Anthony, *Southeast Asia in the Age of Commerce, 1450–1680* (New Haven, CT: Yale University Press, 1988).

Revere, Robert B., ' "No Man's Coast": Ports of Trade in the Eastern Mediterranean', *Trade and Market in Early Empires*, edited by Karl Polanyi (Glencoe, IL: The Free Press, 1957), pp. 38–63.

Reynolds, Frank, 'The Two Wheels of Dhamma: A Study of Early Buddhism', in *The Two Wheels of Dhamma. Essays in the Theravada Tradition in India and Ceylon*, edited by Gananath Obeyesekere, Frank Reynolds and Bardwell L. Smith (Chambersburg, PA: American Academy of Religion, 1972), pp. 6–30.

Roberts, Michael, 'A Tale of Resistance: The Story of the Arrival of the Portuguese in Sri Lanka', *Ethnos*, 54, 1–2 (1989), pp. 69–82.

Roberts, Michael, 'The Collective Consciousness of the Sinhalese During the Kandyan Era: Manichean Images, Associational Logic', *Asian Ethnicity*, 3, 1 (Mar. 2002), pp. 29–46.

Roberts, Michael, *Sinhala Consciousness in the Kandyan Period 1590s to 1815* (Colombo: Vijitha Yapa Publications, 2003).

Rodrigues, Vítor Luís Gaspar, 'A evolução da arte da Guerra dos Portugueses no Oriente (1498–1622)' (PhD dissertation, Insituto de Investigação Científica Tropical, Lisbon, 1998).

Rogers, John, *A Concise History of Sri Lanka* (Cambridge: Cambridge University Press, 2019).

Rohandeera, Mendis, 'Dharma Parakramabahu IX: The False King of Ceylon Inflated by the Portuguese Historians—A Historiographical Perspective', *Vidyodaya Journal of Social Sciences*, 8 (1996), pp. 13–45.

Rosa, Maria de Lurdes, 'D. Jaime, duque de Bragança: entre a cortina e a vidraça', in *O tempo de Vasco da Gama*, edited by Diogo Ramada Curto (Lisbon: Difel, 1998), pp. 319–32.

Rosa, Maria de Lourdes, 'Velhos, novos e mutáveis sagrados… um olhar antropológico sobre formas "religiosas" de percepção e interpretação da conquista africana (1415–1521)', *Lusitania Sacra*, 2a série, 18 (2006), pp. 13–85.

Rubel, Paula G. and Abraham Rosman, eds., *Translating Cultures. Perspectives on Translation and Anthropology* (London: Bloomsbury, 2003).

Russell-Wood, A. J. R., *A World on the Move. The Portuguese in Africa, Asia, and America, 1415–1800* (Baltimore, MD: Johns Hopkins University Press, 1993).

Russell-Wood, A. J. R., 'For God, King and Mammon: The Portuguese Outside of Empire, 1480–1580', in *Vasco da Gama and the Linking of Europe and Asia*, edited by Anthony Disney and Emily Booth (New Delhi: Oxford University Press, 2000), pp. 261–79.

Sabato, Ernesto, *La carta del cantino e la rappresentazione della Terra nei codici e nei libri a stampa della Biblioteca Estense e Universitaria* (Modena: Il Bulino, 1991).

Sahlins, Peter, *Frontières et identités nationales. La France et l'Espagne dans les Pyrénées depuis le XVIIe siècle* (Paris: Belin, 1996).

Saldanha, António de Vasconcelos, 'O problema jurídico-político da incorporação de Ceilão na coroa de Portugal. As doações dos Reinos de Kotte, Kandy e Jaffna (1580–1633)', *Revista de Cultura*, 13/14, Ano V, vol. 1 (1991), pp. 233–57.

Saldanha, António Vasconcelos de, *Iustum Imperium. Dos tratados como fundamento do império dos portugueses no Oriente. Estudo de história do direito internacional e do direito português* (Lisbon/Macao: Fundação Oriente/Instituto Português do Oriente, 1997).

Santos, Catarina Madeira, *'Goa é a chave de toda a Índia'. Perfil político da capital do Estado da Índia (1505–1570)* (Lisbon: CNCDP, 1999).

Santos, Catarina Madeira, *Entre Velha Goa e Pangim: a capital do Estado da Índia e as reformulações da política ultramarina* (Lisbon: CEHCA, 2001).

Santos, Maria Emília Madeira and Vítor Luís Gaspar Rodrigues, 'A feitoria-fortaleza e o comércio transcontinental da coroa portuguesa no século XVI', in *Portugal no Mundo*, edited by Luís de Albuquerque, reprint (Lisbon: Alfa, 1993), vol. II, pp. 557–70.

Saraiva, António José, *História da Cultura em Portugal*, reedited in collaboration with Óscar Lopes and Luís de Albuquerque, 2 vols. (Lisbon: Gradiva, 2000).

Schaub, Jean-Frédéric, *La France espagnole. Les racines hispaniques de l'absolutisme français* (Paris: Seuil, 2003).

Schnepel, Bernhard and Georg Berkemer, 'History of the Model', in *Sharing Sovereignty. The Little Kingdom in South Asia*, edited by Georg Berkemer and Margret Frenz (Berlin: Klaus Schwarz, 2003), pp. 11–20.

Schrikker, Alicia F., *Dutch and British colonial intervention in Sri Lanka, 1780–1815: expansion and reform* (Leiden: Brill, 2007).

Schurhammer, Georg, *Francis Xavier. His Life, His Times*, 4 vols. (Rome: IHSI, 1977).

Scott, Heidi V., *Contested Territory. Mapping Peru in the Sixteenth and Seventeenth Centuries* (Notre Dame, IN: University of Notre Dame Press, 2009).

Seneviratne, H. L., *Rituals of the Kandyan State* (Cambridge: Cambridge University Press, 1978).

Senos, Nuno, *O Paço da Ribeira, 1501–1581* (Lisbon: Editorial Notícias, 2002).

Serrão, Joaquim Veríssimo, *História de Portugal*, 2nd edition, 14 vols. (Lisbon: Verbo, 1977–20).

Silveira, Francisco Rodrigues da, *Reformação da Milícia e Governo do Estado da Índia Oriental*, edited by Benjamin N. Teensma (Lisbon: Fundação Oriente, 1996).

Siriweera, W. I., 'The Theory of the King's Ownership of Land in Ancient Ceylon: An Essay in Historical Revision', *Ceylon Journal of Historical and Social Studies*, New Series, 1 (1971), pp. 48–61.

Siriweera, W. I., 'Land Tenure and Revenue in Medieval Ceylon (A.D. 1000–1500)', *Ceylon Journal of Historical and Social Studies*, New Series, 2 (1972), pp. 1–49.

Siriweera, W. I., *History of Sri Lanka from earliest times up to the sixteenth century* (Colombo: Dayawansa Jayakody, 2002).

Sivasundaram, Sujit, *Islanded: Britain, Sri Lanka, and the Bounds of an Indian Ocean Colony* (Chicago, IL/London: University of Chicago Press, 2013).

Sivasundaram, Sujit, 'Cosmopolitanism and indigeneity in four violent years: the fall of the kingdom of Kandy and the Great Rebellion revisited', in *Sri Lanka at the Crossroads of History*, edited by Zoltán Biedermann and Alan Strathern (London: UCL Press, 2017), pp. 194–215.

Smith, Bardwell L., 'The Ideal Social Order as Portrayed in the Chronicles of Ceylon', in *The Two Wheels of Dhamma. Essays in the Theravada Tradition in India and Ceylon*, edited by Gananath Obeyesekere, Frank Reynolds and Bardwell L. Smith (Chambersburg, PA: American Academy of Religion, 1972), pp. 31–57.

Smith, Monica L., 'Networks, Territories, and the Cartography of Ancient States', *Annals of the Association of American Geographers*, 95, 4 (2005), pp. 832–49.

Smith, Monica L., 'Territories, Corridors, and Networks: A Biological Model for the Premodern State', *Complexity*, 12, 4 (2005), pp. 28–35.

Somaratne, G. P. V., 'Grand Eunuch Ho and Ceylon', *Journal of the Ceylon Branch of the Royal Asiatic Society*, New Series, 15 (1971), pp. 36–47.

Somaratne, G. P. V., *The Political History of the Kingdom of Kotte* (Colombo: Godage and Brothers, 1975).

Somaratne, G. P. V., 'Rules of succession to the Throne of Kotte', *Aquinas Journal*, 7 (1991), pp. 17–32.

Spalding, Karen, *Huarochirí: an Andean Society under Inca and Spanish rule* (Stanford, CA: Stanford University Press, 1984).

Stagl, Justin, 'Szientistische, hermeneutische und phänomenologische Grundlagen der Ethnologie', in *Grundfragen der Ethnologie. Beiträge zur gegenwärtigen Theorie-Diskussion*, edited by J. Stagl and W. Schmied-Kowarzik (Berlin: Dietrich Reimer, 1993), pp. 18–42.

Stein, Burton, *A History of India*, 2nd edition, revised and edited by David Arnold (Oxford: Wiley-Blackwell, 2010).

Stern, Philip J., *The Company-State. Corporate Sovereignty and the Early Modern Foundations of the British Empire in India* (New York: Oxford University Press, 2011).

Stern, Steve J., 'Paradigms of Conquest: History, Historiography, and Politics', *Journal of Latin American Studies*, 24 (1992), pp. 1–34.

Stollberg-Rilinger, Barbara, ed., *Was heißt Kulturgeschichte des Politischen?* (Berlin: Duncker & Humblot, 2005).

Stollberg-Rilinger, Barbara, 'Rituals of Decision Making? Early Modern European Assemblies of Estates as Acts of Symbolic Communication', in *Political Order and the Forms of Communication in Medieval and Early Modern Europe*, edited by Yoshihisa Hattori (Rome: La Viella, 2014), pp. 63–95.

Strathern, Alan, 'Re-reading Queirós: some neglected aspects of the *Conquista*', *Sri Lanka Journal of the Humanities*, 26, 1–2 (2000), pp. 1–28.

Strathern, Alan, '*Os Piedosos* and the Mission in India and Sri Lanka in the 1540s', in *D. João III e o Império. Actas do Congresso Internacional*, edited by Roberto Carneiro and Artur Teodoro de Matos (Lisbon: CHAM/CEPCEP, 2004), pp. 855–64.

Strathern, Alan, 'The Royal "We". A Review of *Sinhala Consciousness in the Kandyan Period 1590s to 1815* by Michael Roberts', *Modern Asian Studies* 39, 4 (2005), pp. 1013–26.

Strathern, Alan, *Kingship and Conversion in Sixteenth-Century Sri Lanka. Portuguese Imperialism in a Buddhist Land* (Cambridge: Cambridge University Press, 2007).

Strathern, Alan, 'Sri Lanka in the long Early Modern Period: Its Place in a Comparative Theory of Second Millenium Eurasian History', *Modern Asian Studies* 43, 4 (2009), pp. 815–69.

Strathern, Alan, 'The digestion of the foreign in Lankan history, c. 500–1818, in *Sri Lanka at the Crossroads of History*, edited by Zoltán Biedermann and Alan Strathern (London: UCL Press, 2017), pp. 216–38.

Strong, John, ' "The Devil was in that Little Bone": The Portuguese Capture and Destruction of the Buddha's Tooth-Relic, Goa, 1561', *Past and Present*, 206, Supplement 5, 1 (2010), pp. 184–98.

Subrahmanyam, Sanjay, 'State Formation and Transformation in Early Modern India and Southeast Asia', *Itinerario*, 12, 1 (1988), pp. 91–109.

Subrahmanyam, Sanjay, *The Political Economy of Commerce: Southern India, 1500–1650* (Cambridge: Cambridge University Press, 1990).

Subrahmanyam, Sanjay, 'The Tail Wags the Dog: Sub-Imperialism and the *Estado da Índia*, 1570–1600', in *Improvising Empire: Portuguese Trade and Settlement in the Bay of Bengal* (New Delhi: Oxford University Press, 1990), pp. 137–60.

Subrahmanyam, Sanjay, *The Portuguese Empire in Asia 1500–1700. A political and economic history* (London: Longman, 1993).

Subrahmanyam, Sanjay, 'An Eastern El-Dorado: The Tirumala-Tirupati Temple complex in early European views and ambitions, 1540–1660', in *Syllables of Sky: Studies in South Indian Civilization in Honour of Velcheru Narayana Rao*, edited by David Shulman (New Delhi: Oxford University Press, 1995), pp. 338–90.

Subrahmanyam, Sanjay, ed., *Sinners and Saints. The Successors of Vasco da Gama* (New Delhi: Oxford University Press, 1995).

Subrahmanyam, Sanjay, 'Connected Histories: Notes towards a reconfiguration of Early Modern Eurasia', *Modern Asian Studies*, 31, 3 (1997), pp. 735–62.

Subrahmanyam, Sanjay, 'Making India Gama: The Project of Dom Aires da Gama (1519) and Its Meaning', *Mare Liberum*, 16 (1998), pp. 43–7.

Subrahmanyam, Sanjay, 'Du Tage au Gange au XVIᵉ siècle: une conjoncture millénariste à l'échelle eurasiatique', in *Annales HSS*, 56, 1 (2001), pp. 51–84.

Subrahmanyam, Sanjay, 'Written on Water: designs and dynamics in the Portuguese *Estado da India*', in *Empires: Perspectives from Archaeology and History*, edited by Susan Alcock et al., (New York: Cambridge University Press, 2001), pp. 42–69.

Subrahmanyam, Sanjay, ed., *Maritime India* (Oxford: Oxford University Press, 2004).

Subrahmanyam, Sanjay, 'A Tale of Three Empires. Mughals, Ottomans, and Habsburgs in a Comparative Context', *Common Knowledge*, 12, 1 (2006), pp. 66–92.

Subrahmanyam, Sanjay, 'Historicizing the Global or Labouring for Invention?', *History Workshop Journal*, 64, 1 (2007), pp. 329–34.

Subrahmanyam, Sanjay, 'Holding the World in Balance: The Connected Histories of the Iberian Empires, 1500–1640', *American Historical Review*, 112, 5 (2007), pp. 1359–85.

Subrahmanyam, Sanjay, 'The birth-pangs of Portuguese Asia: revisiting the fateful "long decade" 1498–1509', *Journal of Global History*, 2, 3 (2007), pp. 261–80.

Subrahmanyam, Sanjay, 'Introduction', in *The Cambridge World History*, vol. 6, The Construction of a Global World, 1400–1800 CE, edited by Jerry H. Bentley, Sanjay Subrahmanyam and Merry E. Wiesner-Hanks (Cambridge: Cambridge University Press, 2015), pp. 1–25.

Subrahmanyam, Sanjay, and Luís Filipe Thomaz, 'Evolution of Empire: The Portuguese in the Indian Ocean during the Sixteenth Century', in *The Economy of Merchant Empires*, edited by James D. Tracy (Cambridge: Cambridge University Press, 1991), pp. 298–331.

Subtil, José Manuel, 'A administração central da Coroa', in *História de Portugal*, edited by José Mattoso (Lisbon: Círculo de Leitores, 1993–4), vol. III, pp. 78–90.

Tambiah, Stanley J., *World Conqueror and World Renouncer: a study of Buddhism and polity in Thailand against a historical background* (Cambridge: Cambridge University Press, 1976).

Tambiah, Stanley J., 'The Galactic Polity in Southeast Asia', *Culture, Thought, and Social Action. An Anthropological Perspective* (Cambridge, MA: Harvard University Press, 1985).

Teixeira, André, 'Os primórdios da presença portuguesa em Baçaim–1534–1554: notas sobre a situação financeira e político-militar do primeiro "território" do Estado da Índia', in *D. João III e o Império. Actas do Congresso Internacional*, edited by Roberto Carneiro and Artur Teodoro de Matos (Lisbon: CHAM/CEPCEP, 2004), pp. 337–65.

Thomaz, Luís Filipe F. R., 'L'idée impériale manuéline', in *La découverte, le Portugal et l'Europe, Actes du Colloque*, edited by Jean Aubin (Paris: Fondation Calouste Gulbenkian, 1990), pp. 35–103.

Thomaz, Luís Filipe F. R., 'Factions, interests and messianism: The politics of Portuguese expansion in the East, 1500–1521', *The Indian Economic and Social History Review*, 28, 1 (1991), pp. 97–109.

Thomaz, Luís Filipe F. R., 'Cipango', *Dicionário de História dos Descobrimentos Portugueses*, edited by Luís de Albuquerque (Lisbon: Caminho, 1994), vol. I, pp. 251–2.

Thomaz, Luís Filipe F. R., *De Ceuta a Timor*, 2nd ed. (Lisbon: Difel, 1994).

Thomaz, Luís Filipe F. R., 'A crise de 1565–1575 na história do Estado da Índia', *Mare Liberum*, 9 (1995), pp. 481–519.

Thomaz, Luís Filipe F. R., 'Estrutura política e administrativa do Estado da Índia', in *De Ceuta a Timor*, 2nd edition (Lisbon: Difel, 1998), pp. 207–43.

Thomaz, Luís Filipe F. R., *A questão da pimenta em meados do século XVI. Um debate político do governo de D. João de Castro* (Lisbon: CEPCEP, 1998), pp. 76–88.

Thomaz, Luís Filipe F. R., 'Precedents and Parallels of the Portuguese *Cartaz* System', in *The Portuguese, Indian Ocean, and European Bridgeheads, 1500–1800: Festschrift in Honour of Professor K. S. Mathew*, edited by Pius Malekandathil and Jamal Mohammed (Tellicherry: IRSSH, 2001), pp. 67–85.

Thomaz, Luís Filipe F. R., 'O malogrado estabelecimento oficial dos portugueses em Sunda e a islamização de Java', in *Aquém e Além da Taprobana. Estudos luso-orientais à memória de Jean Aubin e Denys Lombard*, edited by Luís Filipe Thomaz (Lisbon: CHAM, 2002), pp. 381–667.

Thomaz, Luís Filipe F. R., 'O "testamento político" de Diogo Pereira, *o Malabar*, e o projecto oriental dos Gamas', *Anais de História de Além-Mar*, 5 (2004), pp. 61–160.

Tilly, Charles, *The Formation of National States in Western Europe* (Princeton, NJ: Princeton University Press, 1972).

Tomás y Valiente, Francisco, 'El sistema polisinodial: el todo y las partes', in *Historia de España Menéndez Pidal*, edited by José María Jover Zamora, vol. 25, La España de Felipe IV, 3rd edition (Madrid: Espasa Calpe, 1982), pp. 124–50.

Tomlinson, Gary, 'Unlearning the Aztec *cantares* (preliminaries to a postcolonial history)', in *Subject and Object in Renaissance Culture*, edited by Margreta de Grazia, Maureen Quilligan and Peter Stallybrass (Cambridge: Cambridge University Press, 1996), pp. 260–86.

Trivellato, Francesca, 'Is There a Future for Italian Microhistory in the Age of Global History?', *California Italian Studies*, 2, 1 (2011), online publication.

Turnbull, David, *Maps are territories. Science is an atlas* (Chicago, IL/London: University of Chicago Press, 1993).

*University of Ceylon History of Ceylon*, vol. I, parts 1 and 2, edited by H. C. Ray (Colombo: Ceylon University Press, 1959–1960).

*University of Peradeniya History of Sri Lanka*, vol. II, edited by K. M. de Silva (Peradeniya: University of Peradeniya, 1995).

Valladares, Rafael, *Castilla y Portugal en Asia (1580–1680). Declive imperial y adaptación* (Leuven: Leuven University Press, 2001).

Valladares, Rafael, *La conquista de Lisboa. Violencia militar y comunidad política en Portugal, 1578–1583* (Madrid: Marcial Pons, 2008).

Vignati, Antonella, 'Vida e acções de Mathias de Albuquerque Capitão e Viso-Rei da Índia', *Mare Liberum*, 15 (1998), pp. 139–245 and 17 (1999), pp. 267–360.

Voigt, Lisa, ' "Por Andarmos Todos Casy Mesturados": The Politics of Intermingling in Caminha's "Carta" and Colonial American Anthologies', *Early American Literature*, 40, 3 (2005), pp. 407–39.

Waddell, Brodie, 'What is microhistory now?', Blogpost at *Many-headed-monster* (June 2017). https://manyheadedmonster.wordpress.com/2017/06/20/what-is-microhistory-now/ (last accessed 5 November 2017).

Walters, Jonathan, 'Buddhist History: the Sri Lankan Pali *Vamsas* and their Commentary', in *Querying the Medieval. Texts and the History of Practices in South Asia*, edited by Ronald Inden, Jonathan Walters, and Daud Ali (Oxford: Oxford University Press, 2000), pp. 125–54.

Waquet, Jean-Claude, Odile Goerg and Rebecca Rogers, eds., *Les espaces de l'historien. Études d'historiographie* (Strasbourg: Presses Universitaires de Strasbourg, 2000).

Washbrook, David, 'Problems in global history', in *Writing the History of the Global. Challenges for the 21st century*, edited by Maxine Berg (Oxford: Oxford University Press, 2013), pp. 21–31.

Weerakoddy, D. P. M., 'Greek and Roman Notices of Sri Lanka and their historical Context', *Sri Lanka Journal of the Humanities*, 20 (1994), pp. 65–86.

Weigel, Sigrid, 'Bilder als Hauptakteure auf dem Schauplatz der Erkenntnis. Zur poiesis und episteme sprachlicher und visueller Bilder' in *Ästhetik Erfahrung*, edited by Jörg Huber

(Zurich/Vienna/New York: Institut für Theorie der Gestaltung und Kunst/Voldemeer/ Springer, 2004), pp. 191–212.

Werake, K. M. M., 'A re-examination of Chinese Relations with Sri Lanka during the 15th century A. D.', in *Modern Sri Lanka Studies*, 2, 1–2 (1987), pp. 89–102.

White, Richard, *The Middle Ground: Indians, Empires, and Republics in the Great Lakes Region, 1650–1815* (Cambridge: Cambridge University Press, 1991).

Winius, George D., *The Fatal History of Portuguese Ceylon. Transition to Dutch Rule* (Cambridge, MA: Harvard University Press, 1971).

Winius, George D., 'Few Thanks to the King: The Building of Portuguese India', in *Vasco da Gama and the Linking of Europe and Asia*, edited by Anthony Disney and Emily Booth (New Delhi: Oxford University Press, 2000), pp. 484–95.

Wolf, Eric R., *Europe and the People Without History* (Berkeley, CA: University of California Press, 1982).

Wolfe, Patrick, 'Settler Colonialism and the Elimination of the Native', *Journal of Genocide Research*, 8, 4 (2006), pp. 387–409.

Wolters, O. W., *History, culture, and region in Southeast Asian perspectives*, 2nd revised edition (Ithaca, NY: Cornell University Press, 1999).

Wong, R. Bin, 'Regions and global history', in *Writing the History of the Global. Challenges for the 21st century*, edited by Maxine Berg (Oxford: Oxford University Press, 2013), pp. 83–105.

Wood, Stephanie, *Transcending Conquest. Nahua Views of Spanish Colonial Mexico* (Norman, OK: University of Oklahoma Press, 2003).

Woodward, David, 'Reality, Symbolism, Time, and Space in Medieval World Maps', *Annals of the Association of American Geographers*, 75, 4 (1985), pp. 510–21.

Woodward, David, 'Maps and the rationalization of space', in *Circa 1492. Art in the Age of Exploration*, edited by J. A. Levenson (New Haven, CT: Yale University Press, 1991), pp. 83–8.

Woodward, David, 'Cartography and the Renaissance: Continuity and Change', in *The History of Cartography*, vol. III, *Cartography in the European Renaissance*, edited by David Woodward (Chicago, IL/London: University of Chicago Press, 2007), pp. 3–24.

Xavier, Ângela Barreto, '"Aparejo y disposición para se reformar y criar outro nuevo mundo." A evangelização dos indianos e a política imperial joanina', in *D. João III e o Império. Actas do Congresso Internacional*, edited by Roberto Carneiro and Artur Teodoro de Matos (Lisbon: CHAM/CEPCEP, 2004), pp. 783–805.

Xavier, Ângela Barreto, *A invenção de Goa: poder imperial e conversões culturais nos séculos XVI e XVII* (Lisbon: ICS, 2008).

Xavier, Ângela Barreto and Ines G. Županov, *Catholic Orientalism: Portuguese Empire, Indian Knowledge (16th–18th Centuries)* (New Delhi: Oxford University Press, 2015).

Yates, Frances A., *Astraea. The Imperial Theme in the Sixteenth Century* (London: Routledge and Kegan Paul, 1975).

# Index

Lightning Source UK Ltd.
Milton Keynes UK
UKHW020705250122
397662UK00002B/166